Personality
STRATEGIES FOR THE STUDY OF MAN

THE DORSEY SERIES IN PSYCHOLOGY

Editor   HOWARD F. HUNT   Columbia University

Personality

STRATEGIES FOR THE STUDY OF MAN

ROBERT M. LIEBERT
State University of New York
at Stony Brook

MICHAEL D. SPIEGLER
University of Texas
at Austin

1974   Revised Edition

THE DORSEY PRESS   Homewood, Illinois   60430
Irwin-Dorsey International   London, England   WC2H 9NJ
Irwin-Dorsey Limited   Georgetown, Ontario   L7G 4B3

Revised Edition

First Printing, April 1974

Cover design by Judith Ann Skenazy

ISBN 0-256-01536-8
Library of Congress Catalog Card No. 73–93359

Printed in the United States of America

To our parents

Preface

Revising a book is like having a second child. In guiding its development one can draw on past experiences, see earlier mistakes, and attempt to do things not done in raising the first offspring. At the same time, much of one's original goals and basic philosophy remains unchanged and there is comfort in knowing that the process has been undertaken before without catastrophe. So it has been with this edition of *Personality*.

Our fundamental aim continues to be fourfold: (*a*) to introduce the undergraduate psychology major to important theoretical and practical issues in the study of personality, (*b*) to provide the student who will not take further psychology courses with interesting and accurate information about the application of psychology to important human concerns, (*c*) to present selected examples of research which typify both good scientific methodology and the investigation of meaningful problems, and (*d*) to prepare and interest the student in more advanced study.

To meet these goals more effectively than before, major organizational changes have been made. One involves presenting each major theoretical viewpoint in terms of the larger conceptual *strategy* that underlies it: *psychoanalytic, dispositional, phenomenological,* or *behavioral*. Presentation of these four strategies and a general overview of the psychology of personality at the outset constitute the five sections of the book. To help orient the reader toward viewing man's personality from a variety of broad models, each of the strategy sections begins with a concise introduction which also serves as a summary; our own experience suggests that it is most effective to have students read the introduction both before reading each of the major chapters in the section and then again after the basic material has been read, when it can serve as an aid for integrating what has been learned.

This edition, like its predecessor, attempts to take a relatively even-handed view of the various strategies; each is presented in a favorable light and in the tone and format of its adherents (e.g., the presence of extensive case study material in the psychoanalytic section and the emphasis on experimental research in the behavioral section were dictated by the orientation of those psychologists whose work is representative of each strategy). At the same time we have increasingly recognized the need to make readers aware of the limitations or liabilities of each view without disrupting the affirmative presentation. To accomplish this, a brief "Liabilities" section that presents some of the strategy's major weaknesses as voiced by critics appears at the end of every section.

We believe that any comprehensive strategy for the study of man must come to grips with four issues: a clear *theoretical statement,* a set of procedures for *personality assessment,* a systematic body of *research,* and a basis for understanding and implementing *personality change.* We have substantially added to and reorganized the text in order to bring the critical interplay of these four aspects of the study of personality into sharper focus. The scientific investigation of personality is thus presented within a framework of the four basic strategies—psychoanalytic, dispositional, phenomenological, and behavioral—and four fundamental issues or aspects—theory, assessment, research, and personality change.

As in the first edition of *Personality,* complete coverage is *not* a goal of the book; even if such a goal could be attained, which is highly doubtful, we do not believe that it is either a necessary or effective way to introduce the reader to the field of personality. Instead, the emphasis continues to be on presenting some relatively enduring principles and issues and to illustrate them with representative contemporary and "classic" examples.

Personality courses are among the most popular offerings of a psychology department, but they are often disappointing to the student who wants information which bears on his own life. To serve this need (which we feel is a legitimate one), we have tried to illustrate concepts and principles through examples that "hit home" to the contemporary college student. We have also expanded a feature of the first edition which we believe capitalizes on, and perhaps helps to stimulate, the college student's intellectual skepticism. Periodically, the reader is invited to perform small, easily implemented *Demonstrations,* so that he may personally examine the validity of various propositions discussed in the text. These "personalized studies" have been repeatedly tested in our personality classes and revised when student feedback indicated that changes were called for. A Demonstration is included in each of the strategy's introductory chapters in an effort to involve the student directly in the "way of thinking" presented by each strategy.

We believe that visual illustrations which are integrated with text material and present information more concisely or vividly than words alone could do may be used to advantage. We have also become increasingly aware that a book's appealing format serves more than a cosmetic function; it can make reading easier and more enjoyable and hence aid learning. Accordingly, we have endeavored to improve upon both of these aspects in the present edition of *Personality*.

On the basis of four more years of teaching and research experience in the field of personality, we continue to believe, perhaps more strongly than before, that rigorous science, sophisticated theory, and clarity of presentation need not be antagonistic goals for the scientist or the teacher. It is, of course, all too easy to find complicated jargon and abtruse formulations in the literature of psychology. (We are reminded of the "Peanuts" cartoon in which Peppermint Patty inquires about the book Franklin is reading. Franklin tells her that it is a book about psychology and from what he can understand of it, it seems good. To which Patty quips, "Forget it, Franklin . . . no book on psychology can be any good if one can understand it!") We have tried to present our subject matter in clear and understandable language, without doing an injustice to either the material or its readers. Although the book is written for undergraduates, we hope that graduate students will find it useful for review of some of the more important and enduring issues in the field of personality and that any interested person will find it comprehensible.

We wish to acknowledge our debt to the many undergraduates in our personality classes whose comments, questions, and challenges regarding the first edition had a definite influence in the changes we made in the present volume. We appreciate the helpful criticisms and intellectual exchanges about personality with our colleagues Arnold Buss, David Cohen, Linda Davis, Robert Kaleta, Ann Booker Loper, Robert Plomin, Rita Wicks Poulos, and Lee Willerman. Our thanks are extended to Brenda Romines and Mary Jane White for typing various parts of the manuscript and putting up with perpetual "rush jobs." Special thanks are due Peggy McCarthy for a thoughtful and critical reading of the galley proofs and for shouldering a major responsibility in organizing the subject index. Once again, Betty Scott Berry's expertise and efficiency greatly facilitated the final stages of production. We are especially grateful to Diane Liebert and Judy Skenazy who aided our writing in their roles as editors and critics as well as loving and understanding mates.

Four other people influenced the writing of this book from its earliest inception. Whether by virtue of their ways of rearing us, the dispositions they imparted to us, their willingness to accept us as individuals with views of our own, or the particular behaviors they modeled, shaped, and reinforced for us, we and this book are partially the product of our parents. We are deeply grateful for their contribution and want to acknowledge it by dedicating *Personality: Strategies for the Study of Man* to them.

March 1974

R. M. LIEBERT
M. D. SPIEGLER

Contents

section I

Introduction

1

Strategies for the Study of Personality

In the theater of ancient Rome the actors used no makeup. Instead they wore one of a small number of masks, or *persona,* that told the audience to expect a consistent pattern of attitudes and behavior from the player who wore it. Soon persona came to refer not only to the masks but also to the roles they implied; and, finally, they referred to the actors themselves (cf. Burnham, 1968).

"Persona" is the source of the English word *personality,* and the link is more than historical. The term as we use it today also implies that we expect from other people a consistent pattern of attitudes and behavior or at least what Gordon Allport called an "orderly arrangement" in the behavior of those whom we know. All people exhibit recognizable individual actions that serve to identify them. No doubt "personality," as the term is used outside of psychology classrooms and books, includes a person's physical appearance, but that is probably not an essential part of its meaning, since we can readily imagine (at least as understandable fiction) that a person could be transformed into an entirely different physical form and still maintain all of the essential characteristics which distinguish him from others.[1]

Where, though, do these individual characteristics and regularities come from? Are they ever truly unique, or just particular combina-

---

[1] This is the notion underlying the concept of an afterlife in Christianity and of reincarnation in Oriental religions. A contemporary example can be found in Stephen Leacock's highly amusing novel *Turnabout,* in which a man and woman exchange bodies.

3

tions of characteristics all people possess? Are they learned, inherited, or both? Can personality be altered, and, if so, how? These questions have puzzled thoughtful people for thousands of years. Originally the quest for answers to them was the domain of philosophy and religion, and these fields continue to be interested in such problems. But scientific psychology, born about 100 years ago, has also turned its attention to personality.

This book offers a general introduction to the psychological study of personality and deals with the issues involved in developing an approach to the systematic study of human behavior. So many approaches to personality have been advanced by psychologists, philosophers, and theologians and by social commentators of other disciplines that it would be impossible to discuss all of these positions in detail. Even if complete coverage were possible, a mere catalog of viewpoints would probably not be the best way to introduce the scientific study of personality. Therefore, instead of detailing an exhaustive list of approaches, we have stressed the major *strategies* which psychologists have followed in developing conceptualizations of human behavior. This format is designed to give a general picture of the diversity of existing positions, the points they emphasize, the nature of the evidence they consider, and the assumptions they make. In this way we have tried to explain both the logical and empirical bases which underlie major theoretical positions and, at the same time, to summarize existing knowledge about the causes of human behavior.

To proceed systematically, the study of personality, like other scientific endeavors, requires a strategy. All of the approaches to personality that we shall discuss can be examined in terms of their explicit or implicit strategies, and to understand and evaluate them we must be familiar with their strategic components. Thus, we shall first consider the elements involved in a strategy for studying personality.

Strategy, as we shall use the term here, refers to a four-phase plan for understanding human personality. It includes a *theory* of personality, an approach to the *assessment* or measurement of personality, *research* procedures for testing hypotheses or propositions derived from the theory, and methods of *changing personality* (i.e., therapeutic interventions). There is considerable overlap in the role played by each of the four phases of the study of personality. For instance, theory provides the hypotheses which research tests, and the form of those hypotheses determines, in part, the methods of research which are suitable. In order to do research, assessment techniques must be employed. The model of personality measurement used is dictated by the assumptions about personality made in the theory. The success of the personality change techniques serves to partially validate the therapeutic principles which are derived from the theory. The interdependence of theory, assessment, research, and personality change is indeed complex, and it becomes difficult to talk about one phase without referring to one or more of the other three phases. Our purpose in discussing each phase separately is primarily pedagogical.

THE SCOPE OF THE STUDY OF PERSONALITY

Interest in understanding ourselves and our fellow men has compelling justification. To begin with, it is natural for us to be curious about our own behavior, what determines our personalities, and "how we got that way." Furthermore, our daily lives are filled with concerns that relate to the assessment and prediction of personality. Virtually all social interaction requires that we evaluate and try to predict the behavior of other persons with whom we must deal. For example, on the basis of relatively short interactions, college students must attempt to determine whether a new acquaintance will make a suitable roommate or whether a given professor will be sympathetic to a student handing in a term paper two weeks after it is due.

A number of distinctions have been erected by psychologists who are concerned with human behavior. Interest in interpersonal relations, attitude change, and the influence of major social forces has typically fallen in the domain of *social psychology*. *Developmental psychology* places emphasis on the historical antecedents of a person's behavior and is concerned with maturational and social influences as human beings advance from infancy through childhood and adolescence to adulthood and old age. When someone's behavior is markedly different from the usual norms of his society, and especially when these differences may jeopardize himself or others, then the phenomena are of particular interest to workers in the field of *abnormal psychology,* including the theoretical and experimental work of *psychopathology* and the applied work of *clinical psychology.* Applied fields, such as *human engineering, industrial psychology, personnel psychology, educational psychology,* and *school psychology,* are concerned with specific human enterprises. Additionally, *experimental psychology* may involve the study of single aspects of the organism, such as physiology, sensation and perception, learning, motivation, and emotion.

Because of these distinctions, the term *personality psychology* has typically been reserved for the study of "normal" behavior in all its aspects, particularly when the single individual rather than a larger social unit is the primary object of interest. In this book, however, we shall often cross these traditional boundaries in order to present the largest possible framework for the understanding of human behavior.

DEFINING PERSONALITY

Thus far we have spoken of *personality* without specifically defining the term. There are numerous extant definitions, and which is selected depends upon one's theoretical orientation, or "model of man." A deterministic, biologically oriented model, for example, leads to a definition that stresses heredity as an important determinant of personality. On the other hand, if we view man as an adaptive being whose behavior is primarily controlled by the situation in which he finds himself, then our definition might stress such phenomena as socialization, imitation, and learning.

It is not necessary for the beginning student of personality to start with *a* definition. In fact, a complete definition of personality would involve a statement of a theory of personality. To fully understand what a particular psychologist means by the term *personality*, it is necessary to examine his theoretical approach. For example, conspicuously missing from the small sample of definitions presented below is the name of Sigmund Freud. Since for Freud personality is synonymous with the *psyche* (mind), his theory of personality (see Chapter 4) is a theory of psychology in general. Freud posited that personality is made up of the *id, ego,* and *superego,* three aspects of the psyche, and that it is their interaction which determines behavior. Much of Freud's personality theory deals with these three aspects and their interrelationship and, therefore, Freud's definition of personality is his theory of personality.

Many personality psychologists have, however, given concise, condensed definitions of personality, usually acknowledging that they are incomplete. The following are examples of such definitions (Sanford, 1963):

> *Allport:* Personality is the dynamic organization within the individual of those psychophysical systems that determine his unique adjustments to his environment (pp. 494–95).
>
> *Newcomb:* . . . personality . . . is known only as we observe individual behavior. (I am using the term "personality," by the way, in the inclusive sense of referring to the individual's organization of predispositions to behavior.) What I want to suggest is that the *kind* of behavior from which we can learn most about personality is role behavior. By observing John Doe in such capacities as husband, host, employee, and employer, we can discover those kinds of order and regularity in his behavior which are the goal of the student of personality (p. 496).
>
> *Eysenck:* Personality is the more or less stable and enduring

organization of a person's character, temperament, intellect and physique, which determines his unique adjustment to his environment (p. 496).

Bronfenbrenner: A conception of personality as a system of relatively enduring dispositions to experience, discriminate, or manipulate actual or perceived aspects of the individual's environment (including himself) (p. 497).

Sullivan: . . . the relatively enduring pattern of recurrent interpersonal situations which characterize a human life (p. 497).

Cattell: Personality is that which permits a prediction of what a person will do in a given situation. . . . Personality is . . . concerned with *all* the behavior of the individual, both overt and under the skin (p. 496).

Hilgard: . . . the sum total of individual characteristics and ways of behaving which in their organization or patterning describe an individual's unique adjustment to his environment (p. 497).

Even from this brief sample, several pervasive issues with respect to the definition of personality become apparent.

Overt Behavior and Private Experience

In defining personality and developing a theoretical description of it, we must decide whether our interest will be limited to overt behavior or whether we can talk about internal events as well. It is obvious that our direct knowledge of others is limited to what we can see of their behavior and that we can never directly know what is "inside" a person. We may say that Tom is happy in order to provide a summary label for his smiles, jovial conversation, or his invitation to take us all out for a beer, but we are speaking of his overt behavior and not necessarily of any private, internal state that he is experiencing. Psychologists who subscribe to the *behavioral* view (which holds that our primary concern should be with observable responses rather than presumed internal states [see Chapters 13–16]) argue that the scientific study of personality can be no more than an examination of observable responses. Others, though, have argued that personality must refer to some private experiences as well. Tom, who *appears* happy, may in fact be miserable inside; a prim and proper girl may be seething with sexuality; and, in general, a man's behavior may not reflect his "real" personality. Although this orientation has a good deal of intuitive appeal, the problem of measuring private experiences is a thorny one.

Generality of Personality

Can we talk about personality in terms of enduring dispositions? In our daily language we often hear such things as "John is quiet" or "Sharon is irresponsible." People talk as if these were properties of the individual rather like the color of his eyes, which is always apparent and virtually unchangeable. But such statements are not likely to be true without exception. John may be very outspoken about his hobby, stamp collecting, and Sharon may be very careful in keeping her club's records despite the fact that she has not gotten a single class assignment in on time in the past three years. Both a definition and a theory of personality must therefore account for the inconsistencies as well as the similarities in a given person's behavior across situations and time. Some theorists have minimized the importance of situational differences, while others have argued that such differences are not sources of spurious "error" but rather are the primary data for understanding why a person acts as he does.

The Idiographic-Nomothetic Distinction

All personality psychologists would agree that each individual's personality, however it is defined, is unique. There is, however, controversy over the implications of this fact for the study of personality. If no individual is exactly like any other, does this imply that personality should be studied by making exhaustive investigations of single individuals with the goal of understanding their behavior completely? Such research would lead to laws about the behavior of a specific person. Usually science deals with general laws, implying that personality should be studied by investigating specific aspects of personality in a wide variety of persons with the aim of formulating laws of behavior which hold for people in general. This controversy is between the *idiographic* and the *nomothetic* approaches, respectively (from the Greek *idios* meaning personal and *nomos* meaning law), and we shall discuss both points of view in this book.

Prediction, Control, and Understanding

In developing a perspective of personality we must decide whether it is proper to describe our goal as solely *prediction* and *control* of behavior or whether an additional goal, usually called *understanding,* is necessary for an adequate theory of personality. Whereas prediction and control are easily defined and specified, the meaning of "understanding" is elusive and ambiguous. By understanding we usually mean comprehension of the processes involved in a phenomenon, but the level of comprehension which is sufficient for a person to say "I understand" varies from individual to individual. Understanding is thus a highly subjective matter.

Observation and Inference

Although the terms *personality* and *behavior* are often used interchangeably, there is an essential difference. *Personality* is an abstraction and is not observed directly; instead, it is *inferred from behavior which is observed.* "Personality" is an example of a *theoretical construct.*[2] Theoretical constructs do not actually exist, nor can they be seen or touched. They are merely useful inventions which help to give order to phenomena which have been observed. Theoretical constructs are often shorthand summaries of relationships among many different variables, and they therefore serve to facilitate communication about these relationships. Many of the concepts to be discussed in this book are theoretical constructs.

Why is it necessary or even desirable to use such convenient fictions? A major reason is that they economically and parsimoniously tie together meaningful relationships among observations that would otherwise soon become a hopeless quagmire of raw facts. As seen in Figure 1–1 (page 10), the advantage of using the theoretical construct "anxiety" is striking even in the case of only three situations and three outcomes.

Personality and Value Judgments

Before leaving the problem of the definition of our subject matter, it is important to note that the term *personality,* as we shall use it in this book, and as it is used by all personality psychologists, does not imply any *evaluation* of a person's character, social graces, or abilities. When the layman speaks of Larry as having a "great personality" he may be referring to his pleasant disposition, his generosity, or his concern for the welfare of others, but this evaluative use of the word is generally outside the realm of the scientific study of personality.

THE ROLE OF THEORY

It is often because of a lack of theory that problems go unresearched or unresolved. It is extremely difficult to investigate a phenomenon unless one has at least some tentative ideas about its

---

[2] At least since the publication of a classic article by MacCorquodale and Meehl (1948), a distinction has often been drawn between two types of theoretical constructs. *Hypothetical constructs* are theoretical constructs which are hypothesized to actually exist, although they cannot be directly observed at the present time. In contrast, *intervening variables* ". . . involve no hypothesis as to the existence of unobserved entities or the occurrence of unobserved processes . . ." (MacCorquodale & Meehl, 1948, p. 103).

FIGURE 1–1

An Illustration of the Advantages of Using Anxiety as a Theoretical Construct, Defined Differently in a Number of Circumstances (B), over a Mere Listing of Observed, Separate Relationships (A)

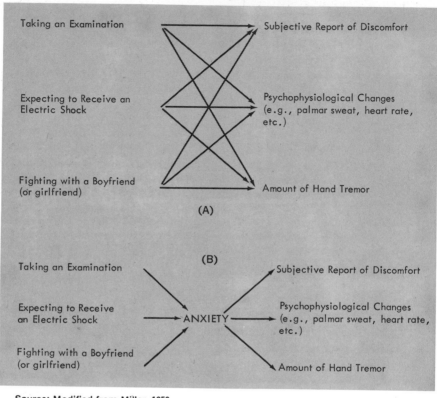

Source: Modified from Miller, 1959.

nature, its relationship with other phenomena, and so on. Consider the undergraduate psychology student in an independent study course who was interested in the effects of popular music on teen-agers. He spent the entire semester trying to design a workable experiment to investigate the problem and never did succeed. Among other things, he failed to delimit his area of study and made no attempt at formulating hypotheses about the relationship of various aspects of popular music to other measurable events. In other words, he did not begin with a theory! While it is probably true that the student was justifiably reluctant to formulate a complete theory concerning the effects of popular music on teen-agers because he felt that he lacked sufficient training or knowledge to do so (a feeling that he shared with many scientists), he should have at least formulated a tentative plan for approaching the problem. The student would then have been able to perform some experiment to test his neophyte hypotheses.

What, more generally, is the role of theory? A theory in psychology, or any other science, must first organize and condense already existing facts and information, and in this capacity it plays mainly a descriptive role. A given phenomenon can be described in many ways. Condensation of any event will require assumptions, and the theory which makes the least number of assumptions, all other things being equal, is usually considered the "best" theory. (This assertion, which is itself an assumption, is often referred to as the "law of parsimony.")

A theory should predict future events as well as account for past observations. A second purpose of theory is therefore to provide a basis for the prediction of events and outcomes that have not yet been investigated. This purpose clearly implies that hypotheses derived from a theory must be *testable* and capable of being refuted, or *falsified*. Not only must the theory make specific predictions, but it must also translate its assumptions and predictions into *empirical hypotheses* that can actually be tested. Theories often fail to survive as much because they are untestable as because they are disconfirmed.

Alternatively, theories that are poorly formulated or based on an inadequate strategy may be improperly tested and thus be "self-fulfilling." George A. Kelly (1955), whose Theory of Personal Constructs we shall discuss in a later chapter, illustrates the way in which an implicit theoretical construct about others may be "confirmed" in a rather redundant fashion.

> A man construes his neighbor's behavior as hostile. By that he means that his neighbor, given the proper opportunity will do him harm. He tries out his construction of his neighbor's attitude by throwing rocks at his neighbor's dog. His neighbor responds with an angry rebuke. The man may then believe that he has validated his construction of his neighbor as a hostile person.
>
> The man's construction of his neighbor as a hostile person may appear to be "validated" by another kind of fallacy. The man reasons, "If my neighbor is hostile, he will be eager to know when I get into trouble, when I am ill, or when I am in any way vulnerable. I will watch to see if this isn't so." The next morning the man meets his neighbor and is greeted with the conventional, "How are you?" Sure enough, the neighbor is doing just what was predicted of a hostile person (pp. 12–13).

It is probably true that we all have an *implicit* theory and definition of personality which we use in everyday interpersonal relations.

Individual implicit personality theories differ from the theories we shall discuss in this book in several important respects. First, the theories we shall examine in later chapters are formalized and set down in terms that can be communicated to others. It is not that we cannot formalize or communicate our own personal theories of human behavior to others; it is just that we generally do not do so. Second, formalized theories are based on observations of many different people. Although we may meet different individuals in our daily lives, we usually do not make an explicit effort to observe and take note of their behavior. Third, most personal theories are based more on the observation of ourselves than on observation of other persons. Finally, formalized personality theories are tested repeatedly in research under relatively rigorous standards, often by critics of the theories. Implicit personality theories are not subjected to such testing.

There is much philosophical debate concerning the nature of "proving" or "disproving" a theory, and in order to avoid getting into the fray of a yet raging conflict, we will simply make several conservative statements in this regard. First, *a theory,* like a hypothesis, *is never proved or disproved* by empirical evidence. The most that research can do is to find support for a theory, while the absence of such findings does not usually refute the theory.[3] With each new substantiating piece of evidence the psychologist gains more confidence in the theory. If after a number of experimental tests a theory has failed to receive support, the psychologist would be forced to turn to a new theory or to revise the existing one. In this case, for all practical purposes the theory would have been rendered useless. Strictly speaking, though, it would not have been proven false.

In practice, supportive evidence, or positive results, seems to carry more weight with scientists than does nonsupportive evidence, or negative results. If one were to make a tally sheet of the positive and negative findings of research relevant to a particular theory, it would be necessary to have substantially more negative results than positive results (perhaps in a ratio of 50 or even 100 to 1) for a scientist to feel that his theory was no longer (or perhaps never was) useful. It is a fact of science that theories, once adopted, die slowly.

We have been speaking of the importance of research in testing a theory, but it should be kept in mind that whole theories are never tested by experimentation. Rather, a hypothesis, or set of hypotheses, relevant to a specific aspect of the theory, is investigated. Because

---

[3] A theory can be decisively disconfirmed if some empirical consequence that is *absolutely* necessary for the theory turns out not to occur. However, psychological theories are rarely this determinate and "tight."

of this, proponents of a theory must restrict their research conclusions to what has actually been shown. This is important, since it is often tempting, when research has been conducted within a particular theoretical perspective, to interpret the results as providing more general support for the theory than can be reasonably derived from the data available.

For example, many personality psychologists have attempted to find the basic elements of personality structure by asking persons to rate close friends on a variety of descriptive scales. Then, using a statistical technique for summarizing data called *factor analysis* (see Chapter 7), they looked for common elements, or *factors*, of description. It was found that the same five factors emerged in many different studies. They were extroversion, agreeableness, conscientiousness, emotional stability, and culture (Mischel, 1968). This line of research was based on the general theory that persons do in fact possess a limited number of stable personality characteristics, or traits.

Do these highly consistent results confirm the general theoretical position? A sophisticated analysis by Passini and Norman (1966) revealed that they may not. The previous studies all assumed that one person's description of another was determined primarily by the actual characteristics (personality) of the person being rated. Passini and Norman created a situation in which ratings of others could not be based on extensive knowledge of them because the raters were asked to describe complete strangers! Nonetheless, the same pattern of five factors emerged. Thus, while the *results* of the earlier studies were not challenged, the original *interpretation* was forced to give way to a simpler one, namely, that the structure found revealed the pervasive character of the *labels* we use to describe all persons rather than the way people really are.

PERSONALITY ASSESSMENT: DIRECT VS. INDIRECT

All assessment of personality is indirect in the sense that "personality" per se cannot be observed directly because it is a theoretical construct and thus exists only conceptually. The unit of observation (e.g., a verbal report) used to assess a personality construct is at least one step removed from that construct. The statement "I am happy" (observation) may yield information about the inner state of happiness (personality construct), but few people would say that the two are equivalent.

In another sense, personality assessment techniques do vary in the directness of their approach to finding answers to questions, just as our own everyday methods of acquiring information from others can be relatively indirect (e.g., "Are you doing anything Saturday night?") or direct (e.g., "Would you like to go out with me Saturday night?"). As applied to methods of personality assessment, the terms *direct* and *indirect* are always relative.

The most direct method of personality assessment involves the observation of overt behavior. For example, if we were interested in assessing an individual's tolerance for frustration, we might observe him in a situation in which he was frustrated in his attempt to complete a task and measure the degree to which he persevered. However, many personality phenomena are not so closely tied to overt behavior.

In the case of private experiences, one of the most direct methods of personality assessment is to ask the person how he feels, what he is thinking, why he is acting in a particular way, and so on. Direct self-reports are useful in many circumstances, both conceptually and as real predictors of behavior. As Dement (1965) has noted: "We accept . . . these concepts without qualification because long experience has shown over and over that they *do* correlate with observable events in the real world. Their function is to bridge the gap between sensory input and motor output; to help order the intervening processes that govern human behavior" (p. 142). For example, a wide variety of external stimulation, ranging from pinpricks to burning torches to sharp blows, will lead most adults to say "ouch" (or some other appropriate four-letter word). We observe quickly that we can predict many of the events that a person has not yet experienced which will lead him to report pain. The assumption that the individual *really* is experiencing an intense internal feeling proves, in this example, to be highly serviceable. Objective evidence that the individual is in fact experiencing internal sensations with particular characteristics cannot be provided; on the other hand, such rigorous proof hardly appears necessary in view of the obvious utility of assuming that his feelings are real.

The problem is that we may not always be able to "trust" self-reports. There are many circumstances in which an individual will distort both his feelings and his own stated recollection of his behavior to make them more compatible with perceived social demands. Social psychological studies, for example, have found that after an election has been narrowly won by one candidate, an overwhelming majority of voters will claim that they voted for the winner. It is improbable that these citizens have actually forgotten how their ballots were cast. Rather, it seems likely that they are deliberately modifying their statements so as to be in the "winner's circle." The possible operation of such distorting psychological processes has been extensively formalized in psychoanalytic theory. But even apart from such formalization, everyday experiences suggest that there are many circumstances in which one would be ill-advised to place heavy reliance on an individual's report of events of which he alone has direct knowledge.

In virtually all circumstances in which accurate representation of one's feelings might lead to negative consequences, psychological research and common experience alike suggest that an individual's statements about himself may not provide dependable information. Consider the well-known experiments on conformity (e.g., Asch, 1956) in which naive subjects and confederates of the experimenter are asked to make perceptual judgments, such as determining which of two lines is longer. When the confederates declare the objectively shorter line to be the "longer" one, subjects frequently will conform to the majority's "misperception" and, furthermore, they will occasionally insist that they actually "saw" the lines the way they judged them. A more common example occurs when we are asked whether we know a particular fact which we have never been aware of, yet answer in the affirmative so as not to appear ignorant.

Another limitation of self-report measures of personality arises from the fact that such self-descriptions are of necessity mediated by language. One must understand the connotative use of the individual's verbal expression before his descriptions can have much value. If someone says that he is "hot," he may be referring either to a feeling of heightened temperature or of heightened sexual arousal.

When there is reason to believe that direct self-reports will be invalid or inaccurate indicators of personality phenomena, indirect personality assessment techniques are used. In most cases these techniques "disguise" their purpose so that the person being assessed cannot easily distort the measurement. Projective techniques, which are discussed in Chapter 5, are a prime example of indirect personality assessment.

THE IMPORTANCE OF RESEARCH

Occasionally the beginning student of personality feels that carefully controlled research is unnecessary to validate "obvious" propositions. Often, however, the seemingly obvious does not hold up under careful examination. The following Demonstration[4] can serve to illustrate the manner in which impressions may appear very powerful yet, like cotton candy, prove to have very little substance.

---

[4] This book contains a number of Demonstrations in which you can actually participate and which will allow you to illustrate for yourself both the principles and the problems associated with the study of personality.

Demonstration 1–1

AN ILLUSTRATION OF ERRONEOUS IMPRESSIONS

Most of us have had the experience of reading horoscopes in the newspapers and may well have commented that it is difficult to imagine anyone being "taken in" by these overly general descriptions and predictions. It is possible, however, that a more sophisticated version of the same kind of generalized descriptions can be extremely effective and even lead persons to believe that they have an entirely unique description of themselves. Testing this hypothesis, Ulrich, Stachnik, and Stainton (1963) asked students in educational psychology classes to take two personality tests. A week later the students were given a written interpretation of their test scores which appeared to represent the careful efforts of the professor. As a second part of the study, other students were given instructions in administering the same two personality tests to a friend. For both phases of the study, the people whose personalities were "being interpreted" were asked to rate the accuracy of the "interpretation" (on a scale ranging from excellent to very poor) and to make any additional comments about the "interpretation" which they felt were important.

Despite the individualized appearance of the personality description, *all persons were given exactly the same "interpretation"* (though the order of the statements varied), and, in fact, *no actual interpretations of the tests were made.* The description read:

> You have a strong need for other people to like you and for them to admire you. You have a tendency to be critical of yourself. You have a great deal of unused capacity which you have not turned to your advantage. While you have some personality weaknesses, you are generally able to compensate for them. Your sexual adjustment has presented some problems for you. Disciplined and controlled on the outside, you tend to be worrisome and insecure inside. At times you have serious doubts as to whether you have made the right decision or done the right thing. You prefer a certain amount of change and variety and become dissatisfied when hemmed in by restrictions and limitations. You pride yourself as being an independent thinker and do not accept others' opinions without satisfactory proof. You have found it unwise to be too frank in revealing yourself to others. At times you are extroverted, affable, sociable, while at other times you are introverted, weary, and reserved. Some of your aspirations tend to be pretty unrealistic (Ulrich et al., 1963, p. 832).

When the students who had been administered the personality tests by the professor rated the "interpretations," virtually all rated them as good or excellent. In the second phase of the study, approximately 75 percent of the subjects who had been tested by admittedly inexperienced students also rated the assessments of themselves as good or excellent. Furthermore, the comments that subjects made clearly indicated an acceptance of these interpretations as accurate and individualized descriptions of their own personalities. One student who had been given his tests and interpretation by the professor said: "On the nose! Very good. I wish you had said more, but what you did mention was all true without a doubt. I wish you could go further into this personality sometime." A subject who had been given the tests and interpretation by a student commented: "I believe this interpretation fits me individually, as there are too many facets which fit me too well to be a generalization" (Ulrich et al., 1963, p. 833).

More recently Snyder and Larson (1972) have replicated this study, extending it to show that college students accept these global evaluations as relevant regardless of whether they are presented by a psychologist in his office or a graduate student in the laboratory. Indeed, in the Snyder and Larson study, even among students who had been led to believe that their tests had been computer scored (rather than evaluated by a human scorer), most rated these statements as between good and excellent. From their own and earlier experiments of this sort, Snyder and Larson (1972) conclude that the evidence provides

> . . . an object lesson for the users of psychological tests. People place great faith in the results of psychological tests, and their acceptance of the results as being true for them is fairly independent of test setting, administrator, and scorer. Furthermore, it must be realized that presentation of the results of psychological tests, typically presented to the individual as being for him personally, maximizes the acceptance of the psychological interpretation. Thus, the individual's acceptance of the interpretation cannot be taken as a meaningful "validation" of either the psychologist or his tests (p. 388).

To replicate this experiment for yourself, tell a friend that you are learning how to use personality tests in class and have him make two different drawings for you. First, ask your friend to draw a picture of himself, and then another picture of himself, but this time as he would like to look. (The Draw-a-Person test is a projective technique which uses this procedure to assess personality; we shall have more to say about projective techniques in Chapter 5.) Then, in your own handwriting, copy the interpretation used by Ulrich et al. (see page 16), and about a week later offer this assessment to your friend. After he has had an opportunity to read it, ask him to rate the interpretation (excellent, good, average, poor, or very poor) and give you some feedback as to how well you are doing as a "psychological examiner." After this part of your experiment is completed, it is important that you reveal to your friend the real nature of the experiment. Complete explanation of the experimental deception, often called "debriefing," may evoke further comments of interest and also remove the possibility that permanent misconceptions about psychological testing will result.

PLAN OF THE BOOK

The book is divided into five sections. Section I includes this introductory chapter and the next chapter, which deals with methods of personality research which will be illustrated throughout the book. Each of the four succeeding sections is devoted to a description of the theory, assessment techniques, research methods, and change procedures which characterize one of the four strategies for the study of personality—*psychoanalytic, dispositional, phenomenological,* and *behavioral.* The strategy sections begin with brief introductory chapters which also serve as summaries; they should be read before the major chapters in the section and then again after the basic material has been read in order to help integrate what has been learned.

The format, emphasis, and writing style of Sections II through V vary somewhat so as to be consistent with the "flavor" and "customs" of each of the four strategies. Each strategy is presented in a positive light emphasizing its assets, thereby affording the reader an opportunity to evaluate the merits and limitations of the strategy on his own. The authors believe that this approach will provide an optimal introduction to the scientific study of personality. A brief discussion of several of the more cogent liabilities of each strategy appears at the end of Sections II through V. These discussions are not intended to be complete critiques and evaluations of the strategies; rather, they are presented to illustrate the limitations and problems each strategy faces when it is applied to the study of human personality.

2

Methods of Personality Research

Three major research methods have been used to study personality —the *experimental, correlational,* and *case study* methods. The experimental method involves the direct manipulation of experiences or "treatments" to which people are exposed and thus allows us to identify clear causal relationships between these experiences and subsequent behavior. The correlational method also examines the relationship between two or more events; however, though it provides a great deal of information, it does not usually allow us to draw causal inferences with certainty. The case study method involves a careful description of the behavior of one person and achieves a depth of information not usually available in either experimental or correlational research. We shall see, though, that the price paid for the case study approach is a severe limitation on the extension of conclusions drawn about the person studied to people in general.

These three methods have one essential element in common— they all involve *observation* of one sort or another. The differences lie in the manner in which the observations are made and in the way the data from the observations are analyzed. These research approaches will be discussed so that the reader may be in a better position to critically examine the personality research described in the remainder of the text.

THE EXPERIMENTAL METHOD

To introduce the components of experimental personality research, we shall consider a study in which the investigators were interested in persons' feelings of responsibility during an emergency (Darley & Latané, 1968). This study was instigated by a provocative social event, which Darley and Latané describe in the following way:

> Several years ago, a young woman was stabbed to death in the middle of a street in a residential section of New York City. Although such murders are not entirely routine, the incident received little public attention until several weeks later when the New York *Times* disclosed another side of the case; at least 38 witnesses had observed the attack—and none had even attempted to intervene. Although the attacker took more than half an hour to kill Kitty Genovese, not one of the 38 people who watched from the safety of their own apartments came out to assist her. Not one even lifted the telephone to call the police (p. 377).

The surprising lack of intervention by any of the observers in this case appears to be inconsistent with all of the humanitarian and co-operative norms which our society attempts to foster. The incident itself may provoke several alternative explanations, or *hypotheses,* to account for the fact that no assistance was rendered to the victim. For example, it is possible that, contrary to our common beliefs, persons are simply not willing to assist others whom they do not know, even in an obvious emergency. But this is a very general hypothesis, and the events described above did not happen in a vacuum. Perhaps, then, some identifiable characteristics of the situation diminished persons' willingness to come to the aid of the victim. She might have been helped if "things had been different." Different in what way? At this point the investigators must formulate, in fairly precise terms, some specific characteristics of the situation which might have reduced the willingness of others to provide assistance and feel responsibility. The following were suggested:

> In certain circumstances the norms favoring intervention may be weakened. . . . One of these circumstances may be the presence of other onlookers. For example . . . each observer, by seeing lights and figures in other apartment house windows, knew that others were also watching. However, there was no way to tell how the other observers were reacting. These two facts provide several reasons why any individual may have delayed or failed to help. The responsibility for helping was diffused among the observers; there was also a diffusion of any potential blame for not taking action; and finally, it was possible that somebody, unperceived, had already initiated helping action (p. 377).

These possibilities may now be seen to converge upon a single, testable *experimental hypothesis,* namely, that "the more bystanders to an emergency, the less likely, or the more slowly, any one bystander will intervene to provide aid" (p. 378). At this point the hypothesis is still untested. It is no more than an idea or possibility, but the idea is now well formulated as a specific proposition and can be tested in a new, *controlled situation. Control* in psychological research has three different meanings: control over the behavior of the subject under study (what he is allowed to do), control over the behavior that is observed and recorded, and control over the influences of the environment, or the circumstances present in the situation.

The controlled situation must meet all of the logical demands of the proposition but exclude other factors which have not been hypothesized to be relevant. What are the demands in the present example? First, a situation must be created in which subjects can be made to perceive a true emergency as occurring in their presence. Second, it must be possible for each subject to be aware of the number of other "bystanders" present. Third, subjects must be unable to get information about the reactions or behavior of the other bystanders. Finally, precise measurement of the variables of interest (the speed and frequency of reaction to the seeming "emergency") must be possible.

To meet these requirements in the Darley and Latané experiment, college students were told that they were going to participate in a discussion of personal problems dealing with college life. When a subject arrived for the experiment, he was taken to a small room, instructed to put on headphones with an attached microphone, and told to listen for instructions. By means of the headphones, the experimenter explained how the "discussion" was to be run. Subjects were told that the purpose of their being placed in individual rooms was to preserve anonymity (actually other persons were simulated by tape-recorded statements) and that, in order to foster more open discussion, the experimenter would not listen to the discussion while it was in progress. Finally, each person was to speak for two minutes, in turn, during which time only his microphone was turned on. Thus, only one person at a time could be heard.

The first person to speak, the "victim" to be, mentioned in the course of his comments that he was subject to seizures similar to epilepsy. After the subject spoke (always last), it was the victim's turn again. Following several brief, calm, and coherent comments, the victim began to stutter and his words became increasingly incoherent as he verbally feigned a seizure.

Each subject was placed in the situation just described, but the number of other people the subject believed were participating in the discussion varied. In one condition, subjects heard only the victim's voice (two-person group); in a second condition, subjects listened to one other voice besides the victim's (three-person group); subjects in a third condition heard four other voices besides the victim's (six-person group). Thus, the *independent variable,* the condition which the experimenter *manipulated,* or had under his control, was the number of persons whom subjects thought to be participating in the discussion.

A *dependent variable* is that part of a subject's behavior which changes as the independent variable changes. The name *dependent variable* comes from the fact that the variable depends on, or is controlled by, the conditions set up by the experimenter. In our example, the dependent variables were the *speed* and *frequency* of reaction to the "emergency." The speed of reaction was defined as the time that elapsed from the beginning of the victim's seizure until the subject left his room to summon aid. The frequency of reaction was simply the proportion of subjects in each group who summoned aid within six minutes after the emergency began.

An *experimental hypothesis* involves a statement about the effect of manipulating the independent variable upon the dependent variable. It was hypothesized in the experiment that the more witnesses to an emergency (the independent variable), the less likely and the more slowly will any one witness intercede (the dependent variables). If the three groups of subjects differed (on the dependent variables) from one another in the predicted direction (i.e., the most aid coming from subjects in the two-person group and the least from those in the six-person group), the experimenters would then want to be in a position to say that the difference was due to the independent variable and only to the independent variable. Suppose, for example, the two-person group had a higher percentage of "civic-minded" subjects than either of the other groups. In that case, the greater aid given by these persons might be due to a difference in the characteristics of the sample of subjects rather than to the number of people in the discussion group. Or, if the six-person group heard a less convincing seizure by the victim, this might account for their reluctance to help him. To eliminate or minimize the possibility of such alternative explanations being as viable as the experimental hypothesis, every effort was made to equate the groups with respect to characteristics of the subjects. (Usually this is accomplished by assigning them *randomly* to groups.)

Once the groups have been made as similar as possible, it is necessary for all subjects to receive exactly the same treatment except for the independent variable. The only difference between the three groups in our example was the number of people perceived to be part of the discussion. To ensure the same treatment for all groups, standard procedures were employed. For example, by using tape-recorded simulation of other discussants, all subjects were exposed to identical voices.

The major results of Darley and Latané's experiment are shown in Table 2–1. From this table it can be seen that the experimental hypothesis was confirmed for both dependent variables. The two-person group had the highest percentage of subjects responding to the emergency and the fastest average reaction time, while the six-person group had the lowest percentage of subjects responding and the slowest average reaction time.

In considering these data, it is important to keep in mind that *on the average* people who were supposedly alone with the victim were more helpful than people who thought four other persons were also witnessing the victim's plight. When experimentation is done with groups of subjects, the average (usually the *mean*) performances of the groups are compared. There may have been subjects in the two-person condition who took longer to respond to the emergency than some of the subjects in the six-person condition. But, when the average performance of the subjects in each treatment condition was examined, the two-person group was considerably more helpful than the six-person group.

TABLE 2–1

Effects of Group Size on Likelihood and Speed of Response

Group Size	Percent Responding by End of Seizure	Mean Time in Seconds
2 (subject and victim).................	85	52
3 (subject, victim, and 1 other)........	62	93
6 (subject, victim, and 4 others).......	31	166

Source: After Darley and Latané, 1968.

In reporting the results of research, the phrase *significant difference* is often used in comparing treatment groups. When employed in this context, the word *significant* does not refer to importance (i.e., social significance). A statistically significant difference is one that has a low probability of occurring by chance alone and thus reflects a difference which could be reliably expected in other samples—that is, a "real" difference. If all relevant variables other than the independent variables are controlled for (by holding them constant for all groups, for example), then the experimenter can conclude that the difference is a function of the independent variables which he has manipulated.[1]

Traditionally in psychological research, a difference is considered *statistically significant* and therefore admissible as evidence if the odds are 5 in 100 or less that the difference is not a chance finding.

---

[1] For a more detailed discussion of statistical significance as well as other statistical and methodological concepts touched upon in this chapter, the interested reader should see Neale and Liebert's *Science and Behavior* (1973).

This level of significance is called the .05 level (commonly written "$p < .05$" and read "probability less than 5 percent"). Generally, the greater the likelihood that a difference is not due to chance alone, the more confidence an experimenter places in his results.[2]

For practical purposes, small differences are often meaningless. It would be difficult, for example, to think of a group who on the average summoned aid a second faster than another group as being more concerned with helping in an emergency. Optimally, manipulating independent variables will lead to both statistically significant and practically meaningful differences among experimental conditions, as was the case in Darley and Latané's study. The difference between 52 and 166 seconds certainly could mean the difference between the victim's living or dying in a real emergency.

People sometimes criticize psychological research because it frequently deals with questions more in terms of "science for science's sake" than of relevancy to man's daily life and its problems. The subject matter of psychological research may seem too abstract to be relevant to everyday human behavior. Or, the research problem may appear important to the "man on the street," but the method of investigation may seem wholly artificial and therefore devoid of meaning for him. Is it reasonable to translate an interest in the behavior of witnesses to crime and brutality into an experimental investigation of the reactions of college students to the verbal anguish of another person heard over headphones? Can we generalize from this laboratory setting to the streets of our large urban centers? Would it not be better to observe bystander behavior in an actual incident like the one which prompted the experiment? It is true that something is lost when an investigation of human behavior moves into less authentic circumstances. However, *although in laboratory experiments we gain less information about the total problem at hand, we gain more reliable information about a specific aspect of the problem.*

THE CORRELATIONAL METHOD

Correlation, as the name implies, deals with the co-, or joint, relationship between two or more variables. The method answers research questions put in the form of: "Do variable X and variable Y go together or vary together?" Questions of relationship are frequently asked in psychology. Is there a relationship between late toilet training and compulsiveness in adulthood? Is the frequency

---

[2] Some caution must be employed in carrying this rule to extremes, for when very large samples of subjects are employed (e.g., several hundred or more), extremely small differences *can* be statistically significant. The question still remains whether such a difference is *important.*

of dating in college related to marital success and happiness? The correlational method is characterized by the fact that all subjects are observed under identical conditions. *Rather than manipulate variables, the researcher makes measurements (observations) of already existing characteristics of the subjects.*

The major drawback of correlational research is that cause and effect relationships usually cannot be identified. When two variables are correlated (vary together), we do not know which is the cause of the other or whether both are caused by something else. There is, for example, a high positive correlation between the number of churches in a city and the number of crimes committed in that city; the more churches a city has, the more crimes are committed in it. Does this mean that religion fosters crime? Probably not. That crime fosters religion? Unlikely. The relationship is due to a third variable —population—the growth of which leads to an increase in both churches and crime. Or consider the high positive correlation between the number of drownings on any given day and the consumption of ice cream on that day. Here, too, a third variable—temperature—is responsible for the relationship. The warmer the weather, the more people who are swimming (and thus the more people who drown) and the more ice cream that is eaten. The fact that we cannot infer causation directly from correlational evidence does not mean that a cause and effect relationship does not exist; it merely means that, in contrast to the experimental method, a correlation does not enable us to identify the nature and direction of causal relationships without further information.

When studying the correlation between variables, the psychologist wants to know the *direction* and *magnitude* of the relationship. The direction of the correlation indicates the manner in which the variables[3] relate to each other. A *positive correlation* between variable X and variable Y means that high scores on X tend to be associated with high scores on Y and low scores on X tend to go along with low scores on Y. For example, a positive correlation is regularly found between a person's height and weight. Conversely, a *negative correlation* is one in which high scores on X tend to be associated with low scores on Y and low scores on X tend to go with high scores on Y. Age and quickness of reflexes are negatively correlated; as people grow older, their reflexes become slower.

The Pearson product-moment *correlation coefficient* is the most commonly used statistic to indicate both the direction and magnitude of a relationship. The direction of the correlation is indicated by

---

[3] It should be noted that any number of variables can be correlated with one another. However, for the sake of illustration, the examples in this section refer to the simplest case—that is, only two variables.

the sign of the coefficient, while its magnitude is indicated by the absolute value (i.e., disregarding algebraic sign) of the coefficient. The correlation coefficient may range from a value of $+1.00$, which indicates a perfect positive relationship, to a value of -1.00, which indicates a perfect negative relationship. When the coefficient is equal to 1.00 ($+$ or $-$), either variable can be exactly predicted from the other. As the coefficient decreases in absolute value from 1.00, the ability to predict one variable from the other decreases. In the extreme, a product-moment correlation of 0.00 indicates that the variables are unrelated. Knowledge of one would not assist us at all in predicting the other. It must be emphasized that how closely two variables are related depends only on the absolute size of the correlation coefficient. Thus, correlation coefficients of $+.60$ and $-.60$ are equivalent with respect to the extent to which one variable can be anticipated from the other. (Of course, the direction of the correlation must be known to make the prediction.)

Because correlation coefficients range in absolute value between 0 and 1.00, it is tempting to view them as percentages (i.e., when multiplied by 100) and thereby to assume that a correlation of .50 is twice as large as one of .25. This is an error. The appropriate rule of thumb is to compare *squared* correlation coefficients as an estimate of the ability to predict one variable, knowing the value of the other. This is what is technically called the percentage of variance that the two variables have in common. A correlation of .71 would be considered twice as large as a correlation of .50—i.e., $(.71)^2 = .50$ (rounded off) and $(.50)^2 = .25$.

It is often convenient and instructive to plot a correlation graphically as a *scatter diagram*. Figure 2–1 presents several such scatter diagrams. The horizontal axis represents the values of one variable, while the vertical axis represents the values of the other. Each point corresponds to the scores of one subject on the two variables. Notice that in the case of perfect positive or perfect negative correlation, all the points fall in a straight line. Thus, by knowing a person's score on one of the variables (it makes no difference which one), we can perfectly predict his score on the other variable. Where there is perfect correlation, either positive or negative, the plot shows no "scatter" (i.e., deviation from the perfect line of correlation). In the case of a moderately large correlation, there is some scatter about the line of perfect correlation, but the scores tend to fall within a narrow ellipse. Finally, where there is virtually no correlation, there is much scatter of the scores, and the plotted points tend to lie within a circle.

Correlational research does not always employ the correlation coefficient. The method of correlation is a research method and not a statistical procedure. *As long as each subject is treated in the same way and measurements are made of already existing characteristics*

FIGURE 2–1

Scatter Diagrams Showing Various Degrees of Relationship

(a) Perfect Positive (+1.00)

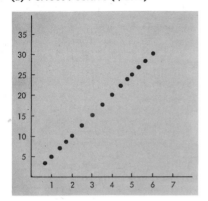

(b) Perfect Negative (−1.00)

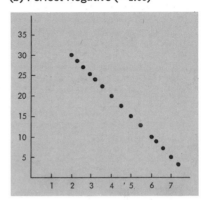

(c) Moderate Positive (+.67)

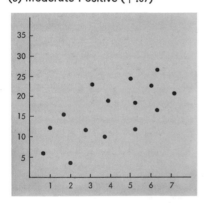

(d) Moderate Negative (−.67)

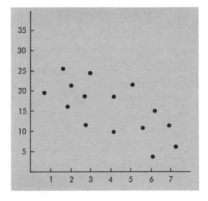

(e) Unrelated (0.00)

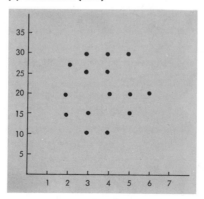

of the subjects, we are dealing with correlational research. The correlation coefficient has been discussed in some detail because of its frequent use and because it illustrates the underlying principles of correlation.

Correlational research can be viewed as compromising the control provided by experimentation for an economical means of making a broad inspection of a problem. By substituting measurement of already existing characteristics of the subject for experimental manipulation, the correlational strategy often permits much of the naturalness of the situation to remain. As we have seen, lack of control has its drawbacks, but among its strong points is that an absence of control may bring the investigation closer to "real life" than the controlled experiment can.

Behavior is almost always *multiply determined* (i.e., caused by a number of variables operating at the same time and in conjunction with one another), and the correlational design can easily take this "fact of nature" into account by studying the relationship of many variables with one another. Although experimentation can also deal with multideterminants by manipulating more than one independent variable at a time, it is rare in practice for a single experiment to employ more than three independent variables, and many experiments have only one.

Generally, there are three reasons that correlation is used instead of experimentation. First, there are a number of variables which do not lend themselves to manipulation by the experimenter without becoming highly artificial. (Variables such as sex, age, and birth order are usually unmanipulable.) In the study of child-rearing practices, for example, it is virtually impossible to place rigid controls over the home environment and the relationships of parents and children. Sometimes it is questionable whether an experimental manipulation will work, whereas the "natural manipulation" of the variables is certain to have an effect on the subject. This is another case where the correlational method may be favorably compared with the experimental approach. For example, the 1964 U.S. Surgeon General's report dealing with the relationship between cigarette smoking and lung cancer was an event which provided a credible account of the health hazards of tobacco which could not have easily been simulated in the laboratory. After the report appeared, it was possible to relate giving up cigarettes to familiarity with the evidence—a unique opportunity to study attitude change under conditions of intense personal involvement. A second reason that correlation is used in place of experimentation is that there are situations where direct manipulation is possible but unethical, as in cases where a subject would have to suffer severe pain or physical injury. Psychological investigations of death, suicide, and mourning have necessarily been correlational in nature, since these variables cannot be controlled by the experimenter.

Third, psychologists use a correlational method instead of an experimental one when it is initially more economical to do so. Rather than create a particular condition in his subjects, the investigator may find that much time, money, and effort can be saved if measurements can first be taken of subjects who are already in that condition. Thus, a psychologist interested in the relationship between anxiety and test performance might administer questionnaires during a class examination to tap the already present state of anxiety in the subjects and then correlate these scores with the grade on the examination. This approach is to be distinguished from one creating different levels of anxiety in the subjects by telling some of them, for example, that the results of the test will have an important influence on their being accepted into graduate school and telling others that the results will be kept confidential.

Whether a correlational approach is truly efficient in the long run will depend on the price paid for the lack of adequate controls. Pilot studies which are correlational in nature can serve to direct the investigator toward behavior which may have been previously ignored or overlooked and to suggest hypotheses which can then be tested in experimental settings. Tentative hypotheses about certain relationships can also be subjected to correlational study before experimentation is undertaken.

Sometimes a researcher has the opportunity to see how relationships investigated under highly controlled laboratory conditions apply to real-life situations. The massive power failure which encompassed much of the eastern seaboard of the United States on November 9–10, 1965 offered a rare opportunity for a field investigation of an in-process crisis. One group of alert psychologists capitalized on this "natural manipulation" to test their laboratory findings concerning individual differences in anxiety and affiliation in relation to birth order (Zucker, Manosevitz, & Lanyon, 1968). The blackout occurred in New York City about 5:30 P.M., at the height of the transportation rush hour. The result was that thousands of people on their way home from work were forced to spend the night in public places. In the early morning hours, Zucker and his colleagues asked persons in a large bus terminal and a hotel lobby, both of which were illuminated by emergency power, to complete a questionnaire concerning such information as age, education, birth order, and so on, and their feelings about being stranded for the night. The subjects were asked to rate their preference for being alone or with other people, on a five-point scale, and to assess their anxiety by responding to the following question, also on a five-point scale: "How nervous or uneasy did you feel during this experience (i.e., the blackout experience over the course of the evening)?" The investigators also noted, before approaching a subject, whether he was talking to or standing with someone else, and this information became a dichotomous index of actual gregariousness (i.e., affiliative or nonaffiliative) at the time of the data collection.

Previous research had shown that firstborns tend to be more anxious than later borns when they are placed in an anxiety-arousing situation, and Zucker and his associates found some further evidence for this relationship. Additionally, the results of numerous laboratory studies had shown that firstborns express a greater preference for being with other people than for being alone when exposed to stress-inducing conditions. This hypothesis received support for women only in the actual crisis situation.

Correlation and Causation: A Recapitulation and Some Alternatives

We have said that when a substantial correlation between variable X and variable Y is found, one of three possibilities exists with regard to cause and effect. X may cause Y. Y may cause X. Or Z, a third variable, may be responsible for both X and Y. Nonetheless, other available knowledge, often coupled with sophisticated statistical techniques, may allow us to draw some types of causal information from correlations.

In the case of the correlation of certain variables, at least one of the three possibilities for causation may be manifestly absurd. If a high correlation between sex and intelligence is found, the possibility that intelligence causes sex can be immediately dismissed for obvious reasons. The alternatives are then narrowed to two. An individual's sex may determine his intelligence. Or, parents may treat children differently with respect to the educational advantages given them as a function of their sex. In this latter case, sex is only an indirect causative factor, and differential familial treatment would be the direct cause of variations in intelligence.

It is also true that when one variable precedes another in time, the second cannot cause the first. For this reason it is possible to obtain some causal information by repeating a correlational study more than once, over fairly wide spans of time. Through statistical analyses of these *time-lagged correlations* causal relationships may be identified. Consider the question of whether exposure to violence on television causes young viewers to become more aggressive. It has been known for some time that there is a correlation between the amount of such viewing which youngsters engage in and their aggressive behavior toward others (e.g., Eron, 1963). Still, it is possible that being aggressive makes a youngster more likely to be interested in and to watch violent entertainment, rather than vice versa. To disentangle these two possibilities, one team of investigators (Lefkowitz, Eron, Walder, & Huesmann, 1972) measured the relationship between television violence viewing and aggressive behavior for a large sample of boys not once, but twice: when the boys were 9 years old and again when they were 19. Then the investigators compared the correlation between early viewing and later behavior with the one between early behavior and later viewing. Since the former correlation was statistically significant while the latter was not (see Figure 2–2), the evidence suggested that viewing television violence *caused* aggressive behavior and the building of aggressive habits, rather than the other way around. Thus, depending on the nature of the variables under investigation, some information concerning causation may be gleaned from correlational research.

FIGURE 2–2

The Correlations between Television Violence Watched and Aggressive Behavior for 211 Boys over a 10–Year Lag

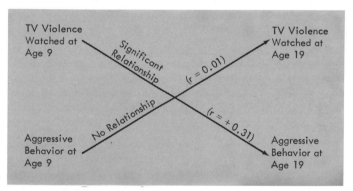

Source: Based on Lefkowitz et al., 1972.

There are instances, too, in which it is not necessary to know whether one of the measured variables is causing another or whether an "outside" variable is responsible. One such case is in applied areas of psychology in which prediction of a criterion is all that is required. For example, a college admissions committee needs information to predict success in college. Typically there is a high positive correlation between grades in high school and scores on entrance examinations and academic achievement in college. Using this information, the committee can do its job effectively without reference to the causes of college academic achievement.

THE CASE STUDY METHOD

A familiar and quite commonplace method of studying personality is the biography. When a detailed account of a single individual is used in personality research, in a hospital by physicians, or in a community service agency by a social worker, it is typically called a *case study*. Although the case study is the least systematic and least controlled research method and is mainly descriptive in nature, it does have a place in the scientific study of personality (cf. Ross, 1963).

There are numerous instances of case studies being used *didactically* as examples of prototypical behavior. For example, in an attempt to illustrate the classification of abnormal behavior, the following short case study was used as an example of an obsessive-compulsive reaction, which is characterized by the presence of persistent, disturbing thoughts and the urge to perform stereotyped acts repeatedly.

> Michael R., a twenty-three-year-old single man, applied for treatment to a psychiatric clinic in a medium-sized midwestern town. He was living alone in a small apartment in that town.
>
> Michael was the older of two children born to a rather vitriolic couple. His father was an ex-college athlete and part-time alcoholic, whose only interest in his children was the thought of developing their athletic ability. His mother was a violent-tempered woman who frequently flew into tantrums, which usually were initiated by the father's alcoholic disorderliness. Harsh physical punishment was not at all uncommon, and Michael had the occasional experience of being thrown bodily out of the house and being locked out a whole night, even for minor misdemeanors. His younger sister was an accomplished athlete, while Michael was clumsy, unco-ordinated, and eventually, uninterested. This situation provoked jealousy and hostility in Michael, and prohibited a warm relationship with his sister, who was the father's favorite. Although of very superior intelligence, Michael had a great deal of difficulty in school, generally because of disciplinary matters. He preferred sketching and painting to any of the formal courses offered, and persisted despite the taunt of his family and schoolmates. Michael chose to attend the nearby state university, which offered a fine program in art education. He graduated from that school, but was very dissatisfied with his progress, and felt that he had not learned anything. He then took a job as an elevator operator, forsaking any attempt to find employment which would utilize his artistic ability.
>
> Throughout his life, Michael had an intense fear of stinging insects such as wasps and hornets. If he passed a man on the street who appeared to have an athletic physique, he would be beset with the fear that the man would attack him. He also had a fear of heat and fire, and this fear was accompanied by the persistent thought that he would step on discarded lighted matches or cigarettes. He was extremely neat and orderly in all his affairs, carrying this to

the point where everything had to be "lined up" neatly. He realized that these concerns were unreal and irrational, but nevertheless they persisted. He was always dissatisfied with his social relationships, feeling that others ridiculed, belittled, and disliked him. He did little or no dating, and never had a genuinely warm friendship with anyone.

When applying for treatment, Michael entered the room with a list of the things which bothered him, and he proceeded to read this list to the interviewer. The list was divided into four sub-categories, namely, "anxiety, sexual thoughts, anger, and miscellaneous." It was felt that Michael was in need of therapy, and might possibly benefit from it, although many potential difficulties were recognized in his rigid attitudes. However, because he was making plans to move back to his home town soon thereafter, Michael was advised to seek treatment in the latter community (Zax & Stricker, 1963, pp. 169–70).

Such a use of the case study helps to bring the student out of the realm of abstract conceptions and into the realm of concrete examples. A danger in this technique is that it may lead to the false conclusion that all cases of a particular genre are exactly the same. This problem can be somewhat circumvented when more than one case study is presented and the commonalities among them as well as the idiosyncrasies of each are pointed out.

Case studies can also be extremely useful in *illustrating procedures,* such as methods of personality change, where it is often insufficient to merely learn the principles involved. One must also be able to see how the principles are applied. Ayllon (1965) illustrates the management of "some behavioral problems associated with eating in chronic schizophrenic patients" in the following case study.

Anne was a near mute catatonic who for the last 16 years would not eat unless a nurse led her to the dining room, gave her a tray, silverware, and food, and seated her at the table, then urged her to eat and occasionally spoonfed her.

A 14 day baseline of Anne's behavior associated with meals was obtained. Not once during this period did she go to the dining room on her own, nor did she help herself to food. This information suggested that her difficulty in both these behaviors was being maintained by the attention she received from the nurses as a function of this difficulty. The nurses were instructed not to take the patient to the dining room but to help her as much as before once she entered the dining room.

During the 21st week of this program, it was decided to shape her behavior in the dining room so that the patient would go through the cafeteria line completely on her own, without the nurse's assistance (for four weeks previous to shaping, no records were taken once she had entered the dining room). The nurses were instructed not to help the patient in the dining room, but to reinforce her by dropping some candy on her tray, only after she had picked up a tray, silverware, and one edible item (p. 74).

Case studies have also been used to present data concerning an unusual case. Probably the most famous of these is "A Case of Multiple Personality" (Thigpen & Cleckley, 1954), an account of a 25-year-old married woman, "Eve White," who displayed three very distinct personalities. Eve White had been seen in psychotherapy for several months because of severe headaches and blackouts. Her therapist described her as a "retiring and gently conventional figure." One day during an interview,

> As if seized by a sudden pain she put both hands to her head. After a tense moment of silence, her hands dropped. There was a quick, reckless smile and, in a bright voice that sparkled, she said, "Hi there, Doc!" The demure and constrained posture of Eve White had melted into buoyant repose. . . . This new and apparently carefree girl spoke casually of Eve White and her problems, always, using *she* or *her* in every reference, always respecting the strict bounds of a separate identity. When asked her own name she immediately replied, "Oh, I'm Eve Black" (p. 137).

Following this startling discovery, Eve was observed over a period of 14 months in a series of interviews amounting to approximately 100 hours. (During this time, still a third personality emerged.) This case study is valuable because it is one of only a few detailed accounts of a rare phenomenon, a true multiple personality.

Recently, fictional case studies of abnormal behavior (particularly in children) have become very popular. The writer draws upon the case studies of a number of individuals and upon his experience in treating them. Good examples include *Jordi, Lisa and David, One Little Boy,* and *I Never Promised You a Rose Garden.*

Case studies are sometimes used to test hypotheses and support theories, but the justification of such use is questionable. Freud used case studies extensively to support psychoanalytic theory, and, in fact, they were the only evidence he presented for his hypotheses. His case studies, including that of Little Hans, to be discussed in a later chapter, all suffer from the critical flaw of being open to many interpretations. While Freud used these studies as evidence for his hypotheses, others can (and have) explained the same observations from an entirely different theoretical viewpoint. For this reason, and others which will be mentioned shortly, case studies are poor substitutes for controlled experimentation when one's purpose is to muster support for a theory.

On the other hand, case studies can sometimes be helpful in *disconfirming* the implications of a theory. When a theory purports to be universally true (i.e., to hold in all cases), case studies can provide *negative instances* of the theory. A single negative instance—an example that is covered by the domain of the theory yet does not conform to the theory—is sufficient to disprove the claim of universality. For instance, Freud conceived of the Oedipus complex (discussed in detail in Chapter 4) as a universal phenomenon. Accordingly, the anthropological studies which demonstrated that there are cultures in which young boys do not exhibit the Oedipus complex have been viewed by some as casting serious doubt on Freud's original hypothesis. Of course, a somewhat modified position may still be tenable (e.g., limiting the phenomenon to Western society).

As a method of personality research, the case study has several advantages. First, it is an excellent method for examining the personality of a single individual in great detail. For example, in a clinical setting, where the focus of interest is on one and only one person, the case study is found to be quite useful.

A second advantage of the case study, intimately related to the first, is that it allows an individual's idiosyncrasies, complexities, and contradictions to be examined. However general the laws of human behavior are, each person is very much a unique individual. An idiographic approach would focus upon a particular person rather than upon persons in general. Occasionally, a psychologist primarily interested in making statements about man's behavior in general will use a large number of case studies, and in this situation the inconsistencies which appear may be of special significance.

It is ironic that the most glaring deficiency of the case study method can be its most redeeming quality. Here we are speaking of the *lack of control* which usually characterizes case studies. By allowing circumstances to vary as they will, the case study has a greater potential for revealing new and perhaps serendipitous findings. This is especially true with regard to control over the dependent measures. If the dependent measures are specified in advance and only those measures are collected, the experimenter may miss some vital observations which are not measured. In fact, it is often the case that unexpected data become even more significant than the anticipated data and subsequently become the subject of further investigation.

Usually the case study method does not specify the observations to be made but rather attempts to record as much of the entire situation as possible. (In this regard, such modern techniques as video tape recording make this goal more realistic.) The advantage of placing no restrictions on the measures to be taken is sometimes outweighed by the problem of sorting through the data and making sense out of them. (Anyone who has sat down for an evening of editing reels of home movies has some idea of what a problem this could turn out to be.)

Still another advantage of the case study method should have become apparent in the foregoing discussion. The case study typically deals with a person in his natural environment as opposed to an artificial laboratory setting. Since ultimately theories of personality are intended to explain the behavior of persons in "real-life" situations, it is apparent that case studies have compelling *external validity*. That is, they directly examine the phenomena of ultimate interest.

The case study can be recommended as a method for personality research for at least one additional reason. It can include among its data the richness and complexity of personality. Although such data may not be specific enough to be used in *support* of a theory, they often are the source of hypotheses about man's behavior. These hypotheses, once formulated on the basis of the case study material, can then be tested by a more controlled and rigorous research method.

There are several distinct limitations of the case study method. First, to circumvent the major practical problem of being in the right place at the right time, the psychologist typically waits for the critical event to happen and at some later time collects his observations. These observations are in the form of detailed *retrospective* reports by the subject and any other people who happened to observe him. The problem with such *post hoc* data collection is that the observers (the subject and others) tend to forget what has happened and to lose the feelings that accompanied the original critical situation. Additionally, observers not only forget details, but their "stories" also tend to change with the passage of time. Things are now seen in a different perspective, especially when the incident under study has been somewhat stressful for the subject. Memories are mixed with present thoughts and feelings in a process similar to that which occurs when someone tries to reconstruct a dream after he has awakened. Thus, unless the data for the case study are gathered at the time the crucial incident occurs, the accuracy of the case material is open to question. The case of Eve White, mentioned previously, is an example of a *non*retrospective case study. Once it was decided that she was to be the subject of an extensive investigation, the data were systematically collected at each interview.

A second limitation of the case study method is that the data it yields are unique in that they generally come from a single individual, and therefore it is difficult to generalize from them to other people. A third limitation is the fact that case studies are open to a variety of interpretations, since there are no definite guidelines for deciding among two or more seemingly tenable hypotheses which account for the same data. Finally, the data from case studies are qualitative rather than quantitative, and quantification is an important element of scientific research since it leads to finer, more precise descriptions of behavior.

Whether the disadvantages of the case study method outweigh its advantages for studying personality depends upon the purpose of the investigation. At the very least, it is reasonable to think of the case study as a preliminary and adjunct research method.

CONVERGING METHODS IN PERSONALITY RESEARCH

Our descriptions and examples of experimental, correlational, and case study approaches to personality research thus far have been relatively pure instances. In practice, however, the personality psychologist will rarely rely on only one method (or only one study) to reach his conclusions. Instead, several methods may be used in various studies, and methods may be modified so as to maximize the amount of information obtained about a particular phenomenon.

Consider the question, raised earlier, of the possible effects of television violence on aggressive behavior. Here investigators have approached the problem by generating a converging line of evidence. The earliest studies were simply case reports of individual youngsters who had apparently become more aggressive by learning from or copying antisocial behavior which they had seen on television. Subsequent laboratory experiments then revealed that brief exposure to violent entertainment made youngsters more aggressive in play. Next, correlational evidence was introduced, showing a relationship between home viewing of TV violence and aggressive behavior. Recently, time-lagged correlational and experimental field studies have added further support for the hypothesis that viewing violence on television causes aggression. While no one of these investigations or methods could have made a strong case for a socially significant causal relationship, their combination is highly persuasive (cf. Liebert, Neale, & Davidson, 1973).

Although each of the strategies for the study of personality to be discussed in subsequent sections of the book tends to favor particular types of research, we shall see numerous examples of the use of converging lines of evidence from varied research methods in order to support hypotheses developed within each strategy.

section **II**

The
Psychoanalytic
Strategy

3

The Psychoanalytic Strategy
INTRODUCTION

As was discussed in Chapter 1, the purpose of this book is to introduce the study of personality by presenting four basic strategies which are used in the field and to illustrate each strategy with representative examples of theory, assessment, research, and personality change from the viewpoint of that strategy. In this section, only one major theory and approach to personality change will be presented: Sigmund Freud's psychoanalysis. Whereas each of the other three strategies encompasses a number of theoretical perspectives, the psychoanalytic strategy is dominated by this single view.

WHAT IS PSYCHOANALYSIS?

Psychoanalysis is, first of all, a strategy which emphasizes the importance of *intrapsychic events* (i.e., events within the mind) as central to personality. Beyond this general characteristic (shared with the phenomenological strategy discussed in Section IV), the term *psychoanalysis* has three common referents. First, it refers to a theory of personality (particularly personality development from its earliest stages in childhood) which was originally advanced by Freud and has subsequently been modified by other psychoanalysts who are called *neo-Freudians* or *neoanalysts*. (Those psychologists who have not deviated from Freud's position are called *orthodox Freudians* or simply *Freudians*.) Unless otherwise stated, the next two chapters will deal with Freudian psychoanalysis, since it illustrates better than any of the neo-Freudian theories the psychoanalytic strategy for the study of personality.

The second meaning of psychoanalysis is a method of scientific investigation, a way of studying intrapsychic phenomena. This includes *psychoanalyzing* a person's random thoughts, dreams, mistakes, and other forms of behavior so as to determine their intrapsychic significance, or meaning for the person. This process is the same as that used to bring about personality change, and psychoanalysis as therapy is the third meaning of the term.

INTENTION: THE FOCUS OF PSYCHOANALYTIC THEORY

Man is an inquisitive being. His questions, both explicit and implicit, can be broadly classified into two categories. One type of question is aimed at specifying operational and procedural details about events, phenomena, objects, or behavior and uses interrogatives such as *what, who, when, where,* and *how.* (A detective investigating a homicide case needs to know exactly what occurred, the time and place of the murder, how the victim was killed, and, naturally, "Who done it?") Answers to descriptive questions serve us pragmatically in that they allow us to *predict* events and have some *control* over them, thereby enabling us to function efficiently in our daily endeavors.

The other type of question is asked to gain "understanding," to learn *why* things happen the way they do. (Our homicide detective will also be interested in the murderer's *motive.*) Such questions are most frequently asked about some event after it has occurred, and therefore they are of less practical use to us since they do not allow us to predict or gain control of the event. Rather, these questions are posed to satisfy our curiosity and our desire for explanations. Most people want to know the reasons behind events which affect them, and the uncertainty of not knowing "why" may serve as an impetus to seek an explanation or "understanding." The psychoanalytic approach to personality is very much concerned with the reasons behind man's behavior and therefore with understanding personality.

"Why-questions" about behavior are implicitly asking about *intentions.* For example, a hitchhiker who has just gotten a ride might ask himself *why* the motorist had stopped for him. The hitchhiker is curious about the motorist's *intention* in giving him a ride. "Did he want company?" "Did he feel sorry for me?" "Is he going to ask me to do something for him in return?"

Intention is a critical notion in all sorts of personal relations. Historically, it is one of the most appealing and seemingly natural ways to conceptualize our own behavior and the behavior of others. Our legal system places great emphasis on the degree to which harmful acts are premeditated. For example, the law prescribes incarceration for as little as one year for killing another man if intent cannot be shown. But if intent to murder is clearly established, the penalty can be upwards of 20 years imprisonment or even death. In everyday life we often base judgments about other people and their behavior by evaluating the "worthiness" of their intentions. Consider such common questions as: "Why did she offer to help me with my work . . . because she likes me or because she felt she owed me something?"

In Western society, the importance of intent is learned early. Jean Piaget, a famous Swiss developmental psychologist, has found that children as young as seven may acknowledge that a small amount of purposeful damage is "naughtier" than substantial damage that occurs through ignorance, oversight, or accident. Our culture is filled with customs and attitudes which reflect the high status given to noble intentions, even when their outcome is undesirable. When given a gift, it is the *thought* (the giver's intent) that counts, and parents feel justified in severely punishing a child *because* they love him.

From the preceding examples, it is evident that knowing other people's intentions is important in daily interpersonal relations. We are also concerned with the extent to which others understand our own intentions. When a man walks hurriedly past a close friend without stopping to say hello, he is likely to explain his "behavior" the next time he sees his friend. If the man had been late for an important appointment, for example, he would tell his friend that he did not *mean* to be rude but was concerned about being late for his appointment. Actually, he is explaining his intention rather than his behavior.

Just as we sometimes explicitly make our intentions for a given act clear to another person, so too are there times when we try to conceal our intentions. A student who volunteers to do some additional research for a class in the hope of getting on the teacher's good side might tell his teacher that he is very interested in the topic.

Informing another person about the purpose of our behavior does not guarantee that he will accept our statement of intent as valid. If the man on his way to an appointment had had an argument with his close friend the night before, his friend might not be so sure that the man was merely concerned with his important engagement. Similarly, if the "diligent" student had shown little interest in the course throughout the semester, the teacher might question the student's motivation in volunteering to do extra work. In each case, there is a question raised as to the validity of a person's report of his intentions. The issue becomes one of finding the "true" intent of the act, the "real" reason it was performed. People frequently use the word "really" to emphasize the validity of a statement of intent. "Do you really like how I'm dressed?" "He really meant well." "I really love her."

The psychoanalytic strategy is characterized by the fact that it emphasizes the importance of questions of motivation and intention for understanding personality. In turn, these interests lead to the other emphases of the strategy. As implied, for example, by terms like *really,* a person may not always be aware of his own intentions and motivations; some of the most important aspects of an individual's personality may be *unconscious* and therefore the products of motivations of which he is entirely unaware.

Intention is always inferred from behavior. But people vary in the degree to which they use behavior to evaluate interpersonal interactions or go beyond the behavior to infer intentions. Demonstration 3–1 will give you an opportunity to explore your relative use of behavior and intentions to evaluate personal interactions.

Demonstration 3–1

INTENTION VERSUS BEHAVIOR

In our daily lives we have many interactions with people: roommate, shoe salesman, friend, teacher, bus driver. In each interaction we have certain expectations, either explicit or implicit, about what should take place. For example, the bus driver is supposed to get us to work on time, a teacher is supposed to assign grades, a friend should listen sympathetically to problems, and so on. Some of our expectations are doubtless satisfied (e.g., teachers almost never forget to give grades), while others are not (e.g., friends are not always eager to hear about our frustrations). When our expectations about how another person is supposed to act are not met, our reactions and feelings about that person are based on two sources of information: his *behavior* (what he has done or failed to do), and his *intent* (what he meant to do).

Suppose a bus driver failed to stop at your corner. You might have been very annoyed if you were consequently late for an appointment. It would have made little difference to you in that situation that the driver "had good intentions" of stopping. The driver's intent was at odds with his behavior, and your reaction of annoyance was based on the bus driver's *behavior* of driving past your corner and not on his intent.

It is important to note that in this instance the driver did not explicitly state his intention to stop, but the intention was a reasonable inference. *Intent frequently has to be inferred.* In the next example, the person's intention is explicitly stated.

Suppose you met a friend at lunch, hoping to share with him the events of your frustrating morning. Your friend said he wanted to listen (intent) but that he had to rush off (behavior) to study for a physics test scheduled that afternoon. You appreciated your friend's desire to listen to you and wished him well on his exam. Here again, a person's intent and behavior were inconsistent, but in this situation you evaluated the interaction in terms of your friend's *intention* to listen rather than his behavior of rushing off.

A third way of reacting to an inconsistency between intention and behavior would take both factors into account. In the preceding example, if your friend had left to play tennis, it is likely that you would have felt less good about your interaction with him than if he had "had" to leave for an exam. You would have understood that your friend had an appointment to play tennis but, at the same time, would have thought that he might have given your feelings and needs higher priority. By considering both behavior (your friend's playing tennis) and intention (he would have liked to listen to you), you would have viewed the situation differently than if you had taken only his intention or only his behavior into account.

The purpose of this Demonstration is to sensitize you to the role which other people's intentions and behavior and the relation between the two play in some of your daily interpersonal transactions. To achieve this, you will first compile a list of people with whom you have dealt recently and whom you either know very well or with whom you merely have a passing acquaintance. Then you will consider interactions you have had with these people in which their intentions and behavior were inconsistent.

Procedure

1. First, make a list of the people with whom you have interacted over the past few weeks. Try to include as many persons as you can, but there is no need for the list to be exhaustive.

2. Next, divide the people on your list into three categories:

"Close"—people you know well, interact with frequently and regularly, think about, and so on (e.g., roommate, good friend, parent);

"Distant"—people you do not know well, interact with infrequently and irregularly, may have met only once or twice, have only brief business-type dealings with (e.g., salesman, teacher with whom you have minimal personal contact);

"Other"—people who do not fit into either the "close" or the "distant" category (as defined above), whom you would not consider intimate acquaintances but also with whom you have had more than just a brief encounter (e.g., many classmates, people who live in your dorm, your mailman). The people in this category will *not* be used in the Demonstration.

Keep in mind that the object of this preliminary step in the Demonstration is to provide you with a list of a number of people whom you have recently interacted with and whom you would consider either "close" or "distant." Thus, if you are having difficulty coming up with six to eight people in *each* of the two categories, you may be using too stringent criteria for either "close" or "distant" relationship. If this seems to be the case, adjust your criteria accordingly.

3. Having compiled a sizable list of persons whom you might construe as "close" and "distant," you are ready to proceed with the major part of the Demonstration. This involves identifying as many interactions as you can with the persons on your "close" and "distant" lists *in which the persons' intentions and behavior were somehow inconsistent with each other*. Certainly all of your interpersonal interactions will not meet this requirement. Your goal should be to come up with at least four instances of intention-behavior discrepancies for each of the two categories of people (i.e., four for "close" and four for "distant") and more if possible.

4. For recording each of the intention-behavior discrepancies, make a large copy of the chart in Table 3–1 (omitting the examples, of course). Then, for each interaction in which intention and behavior were inconsistent, record the information outlined below. Note that the top half of the chart is designated for interactions with "close" acquaintances and the bottom half for interactions with "distant" acquaintances.

TABLE 3–1

Sample Chart for Demonstration 3–1

	I Other Person	II Nature of Interaction	III Other's Behavior	IV Other's Intent	V Your Evaluation	VI Basis for Evaluation
"Close" Relationships	Dick	Met Dick after having rough morning	Went to study	Wanted to talk with me	Understood why he couldn't talk and felt okay about it	I
	Dick	Met Dick after having rough morning	Went to tennis game	Wanted to talk with me	Appreciated that he had a tennis date but was a bit angry with him	B and I
"Distant" Relationships	Bus driver	On bus going to appointment	Drove past my stop	To stop	Annoyed at the driver for making me late to my appointment	B

In Column I: give the name of the person with whom you had the interaction.

In Column II: give a brief description of the interaction.

In Column III: give a brief description of the other person's behavior.

In Column IV: give a brief description of the other person's intention.

In Column V: give a brief description of how you evaluated the incident—that is, how you felt about and reacted to the other person and to the outcome of the incident.

In Column VI: state whether the basis for your evaluation in Column V was primarily the other person's behavior (B), primarily the other person's intention (I), or definitely a combination of behavior and intention (B & I).

The examples written in Table 3–1 are taken from those discussed in the introduction to the Demonstration.

Discussion

By the time you complete the Demonstration you should have gained a greater understanding of the difference between intention and behavior which is an essential distinction made by the psychoanalytic strategy. We usually do not differentiate between intention and behavior when they are consistent with each other. However, when they are discrepant, as was the case in each of the interactions you considered in the Demonstration, a need arises not only to distinguish between them but also to decide whether to evaluate the situation and its consequences for ourselves in terms of the person's intent, his behavior, or some combination of the two. The Demonstration should have given you an indication of how you tend to use intention and behavior in dealing with situations in which they are inconsistent. Is there any pattern in your reliance on intention versus behavior? There are any number of variables which might affect this, and one has been built into the Demonstration. By comparing your Column VI entries for "close" relationships with those for "distant" relationships, you may find that you tend to use intention as a basis for your evaluation of situations involving one of these groups of people, and behavior for the other group. Clearly this is an individual matter. The more interactions you have considered, the greater is the likelihood that consistent patterns or trends will emerge. You might wish to examine your relative use of intention and behavior in relation to other factors, such as the importance of the interaction to you, the sex of the other person, whether or not your evaluation of the other person's intention-behavior discrepancy had direct consequences for him (e.g., you commented to him on how you felt), and so on.

In addition to what you have already done in Demonstration 3–1, you might also wish to examine those instances in which your own intentions and behavior were inconsistent. How did you evaluate such situations? How did others who were aware of your inconsistencies react with regard to the relative emphasis they placed on your intention versus your behavior?

PSYCHOANALYTIC ASSESSMENT

If we are to deal with an individual's private motivations, we must decide the degree to which he himself is aware of them. To get a feel for the problem of people's degree of awareness about their motives and attitudes, you might ask yourself such questions as: Why am I attending college? Why do I like (dislike) my roommate (friend, relative)? (If the answers to these questions are readily apparent, try inserting the word "really" before the words *attending* and *like*.) Can people be ignorant of their own motives and unaware or mistaken about their feelings regarding other persons, places, or events? It is now commonplace, for example, to speculate that an individual who expresses an excessive degree of certainty about his own abilities, like the roaring lion, is expressing not self-confidence but self-doubt. Are there grounds for such assumptions? How often do they hold? What is the value and what are the limitations of looking at people in this light? The answers to these crucial questions about *unconscious* processes are the burden of the psychoanalytic strategy.

On the dimension of direct versus indirect approaches to personality assessment, described in Chapter 1, the psychoanalytic strategy relies almost exclusively on the indirect approach. There are two reasons for this orientation. First, an individual's reports cannot be trusted because various considerations, such as misperceptions and social pressures, might lead him to be inaccurate. Second, there may be reason to assume that the person himself cannot accurately verbalize his own motives and internal conditions. For these reasons, private events are usually assessed by indirect techniques (e.g., analysis of dreams, projective techniques) .

Another characteristic of psychoanalytic personality assessment is that it assumes that observations are *nonadditive* (Mischel, 1971). This means that the strength of a personality attribute, such as generosity, cannot necessarily be measured by summing various observations (overt behaviors) which are taken to indicate the presence of the attribute. Suppose Eric frequently helped his friends, gave expensive Christmas gifts to his relatives, and donated money to half a dozen charities each year, whereas Erica rarely offered aid to friends, sent Christmas cards but no presents, and was an ardent adherent of the saying "Charity begins at home." If a nonadditive measurement model is used, Eric would not necessarily be considered more generous than Erica. In fact, it might be inferred that Eric's behavior is indicative of an underlying stinginess and that his generous behavior serves to cover up this more reprehensible personality characteristic.

To summarize, personality assessment in the psychoanalytic strategy involves making observations of behavior from which are inferred in an indirect and nonadditive manner the underlying processes which cause behavior.

PSYCHOANALYTIC RESEARCH

The psychoanalytic strategy has employed primarily the case study method to substantiate its theoretical propositions. As a consequence, a huge amount of data about single individuals has been collected; no other personality strategy has led to such a wealth of observations. Most of these observations have been made in the course of psychotherapy. Consistency is sought both within an individual subject (e.g., the recurrence of a particular theme or symbol) and among subjects (e.g., themes common to many subjects, such as feelings of jealousy between a child and his same-sexed parent) . After hearing a patient repeat a given theme a number of times, the therapist will present the patient with an interpretation of its meaning. The validity of the interpretation is partially assessed by the degree to which the patient accepts it as true and it leads to a change in the patient's behavior. In turn, interpretations that are frequently made by a number of therapists and have been validated in the manner just described become principles of the theory. The validity of these principles may be further tested by seeing how well they fit with such cultural phenomena as taboos and folktales and with data which have been gathered from correlational and experimental investigations.

PSYCHOANALYTIC PERSONALITY CHANGE

If personality is made up of motivations and intentions, many of which are unconscious, then in order to change personality, the intrapsychic events accounting for it must be modified. Personality change in the psychoanalytic strategy involves dealing with thoughts, feelings, wishes, biological drives, and intentions, particularly those which are unconscious.

How can events about which a person is unaware be dealt with? The answer is that they cannot, and therefore a major aim of psychoanalytic personality change procedures is to make the person aware of his unconscious processes and motives—to make conscious what is unconscious. Personality change comes about primarily through the lengthy process of having the person discover and come to understand (gain insight into) his inner motivations. Frequently it is discovered in the course of psychoanalytic psychotherapy that the person's motives are based on early childhood adjustment problems and conflicts, and he must learn to accept the fact that such motives are no longer relevant to his life and are therefore unrealistic guides for his present behavior. Like the procedures for personality assessment used in the psychoanalytic strategy, the psychoanalytic techniques of personality change are indirect. Whereas the ultimate goal is to change *behavior* (from which personality change can be inferred), the change is brought about by modifying the intrapsychic events which are presumed to cause behavior.

4

The Psychoanalytic Strategy
THEORY AND RELATED RESEARCH

Before psychoanalytic personality theory is examined in detail, a brief overview of its major characteristics will be presented. Psychoanalysis can be usefully conceptualized as being deterministic, dynamic, organizational, and developmental.

First, psychoanalytic theory is a *deterministic* point of view. Freud held that all behavior is determined, or caused, by some force within us and that all behavior therefore has meaning. One of Freud's earliest and most widely cited clinical observations was the finding that even the simplest occurrences of human behavior can be traced to complicated psychological factors of which the individual may be totally unaware. Perhaps the best known of these occurrences are the so-called Freudian slips made in speech, writing, and reading. The errors presumably reveal something about the person's "inner" thoughts, or "real" intent. Examples in which the unconscious ideas are obvious include substituting "play-body" for "playboy" and "Fraud" for "Freud." In regard to omissions in writing, Freud (1951)[1] interestingly noted:

> Even the Bible did not escape misprints. Thus we have the "Wicked Bible," so called from the fact that the negative was left out of the seventh commandment. This authorized edition of the Bible was published in London in 1631, and it is said that the printer had to pay a fine of two thousand pounds for the omission (p. 63).

---

[1] The dates refer to the actual references used and thus do not always correspond to the original publication of the work.

Among the clearest examples of the thoroughgoing determinism which Freud (1963) used are those related to the "accidental" forgetting and losing of objects:

> If anyone forgets a proper name which is familiar to him normally or if, in spite of all his efforts, he finds it difficult to keep it in mind, it is plausible to suppose that he has something against the person who bears the name so that he prefers not to think of him (p. 52).

> We lose an object if we have quarreled with the person who gave it to us and do not want to be reminded of him; or if we no longer like the object itself and want to have an excuse for getting another and better one instead. The same intention directed against an object can also play a part, of course, in cases of dropping, breaking, or destroying things (p. 54).

> Here is the best example, perhaps, of such an occasion. A youngish man told me the following story: "Some years ago there were misunderstandings between me and my wife. I found her too cold, and although I willingly recognized her excellent qualities we lived together without any tender feelings. One day, returning from a walk, she gave me a book she had bought because she thought it would interest me. I thanked her for this mark of 'attention,' promised to read the book and put it on one side. After that I could never find it again. Months passed by, in which I occasionally remembered the lost book and made vain attempts to find it. About six months later my dear mother, who was not living with us, fell ill. My wife left home to nurse her mother-in-law. The patient's condition became serious and gave my wife an opportunity of showing the best side of herself. One evening I returned home full of enthusiasm and gratitude for what my wife had accomplished. I walked up to my desk, and without any definite intention but with a kind of somnambulistic certainty opened one of the drawers. On the very top I found the long-lost book I had mislaid" (p. 55).

Freud noted that he could "multiply this collection of examples indefinitely," and he used incidents like these as an indirect assessment technique to understand facets of an individual's personality that would otherwise be unavailable to anyone else.

A second major characteristic of psychoanalytic theory is that it is a *dynamic* point of view. "Dynamic" in the present context refers to the exchange and transformation of energy within the personality. Like most other personality theorists, Freud thought that it was essential for a comprehensive understanding of personality to have a statement of the source of motivation for human actions. Freud postulated that this source of motivation was a unitary energy source, called *psychic energy,* which can be found within the individual.

Third, psychoanalysis is *organizational.* Freud believed that personality is organized into three basic functions—the *id, ego,* and *superego*—and that it is the dynamic interaction or conflict among them which determines behavior. Also, these personality functions operate at three levels of awareness—*unconscious, preconscious,* and *conscious.*

Fourth, psychoanalytic theory is *developmental.* Freud held that human development follows a more or less set course from birth, and he divided development into a series of stages which all persons must pass through. Freud's theory is also developmental in the sense that it stresses the importance, indeed the dominance, of an individual's early childhood development as a determinant of his adult personality.

DRIVES AND LIBIDO

The psychoanalytic term *drive*[2] refers to an inborn, intrapsychic force which, when operative, produces a state of excitation or tension. Like much of his theory, Freud's formulations of drives underwent considerable revision in the more than 40 years he was engaged in developing them. Freud's early formulation divided drives into two classes. The first class of drives are self-preservative, dealing with the basic physical needs of existence, including breathing, hunger and thirst, and the excretory functions. When these drives are not satisfied, the organism experiences tension, as when one holds his breath or has not eaten in some time and feels hunger pangs. Usually, objects or circumstances to satisfy these drives are available in direct form; their satisfaction is typically simple and straightforward, allowing relatively little tension to build up. However, under unusual circumstances a drive such as hunger can become strong and exert a powerful influence on behavior. When the plane carrying a Uruguayan Rugby team and their supporters to a series of matches in Chile crashed in the Andes Mountains in October 1972, the passengers and crew were given up for lost. Miraculously, 16 men survived for 73 days in subfreezing temperatures with no fuel and only enough food to be rationed for 20 days. When they were finally rescued, it

---

[2] "Drives" are frequently referred to as *instincts* in the psychoanalytic literature, but the latter translation of the German *Trieb* can be misleading. Unlike the common usage of "instinct" as an inherited predisposition to behave in a characteristic way, a "drive" refers only to a source of internal excitation and not to the motor response which follows. More in keeping with the psychoanalytic usage, "drive" connotes a force whose energy can be modified and can be expressed in a variety of responses. The sex drive, for example, can be satisfied rather directly through sexual intercourse or masturbation and indirectly through such artistic endeavors as painting and sculpting (see discussion of sublimation on page 74–75).

was discovered that the survivors had remained alive by eating parts of the bodies of those who had died.

The second group of drives are those related to sexual urges; the psychic energy of sexual drives is called *libido*. In this context, "sexual" refers to all pleasurable actions and thoughts, including, but not confined to, eroticism. Libido is also the energy for all mental activity (e.g., thinking, perceiving, imagining, remembering, problem solving) and is somewhat analagous to, though not the same as, physical energy.

Freud contended that most of man's basic motivation is sexual in nature. Societies place obstacles in the way of living completely or even predominantly in terms of satisfying one's pleasure-seeking drives. In capsule form, Freud's theory of personality deals with the manner in which man handles his sexual needs in relation to his society, which usually prevents direct expression of these needs. Each individual's personality is a function of his particular compromise between his sexual drives and society's restraints on them.

For many years Freud's theorizing was concentrated exclusively on the sexual drive. Later, around 1920, he revised his theory of motivation to include the aggressive drive along with the sexual drive.[3] The aggressive drive was hypothesized to account for the destructive aspects of man's behavior. It possesses its own kind of psychic energy, although Freud gave this energy no special name. Freud's dual theory of drives assumes that both the sexual and aggressive drives are involved in the motivation of all behavior, although their contributions are not necessarily equal. (Had Freud lived in contemporary America, he might well have cited as one piece of evidence for the close interrelationship of the sexual and aggressive drives the common use of the word *fuck* to express anger.) Like the sexual drive, the aggressive drive is said to build up tension which must be released and develops in a manner parallel to that of the sexual drive. However, Freud's formulation of the development of the aggressive drive was never as clear-cut or complete as that of the sexual drive, and accordingly our subsequent discussion will focus on the latter.

Psychic energy is conceptualized as potentially building up in pressure or thrust in very much the same way as water might develop tremendous pressure in a series of pipes when no external valve is open. If there is an increase in pressure and there is no outlet for this pressure, the pipe will burst. Further, it will burst at its weakest point. Psychoanalytic theory argues that increase in the pressure, or tension, of psychic energy is a natural consequence of an intrapsychic

---

[3] Freud also called the aggressive drive the death drive (death instinct), or *Thanatos,* which is in opposition to the life drive (sexual drive), or *Eros.*

conflict. Reduction of this tension is necessary for an individual's functioning, and it also produces a highly pleasurable experience, since tension is experienced as unpleasant or painful. Tension reduction, which assumes a prominent place in psychoanalytic theorizing, is formally called the *pleasure principle*. If the individual's psychic energy does not have an opportunity to discharge in normal or socially acceptable ways, then the pressure will increase and finally, as with the water pipe analogy, will burst out violently at the weakest point in the personality.

Freud's psychic energy system is a *closed* system. That is, each person may be thought of as possessing a fixed quantity of psychic energy which is invested in given objects, persons, and ideas. Psychic energy cannot literally be *cathected*,[4] or attached to people and objects in the external world, but within the mind it can be cathected to their mental representations in the form of thoughts, images, and fantasies. The strength of a cathexis (i.e., the amount of energy invested) is a measure of the importance of the object. Since there is only a limited amount of psychic energy, the greater a given cathexis, the less psychic energy there is available for other cathexes and mental activities. Hence, the young man who is constantly thinking of his girl friend has difficulty doing other things, such as reading an assignment in his personality textbook. Cathexes are not permanent, so that if psychic energy is no longer cathected to one object it is free to be reinvested in another.

PSYCHOSEXUAL DEVELOPMENT

Psychoanalytic thinking places a great premium on the importance of early experience and suggests that many of the early social and personal experiences of the child become the models for his later personality.

While Freud expressed relatively little interest in the facts of the intrauterine environment and the birth process, several of his followers assigned a very critical role in the development of personality to these aspects. One psychoanalytic theorist, Fodor (1949), even asserted that the violence of parental sexual intercourse during pregnancy may have a traumatic effect which can be traced throughout the child's later life and revealed through his dreams.

Otto Rank (1929), whose name is most often associated with the concept of the *birth trauma,* argued that the initial biological separation of the child from his mother which is experienced at birth becomes the prototype for all later anxiety. Biological separation

---

[4] *Cathect* is the verb form of cathexis and refers to investing psychic energy in an object; *cathexes* is the plural of cathexis.

becomes a representation in later life for loss and separation. Rank suggested that every enjoyable act is oriented toward regaining the pleasure of the intrauterine environment. For example, for the male sexual intercourse symbolically represents a return to the mother's womb.

Freud himself suggested that before birth the child is in fact leading a relatively calm, peaceful, and undisturbed existence. In a warm, safe environment, he sleeps, exercises, and evacuates when he pleases. After birth this "ideal" existence changes radically. His needs and desires are to a large degree now under the control of others, particularly his parents, and immediate satisfaction and tension reduction is rarely, if ever, possible as it was during the previous nine months. Further, at the time of birth the child has not yet developed ways to cope with the immediate pressures (anxiety) that face him.

Stages of Psychosexual Development

Freud divided human development into a series of universal stages which all persons pass through from infancy to adulthood. The stages are delimited by the *erogenous zone* (an area of the body which is particularly sensitive to erotic stimulation) which is dominant at the time. That is to say, at any particular time in the developmental sequence, one body area—specifically, the mouth, the anus, or the genital region—seems to outweigh other areas as a source of pleasure. The stages of development are called *psychosexual* to indicate that the development is actually that of the sexual drive as it moves through the erogenous zones.

At each psychosexual stage a particular *conflict* must be resolved before the person can pass on to the next stage. The individual's libido is invested in behavior involving the erogenous zone which is predominant at the time; however, since each individual has a fixed amount of libido, the libido must be freed from the primary erogenous zone of the stage it is in (a consequence of resolving the conflict) so that it can be reinvested in the primary erogenous zone of the next stage. Freud used the analogy of military troops on the march to explain this process. As the troops march, they are met by opposition (conflict). If they are highly successful in winning the battle (resolving the conflict), virtually all of the troops (libido) will move on to the next battle (stage). The greater the difficulty in winning the battle, the more troops will be left behind on the battlefield and the fewer troops will be able to move on to the next confrontation.

In psychosexual development there are two basic reasons for an individual to have difficulty in leaving one stage and going on to the next. Either the person's needs relevant to the psychosexual stage have not been met (frustration), or his needs have been so well satisfied that he is reluctant to leave the stage (overindulgence). Frustration or overindulgence results in *fixation* at a psychosexual stage. Fixation involves leaving a portion of libido permanently invested in a stage of development which has passed and is analogous to the dead troops left behind in battle. The amount of libido fixated is dependent on the severity of the conflict.

Inevitably, some libido is fixated at each psychosexual stage. When the proportion of libido fixated at an earlier stage of development is small, only vestiges of earlier modes of obtaining satisfaction are seen in later behavior. However, when a substantial proportion of libido is fixated at an earlier stage, the individual's personality may become dominated by modes of obtaining satisfaction or tension reduction which were used in the earlier stage.

Oral Stage

During the first year of life, the child's mouth is the most prominent source of both his tension reduction (e.g., eating) and his pleasurable sensations (e.g., sucking). The child is said to be in the *oral stage* of development since the libido is centered in the oral cavity. Many neo-Freudians have broadened Freud's basic notions concerning the oral stage. As Strupp (1967) puts it, "the focal point of the child's personality organization at this period is not necessarily the mouth per se but *the total constellation of immaturity, dependency, the wish to be mothered, the pleasure of being held, the enjoyment of human closeness and warmth*" (p. 23).

These early experiences, attitudes, and aspects of social interaction are the prototypes for all future social behavior. Individuals who are fixated at the oral stage are likely to hold an optimistic view of the world, to develop dependent relationships in adulthood, to be unusually friendly and generous, and to expect the world, in turn, to "mother them." It is important to note that this type of theorizing, which is central to psychoanalytic thinking, lays the groundwork for explaining whole patterns of behavior in terms of early events and sets the tone for categorizing adults into character types (e.g., an oral character).

Some neo-Freudians have divided the oral stage into two phases. Thus far in the discussion only the first phase, *oral eroticism,* has been described. It is characterized by the pleasure of sucking and oral incorporation. The second phase, *oral sadism,* commences with the eruption of teeth and may be viewed as representing the development of the aggressive drive. Biting and chewing now become part of the child's behavioral repertoire, and he is able to behave aggressively and destructively. A person fixated at this second phase of the oral stage is likely to be pessimistic, cynical, and aggressive in later life.

Weaning is the crucial conflict of the oral stage. The more difficult it is for the child to leave his mother's breast or his bottle and its accompanying sucking pleasure, the greater will be the proportion of his libido which is fixated at the oral stage.

Anal Stage

With the weaning of the child, the libido shifts from the oral region to the area of the anus. Pleasure is obtained at first from expelling feces and later from retaining them. This is not to say that the child did not derive similar pleasure during the oral stage. However, during the second and third years of life, anal pleasure predominates just as oral pleasure predominated during the first year of life. Up until the anal stage, relatively few demands are made on the child. During the second year of life, however, parents in most Western cultures begin to make demands on their offspring, particularly with respect to bowel and bladder control. The conflict in the anal stage pits the sexual drive for pleasure, derived from the tension reduced by defecation, against the constraints of society, which require that the child develop self-control with respect to excretion.

If the child is able to easily accede to his parents' toilet training demands, he will develop the basis for successful self-control. However, the child may have difficulty in developing sphincter control and thus meeting the increasing demands of his parents. Two fundamental strategies for coping with the frustrations of toilet training are open to the child. He may attempt to "counterattack" by defecating at moments which are particularly inconvenient for his parents (e.g., immediately *after* being taken off the "potty"). If the child discovers that this is a successful means of social control, he may come to employ the same type of strategy for handling frustration in general. It is interesting to note, for example, that in our culture verbal statements of extreme anger and hostility are often expressed in colloquial terms which refer to the anal function. A person who makes excessive use of such hostile outbursts in later life would be labeled an *anal aggressive character*.

Alternatively, the child may adopt the strategy of meeting his parents' demands by complete retention of his feces. This in itself is pleasurable (i.e., gentle pressure against the intestinal walls), and, in addition, it may prove to be a powerful way of manipulating his parents (e.g., through their increased concern over his failure to have a bowel movement). If the tactic is successful, it may set the stage for similar behavior patterns in later life. Persons who are stingy, hoarding, and stubborn are often termed *anal retentive characters.*

An important implication of the psychoanalytic theory of psychosexual development is that the character types presumed to have developed in childhood due to fixated libido will be found among adults. The major empirical research strategy which has been used to validate the hypothesis of character types involves examining adults' responses to personality inventories to see whether the behaviors which are postulated to make up each character type actually occur together. For example, do the key anal traits of obstinacy, orderliness, and parsimony occur in the same individuals? Correlational studies of this kind have provided some support for the hypothesis of oral and anal character types, although the evidence is substantially stronger for the latter (Kline, 1972).

Phallic Stage

During the fourth and fifth years of life, the libido is centered in the genital region. Children at this age are frequently observed examining their genitalia, masturbating, and asking questions about birth and sex. The conflict in the phallic stage is the last and the most crucial one with which the young child must cope. The conflict involves the child's unconscious wish to possess his opposite-sexed parent and at the same time to eliminate his same-sexed parent. Freud called this situation the *Oedipus complex.* The name is derived from the Greek myth[5] in which Oedipus unknowingly kills his father and marries his mother.

THE OEDIPUS COMPLEX.   The Oedipus complex operates somewhat differently for males and females. The little boy's first love object is his mother. As the libido centers in the genital zone, his love for his mother becomes erotically tinged and therefore incestuous. However, the boy's father stands in the way of his sexual desires for his mother, and thus the father becomes his rival or enemy. Concomitant with his antagonism for and wish to eliminate his father are the boy's fears that his father will retaliate. The little boy's casual observations that women lack penises suggest to him that his father's revenge will be extracted in the form of castration. This threat of castration, experienced as *castration anxiety,* forces the boy to give up his wish to possess his mother. The resolution of the Oedipus complex is said to occur when the boy *represses* (puts out of consciousness) his incestuous desires for his mother and identifies with his father. The latter process is called *defensive identification*

---

[5] The myth has been popularized by Sophocles' tragedy *Oedipus Rex.*

and follows from the boy's unconscious "reasoning": "I cannot directly possess my mother, for fear of being castrated by my father. I can, however, possess her vicariously. I can get some of the joy of possessing my mother *by becoming like my father.*" The boy thus resolves his conflict by incorporating his father's behaviors, attitudes, and values, thereby simultaneously eliminating his castration anxiety, possessing his mother vicariously, and assimilating those behaviors necessary for appropriate sex-role behavior.

The Oedipus complex for the little girl, sometimes called the *Electra complex,*[6] is considerably more complicated and less clear than for the young boy.[7] The little girl's first object of love is also her mother. However, during the phallic stage, when her libido is centered in the genital zone, the little girl is likely to discover that while her father and other males (such as a brother) have penises, she and her mother (and other women) do not. She reasons that she must have had a penis at one time, and she blames her mother for her apparent castration. This, along with other disappointments in her mother, such as those revolving around conflicts in earlier psychosexual stages, leads to some loss of love for her mother and subsequent increased love for her father. Her love for her father, which is erotically tinged, is coupled with envy because he has a penis. *Penis envy* is, in some sense, the counterpart of castration anxiety. However, unlike castration anxiety, which motivates the little boy to renounce his incestuous desires, penis envy carries with it no threat of retaliation by the mother, since the ultimate punishment, castration, has no meaning for the girl.

It is not clear exactly how the feminine Oedipus complex is resolved, although Freud does state that the resolution occurs later in life and that it is never complete. It is obvious that even though the mother does not hold the threat of castration over her daughter, she would express considerable displeasure over incestuous relations between her husband and daughter. Presumably, the impracticability of fulfilling her Oedipal wish causes the girl to repress her desires for her father and to identify with her mother (i.e., defensive identification).

We have presented the general "formula" for the Oedipus complex, but it should be kept in mind that the exact pattern it takes for each individual is a function of his history during the prephallic stages and of the specific familial circumstances during his phallic stage. Freud considered the resolution of the Oedipus complex to be

---

[6] In Greek mythology, Electra persuaded her brother to murder their mother and their mother's lover, who together had killed their father.

[7] In general, Freud had more difficulty theorizing about women than about men.

crucial, since he postulated that all neuroses were due to an incomplete solution.

Of the views advanced by Freud, his ideas concerning infantile sexuality and especially the Oedipus complex are no doubt among the most difficult to comprehend or accept. This was true at the beginning of the century, when Freud introduced his revolutionary theory, as it probably is today for students being introduced to these notions for the first time. It is easy for us to accept the conflicts of the oral and anal stages; though we may not recollect being weaned and toilet trained, there is good evidence in our present behavior that we were. In contrast, not only is it unclear to us that we once had incestuous desires toward our opposite-sexed parent, but the very idea is completely contrary to our present morality. Freud's answer to an allegation such as *"I* never went through the Oedipus complex" was simply that the person cannot remember or accept his Oedipus complex because he has long since repressed memories of it, as part of his resolution of the conflict.

EVIDENCE FOR THE OEDIPUS COMPLEX.   Most of the evidence for the concepts of the Oedipus complex, castration anxiety, and penis envy comes from case studies of patients in psychoanalytic treatment. However, there have been some attempts to study these important psychoanalytic notions nomothetically. In these investigations, a major problem has been to develop adequate research definitions of the concepts. A good definition should meet two requirements. It must be amenable to objective measurement, and it must be closely related to the theoretical concept so that research findings will have a bearing on the theory. In practice it is often difficult to meet both requirements with psychoanalytic concepts, as can be seen in a study by Johnson (1966). He found that significantly more college men than college women returned pencils which they had been loaned during an examination. Although defining penis envy as not returning the pencil (a phallic symbol) has the advantage of amenability to objective measurement, it could be argued that pencil hoarding is too far removed from the theoretical concept of penis envy to have much value. An example of a correlational and an experimental study will be presented to illustrate the nature of more definitive investigations of castration anxiety and penis envy.

Based on the differences between the Oedipal situation for males and females, Hall and Van de Castle (1963) hypothesized that men would have more dreams of castration anxiety than women and that women would have more dreams of the wish to be castrated and penis envy. The content of 120 college students' dreams was examined. Examples of dream material taken to indicate castration anxiety included the dreamer's inability to use either his penis or a symbol of his penis (such as a pen or gun). When another person in the dream had this difficulty, a castration wish was assumed to be indicated. Acquiring a penis or a phallic symbol or changing into a man in the dream was regarded as evidence for penis envy. The content analyses supported the hypothesis under test.

In a very different type of investigation, Sarnoff and Corwin (1959) studied the relationship of castration anxiety and the fear of death. If fear of death is assumed to be a derivative of repressed fear of castration, then the more castration anxiety a person has, the greater should be his fear of death when castration anxiety is aroused. To test this proposition, Sarnoff and Corwin measured male undergraduates' fear of death before and after their castration anxiety was aroused. In the first part of the experiment, subjects indicated their agreement with statements about death (e.g., "I am disturbed when I think of the shortness of life") on a brief Fear of Death scale. Castration anxiety was assessed by means of a projective technique known as the Blacky Pictures (see Chapter 5), in which subjects were asked to choose one of three descriptions of a cartoon which was presumed to depict castration. On the basis of this test, subjects were divided into high and low castration anxiety groups.

In the second part of the experiment, subjects returned four weeks later, ostensibly to rate the esthetic value of some pictures. Half the subjects in each of the castration anxiety groups rated pictures of nude women (high sexual arousal condition), and half rated pictures of fully clothed fashion models (low sexual arousal condition). Following this task, the subjects were again administered the Fear of Death scale. As predicted, under conditions of high sexual arousal, which was presumed to arouse anxiety of castration, those subjects with high castration anxiety showed significantly greater increase in the fear of death than subjects with low castration anxiety. No differences were found when sexual arousal was low. If one assumes that fear of death is an indication of castration anxiety, this study lends support to an important psychoanalytic concept.

Latency Period

Following the resolution of the Oedipus complex, at about the age of five, children of both sexes pass into a period known as *latency*. Latency is *not* a stage of psychosexual development, since during this period, which lasts from the end of the phallic stage to the onset of puberty, the sexual drive is dormant. The libido is channeled into such activities as school, interpersonal relations with children of the same age and sex, hobbies, and so on. Freud said little about this period of life, although other psychoanalytic theorists (e.g., Erikson, Sullivan) have placed considerable emphasis on it.

Genital Stage

The final stage of psychosexual development begins at puberty when the young adolescent starts to mature sexually and lasts through adulthood until the onset of senility, at which time the individual tends to regress to pregenital behavior (i.e., behavior of the oral, anal, or phallic stage). In the genital stage, the libido is again focused in the genital area, but now it is directed toward heterosexual, rather than autoerotic, pleasure. The greater an individual's success in reaching the genital stage without having large amounts of libido fixated in pregenital stages, the greater will be his capacity to lead a "normal" life, free of neurosis, and to enjoy genuine heterosexual relationships.

Although all psychoanalytic theories of personality place a heavy emphasis on the importance of early periods of development for later life, neo-Freudians have tended to de-emphasize the biological and sexual determinants of behavior and to focus upon social development. To illustrate how development can be conceived of with greater stress on social factors within a psychoanalytic framework, the developmental sequence proposed by one prominent neo-Freudian, Erik Erikson, will be outlined briefly. While Erikson does not discount biological and psychosexual influences on the developing individual, he emphasizes the influence of society and culture.

Erikson's "Eight Ages of Man"

Erikson has outlined eight stages of *psychosocial* development, each of which represents an encounter with the environment. Each stage is designated by a conflict between two alternative ways of handling the encounter (e.g., basic trust versus mistrust), one adaptive and the other maladaptive. Unlike the conflicts in each of Freud's psychosexual stages, the eight critical conflicts or encounters with the environment which Erikson outlines are all present at birth in some form. For example, although in the first year of life the child's major problems center around developing basic trust (Erikson's first stage), he is also struggling to develop autonomy (Erikson's second stage), as when he wriggles to be set free if he is held too tightly.

However, under normal conditions, it is not until the second year that he begins to experience the whole *critical oppositon of being an autonomous creature and being a dependent one;* and it is not until then that he is ready for a decisive encounter with his environment, an environment which, in turn, feels called upon to convey to him its particular ideas and concepts of autonomy and coercion in ways decisively contributing to the character and the health of his personality in his culture. It is this encounter, together with the resulting crisis, that we have tentatively described for each stage (Erikson, 1963, p. 271).

Thus, each critical encounter with the environment predominates at a particular period of life, at which time it must be successfully resolved before a person is fully prepared for the conflict which predominates next. Successful resolution is relative and involves developing a "favorable ratio" between the adaptive and maladaptive alternatives (e.g., more basic trust than mistrust).

TABLE 4–1

Erikson's Epigenetic Diagram of the Eight Stages of Psychosocial Development

		1	2	3	4	5	6	7	8
VIII	Maturity								Ego Integrity vs. Despair
VII	Adulthood							Generativity vs. Stagnation	
VI	Young Adulthood						Intimacy vs. Isolation		
V	Puberty and Adolescence					Identity vs. Role Confusion			
IV	Latency				Industry vs. Inferiority				
III	Locomotor– Genital			Initiative vs. Guilt					
II	Muscular– Anal		Autonomy vs. Shame, Doubt						
I	Oral Sensory	Basic Trust vs. Mistrust							

Source: Erikson, 1963.

Erikson's epigenetic diagram of his psychosocial stages, plotted against periods of physical and/or psychosexual development, is presented in Table 4–1. Each row of the table delineates a conflict at its particular time of ascendance. The purpose of the blank boxes is to emphasize the interaction among the stages of psychosocial development. The blank squares appearing to the left of the square containing the name of the conflict represent the influence of conflicts which are no longer predominant, while the blank squares to the right represent the influence of conflicts which have not yet come to the fore.

Basic Trust vs. Mistrust

Initially, according to Erikson, the infant must develop sufficient trust to let his mother, the provider of his food and comfort, out of his sight without anxiety, apprehension, or rage. Such trust involves not only confidence in the predictability of the mother's behavior but also trust in oneself. This conflict occurs during the period of life which Freud referred to as the oral stage of psychosexual development.

Autonomy vs. Shame and Doubt

Next, the individual must develop a sense of autonomy. This sense is originally developed through bladder and bowel control and parallels the anal stage of traditional psychoanalytic theory. If the child fails to meet his parents' expectations in this regard, shame and doubt may result. The shame of being unable to demonstrate the self-control demanded by parents may become the basis for later difficulties, just as the experience of attaining adequate self-control in childhood may lead to feelings of autonomy in later life. Erikson (1963) suggests:

> This stage, therefore, becomes decisive for the ratio of love and hate, cooperation and willfulness, freedom of self-expression and its suppression. From a sense of self-control without loss of self-esteem comes a lasting sense of good will and pride; from a sense of loss of self-control and of foreign overcontrol comes a lasting propensity for doubt and shame (p. 254).

Initiative vs. Guilt

Initiative versus guilt is the last conflict experienced by the preschool child and thus occurs during the period Freud designated as the phallic stage. During this time, the child must learn to appropriately control his feelings of rivalry for his mother's attention and develop a sense of moral responsibility. At this stage, the child initially indulges in fantasies of grandeur, but in actuality he may feel meek and dominated. To overcome these latter feelings he must learn to take role-appropriate initiative by finding pleasurable accomplishment in socially and culturally approved activities, such as creative play or caring for younger siblings.

Industry vs. Inferiority

The conflict between industry and inferiority begins with school life or, in primitive societies, with the onset of formal socialization. The child at this time must apply himself to his lessons, begin to feel some sense of competence relative to his peers, and face his own limitations if he is to emerge as a healthy individual. Note that these important developments occur during the time when, from Freud's point of view, the child is in a period of psychosexual nondevelopment (i.e., latency).

Identity vs. Role Confusion

With the advent of puberty the individual must begin to develop some sense of identity for himself. *Identity,* as the term is used by Erikson, refers to the confidence that others see us as we see ourselves. Of particular importance for identity formation is the selection of an occupation or career, although other factors may be involved. If an identity is not formed, role confusion, which is often characterized by an inability to select a career or further educational goals and overidentification with popular heroes or cliques, may occur. Role confusion can be overcome through interaction with peers or elders who are informed about various occupational opportunities (if this is the locus of the conflict) or who accept the adolescent's perception of himself.

Intimacy vs. Isolation

By young adulthood the individual is expected to be ready for true intimacy. He must develop cooperative social and occupational relationships with others and select a mate. If he cannot develop such relationships, he will be, and feel, isolated. The conflict between intimacy and isolation occurs during the period which Freud referred to as the genital stage. Erikson (1963, p. 265) notes that when Freud was asked what a healthy person should be able to do well he curtly answered, " *'Lieben und Arbeiten'* (to love and to work)." Erikson believes that "we cannot improve on 'the professor's' formula."

Generativity vs. Stagnation

According to Erikson, a mature person must do more than establish intimacy with others. He "needs to be needed" and to assist the younger members of society. *Generativity* is concerned with guiding the next generation, and if it is not accomplished, the individual may feel stagnant and personally impoverished.

Ego Integrity vs. Despair

If all of the preceding conflicts are not suitably handled, despair may result in later life. Disgusted with himself and correctly realizing that it is too late to start another life, the individual lives his last years in a state of incurable remorse. In contrast, to become psychosocially adjusted and have a lasting sense of integrity, the person must develop each of the adaptive qualities of the other seven stages. Erikson (1963) emphasizes that all men, regardless of their culture, can achieve such adjustment: ". . . a wise Indian, a true gentleman, and a mature peasant share and recognize in one another the final stage of integrity" (p. 269).

THE NATURE OF PERSONALITY

Levels of Consciousness

Psychoanalysis divides the mind into three levels of consciousness, or awareness. The *conscious* part of the mind includes all that we are immediately aware of at a given point in time. Freud's conception of the conscious is close to our everyday use of the term, except that he held that only a very small proportion of our thoughts, images, and memories are contained in consciousness. The mind, like an iceberg, is nine-tenths below the surface.

The *preconscious* includes cognitions which are not conscious but can be brought into consciousness with little or no difficulty. For example, as you read these words you are trying to think about the material being presented. However, unless a test on this information is imminent (and perhaps not even then), you could easily begin to think of an upcoming vacation or next week's date. These thoughts were in your preconscious.

Finally, there is the part of the mind which plays the most important role in personality, the *unconscious*.[8] Freud contended that most of our behavior is directed by forces of which we are totally unaware—that is, they are out of consciousness. In contrast to preconscious thoughts, unconscious thoughts enter consciousness only in disguised or symbolic form.

Freud was certainly not the first to postulate the existence of an unconscious, but his emphasis on those aspects of personality of which we are unaware has had a profound influence on the scientific study of personality as well as on everyday conceptions about personality. Freud himself noted that modern man has suffered three blows to his narcissism and self-image. The first blow was dealt by Copernicus, who discovered that the earth was not the center of the universe. Next, Darwin made man an animal among animals.

---

[8] The term *subconscious* is not part of formal psychoanalytic nomenclature, though presumably in its common usage it refers to everything that is below consciousness (i.e., the preconscious and unconscious).

Finally, Freud made us conscious of our unconscious, aware of the degree to which we are controlled by unknown forces within us which are frequently beyond our control. In his popular interpretation of psychoanalysis, *Life Against Death,* Norman O. Brown (1959) has written: "It is a shattering experience for anyone seriously committed to the Western tradition of morality and rationality to take a steadfast, unflinching look at what Freud has to say. It is humiliating to be compelled to admit the grossly seamy side of so many grand ideals. . . . To experience Freud is to partake a second time of the forbidden fruit" (p. xi) .

In Freud's early theorizing, the concept of the unconscious played a major role. Later, around 1920, Freud revised his theory somewhat to posit three basic aspects of personality—the id, ego, and superego. The functions which were formerly relegated to the unconscious were now primarily taken over by the id. Basically, the relationship of the earlier and later constructs is that "all of the id is unconscious, but not all of the unconscious is id" (see Figure 4–1) .

FIGURE 4–1

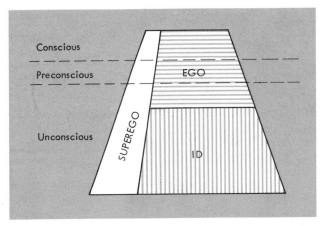

The Relationship of the Personality Functions to the Levels of Awareness

Three Aspects of Personality

Like the levels of consciousness, the id, ego, and superego are theoretical constructs; they do not physically exist within the brain as do such structures as the frontal lobe and the hypothalamus.[9] Although the id, ego, and superego are often referred to as "struc-

---

[9] Freud did believe that all mental functions would be ultimately tied to specific neural structures, but his theory of the divisions of the mind did not depend on the discovery of corresponding anatomical structures.

tures," it is more correct to think of them as *aspects* or *functions* of the personality.

One additional word of caution is called for. The three aspects of personality are frequently discussed in psychoanalytic writing anthropomorphically—that is, *as if* they possessed human capabilities, such as wishing, controlling, tolerating, and *being*. Nevertheless, the id, ego, and superego are not viewed by most psychoanalysts as little men inside us but rather as convenient ways of conceptualizing complex psychological functions.

Id

The *id*[10] is said to be the original system of personality because it contains everything psychological that is present at birth. The id is a reservoir for all drives and derives its power directly from bodily needs and processes. As bodily needs such as hunger and thirst build up, they must be satisfied, and the resulting increase in tension must be discharged. When the id alone governs this discharge, no delay of gratification is possible. The id is regulated by the *pleasure principle:* it cannot tolerate increases in psychic energy and presses for immediate satisfaction.

The id employs two basic techniques to reduce tension—*reflex action* and *primary process*. The primitive id is a reflex apparatus which reacts automatically and immediately to various internal and external irritants to the body, thereby promptly removing the tension or distress which the irritant provides. Reflex action may be observed in such inborn mechanisms as sneezing, blinking, and coughing.

Since the id cannot tolerate any delay of gratification or any tension, it would be expected that very young children would "cry" for care as soon as an appetite or need appears which they cannot satisfy. This seems to be exactly what happens. (Infants are, of course, quite capable of satisfying some of their needs, such as urination.) In addition, when the child's drive requires some object from the outside world, such as food or water, unless the object is immediately available, the id's *primary process* will form a memory image of the required object. For example, when the infant is hungry, the primary process will produce an image of food. This hallucinatory experience is called *wish fulfillment,* and remnants of it can be seen in adulthood, as when a thirsty traveler imagines he sees water.

The primary process is a crude mechanism in that it is not able to differentiate between the actual object required to satisfy a need

---

[10] Literally, the "it," since Freud used the German word *es* in his original description.

and a memory image of the object (e.g., between food and an image of food). Although the id may be temporarily satisfied with a memory image, the primary process does nothing to *actually* reduce tension. Obviously, one cannot eat nor long survive on mental pictures of food. If the infant's needs were met immediately (as they were prior to birth), no problem would arise with the primary process. But inevitably there must be delay of gratification (a mother, for example, cannot be available constantly to nurse or feed her baby), and the infant must learn to tolerate the delay. The capacity to tolerate delay of gratification begins with the infant's growing "realization" that there is an external world—something which is "not me"—which has to be taken into account and considered apart from, but interrelated with, the infant himself. This comes about with the development of the second aspect of the personality, the *ego*.

Ego

The *ego* develops out of the id, which is to say that it "borrows" some of the id's psychic energy for its own functions. Recall that at birth all of the child's psychic energy is contained in the id and is used for primary processes. Therefore, the energy for ego functions must come from the id. An important consequence of the closed nature of the energy system is that as psychic energy is transferred to the ego, there is less psychic energy for id functions. This shift of energy is an intrapsychic phenomenon which cannot, of course, be observed directly. However, it is manifest in such behavior as the child's becoming less demanding of immediate satisfaction of his needs and more willing to delay gratification.

In contrast to the pleasure principle of the id, the ego is governed by the *reality principle* and has as its aim postponing the discharge of energy until an appropriate situation or object in the real world is discovered or produced. The ego does not attempt to thwart the pleasure seeking of the id, but rather it temporarily suspends pleasure for the sake of reality. Whereas the purpose of the primary process is to indicate what object or situation is necessary to satisfy a particular need (e.g., an image of food), the role of the *secondary process* is to create a strategy for actually obtaining the satisfaction (e.g., going to the cookie jar). The ego, then, is characterized by realistic thinking or problem solving and is the seat of intellectual processes. Daydreaming is an example of a secondary process which illustrates the reality-bound nature of the ego. Although we enjoy the pleasurable fantasy of a daydream, we do not mistake the fantasy for reality as we do in a nocturnal dream, which is a primary process.

For a person to function both as an individual and as a member

of his society, he must learn not only to deal with the direct constraints of physical reality but also to adhere to social norms and
prohibitions. Further, he must conform to society's "laws" in the
absence of external monitors (i.e., when there is no realistic fear of
apprehension, punishment, or failure). Beginning around the third
or fourth year of life, children start to judge and evaluate their own
behavior independently of immediate threat or reward. Such self-
control is the province of the third aspect of personality, the superego.

Superego

The *superego* serves as the internal representative of the values of
one's parents and society. It strives for the *ideal* rather than the real.
Independently of the utility of an act, the superego will judge it as
right or wrong, as being or not being in accord with the moral
values of the society.

The superego has two major functions. First, as the representative
of society's demands regarding idealized behavior patterns, the superego, like one's parents, rewards the individual for acceptable behavior in the moral sphere. Second, by creating feelings of guilt, it
punishes him for engaging in actions and thoughts which society
does not sanction.

The role of the superego in the life of an adult is threefold: (1) it
inhibits rather than just postpones, as does the ego, the impulses of
the id, particularly those of a sexual or aggressive nature; (2) it
persuades the ego to attend to moral rather than realistic goals and
thus presumably accounts for various types of self-sacrifice and al-
truism; and (3) it directs the individual toward the pursuit of per-
fection.

Prior to Freud's treatment of the subject, internal restraints on
one's actions of the kind we call "ethical" or "moral" were presumed
to come from a "still, small voice" which had been provided by God
(Brown, 1965). Freud argued that moral conscience is not born with
man and, in fact, that quite the reverse is true. The neonate has no
concern for the welfare of others and is interested only in his own
immediate satisfactions. Moral concerns must somehow be acquired
after birth.

The development of the superego involves the child's "taking in,"
or incorporating, the values of his parents in a way analogous to the
incorporation of food from the outside world into the body. This
process begins about the fourth year of life and is closely related to
the solution of the Oedipus complex. Through defensive identification with the same-sexed parent, the child acquires the parent's moral

values as well as appropriate sex-role behavior. Identification with both parents occurs through another process, called *anaclitic identification,* in which the child comes to value his parents (and, by association, their standards and ideals) because of the love, warmth, and comfort they provide for him.

A Note on the Validity of the Three Aspects of Personality

If Freud was correct that personality can usefully be viewed as being a joint function of three aspects or functions—id, ego, and superego—then this should be evident in behavior. Although casual observation reveals that there are desiring (id), rational (ego), and ideal (superego) aspects in much of human behavior, there has been little empirical investigation of Freud's hypothesis. Again, it appears that difficulty in providing adequate research definitions for the concepts is the major obstacle.

Some tentative findings by Cattell (1957; Pawlik & Cattell, 1964) and his associates suggest the possibility of using factor analysis to investigate the role of id, ego, and superego aspects in behavior. Basically, factor analysis is a research strategy (see Chapter 7) that involves giving a large sample of subjects many different tests and then examining their performances to see if they can be explained by a small number of basic traits which the subjects possess. Using a series of laboratory tasks to study motivation, Pawlik and Cattell (1964) found that three main factors summarized the relationship of the subjects' performances on the various tasks. These factors were described as "high self-assertion," "immature self-centered temperament," and "restrained acceptance of external norms." Pawlik and Cattell conclude, "Although we did not start our studies with any predilections for psychoanalytic theory, it is a striking fact that the psychoanalytic descriptions of Ego, Id and Superego would fit very well the three major patterns found in this research" (p. 16).

The Relationships among the Aspects of Personality

To briefly summarize the development of the aspects of personality, recall that at birth only the id exists. Later, in response to the demands of reality, the ego develops out of the id. Finally, the superego develops as an outgrowth of the ego and serves as the societal or moral representative in the personality. When all three aspects have developed, the psychic energy which once belonged solely to the id is divided among the id, ego, and superego and fluctuates among them. As depicted in Figure 4–2, the ego serves as a mediator among the three basic forces acting upon an individual—the demands of

FIGURE 4–2

The Ego as the Mediator of Personality

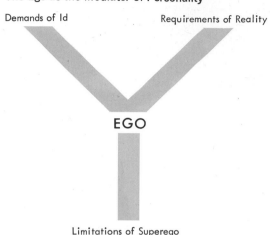

Demands of Id   Requirements of Reality

EGO

Limitations of Superego

the id, the requirements of reality (of the external environment),
and the limitations imposed by the superego. It is therefore the task
of the ego to see that instinctual needs are met in a realistic and, at
the same time, socially approved manner.

An intrapsychic *conflict* occurs when the direction and discharge
of energy demanded by one aspect of the personality is at odds with
the requirements of one or both of the other aspects. All the possibilities for conflict are presented in Table 4–2. In principle, conflicts could be resolved by the complete elimination of a drive, the
redirection of the drive from its original aim (e.g., incestuous goals),
or the expression of the drive in undiluted form. In psychoanalytic
theory, the first alternative is assumed never to occur. A drive can
be banished from conscious awareness but not from the total personality. The battle, then, is between redirection and unbridled expression of the drive.

Redirection of a drive involves arbitration among the forces acting within and upon the personality, and this requires the expenditure of psychic energy. Since a person has only a fixed amount of
psychic energy, the more successfully his ego minimizes intrapsychic
conflicts, the more energy will be "left over" for positive cathexes
and higher mental functions of the ego, such as creativity. If redirection of an impulse is not possible, then the ego is likely to be
overwhelmed with excitation and the person will feel intense anxiety. However, this rarely occurs in adults because anxiety serves as
a signal for the ego to defend itself.

TABLE 4–2

Possible Conflicts among the Aspects of Personality

Conflict	Example
ID vs. EGO	Choosing between a small immediate reward and a larger reward which requires some period of waiting (i.e., delay of gratification).
ID vs. SUPEREGO	Deciding whether to return the difference when you are overpaid or undercharged.
EGO vs. SUPEREGO	Choosing between acting in a realistic way (e.g., telling a "white lie") and adhering to a potentially costly or unrealistic standard (e.g., always telling the truth).
ID and EGO vs. SUPEREGO	Deciding whether to retaliate against the attack of a weak opponent or to "turn the other cheek."
ID and SUPEREGO vs. EGO	Deciding whether to act in a realistic way that conflicts both with your desires and your moral convictions (e.g., the decision faced by devout Roman Catholics as to the use of contraceptive devices).
EGO and SUPEREGO vs. ID	Choosing whether to "act on the impulse" to steal something you want and cannot afford. The ego would presumably be increasingly involved in such a conflict as the probability of being apprehended increases.

ANXIETY AND DEFENSE

The experience of anxiety is all too well known to each of us. In his early theorizing (during the 1890s), Freud viewed anxiety as the result of repressed libido which was transformed into anxiety. Some 30 years later he revised his theory to state that the reverse was true —anxiety led to repression. Freud's later formulation, which was published in 1926 in a short book entitled *The Problem of Anxiety,* held that anxiety was a *signal* of impending danger. While the source of the danger could be either external or internal, Freud, not surprisingly, thought that it was usually the result of an id impulse seeking expression. Due to the intense id impulse, the ego is in danger of being overwhelmed by stimulation (tension) which it cannot master or discharge.

This *signal anxiety* originates in early childhood. During the period when the infant is incapable of delaying gratification (i.e., before the ego develops), he finds himself occasionally overwhelmed by the tension of an id impulse seeking expression (e.g., hunger drive) if someone such as his mother is not present to satisfy his needs. This trauma is accompanied by intense stimulation which is called *primary anxiety*. Later, the child learns to anticipate the danger (e.g., when he sees his mother leaving the room) and to react with anxiety. However, now the anxiety is less intense than that which accompanied the actual traumatic experience and serves as a warning to the ego to somehow prevent the recurrence of the trauma and the accompanying overwhelming stimulation. The ego is "motivated" to deal with the danger because the signal anxiety is unpleasant.

Freud made a distinction among three types of anxiety which occur in adulthood. *Neurotic anxiety* results from an id-ego conflict in which the id seeks to discharge an impulse (e.g., to defecate) and the ego tries to place reality restraints on the impulse (e.g., waiting until a toilet is available). *Moral anxiety* is generated by an id-superego conflict in which the id impulse (e.g., to shoplift) is in opposition to the moral and ideal standards of society (e.g., "Thou shalt not steal") and is experienced by the individual as guilt or shame. *Objective anxiety* is produced when a realistic, external threat is present, such as enemy troops, automobiles on a freeway, or wild animals. In each case, anxiety is a signal of impending danger. In objective anxiety, the danger is external and can be dealt with by taking realistic steps to eliminate or reduce the actual threat. Neurotic and moral anxiety, however, are due to an impending intrapsychic danger, and they must be coped with by internal means, namely, the defense mechanisms of the ego.

Common Ego Defense Mechanisms

Defense mechanisms refer to *unconscious* processes of the ego which keep disturbing and unacceptable impulses from being expressed directly. Although it is helpful for didactic purposes to distinguish among specific ego defense mechanisms, people rarely defend themselves against anxiety with a single mechanism. An individual's characteristic modes of defense are typically a combination of different defense mechanisms. Furthermore, as will become apparent in the following examples, there is considerable overlap in the way the defense mechanisms operate to protect the ego from overwhelming anxiety.

Sublimation

By the process of *sublimation,* impulses are altered by being channeled to completely acceptable, and even admired, social behaviors. Sublimation deprives an impulse of its primitive character while at the same time allowing it some expression. Psychoanalysts consider that many vigorously pursued human activities reflect the sublimation of id impulses. The surgeon and the soldier, for example, may both be regarded as having found a socially acceptable outlet for sadistic impulses—the gynecologist and the movie censor as having sublimated their sexual drives—in their professional activities. More common ways of sublimating aggression include engaging in or even observing competitive contact sports, such as boxing and football. Common sublimations of sex are said to be painting and creative writing.

Sublimation is the only truly successful defense mechanism because it succeeds in permanently redirecting undesirable impulses. All other defense mechanisms are to some degree unsuccessful in that they require a continual warding off of the threatening impulses.

Repression

Repression is the process whereby a dangerous impulse is actively and totally excluded from consciousness. As a solution to conflict it is characterized by a continual struggle to contain primitive desires. Psychoanalytic theory acknowledges that repression may occur in "healthy" individuals but contends that, unlike sublimation, it exacts a severe price.

> Many impulses in the healthy personality are thus permanently banned from awareness, but at the expense of being excluded from the development of the total personality. It is as if the ego had slammed the door against a dimly perceived threatening intruder, but once the door has been shut, the ego will never know whether the intruder was indeed as threatening as he was believed to be, or, whether it is worth spending energy in keeping him out. . . . Once this energy is used for repressive purposes, it cannot be used as "free" energy in the task of adaptation (Strupp, 1967, p. 51).

In Freud's early writing, "repression" was used as a general term and considered to be synonymous with "ego defense." In a sense, then, other defense mechanisms may be construed as types of repression.

EXPERIMENTAL EVIDENCE FOR REPRESSION. Repression has been the subject of numerous laboratory investigations (e.g., D'Zurilla, 1965; Worchel, 1955; Zeller, 1950, 1951). The typical experimental paradigm, which is outlined in Table 4–3, can be divided into three phases. In the first phase, experimental and control subjects learn a list of words and then are tested for their recall of the words (Recall Test 1). Since subjects have been treated in the same way to this point, no differences between the recall of experimental and control subjects are expected. During the second phase, experimental

TABLE 4–3

Experimental Paradigm for Demonstrating the Existence of Repression

Procedures			
Experimental Subjects	Control Subjects	Prediction	Interpretation
Phase 1 { Learn list of words	Learn list of words		
Recall Test 1	Recall Test 1	No differences between experimental and control subjects.	Groups are equivalent.
Phase 2 { Ego-threatening task	Neutral task		
Recall Test 2	Recall Test 2	Experimental subjects recall less than control subjects.	Ego-threat and resultant anxiety lead experimental subjects to repress words associated with threat.
Debriefing (threat removed)	Debriefing		
Phase 3 { Recall Test 3	Recall Test 3	No differences between experimental and control subjects.	When threat is removed, repression is lifted and memory of repressed words becomes conscious again.

subjects are exposed to an ego-threatening situation, such as taking a personality test and receiving negative feedback (e.g., "The test indicates that you may be prone to spells of anxiety"). The control subjects are exposed to a similar, but nonthreatening, situation, such as taking a personality test but receiving neutral feedback.

Next, the subjects' recall of the words is assessed again (Recall Test 2), and this time it is predicted that experimental subjects who have been ego-threatened will recall fewer words than control subjects. It is assumed that the words have become associated with the ego-threat for the experimental group, since both occurred in the same situation and in close temporal proximity, and that the words which elicit anxiety due to the threat have therefore been repressed.

The theory of repression would also predict that if the threat were removed and anxiety was thus reduced, the repressed material would return to consciousness. To test this conceptual hypothesis, in the third phase of the study subjects are debriefed by telling them that they have been given *false* feedback and then tested once more for their recall of the list of words (Recall Test 3). Now it is expected that there will be no differences in recall between the experimental and control subjects.

In general, studies have obtained results consistent with the predictions. Ego-threat leads to lowered recall in Test 2, and removal of the threat restores recall to its prethreat level in Test 3. These results have been interpreted to support the concept of repression.[11]

Reaction Formation

One way of warding off an unacceptable impulse is to overemphasize its opposite in thought and behavior. Someone threatened by his desire to dominate and be aggressive in social situations might think of himself as a timid and shy person, act passively, and be unable to refuse requests made of him no matter how unreasonable they were. Timidity and passivity would be a *reaction formation* against a strong aggressive drive.

It is often difficult to tell whether a given act is an undisguised manifestation of an impulse or a manifestation of its opposite. An important hallmark of reaction formation is the persistence or excess of the behavior in question—"going overboard." As Shakespeare (in *Hamlet*), who antedated Freud and the concept of reaction formation by more than 300 years, observed: "The lady doth protest too much." So, too, the apparently puritanical female, particularly one who responds to sexual advances with numerous gasps, may well

---

[11] Other studies (e.g., Holmes, 1972; Holmes & Schallow, 1969) have suggested that there are equally plausible alternative explanations which will account for these experimental findings.

be seething with erotic desire and sexuality. Similarly, an individual's avowed love for a sibling or spouse may sometimes be interpreted as profound but disguised hate.

Undoing

The aim of *undoing* is to make retribution for the harm caused by an unacceptable act or the potential harm inherent in the thought of the unacceptable act. Brenner (1957) uses the example of a child who defends himself against his unconscious hostile wishes toward a younger brother by finding injured animals and nursing them back to health. The act of healing sick animals—symbols of the child's brother—unconsciously undoes the harm that his hostile impulses might cause his brother. Undoing frequently involves a ritualistic act which symbolically compensates for an id impulse which is threatening to the ego. Lady Macbeth compulsively washed her hands as if to cleanse herself of the blood she had spilled as a party to murder.

Projection

The defense mechanism of *projection* involves attributing one's own unacceptable and disturbing impulses or wishes to someone or something else. It has often been observed that under stress people tend to see in others precisely those characteristics which they abhor in themselves. It is as if the individual said to himself, "It is he, not I, who has dangerous thoughts and commits unacceptable acts." For example, a student who cheats on an examination may attribute the "high curve" and his low grade to the prevalence of cheating among his classmates. A common type of projection is scapegoating.

As in the case of reaction formation, it is not always clear when projection is operating, since the possibility exists that the person is making an accurate invidious statement about someone else which does not apply to himself. Projection is most readily identified in childhood, as when a boy, having been told by his mother that he has made a mess in the living room, replies by blaming Nubbie, his imaginary playmate, for the disarray.

Displacement

Whereas projection involves attributing one's impulse to another person, *displacement* involves shifting one's impulse which is directed toward an unacceptable and threatening object (or person) to a more acceptable and less threatening object. A common example of displacement is that of the employee who, rather than express his hostility toward the superior who has bawled him out on the job, which is obviously a threatening and unadaptive strategy, redirects his anger toward his wife or children at home. As we shall see in Freud's case of Little Hans (discussed in Chapter 5), displacement is the primary mechanism involved in phobias. According to the psychoanalytic viewpoint, a phobia, or irrational fear, originates with a realistic or unrealistic fear of some object or person which cannot be easily avoided. In order to reduce the intense anxiety which repeated contact with the feared object induces, the individual displaces his fear onto another object which he can easily avoid and which is symbolically related to the originally feared object.

Regression

One frequently used method of coping with frustration and anxiety is to escape to a mode of behavior that is more satisfying and pleasant. *Regression,* according to psychoanalytic theory, involves such a retreat to an earlier period of development, which, for adults, is a pregenital psychosexual stage. Common examples of regression include sleeping, dreaming, smoking, fingernail biting, talking baby talk, getting drunk, overeating, breaking the law, and losing one's temper. Hall (1955) interestingly notes that "some of these regressions are so commonplace that they are taken to be signs of maturity" (p. 96).

Rationalization

After performing an unacceptable act or thinking a threatening thought, people frequently alleviate the anxiety or guilt which ensues by finding a "perfectly reasonable" excuse for their behavior. *Rationalization,* as this defensive strategy is called, is often used as a mechanism for maintaining one's self-esteem. When a young woman is "stood up" by her date, she may tell herself and her friends that she "really" didn't want to go out with the fellow. Such a rationalization has been colloquially labeled "sour grapes," after the fable of the fox who was unable to reach some grapes and therefore concluded that they were sour. Rationalization is an unconscious process, as are all of the ego defense mechanisms, and should not be confused with consciously making up an excuse.

Denial

Still another way to handle painful experiences and thoughts is to deny their existence. Sometimes a person will refuse to believe that a loved one has died and will continue to behave as if he were still alive. A more common form of *denial,* which most people engage in from time to time, involves fantasy or play. People may find temporary relief from reality by daydreaming about how things would be if some unpleasant circumstance had not occurred. Children deny their inferiority through play, as when a young boy assumes the role of a strict father while playing "house."

HUMOR AND THE EXPRESSION OF REPRESSED IMPULSES

Laughter and humor are a pervasive part of human existence. Virtually all people enjoy laughing at a joke, funny story, or humorous incident. A good sense of humor is considered socially desirable, and we tend to look with suspicion on those people who do not laugh at our witticisms. In fact, there is a commonly held notion that laughter is a necessity for psychological well-being.[12] Yet for all its pervasiveness in our daily lives, relatively little scientific study has been made of humor. It is certainly legitimate to ask such questions as what makes a joke funny and why do some people seem to laugh more than others. Although such philosophers as Thomas Hobbes and Immanuel Kant have commented on the nature of humor in their writings, the first, and perhaps the only, comprehensive theory of humor was developed by Freud.

Simply stated, Freud's theory says that humor[13] serves the function of vicariously gratifying a forbidden impulse or wish. The pleasure gained from humor arises from a sudden reduction of inner tension or anxiety, and the abrupt freeing of psychic energy, which was holding the impulse in check, results in laughter. The anxiety is due to intrapsychic conflicts concerning the expression of a strong drive, notably sex or aggression. Freud's observation that more humor is concerned with these two drives than with anything else is probably no less true today than when he made the observation. The id, governed by the pleasure principle alone, demands expression of the impulse, while the superego, the guardian of cultural taboos, fights to inhibit its expression. For a joke to appear funny, it must first arouse some anxiety and then relieve this tension. Consider the following joke:

> Standing on a golf course green, one golfer is vigorously choking another to death. A third party arrives on the scene and casually says to the aggressor, "Excuse me, bud. Your grip's all wrong."

---

[12] Many psychiatric patients seem to lack a sense of humor (e.g., Spiegler, 1973), although little is known about the relationship between humor and psychiatric disorders.

[13] Freud made a distinction between tendentious humor, which serves some aggressive or sexual purpose, and nontendentious (innocent) humor, which involves the pleasure derived from the mental activity of the joke technique (e.g., puns, incongruities, and the like). In this section, we shall be speaking only of humor in the former sense.

In the first part of the joke, the scene is set simply as an act of aggression which, because direct expression of aggression is frowned upon in our culture, leads to anxiety. What follows, the punch line, is funny because the theme is no longer aggression, but rather an unanticipated, casual, and *unrelated* remark. The change of content serves to reduce the tension. In Freud's words: ". . . *this yield of pleasure corresponds to the psychical expenditure that is saved*" (1960, p. 118).

Similar to the defense mechanism of sublimation, in which unconscious and culturally taboo impulses are given an outlet in socially acceptable endeavors, humor, according to psychoanalysis, helps "normal" men control their primitive impulses.

> . . . wit is a product of civilization. It is a bypath for emotional outlet. Jokes that are particularly desirable are those dealing mainly with sex control or with other oppressions put on us by civilization [particularly aggression]. If you can crack a joke of this type and thus give vent to some of your repressed feelings, you and your audience obtain a good, vicarious outlet. It is for this very reason that we can look upon jokes as disguised expressions of something that is very deep and fundamental but which must be held in check by civilization (Brill, 1955, p. 140).

To illustrate how the psychoanalytic theory of humor has been studied in the laboratory, several representative experiments will be described.

If, as Freud suggested, the lowering of inhibitions against impulses plays a major role in the enjoyment of aggressive humor, then the following two hypotheses should hold: " (1) a heightening of inhibitions surrounding expression of aggressive impulses should result in decreased ability to enjoy aggressive humor; (2) this effect should be more pronounced the stronger and the more blatant the aggressive content of the humorous material" (Singer, Gollob, & Levine, 1966, p. 2). To test these predictions, Singer and his associates first asked male undergraduates to rate five etchings by Goya. Half of the subjects looked at brutal and sadistic scenes from the Spanish artist's *Disasters of War* series with the purpose of heightening their inhibitions against such wanton cruelty (inhibition condition). The other half of the subjects viewed five benign social scenes (control condition). Immediately following this phase of the experiment, the students were asked to rate a series of 12 cartoons for funniness and the amount of aggression portrayed. Four of the cartoons concerned highly aggressive interpersonal incidents (e.g., "A woman sits reclining in a chair. Beside her is a rifle aimed at the door with a string running from door to trigger. She says, 'It's not locked, honey!' "). Four other cartoons dealt with mild interpersonal aggression (e.g.,

"A service station attendant is shown wiping the oil dipstick on his customer's tie as he comments, 'Oil's pretty dirty.' ") . The remaining four cartoons had little or no aggressive content (e.g., "A group of people and a zoo keeper are grinning widely in front of the hyena cage. The zoo keeper comments, 'Contagious, isn't it?' ") .

A partial check of the effectiveness of the inhibition-inducing manipulation was made by asking subjects, after the experiment was concluded, to describe how they felt during the initial phase of the experiment. It was found that significantly more inhibition than control subjects said they had felt "revulsion," "disgust," or "depression" while viewing the Goya works. When inhibition is defined as these emotional reactions, the experimental hypotheses received support. The subjects in the inhibition condition rated the mildly aggressive cartoons as slightly less funny and the highly aggressive cartoons as considerably less funny than did the subjects in the control condition. It appears, then, that persons do find aggressive humor less funny when their inhibitions concerning the expression of aggression are heightened. Furthermore, when these inhibitions are sensitized, the more aggressive the content of the humor, the less funny it will seem.

In the case of aggressive or sexual humor, Freud contended that in order for it to be considered funny rather than revolting or disgusting it must somehow distract the person so that he is not fully aware of the unacceptable impulses involved. Otherwise, the anxiety induced by the joke would be too great, and the ego defense mechanisms would be mobilized to mitigate the tension to the point where relief from it would not give rise to the pleasurable experience of humor.

It is no doubt a common occurrence for people to laugh at a joke and then, after some time has passed, to find it distasteful rather than humorous when they think about its more unacceptable aspects. The so-called sick jokes, which involve human cruelty or ridicule, usually lead to such an experience (e.g., Son: "Why is mommy so pale?" Father: "Shut up and keep digging.") . Gollob and Levine (1967) put these ideas to an experimental test by having female subjects rate the funniness of cartoons (very similar to the ones employed by Singer et al., 1966) both before and after they had had their attention drawn to the aggressive content by being asked to explain the joke. The results of this study showed that whereas high-aggressive cartoons were judged to be most funny initially, after the subjects were asked to explain them (10 days later) they were rated less funny than either low-aggressive or nonsense cartoons.

Freud's idea that humor involves an emotional release has more recently been couched in terms of the concept of physiological arousal. Humorous situations contain elements which make for heightened arousal, while other elements serve to reduce the level of arousal. It follows that the greater a person's arousal before relief, the greater will be the funniness of the humor. In an ingenious experiment, Shurcliff (1968) tested this hypothesis.

Using anxiety as an index of arousal, Shurcliff divided his subjects into three experimental groups corresponding to the degree of anxiety which was experimentally induced. The subjects were brought individually to the laboratory, ostensibly to assess their reaction to small animals. Three cages were visible to the subjects, but they were arranged in such fashion that only the occupants of the first two cages, white laboratory rats, could be seen. Subjects in the low-anxiety group were told that their task would be to pick up the rat in the third cage and hold it for five seconds. The experimenter emphasized that the rat was docile and that the subject should have no difficulty. Subjects in the moderate-anxiety condition were shown two slides which supposedly contained blood samples from the rats in the first two cages. It was explained to these subjects that they would have to obtain a blood sample from the third rat. They were instructed in how to do this and told that the task was easier than it appeared. Finally, the subjects in the high-anxiety condition also were told that they would have to draw blood from the third rat, but they were shown bottles supposedly containing blood from the first two rats and instructed in the procedure for taking a large quantity of blood with a hypodermic needle. These subjects were cautioned about the difficulty of the task and were told that the rat might bite them.

At the start of the task, the subjects in each condition reached into the third cage and, much to their surprise and relief, discovered a toy rat! They were then asked to rate the humor of the situation as well as their anxiety prior to seeing the toy rat, the latter measure as a check on the effectiveness of the experimental manipulation of inducing different levels of anxiety. As predicted, the higher the subjects' anxiety prior to seeing the "rat" they were to handle, the funnier they found the situation.

These studies, which attempt to validate Freud's theory of humor, are particularly significant because they deal with one of the few aspects of psychoanalytic theory that has been subjected to relatively rigorous testing in laboratory experimentation. Furthermore, at present, there seem to be no viable alternative explanations which do a substantially better job of explaining the empirical results of these investigations.

5

The Psychoanalytic Strategy ASSESSMENT AND PERSONALITY CHANGE

The previous chapter explored the major theoretical propositions of psychoanalysis. This chapter will be devoted to a discussion of the assessment and modification of personality from the psychoanalytic framework. Because psychoanalysis assumes that most of personality is unconscious, it must employ indirect means of assessment. Two basic indirect techniques have already been discussed: one, the analysis of slips of the tongue, forgetting, the loss of objects, and "accidental" mistakes, and the other, the analysis of humor. The present chapter will deal with dream interpretation, the method of personality assessment which Freud thought most useful for examining intrapsychic events, and with projective techniques. Following this, psychoanalytic personality change will be discussed.

DREAMS: THE ROYAL ROAD TO THE UNCONSCIOUS

One-third of our lives is spent in sleeping. It is no wonder then that man has long expressed a fascination with his dreams and the dreams of others, since they represent the only processes occurring during sleep of which he has more or less direct knowledge. Freud's interest in dreams was certainly not new, but, as in the case of humor, his theory was the first comprehensive account of the psychological aspects of dreaming, and it has served as a major impetus for the contemporary study of dreams. Freud believed that his theory of dreams and their interpretation was his most significant scientific contribution.

Freud's Dream Theory

Manifest vs. Latent Content of Dreams

Freud was interested in dreams because of what he thought their content revealed about an individual's personality, particularly its unconscious aspects. He made a clear distinction between two levels of dream content. The *manifest content* is what a person can remember about his dream, whereas the *latent content* refers to the underlying intrapsychic events which led to the manifest content. The latent content of a dream consists primarily of unconscious thoughts, wishes, fantasies, and conflicts which are expressed in disguised form in the manifest content. Because of their unacceptable or threatening nature, these unconscious events cannot enter consciousness directly. They can, however, be expressed incognito, and the manifest content represents the dressed-up version of the "disreputable" determinants of the dream. Latent content becomes manifest through two basic processes, dream work and symbolization.

Dream Work

Dream work refers to the ways in which the latent dream content is transformed into the manifest content. *Condensation* is a type of dream work wherein separate thoughts are compressed and combined into a single, unified thought. The process involves borrowing elements from a number of different sources to form a compound which is far less extensive than the sum of the latent elements from which it was derived. In this way, threatening latent content is disguised so that its threat is not apparent in the manifest dream. An example of condensation would be a man dreaming of being affectionate with his girlfriend who, in the dream, physically was his mother. The man's girlfriend and mother were condensed into a single person. In such a process, the manifest content is said to be *overdetermined* —that is, it is the result of more than one latent source.

Sometimes an important element of the latent content may appear as only a trivial aspect of the manifest content, or vice versa. This process is known as *displacement* and can be illustrated by the example of a woman who receives a telegram which says that her son has been killed in battle and who dreams of merely receiving a telegram without any reference to its contents. If the woman had dreamt that the telegram said her son had been found alive after having been missing in action, this would be an example of the dream work process called *opposites*. The similarity between displacement and opposites as dream work and displacement and reaction formation as defense mechanisms should be noted. Both dream work and defense mechanisms serve to keep unacceptable and threatening material from becoming conscious. Another type of dream work is *visual representation,* which transforms thoughts into pictorial images in a manner similar to that of a rebus, a verbal puzzle in which a set of pictures suggests a word or phrase (see Figure 5–1).

FIGURE 5–1

An Example of a Rebus in Which the Pictures Depict the Syllables of a Word*

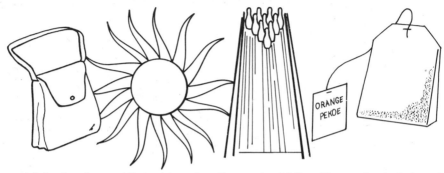

* A simpler rebus would be a picture of a coffee mug (cup) followed by one of a plank of wood (board) to represent the word *cupboard.* The reader who is unable to decipher the word which is visually represented above should consult page i, of this book, on which the word appears.

Upon awakening from a dream and trying to reconstruct it, we sometimes find that the parts of the dream do not fit together logically. According to Freud, this is the result of the dream work which has taken place. Dream work is a type of primary process and therefore does not follow the laws of logic. In reconstructing the dream, the dreamer attempts to fill in the missing elements and otherwise create a coherent overall picture of the dream. In doing so, he changes the dream content even further, and this process is referred to as *secondary elaboration.*

Symbolism

Whereas dream work changes unacceptable latent content into acceptable manifest content, *symbolism* serves to bring the latent element directly into the manifest content but in such a form as to be unrecognizable and therefore unthreatening to the conscious mind. Symbols are objects or ideas which stand for something else, and in psychoanalysis symbols typically substitute for something unconscious and threatening. One aspect of dream interpretation involves "translating" the symbols in the manifest dream. This task is facilitated by the fact that some symbols have universal meanings and therefore represent the same thing in all dreams. Freud believed that these *universal symbols* first came to be connected with their referents in prehistoric times.

Symbols are not the exclusive domain of dreams, and Freud and many others have examined symbolism in myths, fairy tales, literature, and colloquial speech. Some common symbols and their meanings *according to psychoanalytic theory* are presented in Table 5–1. It is apparent from the table that most of the symbols refer to sexual objects and activities, which is in keeping with the central psychoanalytic postulate that man's basic motivation is sexual in nature. Although there are many symbols, according to Freud only a few subjects are symbolized.

TABLE 5–1

Common Psychoanalytic Symbols and Their Latent Meanings

Symbol	Latent Meaning
House	Human body
Smooth-fronted house	Male body
House with ledges and balconies	Female body
King and queen	Parents
Little animals	Children
Children	Genitals
Playing with children	Masturbation
Beginning a journey	Dying
Clothes	Nakedness
The number three	Male genitals
Elongated object (e.g., snake, stick, gun, tree trunk, necktie, pencil)	Penis
Balloon, airplane	Erection
Woods and thickets	Pubic hair
Room	Woman
Suite of rooms	Brothel or harem
Box	Uterus
Fruit	Breast
Climbing stairs or ladder	Sexual intercourse
Baldness, tooth extraction	Castration
Bath	Birth

What evidence exists for sexual symbolism? Do people connect the sexual symbols with sexual objects as psychoanalysis proposes? One line of research which has looked into these questions involves having individuals classify psychoanalytic symbols of male and female genitals as either masculine or feminine. In general, these studies have confirmed that adults and sometimes children are able to categorize sexual symbols according to the gender predicted by psychoanalytic theory at a better than chance level (Kline, 1972).

It would be possible to argue that although the symbols were classified in accord with psychoanalytic theory, the principles which the subjects used to make the classifications were based on cultural differences. This would be the case when psychoanalytic and cultural symbolism coincide. A gun, for example, is a masculine symbol both in psychoanalysis and in our culture. Lessler (1964) examined the possible influence of both psychoanalytic theory and cultural stereotypes on the classification of sexual symbols. He found that the cultural stereotype was used to assign gender when the symbols had cultural referents but that they were classified according to psychoanalytic theory where no cultural bias existed. These results show that cultural sexual stereotypes as well as psychoanalytic sexual symbolism influence people's classification of symbols into masculine and feminine categories. Lessler argues that the results are completely in accord with psychoanalytic theory. Because sexual objects are usually threatening, if a cultural gender referent for the symbol exists, people are more likely to choose it instead of the psychoanalytic sexual meaning (e.g., calling a rolling pin feminine). On the other hand, if no cultural gender meaning is obvious, then people "must" and do use the psychoanalytic sexual meaning (e.g., classifying a cane as masculine).

In another major line of research aimed at validating psychoanalytic symbolism hypotheses, differences between the dreams of men and women have been tested. A good example of such research is Hall and Van de Castle's (1963) study of the effect of the masculine and feminine Oedipal situations on their respective dreams which was described in Chapter 4 (pages 60–61).

The Functions of Dreaming

Why do people dream? Freud talked about three interrelated functions of dreaming: (1) *wish fulfillment,* (2) *the release of unconscious tension,* and (3) *the guarding of sleep.* Every dream is an attempt to fulfill a wish. The wish may be a conscious desire which is not fulfilled during the day (e.g., a person wishes he were out sailing rather than in his office working) or an unconscious desire which is a more direct expression of a repressed drive. Frequently dreams represent a combination of these two sources. Thoughts from the day, called *day residues,* combine with an unconscious impulse to produce the dream. In effect, the unconscious impulse provides the psychic energy for the enactment of the day residues in the form of a dream. The result is that each of the three functions of dreaming is satisfied.

First, the wish is fulfilled in the dream. Recall that nocturnal dreams are primary processes in which the mental representation of the object or activity required to satisfy a wish is not distinguished from the actual object. Thus, when a wish "comes true" in a dream, it is as if it were actually fulfilled. This theoretical proposition is in keeping with the common observation that when we are dreaming we believe that the events are really happening.

Second, the unconscious impulse is allowed expression, albeit in a disguised and acceptable form due to dream work and symbolism. This allows dreams to serve as a safety valve for tensions which have built up in the unconscious.

Third, the individual remains asleep even though unconscious, threatening impulses are becoming conscious in the manifest dream. In a waking state, if threatening impulses began to become conscious, anxiety would be generated. If such anxiety were to be present during dreaming, the person would be awakened. However, through dream work and symbolism the threatening aspects of the latent material are removed. The result is that anxiety is not generated, and the person can continue sleeping without interruption.

Freud's overall interest in unconscious processes is reflected in his ideas regarding the functions of dreaming. Neo-Freudians, who have typically paid more attention to conscious, ego processes, have suggested that an important function of dreaming is problem solving and planning for future actions (e.g., Erikson, 1954; French & Fromm, 1964). Studies of sequential dreams have supported this additional function (e.g., Offenkrantz & Rechtschaffen, 1963).

The Interpretation of Dreams

The interpretation of dreams, the primary method of studying dreams within psychoanalysis, involves examining the manifest content of a reported dream as well as the subject's free associations about the dream to arrive at an understanding of its latent content. The psychoanalyst is aided in his interpretation by his knowledge of symbolism and dream work. These procedures are illustrated in the following dream interpretation by Freud (1961).

The dreamer, a patient of Freud's, was a woman who was still quite young but had been married for a number of years. She had recently received news that a friend of hers, Elise L., a person of about her own age, had become engaged to marry. Shortly thereafter she had the following dream:

> *She was at the theatre with her husband. One side of the stalls* [theater boxes] *was completely empty. Her husband told her that Elise L. and her fiancé had wanted to go too, but had only been able to get bad seats—three for 1 florin 50 kreuzers—and of course they could not take those. She thought it would really not have done any harm if they had* (p. 415).

Freud begins his discussion of this rather brief dream by analyzing the symbolic meaning of the monetary units. He notes first that this particular symbol was partially determined by an unimportant event of the previous day. The dreamer had learned that her sister-in-law had recently been given a gift of 150 florins (exactly 100 times the amount dreamt of) and had hastened to spend this gift on jewelry. Freud notes that *three* tickets are mentioned in the dream, whereas Elise L. and her fiancé would only have required two tickets for themselves. Examination of previous statements made by the dreamer revealed a connection: ". . . her newly-engaged friend was the same number of months—*three*—her junior" (p. 415).

Attention is then given to the statement that one side of the stalls was entirely empty. Recently, when the patient had wished to attend a play, she had rushed out to purchase tickets days ahead of time and, in doing so, had incurred an extra booking fee. When the patient and her husband arrived at the theater, they in fact found that one half of the house was almost entirely empty. This bit of information, according to Freud, raises two important points. First, it accounts in part for the appearance of the fact of "empty stalls" in the dream. More important in terms of psychoanalytic theory, there is the meaning of the empty stalls vis-à-vis the underlying meaning of the dream. In the patient's actual life, her experience with the theater tickets could clearly lead to the conclusion that she had been excessively hasty about running out to buy tickets and therefore had had to pay an additional, unnecessary price. Freud assumes that the same *meaning* may be hidden with respect to her feelings about her own marriage and that, in symbolic form, these feelings are revealed by the dream. Thus, the following final interpretation of the meaning of the dream for the patient is offered:

> "It was *absurd* to marry so early. There was *no need for me to be in such a hurry.* I see from Elise L.'s example that I should have got a husband in the end. Indeed, I should have got one a *hundred times* better" (a *treasure*) "if I had only *waited*" (in antithesis to her sister-in-law's *hurry*). "My money" (or dowry) "could have bought *three* men just as good" (p. 416).

Psychoanalysts, beginning with Freud, have tended to disparage the often used distinction between clinical practice and research. They consider the interpretation of dreams (of the kind presented above) to be valuable both as a clinical technique for the assessment of a patient's conflicts and as a method of research, the results of which may be used to support psychoanalytic theory. Many personality psychologists have argued that such analyses are highly *inferential* and accordingly have eschewed the study of dreams as a legitimate scientific enterprise. However, in the past two decades much impressive evidence has been accumulated to show that dreams and other phenomena associated with sleep may be brought under objective scientific scrutiny.

The Physiology of Sleep and Dreaming

Perhaps the major reason that systematic laboratory research of dreams was slow in developing is that these phenomena appeared to be entirely private events which could be directly observed only by the dreamer himself. It could be argued that dream research cannot be subjected to proper scientific scrutiny unless the dream itself is made to appear objectively, as on a television screen, while the dreamer is asleep.

Such television screens are not likely to become available in the near future, but some remarkable techniques for objectively studying dreams and other sleep-related phenomena have been developed. The two most important of these are the continuous recording of brain-wave patterns from sleeping subjects and the parallel recording of eye movements.

Brain waves are recorded by an instrument called an *electroencephalograph* which produces an *electroencephalogram* (EEG), a tracing, plotted against time, of the frequency and potential (voltage) of electric currents emitted by the brain (see Figure 5–2). The frequency of the electric currents from the brain is measured horizontally on the EEG, so that the closer together the tracings are, the

FIGURE 5–2

Sample EEG Patterns for the Waking State and the Four Stages of Sleep

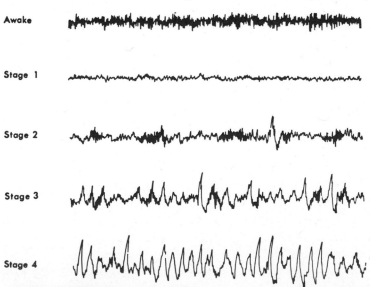

Source: Dement, 1965.

FIGURE 5–3

A Sleeping Subject with EEG and Eye-Movement
Electrodes

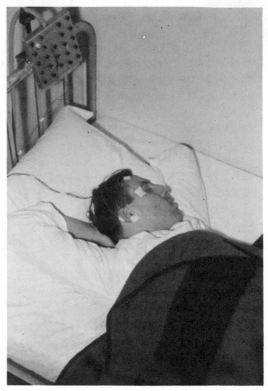

Courtesy of Dr. William Dement

greater is the frequency. The electric potential is measured vertically
on the EEG, so that the greater the amplitude, or height, of the
tracings, the greater the electric potential. EEG recordings are made
by placing electrodes directly on the scalp, a procedure which is pain-
less and noninjurious to the subject, and does not appear to disturb
sleep.

Eye movements have been measured during sleep primarily by
placing small electrodes around the orbits of the eyes and measuring
the differences in electric potential produced by displacement of the
eyeballs. Figure 5–3 shows a subject wearing both brain-wave and
eye-movement electrodes.

Stages of Sleep and Dreaming

It has been known for some time that sleep is not a uniform state
but rather consists of various stages. EEG recordings during sleep

reveal four basic stages of sleep which can be distinguished from the waking state. Figure 5–2 illustrates that as sleep progresses from Stage 1 to Stage 4, there is a progressive development of high-amplitude, low-frequency waves. Originally, this was thought to be correlated with reduction in neural activity and responsiveness as the person went from "light sleep" in Stage 1 to "deep sleep" in Stage 4. More recent evidence makes it clear that although the stages of sleep can be roughly placed on a quantitative continuum of depth, there is a very important exception. Indeed, this exception, which occurs during Stage 1 sleep, is so striking that it has been the primary focus of sleep researchers.

In 1953, Aserinsky and Kleitman were studying the sleep patterns of infants at the University of Chicago and inadvertently discovered the occurrence of occasional periods of rapid movements of the eyes during sleep. Such *rapid eye movement* (REM) activity has been shown to occur only during Stage 1 sleep, although not all of Stage 1 is characterized by REMs.[1] Much research has been directed toward elucidating the characteristics of REM sleep. During this time, there is a considerable amount of neural activity in the cerebral cortex which is similar to that found in the waking state. The autonomic nervous system is activated, including the presence of an irregular heart beat, irregular breathing, and penile erection. These physiological correlates of REM sleep give the impression of "light sleep." At the same time, REM sleep is associated with considerable muscular relaxation. People in REM sleep are relatively insensitive to external stimulation, and when they are awakened they frequently report that they have been in "deep sleep."

Is REM sleep "light" or "deep"? The best available answer seems to be that it is both and neither, which is to say that it is a unique neurophysiological stage which is *qualitatively* different from the other stages of sleep. This *paradoxical sleep,* as it is sometimes called, is found in humans of all ages and in subhuman mammals ranging from the opossum (Snyder, 1965) to the monkey (Weitzmann, 1961). In adult humans, REM sleep occupies slightly more than 20 percent of total sleep time (about 50 percent in infants). It usually occurs in regularly appearing cycles of approximately 90 minutes each, as shown in Figure 5–4. Successive REM periods become progressively longer, with the final period lasting from 25 to 45 minutes. Of course, these are only average figures, and they vary somewhat from individual to individual and from night to night.

The most important psychological correlate of REM sleep is that this is when most dreaming occurs. When Aserinsky and Kleitman

---

[1] REMs occur in almost all Stage 1 sleep except the initial period of Stage 1 when the person first falls asleep.

FIGURE 5–4

Sleep Cycles As They Relate to Stages of Sleep

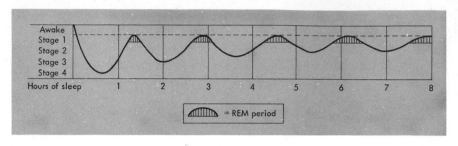

discovered the periodic occurrence of REMs, they believed that it might be related to dreaming. To test this hunch, they awakened adult subjects during REM and NREM (*nonrapid eye movement*) periods and asked them whether they had been dreaming. Of the subjects awakened from REM sleep, 74 percent indicated that they had been dreaming; of those awakened from NREM sleep, only 7 percent indicated that they had been dreaming (Aserinsky & Kleitman, 1955). This finding was of major significance because it was the first time that a reliable relationship had been found between an objective measure of a sleep variable (REM) and recall of dreams. Although the percentage of dream recall for REM and NREM awakenings has varied in different studies, the general finding that REM periods are associated with substantially more dream reports than are NREM periods has been upheld in numerous investigations (Van de Castle, 1971).

Continuing with this work, Dement and his associates reasoned that if dreams actually occur during REM sleep, then the subjective duration of the dream should be proportional to the duration of rapid eye movement observed prior to awakening the subject. The results were very positive:

> In one series of trials, subjects were awakened either 5 minutes or 15 minutes after the onset of REMs and were asked to choose the correct interval on the basis of whatever dream material they recalled. A correct choice was made in 92 of 111 instances. In another series, high correlation coefficients were obtained between the number of words in the dream narratives and the number of minutes of REMP [REM period] preceding the awakenings (Dement, 1965, p. 172).

Besides being an objective indication that there is a high probability that dreaming is occurring, REMs seem able to yield information about the content of dreams. It appears that dreamers scan their dream images in much the same way as they would visually scan similar events in a waking state and that their eyes move accordingly. Dement and Wolpert (1958) found that more frequent individual eye movements were associated with reports of active dreams (e.g., running or fighting) while less frequent individual eye movements were related to reports of passive dreams (e.g., staring at a distant object). Furthermore, when REMs were vertical, subjects tended to report dreams of vertical movement, such as looking up and down a flight of stairs; when the rapid eye movements were horizontal, the dream reports tended to contain horizontal imagery, such as two people throwing a ball back and forth (Dement & Kleitman, 1957).

Does dreaming only occur during REM sleep? The answer to this question depends partially on one's definition of a "dream." Most dictionaries define a dream as a succession of images, thoughts, or emotions passing through the mind during sleep. Using this meaning, reports of dreams after NREM awakenings have been found to be as high as 74 percent. However, if dreams are defined more stringently to include only vivid perceptual experiences (which often involve considerable emotion, improbable events, and a story line), the average percentage of subjects recalling dreams after NREM awakenings drops to less than 20 percent (Van de Castle, 1971). At the present time, research appears to support the existence of at least two types of "dreams"—REM dreams and NREM mentation. REM dreams tend to be lengthier, more vivid hallucinatory experiences with emotional components and are experienced *as if* they were occurring in the waking state. In contrast, NREM mentation tends to consist of relatively short, nonemotional, random thoughts which contain very few characters and a minimum of sensory imagery. NREM mentation frequently deals with events of the very recent past and has been likened to the random, background thoughts one has while engaged in some routine activity, such as getting dressed or preparing a meal (Foulkes, 1966).

Freudian Dream Theory in the Light of Recent Physiological Evidence

Freud's theory of dreams dealt primarily with their psychological aspects. In particular, Freud was interested in what dreams could tell him about the unconscious conflicts and processes of his patients. The recent physiological research on sleep and dreaming described above bears only an indirect relationship to psychoanalytic dream theory. Nevertheless, it is interesting to see to what extent psychoanalytic dream theory is in accord with what is now known about the physiology of sleep and dreams.

Does dreaming serve as a guardian of sleep as Freud postulated?

There is good evidence that most of our vivid and emotionally charged dreams take place during REM periods, which generally occur in regular cycles during the course of each night's sleep. Since this is a more or less automatic function, it is doubtful that dreaming per se keeps us asleep. However, it is also known that during REM sleep people are relatively insensitive to external stimulation. Therefore, it would seem that sleep is somewhat protected at the times when dreaming is most likely to occur.

One way to interpret the heightened neural activity and autonomic arousal that occurs during REM sleep would be in terms of the discharge of unconscious impulses, an important function of dreaming according to Freud. The fact that in males penile erection occurs regularly during REM periods but not during NREM periods (e.g., Fisher, Gross, & Zuch, 1965) *could* be construed as evidence for the discharge of the sexual drive during dreaming.

A corollary to Freud's hypothesis concerning the release of repressed psychic energy through dreaming is that if such an outlet is not provided, then the individual should exhibit signs of abnormal behavior. Studies of dream deprivation have shed some light on this issue. The procedure involves depriving subjects in a sleep laboratory of REM periods. A subject is awakened just as he is beginning to enter a REM period, and then he is allowed to fall back to sleep. Recent studies have shown that healthy subjects can undergo REM deprivation for as long as two weeks without adverse psychological effects. This general finding does not support the corollary to Freud's hypothesis. However, for a while after REM deprivation some subjects exhibit a rebound effect in which they experience considerably more REM periods than they normally do. There appears to be wide variation in subjects' "need" to compensate for lost REM sleep, and some subjects have displayed very little REM rebound. Interestingly, REM rebound may be related to such personality variables as flexibility. One possible hypothesis is that subjects who exhibit little REM rebound and are more flexible are able to release their unconscious impulses, which are normally discharged during dreams, in some other behavior.

The existing physiological evidence on sleep and dreaming is least applicable to Freud's contention that all dreams involve wish fulfillment. It is unlikely that unconscious wishes seek satisfaction at regular intervals, yet it is known that REM dreaming occurs in this manner each night. Although wish fulfillment may be one of the functions of dreams, it is most probable that not all dreams involve wish fulfillment. As neo-Freudians have suggested, dreams may also serve as an arena for problem solving and the rehearsal of future behavior. To illustrate the nature of this adaptive model of dreaming, a recent study designed to test a fundamental hypothesis of the model will be described.

Grieser, Greenberg, and Harrison (1972) investigated the general hypothesis that "dreaming serves to integrate current stressful experiences with similar experiences from the past, thus enabling the individual to use his basic coping mechanisms (defenses) to deal with the current stressful situation" (p. 281). College students were given anagrams to solve, following which they were told which anagrams they had solved and which they had failed to solve. Failure was made ego-threatening by informing the subjects that the task was a test of intelligence in which the average college student was able to do quite well. It was predicted that subjects who were permitted to dream following the experimental task would remember the failed anagrams better than subjects who were prevented from dreaming. This hypothesis follows from the view that dreaming is a period in which the person copes with a stressful situation, such as failure. By coping with the failure a person presumably makes it less ego-threatening. He will therefore have less need to repress the events leading to the failure (i.e., the unsolved anagrams) and will be more likely to remember them.

Grieser et al. found that subjects who were awakened during NREM periods, and thus were able to dream during REM sleep, recalled significantly more failed anagrams than subjects who were awakened during REM periods, and thus were "dream deprived." These results were interpreted as supporting the view that dreams have an adaptive function which enables the dreamer to cope with ego-threatening material.

PROJECTIVE TECHNIQUES

The psychoanalytic approach to personality places a heavy emphasis on unconscious factors in the determination of behavior. Since the individual is by definition not directly aware of these factors, indirect methods of assessment are necessary to uncover the unconscious determinants of behavior. This section explores the use of *projective techniques* in assessing unconscious motives and feelings. While their major application is in clinical settings, projective techniques are also used in personality research.

The Nature of Projective Techniques

All projective techniques are based on the assumption, called the *projective hypothesis,* that when an individual is forced to impose meaning or order on an ambiguous stimulus, his response will be a projection or reflection of his feelings, attitudes, desires, and needs. The principle is similar to the defense mechanism of projection.

There are a variety of existing projective techniques, with a wide range of stimulus materials and responses required of the subject. Some projective techniques require that the subject make *associations* to stimuli such as inkblots or words. Some involve the *construction* of stories about pictures which are open to a variety of interpretations (e.g., the Thematic Apperception Test [TAT]). Other projective techniques require the subject to *complete* sentences (such as "I often feel . . .") or stories. In still other projective techniques, the subject must *express* himself through drawings (e.g., the Draw-a-Person Test) or by acting out a loosely specified role (as in psychodrama). Finally, there are projective techniques in which the subject *chooses* between a variety of stimuli, indicating those he likes best and least (e.g., in the Szondi Test the stimuli are photographs of psychiatric patients with different diagnoses). Table 5–2 summarizes the most common types of projective techniques.

TABLE 5–2

Common Types of Projective Techniques

Type of Task	Stimulus Materials	Instructions	Example
Association	Word (e.g., man)	"After hearing each word, say the first word that comes to mind."	Word association
Construction	Picture	"Tell a story about the picture."	Thematic Apperception Test (TAT)
Completion	Sentence stem (e.g., "I want . . .")	"Complete the sentence."	Incomplete sentences
Expression	Paper and pencil	"Draw a picture of yourself and a person of the opposite sex."	Draw-a-Person Test
Choice	Photographs of people	"Choose the picture you like best and the picture you like least."	Szondi Test

Although there is considerable variety in the type of stimuli presented to the subject and the type of response required of him, all projective techniques share several important characteristics.

1. The stimulus material, be it an inkblot, a picture, or the first part of a sentence, is relatively unstructured and ambiguous. This forces the subject to impose some order or structure of his own.
2. The subject is usually not told the purpose of the test, nor is he usually aware of how his responses will be scored or interpreted.

3. The subject is told that there are no "right" or "wrong" answers.
4. Each response is considered to reveal a true and significant aspect of the individual.
5. The scoring and interpretation of projective methods of personality assessment are generally lengthy and relatively subjective procedures.

Technique vs. Test

It should be noted that the discussion thus far has referred to projective "techniques" rather than projective "tests." Although some projective techniques may appear quite similar to assessment procedures which are commonly called tests (sentence completion techniques, for example, are reminiscent of "fill-in-the-blank" items used in school examinations), others are substantially different from the usual kinds of tests. Additionally, and of more significance, most projective techniques do not meet the generally agreed upon psychometric standards of a test. For example, they are not standardized.

Two different projective techniques will be described in some detail—the Rorschach Inkblots and the Blacky Pictures. The former is the most widely used projective technique, and the latter is unique in that it was developed on the basis of a specific theory of personality, namely, psychoanalysis.

The Rorschach Inkblots

The use of inkblots to learn something about an individual, such as his imaginativeness, was not a new idea when Hermann Rorschach, a Swiss psychiatrist, began his experiments in the early part of the 20th century. Rorschach, however, was the first to make a systematic attempt to assess personality by the use of a standard set of blots. His efforts began with experiments on a variety of geometric forms in different colors. Later, Rorschach shifted his interest to less structured inkblots. The results of his work were first published in his 1921 monograph entitled *Psychodiagnostik,* which was subtitled "Methodology and results of a perceptual-diagnostic experiment (interpretation of accidental forms)." Regrettably, Rorschach died the year after the publication of his monograph, and it was left to others to elaborate on the basic procedures he had outlined.

Description of the Inkblots

The Rorschach Inkblot technique (usually called simply the "Rorschach") consists of 10 nearly symmetrical inkblots, 5 of which have some color and 5 of which are in black and white. The blots are printed and centered on pieces of white cardboard about 7 inches by

FIGURE 5–5

Inkblots Similar to Those Employed by Rorschach

Source: Kleinmuntz, 1967.

10 inches in size. Figure 5–5 presents inkblots similar to the kind used in the Rorschach. The blots were originally made by spilling ink on a piece of paper and then folding the paper in half.

Administration

The Rorschach is usually administered individually, and the administration is typically divided into two basic phases. In the *performance proper,* the examiner merely tells the subject that he is going to be shown a number of inkblots and that his task will be to tell what he sees in each of them. The examiner records *what* the subject tells him he sees in each blot. If the subject asks whether he may turn the card, how many responses he should make for each blot, or similar questions, the examiner tries to respond in such a way as to leave the decision up to the subject.

When the subject has finished responding to all 10 inkblots, the second phase of the administration, the *inquiry,* begins. Starting with the first card again, the examiner reminds the subject of each of his responses and inquires *where* on the blot he saw what he did and *how* he saw each response (i.e., what about the inkblot made it look like it did).

Scoring and Interpretation

A number of different systems for scoring and interpreting responses to the Rorschach have been developed. In one of the more widely used systems (Klopfer & Davidson, 1962), each response is scored for five major characteristics:

1. *location*—where on the card the concept was seen;
2. *determinant*—the qualities of the blot that led to the formation of the concept;

TABLE 5–3

Examples of Scoring and Interpretation of the Rorschach Inkblots

Scoring Characteristic	Examples of Scoring Category	Sample Response	Example of Interpretation*
Location............	Whole	Entire blot used for concept	Ability to organize and integrate material
	Small usual detail	Small part which is easily marked off from the rest of the blot	Need to be exact and accurate
Determinant........	Form	"The outline looks like a bear"	Degree of emotional control
	Movement	"A flying hawk"	Level of ego functioning
Popularity-originality.........	Popular	Response which many people give	Need to be conventional
	Original	Response which few people give and which fits blot well	Superior intelligence
Content.............	Animal figures	"Looks like a house cat"	Passivity and dependence
	Human figures	"It's a man or a woman"	Problem with sexual identity
Form-level..........	High form-level	Concept fits blot well	High intellectual functioning
	Low form-level	Concept is a poor match to blot	Contact with reality tenuous

* Interpretations would be made only if the type of response occurred a number of times (i.e., not just once). See text for further precautions regarding interpretations of Rorschach responses.

3. *popularity-originality*—the frequency with which particular responses are given by subjects in general;
4. *content*—the subject matter of the concept;
5. *form-level*—how accurately the concept is seen and how closely the concept fits the blot.

While scoring the Rorschach is a detailed procedure, interpretation is even more complex. Most often the responses are subjected to a formal analysis in which the way they were arrived at is examined. Table 5–3 presents examples of possible interpretations of responses. It is important to keep in mind that a given response or set of responses is always viewed in relation to the other responses made by the subject and in relation to how other subjects typically respond. The latter criterion can be thought of as "informal norms" which each Rorschach examiner compiles in his memory (they are rarely written down) from his experience with using the Rorschach. Interpretations of Rorschach responses are actually hypotheses. Their validity or usefulness varies with the purpose of the assessment and the individual case. A common way of checking the validity of interpretations based on Rorschach responses is to compare them with interpretations derived from other projective techniques to see whether they are consistent with one another.

The Blacky Pictures Technique

The Blacky Pictures were developed by Gerald S. Blum (1949, 1950) as a means of investigating and assessing the psychoanalytic theory of psychosexual development. The technique employs 12 cartoon drawings depicting the adventures of a dog named Blacky and his family—Mama, Papa, and Tippy, a sibling whose sex and age are not specified. Each cartoon is designed to illustrate one phase of psychosexual development. For example, the Oral Eroticism cartoon shows Blacky nursing; the Anal Sadism cartoon depicts Blacky covering something with earth; the Oedipal Intensity cartoon has Blacky standing behind a bush watching Mama and Papa holding hands; and the Castration Anxiety–Penis Envy cartoon shows Blacky watching a knife come down on Tippy's tail.

The Blacky Pictures are administered in three parts. First, the subject is asked to make up a story for each cartoon. Next, the examiner asks the subject a series of predetermined questions about the cartoon concerning what Blacky is doing, how Blacky is feeling, and why Blacky is acting the way he is. Finally, after each of these steps has been completed for each cartoon, the subject sorts the cartoons into two piles, one containing those he likes, the other those he dislikes. Then he is asked to choose the cartoon he likes best and dislikes most, in each case explaining why he picked the one he did.

Information from all three phases of administration and any comments the subject has made about the cartoons are integrated to arrive at an interpretation. Both scoring and interpretation are primarily subjective procedures and depend to a large extent on the examiner's knowledge of psychoanalytic theory.

The Blacky Pictures have been used with both children and adults for clinical assessment (e.g., in conjunction with psychoanalytic psychotherapy) and personality research dealing with psychosexual development. One type of research has involved validation of the Blacky Pictures and the psychoanalytic theory of psychosexual development. Blum and Miller (1952), for example, used the Blacky Pictures in a correlational study to demonstrate a relationship between oral eroticism and variables which psychoanalysis posits to be part of the oral syndrome, such as preoccupation with gifts, boredom, and ice cream consumption. A second category of studies has used the Blacky Pictures as measures of psychoanalytic concepts, an example being Sarnoff and Corwin's (1959) experiment on castration anxiety and the fear of death, discussed in Chapter 4 (page 61).

PSYCHOANALYTIC PSYCHOTHERAPY

The observations which led Freud to his elaborate theory of personality were made in the context of his clinical practice. In the latter half of the 19th century, the science of neurology was making little progress in treating mental disorders. One of the exceptions to this general state of affairs was the work of Jean Charcot in Paris, with whom Freud studied for about a year. Charcot used hypnosis in his treatment of hysterics. In hysteria, more commonly called *conversion reaction* today, the patient suffers from seemingly physical ailments, such as a paralyzed limb or a defective sense organ, for which no physical cause can be found. Charcot hypnotized his hysteric patients and then directly ordered them (hypnotic suggestion) to renounce their symptoms. The orders were generally effective as long as the patient remained in the hypnotic state. However, upon his awakening, the hysterical symptoms almost inevitably returned. This peculiar and intriguing combination of success and failure seemed extremely important to Freud, and he was eager to find procedures which would make the hypnotic cure both more enduring and more understandable.

Shortly after returning from his studies with Charcot, Freud opened his private medical practice in Vienna and became associated with Josef Breuer, a prominent Viennese physician who also practiced hypnosis, though in a slightly different way. Rather than directly willing a hysteric patient's symptoms away, Breuer asked the hypnotized patient to recall and then to relive in his mind the traumatic experiences which had caused the hysteria. The patient's reenactment of the trauma which produced his neurosis was accompanied by a great emotional release in the form of tears and words and seemingly led to a cure. Unlike the changes in Charcot's patients, these changes persisted after the patient awakened. Breuer hypothesized that it was the recollection of the events and the resulting discharge of dammed-up emotions (later to be called libido by Freud) which led to the alleviation of the symptoms and the cure of the neurosis.[2] The name given this treatment was *catharsis,* which is the Greek word for purification.

---

[2] "Neurosis" is a psychological disorder characterized by much anxiety with which the person has difficulty coping and by abnormal behavior, such as irrational fears (phobias), obsessional thoughts, and, as in hysteria, physical complaints.

Initially Freud treated his patients, who were almost exclusively hysterics, by hypnosis. He rejected Charcot's method of direct influence in favor of Breuer's more indirect "hypnocatharsis." But Freud was not always successful in hypnotizing his patients, and soon he substituted the technique of asking nonhypnotized patients to concentrate on recalling past events that were associated with their illnesses. He found that, given sufficient freedom, patients wandered in their thoughts and recollections and that this led to a superior understanding of the patients' unconscious processes. Freud called this technique *free association,* and it became the fundamental technique of psychoanalysis.

In free association, the patient is told not to censor his thoughts, to say whatever comes to mind without regard to social convention, logic and order, seeming importance or triviality, and any feelings of embarrassment or shame. To facilitate free association, Freud had his patients recline on a couch while he sat behind and out of view of the patient. The reclining position, reminiscent of sleep, is thought to bring a person closer to unconscious primary processes and to stimulate fantasy and memory. With the therapist out of view, the patient is not constantly reminded of his presence, and free association is thereby made easier. This physical setup also gives the therapist more freedom, since he does not have to be as aware of his own reactions.

Today, many types of psychotherapy involve a verbal interchange between patient and therapist. But almost a century ago, when Freud began to practice psychoanalysis, verbal psychotherapy was virtually unknown. Even more startling was the revolutionary change in the patient-therapist relationship which Freud advocated in the treatment of psychological disturbances. Hitherto, the patient had played only a passive role in his cure, while the physician had actively treated him. Freud's new therapeutic procedures reversed these roles. Now it became the patient's job to work (to free-associate and to reenact important childhood experiences) and the therapist's task to act as a compassionate but neutral observer who occasionally made significant interpretations about the origin and nature of the patient's intrapsychic conflicts. Many of Freud's contemporaries reacted in astonishment to this new psychotherapy, and remarked indignantly that Freud *listened* to his patients!

Freud viewed all mental illness as a manifestation of repressed conflicts and dammed-up libido which is seeking expression. However, because of the traumatic or culturally taboo nature of these conflicts, they cannot become conscious. Thus, Freud reasoned that the goal of psychotherapy must be to bring unconscious wishes, thoughts, and emotions, which have long since been repressed, into the conscious part of the mind.

Free association is the initial step in penetrating the unconscious, but free association is not sufficient in and of itself. Unconscious material comes to the conscious surface only in disguised or symbolic form during free association, just as it does in dreams. It is the task of the analyst to translate the symbolism and *interpret* the unconscious material for the patient. Interpretations are also made of dreams, symptoms, behavior in and out of therapy, the patient's relation to the analyst, and past experiences. The analyst's interpretations help to reconstruct childhood experiences which led to the conflict producing the neurosis. In Freud's own words, this process:

> . . . resembles to a great extent an archaeologist's excavation of some dwelling-place that has been destroyed and buried. . . . The two processes are in fact identical, except that the analyst works under better conditions and has more material at his command to assist him, since what he is dealing with is not something destroyed, but something that is still alive. . . . But just as the archaeologist builds up the walls of the building from the foundations that have remained standing, determines the number and position of the columns from the depressions in the floor and reconstructs the mural decorations and paintings from the remains found in the debris, so does the analyst proceed when he draws his inferences from the fragments of memories, from the associations and from the behavior of the subject of analysis (cited in Wolman, 1968, pp. 168–69).

From the analyst's interpretations the patient gains *insight* into the nature and origin of his neurosis. Insight is not a mere intellectual understanding of his personality and its inner conflicts and drives. Rather it is an *emotional experiencing* of parts of the personality which have been unconscious.

Early in his treatment of neurotics, Freud observed that his patients often resisted being cured. *Resistance,* as Freud came to call these impediments to successful treatment, can be both conscious and unconscious. In the former case, the patient is aware that he is somehow impeding his progress in analysis. For example, a patient who does not want to talk about a dream or thought which is passing through his mind is consciously resisting. In unconscious resistance, the patient is not aware that he is "fighting" the treatment. For example, the ego defense mechanisms may keep unconscious material from coming out in free association, or the patient may forget to come to a therapy session (unconsciously motivated forgetting). Unconscious resistance is more difficult to overcome than its conscious counterpart, but at the same time it is more significant since it is another manifestation of the patient's unconscious strivings.

The most important form of unconscious resistance is known as *transference.* Transference refers to all the feelings that the patient experiences toward the analyst which are *distorted displacements* from significant figures in the patient's past.[3] For example, the patient may act *as if* the analyst were his father or mother. Transference can be both positive, involving feelings of love, respect, or admiration, and negative, involving such emotions as hatred, jealousy, and disgust.

Transference is an impediment to psychoanalysis because it is an inappropriate reaction. The analyst is not really the patient's father. At the same time, the inappropriateness of the patient's feelings makes transference an excellent illustration for the patient of his significant earlier experiences and their importance to him. An integral part of psychoanalysis is the interpretation of instances of transference. Relative to other feelings about which the patient is expected to gain insight, the patient's feelings toward the analyst are easily seen as inappropriate in the therapy situation (i.e., the analyst gives the patient no provocation to either love or hate him) but pertinent in another, past situation (i.e., some significant relationship in the patient's childhood). Thus, transference is both a form of resistance and a road to the patient's past and his unconscious representations of the past. In fact, Freud believed that for psychoanalysis to be successful the patient had to experience transference, which was then worked through as part of the treatment.

Freud viewed transference rather narrowly in that he considered all transference to be a reliving of the patient's Oedipus complex. This viewpoint is consonant with Freud's conception that all neurosis has its origin in an unsuccessful resolution of the Oedipus complex. He maintained that persons suffering from nonneurotic disorders, such as psychotic disorders[4] and character disorders,[5] were not amenable to psychoanalytic treatment. These people were presumed either to have regressed to (in psychotic disorders) or to have been fixated at (in character disorders) prephallic stages of psychosexual development. In both cases this meant that much of their psychic energy was invested in earlier conflicts and therefore was unavailable

---

[3] The analyst may also experience feelings toward the patient which are distorted displacements from his own past, and this is known as *countertransference*. In order to minimize the adverse effects of countertransference on the therapy (e.g., a reduction in the analyst's objectivity), psychoanalysts are themselves psychoanalyzed as part of their training. By having insight into their own unconscious processes and conflicts, they are better able to understand and deal with countertransference.

[4] "Psychotic disorders" refer to psychological disorders in which the person's behavior seems to be out of contact with objective reality and is sometimes bizarre in nature (e.g., hearing voices, thinking illogically). Most patients in psychiatric or mental hospitals are diagnosed as psychotic.

[5] "Character disorders" refer to psychological disorders which are characterized by long-standing maladaptive patterns of living.

for transference. But as early as 1920, neo-Freudians began to broaden the definition of transference to include the reenactment of feelings toward significant adults which occurred in any stage of development. The view that persons manifesting nonneurotic disorders could form a transference relationship with the analyst led a number of psychotherapists to begin treating such patients by psychoanalysis (e.g., Sullivan with schizophrenics and Reich with persons suffering from character disorders).

"The Analysis of a Phobia in a Five-year Old Boy"

The major research method of psychoanalytic theory has been the case study. Freud saw patients almost 12 hours per day for many years of his professional career, and he used their case studies both as the source of hypotheses for building his theory and as evidence to support the theory that emerged. It is therefore appropriate, in order to indicate the nature of psychoanalytic evidence, to describe in some detail one such case study. "The Analysis of a Phobia in a Five-year Old Boy" (Freud, 1957) is an unusual case in that Freud saw the boy, Hans, only once. Nonetheless, he relied heavily on this case, and others have widely acclaimed it as a cornerstone of evidence for psychoanalytic theory. Glover (1956) has noted:

> In its time the analysis of Little Hans was a remarkable achievement and the story of the analysis constitutes one of the most valued records in psycho-analytical archives. Our concepts of phobia-formation, of the positive Oedipus complex, of ambivalence, castration anxiety, and repression, to mention but a few, were greatly reinforced and amplified as the result of this analysis (p. 76).

The case material which forms the basis for the analysis was collected by Hans's father, a close friend and intellectual disciple of Freud, who kept detailed records of his son's development and regularly reported to Freud concerning the boy's problems.

The first observation of importance for the case was made when Hans was three. At this time, he began to show considerable interest in his penis, which he referred to as his "widdler." This interest naturally led to tactile examination of the organ, and one day, when he was about three and a half, his mother found him engaged in what was presumably autoerotic play. She threatened him thusly: " 'If you do that, I shall send for Dr. A. to cut off your widdler. And then what will you widdle with' " (Freud, 1957, pp. 7–8). Hans also developed an interest in the widdlers of other people and of animals. He was particularly interested in seeing his mother undressed so that he could inspect her widdler.

When Hans was three and a half, his baby sister, Hanna, was born, a significant event which Freud described as "The most important influence upon the course of Hans's psychosexual development" (p. 113). Two major reactions are recorded in conjunction with this event. First, Hans expressed overt hostility toward the new arrival. Part of the hostility, however, was soon suppressed and disguised by symbolism. Freud notes: "From that time forward fear that yet another baby might arrive found a place among his conscious thoughts . . . his hostility, already suppressed, was represented by a special . . . fear of the bath" (p. 114). Recall that *bath* symbolizes birth (Table 5–1, page 87).

Hans soon developed a network of related irrational fears, or *phobias,* which reflected the intrapsychic conflict which he was now experiencing. First, while in the street, he was "seized with an attack of anxiety," but no object was initially identified with the anxiety. It had, presumably, grown from the periods of depression that occurred when he was separated from his mother, as when Hanna was born, but its character had become changed. "It soon became evident that his anxiety was no longer reconvertible into longing; he was afraid even when his mother went with him" (p. 114). Moreover, a specific fear soon emerged and replaced the generalized longing and anxiety. Freud writes that ". . . indications appeared of what it was to which his libido (now changed to anxiety) had become attached. He gave expression to the quite specific fear that a white horse would bite him" (pp. 114–15).

The onset of the problem was not as sudden as it initially appeared. In fact, it was immediately antedated by a dream to which Freud ascribes considerable importance and which occurred a few days before the first attack of anxiety. In the dream Hans's mother had gone away. Freud comments:

> This dream alone points to the presence of a repressive process of ominous intensity. We cannot explain it, as we can so many other anxiety-dreams, by supposing that the child had in his dream felt anxiety arising from the somatic cause and had made use of the anxiety for the purpose of fulfilling an unconscious wish which would otherwise have been deeply repressed. We must regard it rather as a genuine punishment and repression dream, and, moreover, as a dream which failed in its function [i.e., to maintain sleep], since the child woke from his sleep in a state of anxiety. We can easily reconstruct what actually occurred in the unconscious. The child dreamt of exchanging endearments with his mother and of sleeping with her; but all the pleasure was transformed into anxiety, and all the ideational content into its opposite (p. 118).

Under Freud's direction, Hans's father began the first bit of therapy. Hans was told that his anxiety was a consequence of masturbation, and he was advised to break the habit. Further, he was encouraged to explore his memory, and subsequently he disclosed an incident of the previous summer which appeared to be related to his now profound fear of horses. He recalled hearing a father admonish his daughter: " 'Don't put your finger to the horse; if you do, it'll bite you' " (p. 119). Freud notes the similarity between this expression and the earlier warning regarding masturbation which Hans himself had received from his mother.

Several fantasy incidents soon occurred which were interpreted as symbolic expressions of Hans's sexual desire for his mother. In the first, Hans developed a fantasy in which there were two giraffes and one was heard to cry out because Hans had taken away the other. In the second, he imagined himself forcing into "a forbidden space," and in the third, he was smashing a train window. Freud notes:

> Some kind of vague notion was struggling in the child's mind of something that he might do with his mother by means of which his taking possession of her would be consummated; for this elusive thought he found certain pictorial representations, which had in common the qualities of being violent and forbidden, and the content of which strikes us as fitting in most remarkably well with the hidden truth. We can say only that they were symbolic phantasies of intercourse . . . (pp. 122–23).

At this point Hans was informed by his father that he was really afraid of his father rather than of horses and that this fear existed because he (Hans) simultaneously harbored jealousy of his father and hostile wishes against him. Hans was told that the similarity between his father and the horses might be noted. "The black on the horses' mouths and the things in front of their eyes (the moustaches and eyeglasses which are the privileges of a grown-up man), seemed . . . to have been directly transposed from his father to the horses" (p. 123). After this phase of the analysis, carts, furniture vans, horses that looked big and heavy or moved quickly or *fell down* all came to provoke fear in Hans. Soon a new recollection from the past appeared. Freud writes:

> He went for a walk with his mother, and saw a bus-horse fall down and kick about with its feet. . . . He was terrified, and thought the horse was dead; and from that time on he thought that all horses would fall down. His father pointed out to him that when he saw the horse fall down he must have thought of him, his father, and have wished that he might fall down in the same way and be dead . . . a little while later he played a game consisting of biting his father, and so showed that he accepted the theory. . . . From that time forward his behavior to his father was unconstrained and fearless, and in fact a trifle overbearing (p. 125).

However, the fear of horses did not go away, and a new intrapsychic preoccupation appeared. Hans became concerned about defecation and developed a "lumf" complex. Freud explained these thoughts by "an analogy between a heavily loaded cart and a body loaded with faeces, between the way in which a cart drives out through a gateway and the way in which faeces leave the body, and so on" (p. 127). That the lumf complex was in fact related to procreation was corroborated, Freud argues, by another, newer fantasy. Hans imagined that a plumber unscrewed the bath in which he was sitting and then, with "his big borer," the plumber stuck Hans in the stomach. Soon Hans was afraid of bathing in the big tub in his home, and at the same time confessed the wish that his mother might drop Hanna in the bath while bathing her. His own fear of bathing was said to be a fear of retribution.

How can a fear of heavily laden carts, a preoccupation with lumf, and falling horses be related to one another? Freud offered the following interpretation.

> . . . little Hanna was a lumf herself . . . all babies were lumfs and were born like lumfs. We can now recognize that all furniture vans and drays and buses were only storkbox carts, and were only of interest to Hans as being symbolic representations of pregnancy; and that when a heavy or heavily loaded horse fell down he can have seen in it only one thing—a childbirth, a delivery. Thus, the falling horse was not only his dying father but also his mother in childbirth (p. 128).

The case concludes with Hans's successful resolution of his Oedipus complex, and Freud cites two final incidents which marked this occurrence. First, Hans imagined that the plumber gave him a new and bigger widdler than he had previously possessed. According to Freud, this was "a triumphant, wishful phantasy, and with it he overcame his fear of castration" (p. 131). Second, he dreamt of marrying his mother and having many childern by her. In the dream, Hans's father is "promoted" to marriage with Hans's grandmother, which effectively removes his father as a rival. And so, Freud says, "With this phantasy both the illness and the analysis came to an appropriate end" (p. 132).

LIABILITIES OF THE PSYCHOANALYTIC STRATEGY

Several of the often heard criticisms of the psychoanalytic strategy will be mentioned in this section; each has proved to be a liability or at least a source of controversy for the strategy. They are (1) the vague, nonspecific nature of many psychoanalytic concepts, (2) the failure of psychoanalysts to make several important logical distinctions in presenting evidence to support psychoanalytic theory, (3) the sources of bias which enter into psychoanalytic case studies, (4) the untestability of much of psychoanalytic theory, (5) the low reliability and validity of projective techniques, and (6) the questionable efficacy of psychoanalytic psychotherapy.

Psychoanalytic Concepts Are Vaguely Defined

In general, psychoanalytic terminology is poorly and ambiguously defined. For example, Freud (1965) defines the "unconscious" as any mental event the existence of which we must assume but of which we have no knowledge. This definition gives us no information. Other terms, such as "reaction formation," are defined somewhat more clearly yet do not provide sufficient guidelines for us to be able to as-certain when the phenomenon is occurring. Under what conditions, for example, is affection toward another person a manifestation of under-lying hate as opposed to love?

Psychoanalytic theory can be interpreted on at least two levels, the literal and the metaphorical. For instance, the id is spoken of *as if* it were a little man inside us. Here it is fairly clear that Freud did not expect others to interpret his writing literally. What, however, of the description of the Oedipus complex? Did Freud literally mean that every four-year-old boy wants to have sexual intercourse with his mother? Or, was the description of the Oedipal situation to be taken as an analogy of a complex rivalry between a child and his parents (cf. Fromm and other neo-Freudians [Mullahy, 1948])?

As a result of the imprecise terminology, many critical questions cannot be answered because there is no way to measure or quantify such relevant concepts as libido, cathexis, fixation, conflict, resistance, and transference. How much libido must be invested at the oral stage for a person to be considered an oral character? How much threat of castration must a child experience in order to repress his sexual desire for his mother?

Psychoanalysts Fail to Make Important Logical Distinctions

When presenting the evidence for psychoanalytic theory, psycho-analysts often do not make three important logical distinctions. First, usually no distinction is made between observation and inference. The Oedipus complex is a prime example. Freud observed that at around age four, boys are affectionate toward and seek the attention of their mothers and, to some degree, avoid their fathers. To explain these *observations,* Freud conjectured that the boy's feelings for his mother were due to sexual desires and that his feelings for his father must be related to the rivalry created by this sexual attachment and the implicit threat of castration. This *inference* has the status of a hypothesis, one alternative explanation, and nothing more. Thus, to say that four-year-old boys undergo an Oedipus complex is, in effect, *replacing the observation with the inference.* It would, of course, be a different matter to say that four-year-olds exhibit behavior *consistent with* the Oedipus complex which Freud postulated. The fallacy of presenting inferences as observations when they represent nothing more than a possible explanation is especially acute because there is good evidence that theories other than those of psychoanalysis can provide at least as good and often better explanations of the observed facts (e.g., Sears, 1943).

Second, there is a confusion in psychoanalysis between correlation and causation. It is legitimate to report the observation that during the first year of life a child engages in many behaviors dealing with his mouth (e.g., eating, sucking, crying) and is also dependent on other people for most of his needs. Oral behavior and dependency occur concurrently, and therefore they can be said to be correlated. However, on the basis of this observed relationship, it is not legitimate to conclude that dependency is based on orality (see Chapter 2 for a discussion of correlation and causation).

Psychoanalysis employs many analogies in describing its principles (e.g., troops left in battle, dammed-up libido, a mental censor of ideas), and herein lies a third logical error. Analogy is not proof. Although an analogy may help to describe a new or complex concept, it should not be alluded to as independent verification of the concept, which is frequently done in psychoanalytic writing. That military troops may be permanently lost for future battles in a difficult skirmish does not in any way validate the principle that libido is fixated at a stage in which the child has trouble resolving the relevant conflict.

Psychoanalytic Case Studies Are Biased

The primary method of personality research in the psychoanalytic strategy is the case study, usually of a patient in psychoanalysis. The limitations of the case study method have already been discussed in Chapter 2; here some specific sources of bias which affect psychoanalytic case studies will be mentioned.

The individuals studied in psychoanalysis are not representative of the general population; in fact, they constitute a highly restricted sample. They are typically middle-aged adults with relatively high incomes (private psychoanalysis can easily cost $7,000 or more per year) who are considerably above average in intelligence and highly articulate. Furthermore, the observations made of this highly restricted sample are very limited. The subjects are observed in a psychoanalyst's office, while stretched out on a couch, free-associating for 50 minutes. How typical is that of man's behavior?

Psychoanalytic data may also be biased by the investigator himself. In subtle and sometimes even directly explicit ways, psychoanalysts are prone to lead their subjects in the direction of their hypotheses. The use of direct suggestion and leading questions is readily apparent in the case of Little Hans (Chapter 5). Hans was given numerous interpretations of his behavior by his father and then pressed for verification of the interpretations. For example, it is only after Hans is told of the possible relationship between horses and his father that Hans notes the similarity. Upon inquiring about Hans's thoughts when he saw a horse fall down, his father's question directly suggests an answer: "When the horse fell down, did you think of your daddy?"

If psychoanalytic investigations are based mainly on uncontrolled observations, then it is crucial that the analysis of the observations be reliable. For instance, two or more independent analysts scrutinizing the same data should arrive at similar interpretations. As it turns out, there is little evidence for such reliability. Dream interpretation is a prime example in that the same dream will often be interpreted in different ways by independent, highly competent psychoanalysts (e.g., Lorand, 1946; Schafer, 1950). The low reliability of psychoanalytic interpretations is partially due to the qualitative nature of the data and the interpretations. If these were quantified, even in a rudimentary sense of categorization, it might be possible to obtain more agreement.

Psychoanalytic Theory Is Untestable

In oversimplified terms, all findings can be interpreted within psychoanalysis as substantiating the theoretical proposition being tested. Psychoanalysis has been called a "rubber sheet" theory because it can be stretched to cover any outcome. Suppose the hypothesis under investigation is that people who are fixated at the oral stage are dependent in their relationships with others. If the results of the study show that oral characters are dependent, the hypothesis is obviously confirmed. If the study reveals that oral characters are independent, the hypothesis is also confirmed because independence can be a defense (i.e., a reaction formation) against dependence. Finally, if oral characters are found to be both dependent and independent, then the hypothesis still can be said to receive support because the behavior is a compromise between the drive and its defense.

Projective Techniques Have Low Reliability and Validity

Some of the problems with projective techniques stem from the lack of standardization of procedures for administration, scoring, and interpretation. Subtle changes in the manner in which a projective technique is presented to the subject, including the relationship of the examiner and the subject, can lead to differential performance (e.g., Masling, 1960). In many cases the scoring of projective techniques involves some subjective judgment on the part of the examiner, even when scoring consists of placing responses into already designated categories. Considerably more subjectivity goes into the interpretation of the responses once they have been scored, and it is not surprising that interpretations of projective techniques vary widely with the skill and experience of the examiner as well as between examiners of comparable ability. This implies that projective techniques may be as much a projection of the examiner's own biases, hypotheses, favorite interpretations, and theoretical persuasion as an indication of the personality characteristics of the subject (Anastasi, 1968). The existence of well-developed norms for use in the scoring and interpretation of projective techniques would certainly help with this problem, but few adequate sets of norms are available.

Several thousand studies (Buros, 1965) have been performed to assess the reliability and validity of projective techniques. However, there are few adequate studies which support their reliability. Agreement among scorers and internal consistency (agreement among the items or stimuli of a given technique) is usually low. Reliability over time (retest reliability) has been shown to be equally poor, both when comparisons are made between an examinee's responses and between the themes based on those responses in two separate administrations. As an example of the latter finding, Lindzey and Herman (1955) gave the same subjects the TAT twice, but for the second administration they instructed subjects to write different stories. If the TAT were effectively assessing the subjects' personality dynamics, then the *themes* of the stories should have been the same for each subject in the two administrations even though the stories were different. However, no support for this hypothesis was obtained.

The case for the validity of projective techniques is also largely unsubstantiated by research. The findings of validity studies of techniques such as the Rorschach and the TAT have not been all negative, however. The predictive accuracy of a projective technique appears to be highest when the technique is being used to measure a particular personality characteristic (e.g., achievement motivation with the TAT; see Chapter 9) rather than to generate a general personality description. Nevertheless, a majority of the studies have produced inconsistent and inconclusive findings due to a host of methodological (e.g., Anastasi, 1968; Kleinmuntz, 1967) and statistical (e.g., Cronbach, 1949) problems. In one of the more common types of validity studies, experienced clinicians write personality descriptions about subjects based on the subjects' responses to a projective technique such as the Rorschach. The judges are "blind" with respect to any other information about the subjects. Not only has the agreement between the judges' descriptions been found to be low, but often the descriptions are so general as to be applicable to almost anyone.[1]

The Efficacy of Psychoanalytic Therapy Is Questionable

Eysenck's (1952a, 1961) classic summary of outcome studies of psychotherapy which were predominantly psychoanalytic in nature revealed that there is no good evidence that psychotherapy is more effective than no treatment at all. That is, the proportion of people who are rated by the therapists as improved (about two-thirds) is no higher than the proportion of people who recover from their psychological problems without psychotherapy (a phenomenon called *spontaneous remission*). A more recent study of exclusively psychoanalytic therapy has also found that about two-thirds of patients improve when therapists' ratings are the dependent variable (Feldman, 1968). Some writers (e.g., Bandura, 1969) have pointed out that the two-thirds im-

---

[1] The description would include statements like those appearing in Demonstration 1–1, page 16.

provement rate for treated persons may actually be inflated because "dropouts" from therapy serve to restrict the sample of treated persons to those who are more likely to improve and because therapists are apt to overestimate their successes. At the present time it appears that no evidence exists for the effectiveness of psychoanalysis over and above spontaneous remission rates. The present state of affairs is no different today than it was the year Freud died, when Myerson (1939) wrote: "The neuroses are 'cured' by . . . osteopathy, chiropractic, nux vomica and bromides, benzedrine sulfate, change of scene, a blow on the head, and psychoanalysis, which probably means that none of these has yet established its real worth . . ." (p. 641).

It is true that some people are helped by psychoanalysis, and this fact raises the issue of the efficiency of the process. "Successful" psychoanalysis often takes *years* of intensive effort[2] (as often as four or five sessions per week), and it is not at all clear that such an expenditure of time (not to mention money) is worth the results obtained.

---

[2] The great length of time required for psychoanalysis may account in part for reports of favorable outcomes since spontaneous remission rates increase with the passage of time.

The Dispositional Strategy

6

The Dispositional Strategy
INTRODUCTION

"[He] had a special personal charm, a fine courage that dominated his physical weakness, great gifts as a conversationalist and a persistent gaiety that made for him warm friends. . . ." Reading this description gives us the feeling that we know something about the man described. There is a hint of the enduring qualities which set him apart from others and which might help us to identify him or what he will do in different situations. The description is of Robert Louis Stevenson (Nisenson & DeWitt, 1949, p. 139). It might, of course, be applicable to many other people as well, and there is much that it does not tell us about Stevenson's personality. Still, we feel that it has taught us something about his basic characteristics and the way he was usually *disposed* to behave in social interactions.

In Demonstration 6–1 you will be able to explore some of your own dispositional notions about people's behavior and personality.

Demonstration 6–1

DESCRIBING PEOPLE IN DISPOSITIONAL TERMS

We are all accustomed to using dispositional notions in describing and attempting to explain people's behavior. These usually take the form "So-and-so is a _____ person" or "So-and-so acts that way because he is _____." For example, we might say that "Harry is a *meek* person" or "Susan acts that way because she is *proud.*"

The purpose of this Demonstration is to give you an opportunity to describe in dispositional terms people whom you know. It will allow you

119

to compare the way in which you use dispositions to the way in which psychologists use the dispositional strategy. It will also serve as an introduction to some of the methods, predictions, and general findings of the dispositional strategy.

Procedure

1. Take six sheets of lined paper and write one of the letters "A" through "F" at the top of each sheet. Then make a copy of the work sheet in Table 6–1 (this will be used later in the Demonstration).

TABLE 6–1

Work sheet for Demonstration 6–1

Rank		Name	Number of Adjectives Used	Pervasiveness				Percent of Similarity
				Almost Always 4	Fairly Fre- quently 3	Occa- sionally 2	Rarely 1	
		Self						
Know Best	1st							
	2nd							
	3rd							
	4th							
Know Least	5th							
"Σ" = Sum (total)			Σ =	Σ =	Σ =	Σ =	Σ =	
"M" = Mean			M =		%	%	%	%

2. You will need to designate a particular person of your *own sex* for each of the categories listed below. Write each of their names at the top of the appropriate sheet of paper.

A. Your same-sexed parent or, if you have never known this person, a close biological relative of the same sex (i.e., a "blood relative").

B. A close friend who is not related to you.

C. Someone with whom you are somewhat friendly (i.e., with whom you have a more casual relationship than that with B above).

D. Someone whom you know only in one specific context (e.g., a high school or college teacher).

E. A historical figure whom you admire.

F. Yourself.

3. Beginning with your same-sexed parent (i.e., person A), list all the adjectives you can think of that describe him or her. Write down as many or as few adjectives as seem necessary to describe the person fully. You need not put the adjectives down in any particular order. Repeat this procedure for the persons in categories B through F, in that order.

4. Starting with person A, look over the adjectives to see if any of them are similar or redundant. (For example, "clumsy" and "awkward" have

similar meanings.) When you are unsure, double-check with a standard thesaurus. *Collapse any redundant adjectives either by eliminating one or more of the adjectives or by combining them* (e.g., clumsy-awkward). Repeat this procedure for persons B through F, in that order.

5. Starting again with person A, now rate each of the adjectives or adjective-combinations according to the degree to which each is characteristic of the person. Use the following scale:

$$4 = almost\ always\ characterizes\ the\ person$$
$$3 = fairly\ frequently\ characterizes\ the\ person$$
$$2 = occasionally\ characterizes\ the\ person$$
$$1 = rarely\ characterizes\ the\ person$$

Write the scale number which is most applicable next to each of the adjectives or adjective-combinations. Repeat this procedure for persons B through F, in that order.

6. *Rank* the people A through E (excluding yourself) in terms of how well you know them. The person whom you feel you know best should be given the "1st" rank, the person whom you feel you know second best should be assigned the "2nd" rank, and so on until the person whom you feel you know least well has received the "5th" rank. Write the rank in the upper right-hand corner of each sheet.

7. In the first column of the work sheet (which you copied in step 1), write the names of the five people *other than yourself* (i.e., persons A through E) in order of the degree to which you feel you are familiar with them (see step 6). The person whom you ranked "1st" (i.e., the one you feel you know best) should be listed first, the person whom you ranked "2nd" should be listed next, and so on.

8. On the work sheet, in the "Number of Adjectives Used" column, put the total number of adjectives or adjective-combinations you have used to describe each of the persons (A through F).

Then, at the bottom of the column, put the total number of adjectives or adjective-combinations used to describe all of the people *other than yourself* (i.e., sheets A through E). Divide this total by 5 to obtain the mean number of adjectives which you used to describe the other people and enter this in the appropriate space at the bottom of the work sheet.

9. In the "Pervasiveness" columns of the work sheet, record the number of adjectives for each person (A through F) which fall in each of the four categories. These are the numbers you wrote next to the adjectives in step 5.

Then, at the bottom of the column, put the total number of adjectives in each of the four pervasiveness categories for the five persons *other than yourself.*

Next, compute and record at the bottom of the work sheet the percentage of adjectives which fall into each of the pervasiveness categories. To do this, divide the total number of adjectives for each category by the total number of adjectives used to describe the other persons (i.e., combined across all categories) and then multiply by 100.

10. Looking at all of the sheets on which you have listed adjectives (i.e., A through F), check to see if any of the adjectives are similar or redundant across persons. For example, if you described yourself as generous and your parent as giving, these should now be collapsed to one adjective, either by changing "generous" to "giving" or vice versa or by hyphenating the two adjectives where they both appear (e.g., "generous-giving"). Note that this step is similar to step 4, and a thesaurus

may help you. On sheets A through E (i.e., every sheet except the one for yourself) *circle each adjective or adjective-combination which is the same as one you have used to describe yourself* (on sheet F).

11. Compute the *percentage* of adjectives for each of the other people (A through E) which corresponds to your own, and record it in the "Percent of Similarity" column (i.e., divide the number of adjectives which are the same for yourself and the other person—the ones you have circled—by the total number of adjectives used to describe the other person and then multiply by 100).

Discussion

You may have already noticed a number of interesting features and patterns in your use of dispositional descriptions for others and yourself. To lend some further order to your inspection of what you have done, we shall mention a few of the findings of dispositional psychologists which are related to the Demonstration and which will be discussed in detail later in Section III.

Number of Descriptive Adjectives Used.   Gordon Allport was one of the first to examine the range of dispositional terms, or "trait names," which people use to describe others. He found that we often use a large number of adjectives for this purpose, but that many of them are synonymous. The number can therefore be reduced. To the extent that your own experiences in this Demonstration parallel Allport's findings, you would have been able to reduce the size of your initial lists of descriptive adjectives.

After collapsing redundant adjectives, Allport found that most people actually use a fairly small number of adjectives in describing people they know, the usual range being between 3 and 10. Does your mean number of adjectives fall within this range? How does the number of adjectives you used to describe yourself compare with the mean number of adjectives you used to describe other people?

Dispositions and Genetics.   Dispositional psychologists who take a biological view have found evidence suggesting that certain dispositions are transmitted genetically. Evidence of genetic dispositions might show up in this Demonstration in the degree of similarity ("Percent of Similarity" column of the work sheet) between yourself and your parent. Is this similarity greater than the similarity between yourself and a close friend? A more casual acquaintance?

Relationship to People.   Many people believe that the closer one's relationship to someone, the "better" they know him. Yet there is some evidence from psychological studies that we often feel more comfortable assigning dispositional adjectives to people whom we know less well.

Examine the relationship between the number of adjectives you used to describe a person and how well you feel you know that person. Since the five people other than yourself are listed on the work sheet in descending order of familiarity, you can look down the "Number of Adjectives Used" column to see if a pattern emerges. Is "secondhand" information such as that which you used to describe the historical figure whom you admire sufficient to adequately characterize the person? How well were you able to describe the person you know in only a single context?

Generality of Dispositions.   Dispositional psychologists believe that there is a good deal of generality in human characteristics so that a person who acts in certain ways in one situation will also tend to act in those ways in other situations. One measure of whether you view people from a dispositional perspective is the number of adjectives you used to describe the person whom you know in only one context. Did you feel that you were able to describe his overall characteristics? Or did you feel that there were probably many characteristics of which you were unaware? In the former case you would probably have used about the same number of adjectives as you did to describe a close friend.

Pervasiveness. Allport and others have noted that dispositions vary in the degree to which they seem to pervade a particular personality. Not very many people have dispositions which pervade all that they do and dominate their entire personality ("almost always" category), and we are not likely to ascribe characteristics to people which occur "rarely."

Other Issues. You may find it useful to save these materials and to inspect them again as you read the chapters in this section. Even now, you might wish to consider some further analyses of your own. What are the qualitative differences among the adjectives you use to describe various individuals you know? What differences would you expect if you repeated the Demonstration, but described people of the opposite sex? Examining questions like these will help you to better understand the dispositional strategy for the study of personality.

Descriptions of other people which account for their behavior in terms of dispositions to behave in certain ways are among the first rudimentary views of personality to be found in recorded history. These early conceptualizations of man assume, as do their modern counterparts, that there are enduring, stable personality differences *which reside within the person.* These differences, it is further assumed, can be used to predict and understand much of man's behavior.

HISTORICAL ANTECEDENTS

We are not interested in the merely curious relics of history. However, modern dispositional approaches, perhaps more than the approaches found in other strategies, owe some of their thinking to the ideas of past centuries. It is therefore instructive to examine these ideas before characterizing the approaches which make up the contemporary dispositional strategy for analyzing personality.

Early dispositional views assumed that men could be divided into a relatively small number of types, according to their personalities, and that by knowing a man's type one could predict with reasonable accuracy the way in which he would behave in a variety of circumstances. The ancient Hebrews used this perspective of man to conduct what may have been the first formal effort at personality assessment. In the following quotation from the Old Testament, it is apparent that this perspective was dichotomous, with the goal of describing only two types of men, those who could be ferocious fighters and those who lacked this quality.

And the Lord said unto Gideon, The people that are with thee are too many for me to give the Midianites into their hands. . . . Now therefore go to, proclaim in the ears of the people, saying, Whosoever is fearful and afraid, let him return and depart early from Mount Gilead. And there returned of the people twenty and two thousand; and there remained ten thousand.

And the Lord said unto Gideon, The people are yet too many; bring them down unto the water, and I will try them for thee there. . . . So he brought down the people unto the water: and the Lord said unto Gideon, Every one that lappeth of the water with his tongue, as a dog lappeth, him shalt thou set by himself; likewise every one that boweth down upon his knees to drink. And the number of them that lapped, putting their hand to their mouth, were three hundred men: but all the rest of the people bowed down upon their knees to drink water. And the Lord said unto Gideon, By the three hundred men that lapped will I save you, and deliver the Midianites into thine hand: and let all the other people go every man unto his place (*Judges,* 7:2–7).

A second ancient view, the *theory of the four temperaments,* is closely akin to several contemporary theories and to a goodly number of the layman's conceptions of personality. The position has as its basis the Greek hypothesis that the physical universe can be described in terms of four basic elements: air, earth, fire, and water. Hippocrates, often called the "father of medicine," extended this argument to man himself, by suggesting that the body is composed of four corresponding "humors": blood, black bile, yellow bile, and phlegm. Galen later postulated that an excess of any of these humors led to a characteristic temperament, or "personality type": sanguine (hopeful), melancholic (sad), choleric (hot-tempered), or phlegmatic (apathetic). Although this ancient psychophysiological theory of personality is no longer taken seriously, the four temperaments have survived to this day as part of our language.

Conspicuous even to the ancients, however, was the fact that there are clearly more than four types of people. Thus, extensive catalogs of types emerged. The notion of identifying types of men continued, with only minor changes, as the popular conception of personality for thousands of years. Among the most striking of the modifications that did appear was the hypothesis that one could guess a man's behavior and personality from his physical appearance. In William Shakespeare's play *Julius Caesar,* for example, Caesar advises Marcus Antonius:

> Let me have men about me that are fat;
> Sleek-headed men, and such as sleep o' nights:
> Yond Cassius has a lean and hungry look;
> He thinks too much: such men are dangerous.
>
> (Act I, Scene II)

The belief advanced by Shakespeare's Caesar is still rather popular today; for instance, many people believe that they can identify a "criminal type" by physical appearance.

ASSUMPTIONS OF THE DISPOSITIONAL STRATEGY

The major assumption of the dispositional strategy is that a person's behavior is controlled to a significant degree by relatively stable, enduring dispositions. Dispositions vary from one person to another, but for any given individual they are pervasive and affect all aspects of his behavior. This is true regardless of whether they are referred to as types, traits, needs, motives, or characteristic life-styles, all of which are dispositional names.

Another characteristic of the dispositional strategy is that it assumes an *additive model* of personality assessment (cf. the non-additive model of the psychoanalytic strategy; see Chapter 3). The strength of various dispositions is assumed to be the "sum" of various individual response tendencies. For example, a person who likes to meet strangers, easily approaches teachers to dispute grades on examinations, *and* is often outspoken in class discussions would be considered somewhat more extroverted than a person who likes to meet strangers and argue about grades but prefers not to play a prominent role in large-group discussions.

A third assumption of the dispositional strategy involves the related concepts of *consistency* and *generality,* which refer to the assumed "breadth" of the effect of the disposition on behavior. Dispositions are assumed to be stable, or *consistent,* in the sense that a person who is ambitious at his job today will also tend to be ambitious at his job tomorrow, next week, and next month. In like manner, the dispositional psychologist would expect an individual's behavior to be *general.* A man who is ambitious in his work is also likely to be ambitious and striving in his play (e.g., at golf or sailing) and will probably have high ambitions for his children as well.

IDENTIFYING PERSONALITY DISPOSITIONS

Human behavior can be ordered and divided on a nearly infinite number of dimensions. We can speak of someone as a happy person, an aggressive person, a person who needs to be loved, a benevolent person, a stingy person, and on and on. Which of these dimensions are important? Which are most likely to meet the assumptions of the dispositional strategy?

In principle, there are three possible ways to go about identifying the dimensions of personality which are most likely to be significant psychological dispositions. They can be anticipated from a theory, distilled from common lore, and searched for empirically. Generally, dispositional psychologists have not begun with theories telling them which dimensions to look for; only a few dispositionalists, such as Gordon Allport, have tried to take advantage of common lore. Instead, most dispositional psychologists have favored the empirical approach, carefully searching for dispositions, like prospectors sifting for a find.

There are, however, some fairly clear indicators, or criteria, to test whether a given dimension, a prospective psychological disposition, will be useful. One involves meeting the assumptions of consistency and generality. But consistency and generality are not sufficient. The dimension must also clearly discriminate between or among people. If everyone were happy (or aggressive or ambitious), then these dimensions would be of little use as psychological dispositions, for we could not use them to predict or explain any of the differences in behavior among people. Dispositional approaches are, in fact, very much psychologies of "amount," and dispositions which do not make it possible to talk of people having more or less of some durable characteristic add no predictive power.

DISPOSITIONAL PERSONALITY ASSESSMENT

The dispositional strategy has employed almost all of the major personality assessment techniques. For example, interviews as well as projective and situational tests of various sorts have been adopted for identifying the presence of various characteristics. However, one general type of assessment, written reports and descriptions of behavior, has played a central role in most dispositional assessment enterprises. It includes a wide range of "paper-and-pencil" self-report tests (see Chapter 8) and also "reputational" reports in the form of descriptions provided by an assessee's friends, acquaintances, and sometimes his biographers.

Since dispositions are theoretical constructs, it is not possible to measure them directly. Instead, the personality researcher who adopts the dispositional strategy must devise measures of behavior, often self-report inventories, which yield signs or indicators of various underlying dispositions. At the same time, it is presumed that there is no one "absolute measure" of a disposition; in fact, there should be several different indices. The dispositional psychologist

> . . . explains the behavior of an individual by the values assigned
> him on dimensions considered relevant to the behavior in question.
> These values may be expressed numerically as scores on a test,

or they may be represented by labels that stand for different positions on the dimension. A psychologist might, for example, explain an individual's pattern of deference to certain people and hostility to others in terms of authoritarianism, by saying that he is an authoritarian type of person. Or the psychologist might predict a person's success as a business executive from his scores on measures of intelligence, aggressiveness, and sociability. The use of these and other dimensions implies that the values obtained on them by individuals have consequences over a fairly wide realm of behavior and that these dimensions exist independently of any single method of measurement. Therefore, although a particular test may be the one most frequently used in the measurement of some dimension, it is assumed that there may be other, equally valid measures. Like other theoretical constructs, dimensions are inferred; their definition rests not on any single set of operations but on the *convergence* of a set of operations . . . (Levy, 1970, p. 200).

Convergent and Discriminant Validity

The foregoing remarks are related closely to some of the more formal criteria for measuring the adequacy of an assessment procedure. Specifically, since the appearance of a classic article by Campbell and Fiske (1959), the ultimate criterion for dispositional measurement has been the development of instruments having both *convergent* and *discriminant* validity. The terms are technical, but the idea itself is straightforward. Even if measures of what is presumably the same disposition are quite different in form (e.g., paper-and-pencil, projective, situational), they should *converge* and thus correlate highly with one another; on the other hand, tests designed to measure different dispositions should *discriminate* between them and thus *not* be highly correlated.

As a final remark about dispositional assessment, it should be noted that dispositional psychologists typically believe that their measuring instruments are imperfect and thus will contain error, or "noise," as well as true information about the disposition which is being measured. Part and parcel of this belief is the assumption that estimates of the stability and generality of dispositions, based as they are on imperfect measurements, probably *under*estimate the actual stability and generality of the underlying dispositions.

DISPOSITIONAL RESEARCH

Dispositional research is most often concerned with identifying dimensions that may be useful, with verifying the assumptions of consistency and generality of various characteristics, and with developing improved measurement techniques for personality assessment.

Recall that, in discussing the psychoanalytic strategy, we noted how the approach had dictated that the predominant method of research would be the case study. The dispositional strategy also dictates that one method of research will predominate—the correlational method. The dispositional researcher is interested in how well various behaviors go together, for only when a number of different behaviors are related can he speak of an underlying personality disposition which may be controlling them.

DURABILITY OF DISPOSITIONS AND THE POSSIBILITY OF PERSONALITY CHANGE

Unlike the other three personality strategies discussed in this book, the dispositional strategy has little to say about personality change and is not associated with any form of therapy. There are at least two reasons why this is so. First, it follows logically that any psychologist who emphasizes the stability of personality would view personality change as a difficult—if not impossible—enterprise. Second, many of the psychologists associated with the dispositional strategy have had their strongest links with the academic world rather than with clinical endeavors. The practical contributions of dispositional psychologists have focused on the measurement and prediction of behavior rather than on its control.

While the dispositional strategy has not itself been associated with efforts to change personality, some of the individual psychologists discussed in this section have been actively interested in personality change techniques based on one of the other strategies. At least one dispositionalist, David McClelland, has been personally responsible for developing an imaginative program for altering one disposition, the need to achieve (see Chapter 9).

*****

The dispositions suggested by various psychologists to account for personality can be divided into two broad classes: those that are *attributive* and those that are *propulsive*. Attributive approaches specify dimensions which explain a person's behavior because he *is* that way (e.g., "She behaves that way because she *is* stubborn" or "He doesn't say hello because he *is* shy"). Propulsive explanations, on the other hand, emphasize more dynamic, impelling forces as characterizing the individual—forces which drive (or impede) action. We might say, for example, "She is *driven* to achieve" or "He *needs* affection," implying an active force or agency (at least metaphorically) which controls the individual's behavior.[1]

In the next chapter we shall consider some attributive dispositional approaches to personality—the trait and type approaches; in Chapter 9 we shall turn to the propulsive views based on the concepts of need and motive.

---

[1] To be sure, the distinction between attributive and propulsive dispositions is imperfect: we can say that a person "is" achievement oriented or "needs" to be stubborn. Nonetheless, it seems to be a heuristically useful categorization.

7

The Dispositional Strategy
TRAIT
AND TYPE
APPROACHES

In contemporary writing, both popular and scientific, the terms *trait* and *type* have come to be used in several different ways. Sometimes, "type" and "trait" are used as summary labels for observed differences in behavior. To say of a friend "At parties he is usually the shy type" is merely to conveniently summarize our observations. In the same vein, Guilford (1959) defined a trait as *"any distinguishable, relatively enduring way in which one individual varies from others"* (p. 6). Used in this way, the terms have no necessary theoretical implications and serve merely to facilitate communication. Alternatively, traits and types have been considered by many personality psychologists to be real entities, actually residing within persons. Allport (1966) described this as *heuristic realism* and noted the implication that "the person who confronts us possesses inside his skin generalized action tendencies (or traits) and that it is our job scientifically to discover what they are" (p. 3). Yet another, and perhaps more important, implication lies in this approach; a person's traits are now assumed to *cause* his behavior. Thus, it would become legitimate to say that the individual behaves aggressively at least in part because he has an aggressive trait or is an aggressive type. Our primary interest will be in those dispositional approaches which construe traits and types in this last way, looking for enduring characteristics of the person which *determine* his behavior.

BIOLOGICAL VIEWS OF PERSONALITY

A person's psychological attributes might come from many sources. Some theorists have sought a basis for them in the individual's biological constitution, relating personality to both overt physical characteristics and genetic endowment.

The Logic of the Biological Approach

The basic argument underlying the biological approach to personality is that *there are differences in the physical constitution of individuals and that often these differences cause differences in behavior.* It is apparent that the assertion, if viable, has far-reaching consequences for both predicting and understanding individual differences in personality.

The essence of this view was concisely set forth by Williams (1967) in an essay on "The Biological Approach to the Study of Personality." His argument consists of five main points.

First, there are obviously *interspecies* (comparison of one species to another) biological differences, which suggests the existence of *intraspecies* (within the species) differences.

> It is beyond dispute, of course, that dogs, cats, rats, and monkeys, for example, show species differences with respect to their patterns of conditionability. Stimuli which are highly effective for one species may be of negligible importance for another. If hereditary factors make for inter-species differences, it is entirely reasonable to suppose that intra-species differences exist for the same reason (p. 22).

Second, intraspecies differences have regularly been found in experimental work with animals. Ivan Pavlov, in his pioneering animal experimentation, placed great emphasis on conditioning behavior. Williams argues, however, that a major aspect of Pavlov's findings is the pervasive suggestion of constitutional differences among his dogs, an aspect of his research rarely cited by behavioral psychologists.

> Pavlov found as a result of extensive study of many dogs that they often exhibit innate tendencies to react differently to the same stimulus. He recognized in his dogs four basic types: (1) excitable, (2) inhibitory, (3) equilibrated, and (4) active, as well as intermediate types (p. 21).

Third, there is an impressive battery of evidence that humans show intraspecies differences in their biological and hereditary makeup. For example:

> . . . normal stomachs vary greatly in shape and about six-fold in size. . . . Arising from the aortic arch are two, three, four, and sometimes five and six branch arteries . . . each person exhibits a distinct breathing pattern as shown in the spirograms of different individuals under comparable conditions. . . . The morphology

of the pituitary glands which produce eight different hormones is so variable, when different healthy persons are compared, as to allow for several fold differences in the production of individual hormones . . . the male sex glands vary in weight from 10 to 45 grams in so-called "normal" males . . . (p. 23).

Fourth, behavioral indices of these physiological differences also exist and frequently show up in basic research on the ability of humans to discriminate stimuli.

Investigations involving "cold spots," "warm spots," and "pain spots" on the skin indicate that each individual exhibits a distinctive pattern of each. In a relatively recent study of pain spots in twenty-one healthy young adults, a high degree of variation was observed. . . . One young man "A" showed seven percent of the area tested to be "highly sensitive," while in another, "B," the right hand showed one hundred percent "highly sensitive" areas. On A's hand, forty-nine percent of the area registered "no pain" under standard pain producing test conditions. On B's hand, however, there was no area which registered "no pain" (pp. 23–24).

Fifth, Williams concludes that there should be a greater integration of this pattern of findings and reasoning into psychological research.

It seems indefensible to assume that people are built in separate compartments, one anatomical, one physiological, one biochemical, one psychological, and that these compartments are unrelated or only distantly related to each other. Each human possesses and exhibits unity. Certainly anatomy is basic to physiology and biochemistry, and it may be logically presumed that it is also basic to psychology (pp. 22–23).

The biological-type approaches to personality which will be discussed next are in agreement with this conclusion.

Kretschmer's Approach

In 1921, Ernst Kretschmer, a German psychiatrist, published a volume entitled *Physique and Character.*[1] In it were to be found the rudiments of the first modern biological-type approach to personality. Kretschmer's position, like Freud's before him, was instigated by observations made in the clinical practice of psychiatry. The two major categories of *psychosis* (severe psychological disturbance in which the individual is no longer able to function in society) recognized in Kretschmer's day were *schizophrenia* and *manic-depressive psychosis*. The former diagnosis was ascribed to individuals who showed a loss of emotional behavior, while the latter

[1] The English translation by W. J. H. Sprott (1926) has been used.

category included persons characterized by extreme elation (mania) or extreme depression or sometimes a cyclic movement from one to the other.

Kretschmer believed that he had observed a regular relationship between assigned psychiatric diagnosis and the physique of his patients. He set out to demonstrate this relationship by creating a limited number of categories of physique and then relating these categories to psychiatric diagnosis.

Types of Physique

In order to determine types of physique, Kretschmer and his associates began by developing a "constitutional inventory" consisting of more than 70 items. To illustrate the degree of detail in which they were interested, a portion of the inventory dealing with skin blood vessels is reproduced in Table 7–1. The data themselves were collected in a thoughtful and systematic manner.

> We noticed, and immediately filled in point for point, the foregoing list, the patient standing naked before us in bright daylight, and we ruled a red line under whichever member of the groups of descriptions fitted the case. According to the pronouncedness of the characteristic whether it was strong or weak, we drew a single or a double line, so that we saved the time which a written description would have required, and obtained a diagram that provides a perfectly intelligible survey, which conveyed to us at a glance, later on, with no trouble at all, not only the general impression, but each detail of physique, and thus we could make a comparison between every single point in different diagrams in a second (Kretschmer, 1926, p. 9).

Examinations of this type were carried out on approximately 400 psychiatric patients. The data seemed to reveal three basic physiques: *asthenic, athletic,* and *pyknic* and a small number of anomalous pat-

TABLE 7–1

A Portion of Kretschmer's "Constitutional Inventory" Dealing with Blood Vessels

Skin blood vessels:	clearly visible	dimly visible	invisible
Head:	bluish	dark-red	medium	pale
Hands:	bluish	dark-red	medium	pale
Feet:	bluish	dark-red	medium	pale
Hands and feet:	damp	medium	dry
Body:	damp	medium	dry
Hands and feet:	warm	medium	cold
Body:	warm	medium	cold

Source: Adapted from Kretschmer, 1926.

terns grouped together as *dysplastic*. The asthenic type appeared to be

> . . . a lean narrowly-built man, who looks taller than he is, with narrow shoulders . . . thin muscles and delicately boned hands; a long, narrow, flat chest, on which we can count the ribs . . . thin stomach, devoid of fat . . . the way the weight of the body lags behind the length . . . stands out clearly (p. 21).

In contrast, the following is a "rough impression" of the athletic type.

> A middle-sized to tall man, with particularly wide projecting shoulders, a superb chest, a firm stomach, and a trunk which tapers in its lower region . . . the solid long head is carried upright on a free neck . . . the over-developed musculature stands out through only a thin sheath of fat (pp. 24–25).

The pyknic male bears little resemblance to either of these two. He is a man of

> . . . middle height, rounded figure, a soft broad face . . . the magnificent fat paunch protrudes from the deep vaulted chest which broadens out toward the lower part of the body. . . . It seems then as if the whole mass of the shoulders were slipping downwards and inwards over the swelling chest; and the head also plays a part in this static displacement: it sinks forward between the shoulders . . . the neck no longer seems, as is the case with other types, a slim round column, which carries the chin . . . the point of the chin is directly joined with the upper forehead (p. 29).

Less uniformity is to be found among the dysplastics, who are primarily distinguished by the unusualness of their appearance. Kretschmer noted that

> . . . we describe as dysplastic types a high degree of profile angularity, asthenic emaciation, or athletic sturdiness . . . such forms of growth . . . vary very markedly from the average and commonest form of the type in question . . . not only the extremes, but also the majority of cases fall well outside the typical form; they even impress the laity as rare, surprising, and ugly (p. 65).

Figure 7–1 is a reproduction of Kretschmer's examples of the foregoing types.

Physique and Psychiatric Diagnosis

The remaining problem for Kretschmer and his associates was to relate these body types to the psychiatric diagnosis of the patients. The data revealed a clear pattern. Persons of the asthenic, athletic, and dysplastic body type were more likely to be schizophrenic than

FIGURE 7-1

The Four Body Types Identified by Kretschmer

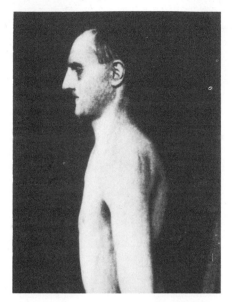

Asthenic

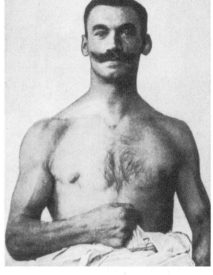

Athletic

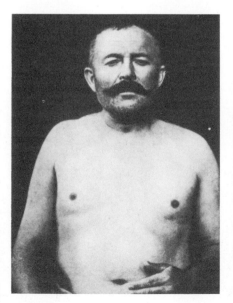

Pyknic

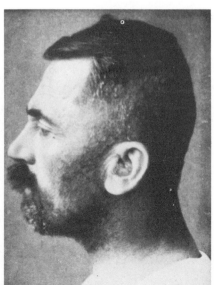

Dysplastic

Source: Kretschmer, 1926.

TABLE 7–2

The Relationship of Physique and Psychiatric Diagnosis
(based on 243 patients)

	Schizophrenic	Manic-Depressive	Total
Asthenic and athletic.....................	91.2%	8.8%	100.0%
Dysplastic...............................	100.0	0.0	100.0
Pyknic..................................	6.5	93.5	100.0

Source: Adapted from Kretschmer, 1926.

manic-depressive. For persons of pyknic build, on the other hand, manic-depressive psychosis was the more probable diagnosis. Some of the data reported by Kretschmer are summarized in Table 7–2.

Kretschmer believed that this striking evidence for a relationship between physique and personality would be paralleled by reliable relationships with "normal" persons, but it remained for William Sheldon to collect the data.

Sheldon's Approach

In developing a comprehensive psychology of constitutional differences, Sheldon (1942) regarded his task as: (1) the development of an adequate classification of physique—the structural, or *static,* aspect of humans; (2) the development of an adequate classification of temperament—the functional, or *dynamic,* aspect of humans; and (3) the empirical search for an enduring, reliable relationship between the static and the dynamic views of man. Sheldon (1942) said:

> . . . physique and temperament are clearly two aspects of the same thing, and we are not surprised if we are led to expect that the dynamics of an individual should be related to the static picture he presents. It is the old notion that structure must somehow determine function. In the face of this expectation it is rather astonishing that in the past so little relation has been discovered between the shape of man and the way he behaves . . . there are dynamic and static variables which correlate sufficiently highly to reaffirm our faith in the possibility of a useful science of constitutional differences (pp. 4–5).

The Primary Components of Physique

Following Kretschmer's lead, Sheldon studied body types by simultaneously examining many physiques to search for regularities. A large number of persons were photographed, under standard conditions, from the front, side, and rear. When the 4,000 photographs from their first study were examined, Sheldon and his colleagues found that, even to the unaided eye, a certain orderliness was apparent. But refining this impression into systematic evidence for distinguishable components of physique required a rigorous procedure. Two formal criteria were introduced.

(1) Could the entire collection of photographs be arranged in an ascending (or descending) progression of strength in the characteristic under consideration, with agreement between experimenters working independently? (2) In the case of a suspected new component of structural variation, is it, upon examination of the photographs, . . . impossible to define this apparently new component in terms of mixtures, regular or dysplastic, of the other components already accepted (Sheldon, 1942, p. 6)?

By means of these criteria, three primary components of body structure were identified: they were named *endomorphy, mesomorphy,* and *ectomorphy.* The names and the statement of their continuity were new, but they were remarkably like the body types found by Kretschmer. As can be seen in Figure 7–2, in the endomorph the digestive system predominates; endomorphs are usually fat and are said to "float high in the water," and their musculature is underdeveloped. Mesomorphs tend to be "hard, firm, upright, and relatively strong and tough." A mesomorph's skin is thick, his blood vessels are large, and his appearance is overwhelmingly one of

FIGURE 7–2

A Comparison of a Predominant Endomorph, Mesomorph, and Ectomorph with a Man of Average Physique

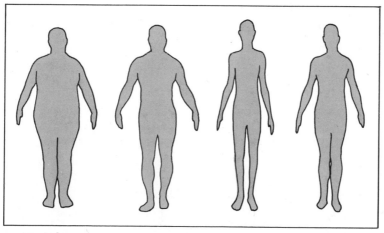

| Predominant Endomorph | Predominant Mesomorph | Predominant Ectomorph | Average Physique |

Source: Drawn from Sheldon, 1942.

sturdiness. Finally, ectomorphs are characterized by "fragility, linearity, flatness of the chest, and delicacy throughout the body."

In Sheldon's scheme, persons are not merely classified as one type or another. Rather, on the basis of many measurements, a person is *somatotyped* by assigning three numbers, each ranging from 1 to 7, which represent the strength of each of the components of body structure. In somatotyping, the first numeral refers to endomorphy, the second to mesomorphy, and the last to ectomorphy. Thus, a muscular, powerful man might approach the somatotype 1–7–1, while an average individual with respect to physique might be somatotyped 4–4–4.

The Primary Components of Temperament

Temperament, according to Sheldon, refers to the dynamic aspects of a man, which may run a long gamut from complex bodily movements to the expression of specific beliefs and attitudes. However, Sheldon argued that between the extremes, there is a level of functioning "where basic patterns of motivation manifest themselves." The problem is to produce a research definition of temperament and to empirically identify its components.

Sheldon began his search for the primary components of temperament with a list of 650 "alleged traits." The list was derived from many sources, including the personal observations and speculations of the investigators. Inspection of the list revealed, however, that many of the trait names were redundant in terms of the ideas which they represented. A list of 50 traits sufficed to encompass the essential content of the original 650. Armed with this list, Sheldon proceeded to rate his first sample of subjects (33 male graduate students and young instructors) for a full academic year. The ratings were based on interviews, observations while they engaged in their ordinary daily activities, and repeated social interactions with the investigators. As with the data on physique, inspection revealed a consistent pattern. Some traits appeared to be regularly related to each other but unrelated to the remaining characteristics in the list. Sheldon (1942) found that

> . . . three groups of traits showed positive intercorrelation among themselves, *and negative correlation with all or nearly all of the other traits.* At this time this was not particularly what we wanted to find, for the writer then entertained a hypothesis that probably at least four primary components existed . . . (p. 14).

The Scale of Temperament that emerged from this first correlational study was modified through eight additional studies. Each successive study looked for additional consistent traits, not yet on the list, which seemed to characterize persons who fell near one of the polar extremes of the previous scale. Finally, using a sample of 100 male subjects, Sheldon selected a list of 60 traits, 20 for each of the components of temperament which had come to be named *viscerotonia, somatotonia,* and *cerebrotonia.* The nature of these components can be seen in the short form of the scale, having 10 traits for each component, which is reproduced in Table 7–3.

TABLE 7–3

A Short Form of Sheldon's Scale of Temperament

I *Viscerotonia*	*II* *Somatotonia*	*III* *Cerebrotonia*
Relaxation in posture and movement	Assertiveness of posture and movement	Restraint in posture and movement, tightness
Love of physical comfort	Love of physical adventure	Overly fast reactions
Slow reaction	The energetic character-	Love of privacy
Love of polite ceremony	istic	Mental overintensity, hy-
Sociophilia	Need for and enjoyment of	perattentionality, appre-
Evenness of emotional flow	exercise	hensiveness
Tolerance	Love of risk and chance	Secretiveness of feeling,
Complacency	Bold directness of manner	emotional restraint
The untempered charac-	Physical courage for com-	Self-conscious motility of
teristic	bat	the eyes and face
Smooth, easy communica-	Competitive aggressive-	Sociophobia
tion of feeling, extraver-	ness	Inhibited social address
sion of viscerotonia	The unrestrained voice	Vocal restraint, and gen-
	Overmaturity of appear-	eral restraint of noise
	ance	Youthful intentness of manner and appearance

Source: Adapted from Sheldon, 1942.

The Relationship between Physique and Temperament

Once adequate taxonomies of both physique and temperament had been developed, the most crucial step remained—the demonstration of a consistent relationship between the two aspects of man. Two hundred white males were selected as subjects and were somatotyped. Over a five-year period, these subjects were rated on Sheldon's Scale of Temperament.

The results were striking. Each of the three body types was *positively related to one and only one* of the temperamental components and *negatively related to the others.* This finding is powerful evidence for the constitutional position, since it demonstrates that "human structure and human behavior are . . . far from unrelated." The reader may want to attempt to guess which class of temperament (viscerotonia, somatotonia, and cerebrotonia) went with each of the three classes of physique (endomorphy, mesomorphy, and ectomorphy) before examining Table 7–4, which summarizes Sheldon's findings.

Table 7–4 is a *correlation matrix* which gives the correlation of each of the body types and temperaments with every other. Only the top half of the matrix is needed, since the lower half. is merely a mirror image of the top half. The diagonal of the matrix contains correlation coefficients of +1.00, which indicates that each variable is perfectly correlated (positively) with itself. Looking at the first row of the matrix, we see that endomorphy is positively related to viscerotonia (+.79) and negatively related to somatotonia (−.29) and cerebrotonia (−.32), the other two classes of temperament. Thus, endomorphy is positively related to *one and only one* of the components of temperament. Furthermore, still looking at the first

TABLE 7–4

The Correlations Sheldon Found among the Primary Components of Physique and Temperament, Using 200 Male Subjects

	Endo-morphy	Viscero-tonia	Meso-morphy	Somato-tonia	Ecto-morphy	Cerebro-tonia
Endomorphy	+1.00	+.79	−.29	−.29	−.41	−.32
Viscerotonia		+1.00	−.23	−.34	−.40	−.37
Mesomorphy			+1.00	+.82	−.63	−.58
Somatotonia				+1.00	−.53	−.62
Ectomorphy					+1.00	+.83
Cerebrotonia						+1.00

Source: Adapted from Sheldon, 1942.

row of the matrix, we see that endomorphy is negatively related to both mesomorphy (−.29) and ectomorphy (−.41), which lends support to the notion that the three basic physiques are relatively independent. That is, the physical attributes which make up the endomorphic physique tend to be different from those which comprise the other two basic physiques. Similarly, an examination of the correlations between viscerotonia and somatotonia (−.34) and viscerotonia and cerebrotonia (−.37) substantiates the relative independence of the three basic temperaments. The relationship which holds for endomorphy and viscerotonia (i.e., high positive) also holds for mesomorphy and somatotonia (+.82) and for ectomorphy and cerebrotonia (+.83).

While Table 7–4 is a concise presentation of Sheldon's findings, it does not fully capture his perspective toward individual cases. Each of the 200 subjects is detailed in a case study in the original report. For example, the only case of 1–1–7 in the sample, a pure ectomorph, is described as

> . . . a weak, inconspicuous youth who has succeeded in making an acceptable integration in the face of what must be regarded as a poor constitutional endowment. He is inoffensive, quiet, defenseless . . . somewhat below average in mental endowment. He has no special gifts of a productive or creative nature, although he is said to possess unusually sensitive appreciation of art. He has a fairly strong endowment of sexuality, which has been expressed mainly in excessive masturbation . . . since he has little access to women, he cleaves to men. He is what might perhaps be called an "intellectual homosexual," but he is not a true homosexual. His masturbational imagery is entirely feminine. . . . He will never offend anyone, and he thus offers one of the essential requisites for success in many endeavors (Sheldon, 1942, p. 290).

The constitutional approach to personality, as reflected in the work of Kretschmer and Sheldon, has as its primary interest the identification of a relationship (correlation) between physiological and psychological endowment. No necessary causal relationship is implied by these correlational data (see Chapter 2). Some personality researchers, however, have specifically avowed genetic causation in personality. The investigations and particular approaches which this outlook has generated have focused mostly upon abnormal behavior, with a particular interest in demonstrating a genetic etiology for schizophrenia.

THE GENETIC APPROACH

The suggestion that an individual's personality dispositions (as well as his physical characteristics) can be transmitted "through the blood" is well known. Is there support for such a belief? The ways of answering this question that at first seem "obvious" are fraught with difficulties.

Suppose a man who is very capable verbally *and* very aggressive has three children. If all three of them were also verbal and aggressive, it would be commonly inferred that they had inherited these dispositions from their father. Yet it is equally possible that the transmission was social rather than biological; the children may have been exposed to a large vocabulary, books, and socially aggressive behavior and thus have *learned* these characteristics during the early years of life. To sort out the relative effects of heredity and environment, circumstances would somehow have to "hold one of them constant" so that the effects of the other could be detected. The *twin study method* of research appears to do just this.

The Twin Study Method

Out of every 85 births, one is a multiple birth producing two children.[2] Approximately two-thirds of all twins are "fraternal," or, technically, *dizygotic,* meaning that they developed from separate ova and sperm. Fraternal twins share only a birthday with their "womb-mates" and are otherwise no more alike genetically than siblings born separately. The smaller remaining group, the "identical," or *monozygotic,* twins, consists of twins who have developed from the same ovum and sperm and consequently have the same genetic endowment. Identical twins have held a fascination for many people, both in and out of science, not only because of their statistical rarity but also because of their tremendous potential for helping us to investigate the extent to which hereditary factors influence behavior.

Twin research in personality involves two major assumptions. First, identical twins are genetically alike, whereas fraternal twins are not. Second, the social and environmental experiences of twins reared together are alike.[3] Therefore, greater similarity on measures of personality between identical twins, as compared with fraternal twins, is a consequence of genetic contribution. Given this reasoning, the research strategy is one of selecting a good dependent measure of personality and determining the degree of *concordance* (similarity) among many pairs of twins who are both identical and fraternal. The largest body of work to date which has followed this approach has involved the search for the etiology of schizophrenia. This research has been spearheaded by the German psychiatrist Franz Kallmann. For many years, the data reported by Kallmann were thought to provide unequivocal evidence for a major genetic component in schizophrenia, the most prevalent form of psychotic behavior.

Kallmann's Data

Kallmann examined large samples of persons diagnosed schizophrenic and determined the percentage who had twins also diagnosed schizophrenic. The results of several of his studies are presented in Table 7–5. Since in all three samples the proportion of persons diagnosed schizophrenic is overwhelmingly higher when the

---

[2] To the extent that new "birth control" drugs can influence the probability of multiple births, these odds may be only approximate today.

[3] It is rare that this assumption is met not only because no two individuals can have truly identical environments but more importantly because identical twins may be more likely to receive similar treatment than fraternal twins. For example, identical twins are often provided with matched clothing, similar haircuts, and so on.

TABLE 7–5

Percentage of Persons Diagnosed Schizophrenic Given a Twin
Also Diagnosed Schizophrenic As Reported by Kallmann

		1946	*1950*	*1954*
Dizygotic	Same sex	17.7		
	Opposite sex	11.5		
	Combined	14.7	14.5	12.5
Monozygotic	Not separated	91.5		
	Separated	77.6		
	Combined	85.8	86.2	86.2

Source: Adapted from Jackson, 1960.

twin also diagnosed schizophrenic is monozygotic, it is easy to see
why many have found in Kallmann's data compelling evidence for
a genetic etiology of schizophrenia.

Despite the powerful correlational data, Kallmann's work has a
number of important failings. Jackson (1960) has correctly observed that inferring genetic causation of schizophrenia from work
such as Kallmann's involves two assumptions:

(1) that individuals have been exposed to stress or psychogenic
trauma similar to that experienced by schizophrenics without developing schizophrenia; (2) that many cases exist of identical twins
who have been reared from infancy or early childhood in separate
and distinct environments and yet both have developed schizophrenia (p. 38).

The first point, Jackson observes, presumes that we know which
psychological conditions ("psychogenic traumas") cause schizophrenia. While there are numerous and divergent speculations on
this point (based on correlational or case study data), there is
neither agreement nor compelling evidence which speaks to the
issue.

With respect to the second assumption, present circumstances are
even less favorable. According to Jackson (1960), a detailed search
of American and European studies performed over the previous 40
years revealed *only two* cases of twins who were reared apart and
who both developed schizophrenic reactions.

The last point requires some amplification when it is juxtaposed
with the "separated" category in Table 7–5. Jackson (1960) notes
that Kallmann's term *separated* refers "only to *separation five years
prior to the psychosis*" and points out that

Because his age group ranged from 15 to 44 years, and because his
average age of subjects is stated to be 33 years . . . it is obvious
that the twins were not apart during their formative years. In-

deed, most remained together well past the usual age for marriage; and even this late in life separation resulted in a significant decrease in concordance for schizophrenia (p. 40).

It appears, then, that Kallmann's data do not allow for an unequivocal separation of the effects of heredity and environment. However, if Kallmann's data are taken together with more recent studies, the suggestion that there is *some* genetic component in schizophrenia is still fairly compelling (Mowrer, 1969). The next genetic personality research which we shall examine is not subject to such sharp criticism.

The Adoption Method

An alternative method for separating out hereditary and environmental influences on personality is often called the *adoption method*. Basically the method involves comparing individuals whose parents[4] had a particular personality characteristic (e.g., schizophrenia) and who have been raised, from a very early age, by foster parents with individuals whose parents did not have the personality characteristic in question but who have been raised in comparable foster-home-type settings. If the former group of subjects develop the particular personality characteristic to a greater degree than the latter (control) group of subjects, it must be concluded that the characteristic has developed because of genetic, rather than environmental, influences.

In a now classic study, Heston (1966; Heston & Denney, 1968) used the adoption method to compare 47 children who were born to women diagnosed schizophrenic and were separated from their mothers within three days after birth with 50 children who were born to mothers with no record of psychiatric disturbance and were also separated shortly after birth. All subjects were born in Oregon between 1915 and 1945. The control subjects were matched to the experimental subjects for sex, type of adoption placement, and length of time spent in child care institutions.

As adults (mean age was approximately 37 years), the subjects were assessed for their current psychological functioning by personal interviews, tests (e.g., personality and IQ tests), and the examination of various public records (e.g., police, hospital, and school records). In addition, friends, relatives, and employers were contacted and interviewed.

The results revealed that five of the subjects born to schizophrenic mothers were classified as schizophrenic, whereas none of the control

---

[4] Usually, only the mother is considered because the identification of the father may not be accurate.

subjects were. (The probability of such a finding occurring by chance alone is less than 5 in 200.) In addition, significantly more subjects whose biological mothers had been schizophrenic were found to be mentally deficient (IQs less than 70), to have diagnoses of sociopathic and neurotic personality disorders, to have spent more than a year in a penal or psychiatric institution, to be felons, and to have been discharged from the armed forces because of psychiatric or conduct disorders. These data are presented graphically in Figure 7–3.

FIGURE 7–3

Some Significant Differences between Foster Children of Schizophrenic and Normal Mothers in Heston's (1966) Study

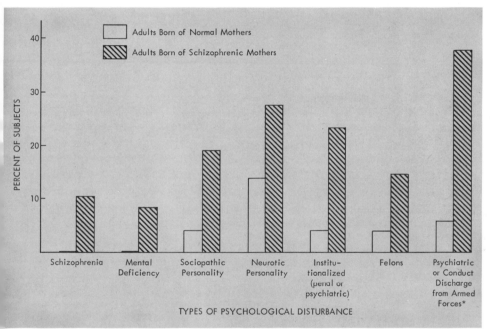

* These are percentages of those subjects in each group who were in the armed forces.
Note: There is overlap among categories such that a given subject may be classified in more than one category of psychological disturbance.
Source: Drawn from data reported in Heston, 1966.

It is important to note that there was considerable overlap of subjects in each of the categories of psychological impairment enumerated above (e.g., one subject was diagnosed as both schizophrenic and mentally deficient). Only 26 of the 47 subjects who had schizophrenic mothers were classified as having at least one type of psychological disturbance. Interestingly, Heston (1966) reports that the remaining 21 subjects born to schizophrenic mothers "were not only successful adults but in comparison to the control group were more spontaneous when interviewed and had more colourful life histories. They held more creative jobs: musician, teacher, home-designer; and followed the more imaginative hobbies: oil painting, music, antique aircraft" (p. 824). Clearly, then, psychological disturbances per se are not transmitted genetically, but only a disposition toward them. (The specific nature of the genetic component for which Heston's data provide evidence remains to be identified.)

The Heritability of Personality Characteristics within the Normal Range

Most early genetic personality research focused upon abnormal behavior. More recently, though, investigators have also begun to ask about genetic determinants of personality within the normal range.

One study, hallmarked by the fact that it was far more sensitive to methodological problems than were its predecessors, was reported by Gottesman in 1963. Gottesman began by enumerating *all* of the same-sexed twins enrolled in public high schools in the Minneapolis–Saint Paul area, thereby drawing his twin sample from a population of over 31,000 children. Voluntary cooperation of more than half of the twin pairs in this sample was then secured. Gottesman legitimately noted that his sample "compares favorably in size with the majority of twin studies reported in the psychological literature. In representativeness, it is superior to the majority" (p. 4).

The next problem was to determine with high certainty which of the pairs were monozygotic (MZ) and which dizygotic (DZ). Most previous researchers had failed to fully appreciate the importance of Gottesman's observation:

> If twins differ in sex or any other known inherited characteristic they cannot be MZ twins. However, if the characteristics are alike, the possibility remains that the twins are DZ. Given a number of simply inherited and widely distributed traits, it is possible to state the probability of monozygosity or dizygosity for a given pair of twins. It is to be noted, however, that all such diagnoses of monozygosity, no matter how many characteristics are identical, will always be statements of probability; that is, the probability of sharing the given number of traits in common (p. 5).

To separate monozygotic from dizygotic twins, Gottesman used the combined criteria of blood typing on nine blood groups, fingerprint ridge count, height and weight, and judgments by geneticists, psychologists, and artists. The probability of a chance likeness on all of these characteristics, given that the twins were actually dizygotic, is about 1 in 200. Thus, Gottesman's procedure resulted in a high probability that he had successfully distinguished between monozygotic and dizygotic pairs. Furthermore, the 68 pairs were found, by this assessment procedure, to consist of 34 monozygotic pairs and 34 dizygotic pairs, precisely the estimate which would be made from prior knowledge of twin frequencies.[5]

The personality measures Gottesman used in his study were derived from three paper-and-pencil tests. The first was the Minnesota Multiphasic Personality Inventory (MMPI), which consists of 550 statements about oneself which must be answered true or false. The MMPI is typically scored for 10 clinical scales, each representing a personality trait (e.g., depression, social introversion-extroversion, and so on). The second test used was Cattell's High School Personality Questionnaire (HSPQ), which was specifically developed for use with persons between the ages of 12 and 17. Its 280 forced-choice items form 14 scales (also representing personality traits), which are said to "cover all the major dimensions involved in any comprehensive view of individual differences in personality" (Gottesman, 1963, p. 7). Finally, subjects' IQ scores were available.

On 5 of the 10 MMPI scales and on the IQ measure monozygotic twins were significantly more alike than dizygotic twins. Paradoxically, though, this pattern did not hold up for the HSPQ where, in fact, the dizygotic twins were somewhat more alike. Overall, Gottesman's results seem to suggest *some* hereditary component on *some* measures of personality, and support for this view has continued to grow.

There is, for example, evidence that children differ in temperament almost from birth (Birns, 1965; Thomas, Chess, & Birch, 1970). Thomas and his associates' findings are illustrative. They followed the development of almost 150 children longitudinally for over a decade, conducting interviews with the youngsters' parents every three months during the first year, every six months until age five, and every year thereafter. The interviews were conducted in such a way that ambiguous statements (e.g., "Tommy 'can't stand' salty food") had to be translated by the parent into more specific behavioral descriptions. Home observations were also conducted by other examiners, who had no familiarity with the subjects' histories, as a check on the reliability of the findings. The data revealed both that individuals show distinct individuality in temperament during the first few weeks of life—as seen, for example, in their responses to unfamiliar objects—and that these characteristics persist over time.

---

[5] Of the total population of twins, one-third would be monozygotic and two-thirds dizygotic. However, among the latter, *half* would be opposite sexed. Thus, an equal number of monozygotic twins (who are, by definition, same sexed) and same-sexed dizygotic twins would be expected.

One disposition in particular, introversion-extroversion, appears to be specifically tied to genetic endowment.

The introversion-extroversion continuum refers to two rather opposite styles in dealing with one's social environment. At one extreme, an introvert would be shy and anxious in all novel social situations and would much prefer to withdraw from people than to approach them. The extrovert, in contrast, would be distinguished by an unusual ease among people, great friendliness, and a marked ability and willingness to introduce himself and seek out people. It has been found that friendly infants tend to become friendly teenagers, while cold infants are also somewhat unfriendly as adolescents (Schaefer & Bayley, 1963). What is more, the genetic evidence suggests that monozygotic twins are more alike than dizygotic twins on this dimension (Freedman & Keller, 1963; Scarr, 1969; Vandenberg, 1966).

Although the discussion thus far has focused upon biological and genetic type and trait positions, these are not the only approaches to the study of dispositions. The monumental trait approach of Gordon Allport, which is considered next, pays little attention to genetic and constitutional variables.

ALLPORT'S TRAIT APPROACH

As noted earlier in this chapter, Allport took a dispositional position whose fundamental assumption is that personality *exists* (heuristic realism) and that the psychologist's job is to find and describe it within the person. In 1966, Allport reexamined the position which he first put forth in 1931. He asserted that the job of finding out "what the other fellow is really like" should not be shunned despite the difficulties it involved.

> The incredible complexity of the structure we seek to understand is enough to discourage the realist, and to tempt him to play some form of positivistic gamesmanship. He is tempted to settle for such elusive formulations as: "If we knew enough about the situation we wouldn't need the concept of personality"; or, "One's personality is merely the way other people see one"; or, "There is no structure in personality but only varying degrees of consistency in the environment." Yet the truly persistent realist prefers not to abandon his commitment to find out what the other fellow is really like (Allport, 1966, p. 3).[6]

Where does the task of finding out what a person is really like begin? According to Allport (1960), personality must reside in a "psychophysical matrix" which is literally within the person.

---

[6] Here Allport is criticizing both the phenomenological and the behavioral strategies.

Human personality has a locus—within the skin. To be sure, its imagination and memory range far and wide, but these acts are well grounded in a psychophysical matrix of some order. On another plane of existence, personality may be freed from its space-time bondage, but on the plane where the psychologist dwells, it must be viewed as an organic unity accessible to study through its acts, its verbal report and even its reflex and physiological functioning (p. 20).

But looking within the skin is not enough of a guideline. We must further decide what units to employ. What are the specific structures for which we search? Allport's answer is that we are looking for *traits*. His original statement of the characteristics of traits appeared in 1931, and Allport still judged it to be defensible in 1966. His eight assertions are:

1. *Traits have more than nominal existence.* They are not just summary labels of observed behavior. Rather, traits exist within the person.
2. *Traits are more generalized than habits.* Brushing one's teeth, Allport notes, may well be a habit but is not properly called a trait (although an underlying trait—for example, cleanliness— might account for it).
3. *Traits are dynamic, or at least determinative, in behavior.* Traits direct action and are not mere structural artifacts. And unlike the intrapsychic structures posited by Freud, they do not require energizing from somewhere else.
4. *Traits may be established empirically.* Allport was steeped in the tradition of experimental psychology and acknowledged unequivocally that theorists must finally defer to their data.
5. *Traits are only relatively independent of other traits.*
6. *Traits are not synonymous with moral or social judgments.*
7. *Traits may be viewed either in the light of the personality which contains them* (i.e., idiographically), *or in the light of their distribution in the population* (i.e., nomothetically).
8. *Acts, and even habits, that are inconsistent with a trait are not proof of the nonexistence of the trait.*

The Dimensions of Traits: Pervasiveness within a Personality

Allport has proposed that an individual's traits may be classified in terms of the degree to which they pervade his personality. He distinguished among three levels of traits, although he acknowledged that "these three graduations are arbitrary and are phrased mainly for convenience of discourse" (1961, p. 365).

The most pervasive traits are referred to as *cardinal dispositions.* A cardinal disposition dominates the individual's entire existence.

It cannot remain hidden, and it often makes its possessor famous. The proper names of historical and fictitious characters which became trait adjectives in our language, such as *quixotic, machiavellian,* and *lesbian,* suggest what is meant by a cardinal disposition, as do the use of the names themselves (e.g., "He is a real Beau Brummel"). According to Allport, few persons have cardinal dispositions.

Central dispositions refer to the relatively small number of traits which tend to be highly characteristic of the individual. They might be thought of as those characteristics which one would enumerate when writing a detailed letter of recommendation. Given this sort of definition and the further suggestion that all persons can be characterized by central dispositions, a vital question becomes: How many central dispositions does the average person have? To answer this question, Allport (1961) asked 93 students " 'to think of some one individual of your own sex whom you know well' " and " 'to describe him or her by writing words, phrases, or sentences that express fairly well what seem to you to be the essential characteristics of this person' " (p. 366). Most students listed between 3 and 10 essential characteristics. The average number was 7.2.

Secondary dispositions are those characteristics of the individual which operate only in limited settings. Preferences for particular kinds of food, fairly specific attitudes, and other "peripheral" or situationally determined characteristics of the person would be placed in this category.

The Dimensions of Traits: Comparison with Other Personalities

Allport argued that traits may be viewed either as characteristics which allow us to compare one person with another (as we might compare body weights) or as unique characteristics of the individual which need not invite, or even permit, comparison with others.

Common Traits

Trait comparisons across people involve the assumption of *common traits* and have often been referred to as part of the psychology of "individual differences." Life situations continually require us to compare people. Businessmen must choose between prospective candidates for a secretarial position; colleges must identify the best applicants for higher education; and in most situations where the job or role is fixed, someone is required to identify the personality or person who "fits." While most of us make such rough and approximate comparisons between persons daily, the researcher committed to discovering common traits must formalize both his criteria for identifying a common trait and his procedures for measuring it.

This task is exemplified in a study by Allport and Allport (1928) in which the investigators were interested in finding a common trait which they labeled *ascendance-submission*. They developed a scale which asked individuals to respond to a variety of situations in which the alternatives for action could be characterized as either dominating another (ascendance) or being dominated oneself (submission). For example:

> Someone tries to push ahead of you in line. You have been waiting for some time, and can't wait much longer. Suppose the intruder is of the same sex as yourself, do you usually:
>
> Remonstrate with the intruder _____
> "Look daggers" at the intruder or make clearly audible
>   comments to your neighbor _____
> Decide not to wait, and go away _____
> Do nothing _____
>
> (Allport, 1961, p. 338)[7]

For Allport the proof of the trait's existence lies in its *reliability*. The reliability of a measure (test) refers to its consistency or repeatability and is customarily expressed as a correlation coefficient. If a test has high *test-retest reliability* (consistency between administrations), when the same test (or an equivalent form) is given to the same persons at a later time, each person should place about the same on the scale on both occasions. Here the correlation is between test administrations. If a test has high *internal reliability,* most of the items in the test tend to be measuring the same thing, and the correlation is between items or groups of items.

Trait theory requires that an individual who is ascendant in one situation should also tend to be so in other situations. Allport has reported that the test for ascendance-submission has a test-retest reliability of +.78 and an internal reliability of +.85, thereby indicating a moderately high degree of reliability for the trait in question.

Common traits, according to Allport, when scaled for the population at large, often have a *normal distribution*. That is, the scores of a large sample, when plotted on a graph, appear to produce a continuous bell-shaped curve, with the majority of cases piling up as average scores in the middle and the number of high and low scores tapering off at the more extreme positions. Allport's test for ascendance-submission appears to be distributed in this way. As seen in Figure 7–4, most people are slightly submissive, but a few are very submissive or very ascendant.

_____

[7] According to Allport, "remonstrate with the intruder" is a moderately ascendant response and is scored +2, " 'look daggers' at the intruder . . ." and "do nothing" are moderately submissive responses and are scored −2, and "decide not to wait, and go away" is an even more submissive response and is scored −3.

FIGURE 7–4

The Distribution of Scores from a Test Measuring Ascendance-Submission

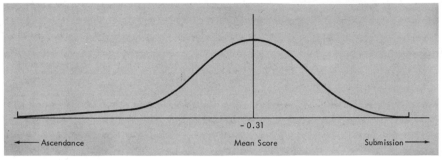

Source: Allport, 1961.

Individual Traits

Allport has used the term *individual traits* to refer to those important characteristics of the individual which do not lend themselves to comparison across persons. Although most of Allport's research has focused upon common traits (nomothetic research), he often stated that such studies can only offer approximations of what persons are really like—that is, we must ultimately study the individual *idiographically* (without comparison to others). He insisted that "the key-qualities which we seek must . . . be *personal,* not universal" adding that:

> . . . I am not repudiating the use of nomothetic factors, nor of test-scales, ratings and dimensions. More of my own research and writing has been devoted to this type of approach to personality than to any other. The resulting "common traits," I find, have utility for *comparative* purposes, for approximations to the modes of adjustment that similarly constituted individuals in similarly constituted societies can be expected to acquire. . . . What I argue is that . . . we must acknowledge the roughness and inadequacy of our universal dimensions. Thereby shall we enhance our own ability to understand, predict and control. By learning to handle the individuality of motives and the uniqueness of personality, we shall become better scientists, not worse (Allport, 1960, p. 148).

This task is accomplished, according to Allport (1966), by searching "for the natural cleavages that mark an individual life" (p. 7), a procedure illustrated in his *Letters from Jenny* (1965). This lengthy case study was based on the personal letters of Jenny Grove Masterson, which

> . . . tell the story of a mother-son relationship and trace the course of a life beset by frustration and defeat. . . . Between the ages of

fifty-eight and seventy she wrote a series of 301 letters to two young friends, a married couple living and teaching in an eastern college town. The tie of friendship extended back to the time when the husband . . . had been the roommate of Jenny's son . . . at college, about ten years before the beginning of the correspondence. . . . The correspondence begins in earnest in March, 1926, and continues without interruption for eleven and a half years, until Jenny's death in October, 1937 (Allport, 1965, p. v) .

The letters were evaluated by 36 judges, who read them in sequence and assigned a total of 198 descriptive adjectives to Jenny based on their overall impression of her personality. Many of the adjectives were synonymous, though, and when they were combined, eight central traits emerged.

It was also possible to compare the impressionistic description with one derived from a more systematic method of analysis. The procedure involved a determination of the frequency with which various key words in the letters were used in conjunction with one another. The resulting data were combined statistically by the method of factor analysis (to be discussed later in this chapter) , yielding seven traits. When the traits derived from the two divergent methods (one impressionistic and the other statistical) were compared, there were differences in terminology, but a marked similarity of description was nevertheless apparent, as can be seen in Table 7–6.

Allport (1966) interprets the similarity of the two analyses as evi-

TABLE 7–6

Evaluation of Jenny's Personality from Her Letters Based on Impressionistic and Factor-Analytic Assessment

Impressionistic Traits	Factorial Traits
Quarrelsome-suspicious Aggressive	Aggression
Self-centered (possessive)	Possessiveness
Sentimental	Need for affiliation Need for family acceptance
Independent-autonomous	Need for autonomy
Esthetic-artistic	Sentience
Self-centered (self-pitying)	Martyrdom
(No parallel)	Sexuality
Dramatic-intense	("Overstate")

Source: Adapted from Allport, 1966.

dence for the validity of the conclusions about Jenny's personality and at the same time construes the disparities found as confirming the utility of the idiographic approach:

> . . . the judges, it seems, gain much from the running style of the letters. Since the style is constant it would not appear in a factorial analysis. . . . The common-sense traits *cynical-morbid* and *dramatic-intense* are judgements of a pervading expressive style in Jenny's personality and seem to be missed by factoring procedure (p. 8).

But is not the assignment of a list of traits to Jenny a mere variation on the nomothetic or comparative approach? Allport argues that it is not. The idiographic approach is not necessarily characterized by an absence of either labels or statistics. It is characterized by the positive quality of letting the behavior of the person under study, rather than an existing battery of tests, measuring instruments, or common traits, dictate the description which will emerge.

Integration of Personality: The Proprium

Allport's fifth characteristic of traits asserts that they are only relatively independent of one another. Since traits interact, it is reasonable to posit the existence of some sort of executive function not unlike Freud's use of the term "ego" or Rogers' concept of "self" (see Chapter 11). These labels have, according to Allport (1961), referred to at least seven different aspects of "selfhood." They are listed in the order of their probable occurrence in the growing child.

1. A sense of the bodily self, as when the child begins to distinguish between his fingers and the objects which they hold.
2. A sense of continuing self-identity, developed as the child begins to understand that *he* is the continuing referent for his own name.
3. A sense of pride or self-esteem, reflected in the young child's delighted "I beat you" (e.g., when he wins a competitive game).
4. A recognition of extensions of self in one's possessions (e.g., "This is *my* bike").
5. A self-image (e.g., "I am naughty").
6. A sense of self as a problem solver, with a rational capacity which can be imposed upon problems.
7. Finally, the individual develops some defining objective (s) which becomes "the cement holding a life together . . . its 'directedness' or 'intentionality.' "

Rather than use terms such as "ego" and "self," which have already been given distinct meanings by other psychologists, Allport suggests the term *proprium* to unite these seven aspects of selfhood. He argues that proprium is an important concept for several reasons. First, the subjective, or felt, side of ourselves is something we all know about; hence it would be foolish for psychologists to ignore it (as some have) merely because it is a difficult notion to study. Second, there is some evidence that a man's performance in a variety of tasks can be significantly influenced by his degree of self-involvement. Third, acknowledging the existence of a proprium opens up lines of research, such as the determination of which *propriate feelings* (feelings of self) are most pervasive, gnawing, or uncomfortable.

TABLE 7–7

Inferiority in College Students

Type of Inferiority Feeling	Percentage Reporting Persistent Inferiority Feelings	
	Men (243)	Women (120)
Physical.............................	39	50
Social...............................	52	57
Intellectual..........................	29	61
Moral...............................	16	15
None at all..........................	12	10

Source: Allport, 1961.

In one study (McKee & Sherriffs, 1957), for example, college students were asked to state the type of inferiority feelings they had (if any) and whether they felt persistent feelings of inferiority about themselves. The results of the study, which appear in Table 7–7, suggest an interesting hierarchy of importance. Also, it appears that in 1957 men had fewer feelings of inferiority than women. Allport (1961) suggested that this latter finding occurs because we are still living in a "man's world" in which the emancipation of women is not yet complete. The situation may well have changed with the advent of women's liberation.

The Transformation of Motives: Functional Autonomy

Allport acknowledges that the personality must be dynamic and that individuals must somehow be impelled to action. However, unlike Freud, Allport holds that motivation is to be found within the structures of personality (traits) rather than as an independent force. Further, motivation for Allport is centered in the present. To these ends, Allport formulated a general law of motivation called the principle of *functional autonomy* which he defined as *"any acquired system of motivation in which the tensions involved are not of the same kind as the antecedent tensions from which the acquired system developed"* (1961, p. 229). The nature of functional autonomy is illustrated in the following example:

> Joe, let us say, is the son of a famous politician. As a young lad he imitates everything his father does, even perhaps giving "speeches." Years pass and the father dies. Joe is now middle-aged and is deeply absorbed in politics. He runs for office, perhaps the selfsame job his father held. What, then, motivates Joe today? Is it his earlier fixation? . . . The chances . . . are that his interest in politics has outgrown its roots in "father identification." There is historical continuity but no longer any functional continuity. Politics is now his dominant passion; it is his style of life; it is a large part of Joe's personality. The original seed has been discarded (Allport, 1961, pp. 228–29).

Allport has distinguished between two levels or forms of functional autonomy, *perseverative* and *propriate*. Perseverative motives refer to biologically derived rhythms, patterns of physical movement, and habits which once were adaptive but no longer serve a useful purpose. Consider two of the lines of evidence which Allport (1961) introduces to support the existence of these motives. First, humans are often observed perseverating on tasks of no extrinsic meaning, as when one tries unsuccessfully to remember the name of a third-grade teacher and is then consumed with the task until the name can be retrieved from memory. Second, our adherence to familiar and routine patterns of behavior, as reflected, for example, in our desire to dine at a set hour each day and in feelings of homesickness, suggests the presence of perseverative functional autonomy. Though perseverative motives are present in all persons as well as in infrahuman species, they are not essential to the fundamental organization of the personality.

In contrast to the "lower-level" perseverative motives, *propriate strivings* or motives refer to acquired interests, values, and attitudes. As their name implies, propriate strivings are intimately tied to the organization of the personality (i.e., to the proprium) and in large measure account for the individual's overall style of life. Propriate strivings play a major role in determining one's behavior. In the earlier example dealing with the son of a famous politician who became a politician himself, the son was motivated by propriate, rather than perseverative, functional autonomy. Allport makes three basic observations which support his concept of propriate motivation.

First, Allport (1961) observes that there are many occasions in which ability turns to interest.

Now the original reason for learning a skill may not be interest at all. For example, a student who first undertakes a field of study in college because it is required, because it pleases his parents, or because it comes at a convenient hour may find himself absorbed in the topic, perhaps for life. The original motives may be entirely lost. What was a means to an end becomes an end itself (pp. 235–36).

Second, Allport notes that acquired interests and values often have selective power. One study has shown, for example, that people with an esthetic interest will read more articles pertaining to art than will less esthetic people (Engstrom & Power, 1959).

Third, Allport (1961) asserts that a person's self-image becomes a major organizing factor in his life.

I am speaking here of the highest levels of organization in personality. Most theories of personality (especially those postulating "unchanging energies") overlook the motivational power of higher-level formations. . . . The more important instance of functional autonomy is found in the complex propriate organization that determines the "total posture" of a mature life system.

A prominent ingredient of this master dynamism is the sense of responsibility one takes for one's life. The way one defines one's role and duties in life determines much of one's daily conduct (p. 237).

What evidence of the presence of such organizing principles exists? Some interesting work on religious orientation by Allport and his colleagues is relevant.

Studies of church attenders have found them to show more ethnic prejudice, on the average, than nonattenders. This finding is obviously contradictory to Christian teachings. Perhaps the controlling factor, Allport argued, is an orientation other than church attendance per se. It was "tentatively assumed that two contrasting but measurable forms of religious orientation exist" (Allport, 1966, pp. 5–6). An *extrinsic* orientation represents "an instrumental value serving the motives of comfort, security, or social status" (p. 6) rather than true devotion. In contrast, an *intrinsic* orientation holds that faith is "a supreme value in its own right" (p. 6).

A scale was devised to assess a person's predominant orientation toward religion. Two of the items from the scale are:

What religion offers me most is comfort when sorrow and misfortune strike.

My religious beliefs are what really lie behind my whole approach to life.

Agreement with the first statement is indicative of an extrinsic orientation, while agreement with the second is indicative of an intrinsic orientation.

The utility of Allport's distinction between intrinsic and extrinsic orientation was determined by correlating religious orientation with various scales of ethnic prejudice. As can be seen in Table 7–8, in each case an extrinsic orientation is positively related to prejudice (extrinsic orientation tends to be associated with prejudice), while an intrinsic orientation is negatively related to prejudice (intrinsic orientation tends to be associated with an absence of prejudice).

TABLE 7–8

The Relationship between Religious Orientation among Church Attenders and Various Forms of Ethnic Prejudice

Denominational Sample	Religious Orientation	Type of Prejudice	Correlation
Unitarian (*N* = 50)*	Extrinsic	Anti-Catholic	+.56
	Intrinsic	Anti-Catholic	−.36
	Extrinsic	Anti-Mexican	+.54
	Intrinsic	Anti-Mexican	−.42
Catholic (*N* = 66)	Extrinsic	Anti-Negro	+.36
	Intrinsic	Anti-Negro	−.49
Nazarene (*N* = 39)	Extrinsic	Anti-Negro	+.41
	Intrinsic	Anti-Negro	−.44
Mixed† (*N* = 207)	Extrinsic	Anti-Semitic	+.65

* Indicates number of subjects in sample.
† From Wilson (1960).
Source: Allport, 1966.

This research, like most of Allport's work, is interesting because of the nature of the topic which it addresses. The method, however, is not a direct outgrowth of Allport's trait approach. One research method, factor analysis, has grown directly out of the general assumptions of the dispositional strategy and was designed to permit identification of personality dimensions directly through research.

FACTOR ANALYSIS AND MULTIVARIATE RESEARCH

The Logic of Factor Analysis

Raymond B. Cattell, a prominent dispositional psychologist, has quipped that "the trouble with measuring traits is that there are too many of them!" (1965, p. 55). Cattell (1965) was referring to the procedure, central to most trait research, "to fancy some particular trait . . . and to concentrate on its relations to all kinds of things"

(p. 55). This procedure, Cattell argues, has many disadvantages, the most salient being that trait researchers cannot compare or integrate their findings with one another, nor agree on what is a referent for such commonly researched traits as "anxiety." If a common method were employed, which allowed for interrelating the various findings of trait research and the simultaneous examination of many traits, this problem would be solved. A statistical technique with these properties is available and has come to be called *factor analysis.* In this section, we shall examine the basic assumptions and principles of factor analysis and consider some research which has been based on this technique.

Cattell and most other researchers who have used factor-analytic techniques believe that there are natural, unitary structures in personality which underlie the various trait names and behaviors which have traditionally been examined. Freud, it will be recalled, assumed the existence of three structures in all persons, while Allport assumed that each individual had a unique (trait) structure. Cattell (1965), in contrast to both, believes that there is a common structure across personalities which must be determined *empirically,* in the same way that the elements of the physical universe were discovered.

> The problem which baffled psychologists for many years was to find a method which would tease out these functionally unitary influences in the chaotic jungle of human behavior. But let us ask how, in the literal tropical jungle, the hunter decides whether the dark blobs which he sees are two or three rotting logs or a single alligator? He watches for movement. *If they move together*—come and disappear together—*he infers a single structure.* Just so, as John Stuart Mill pointed out in his philosophy of science, the scientist should look for "concomitant variation" in seeking unitary concepts (p. 56, italics added).

In the "jungle" of human behavior, however, perfect covariation is rarely to be found. Psychological variables do not seem to *always* go together. We may get a fleeting glimpse of some strong covariations but never the perfect data generated by Cattell's alligator. The correlational method allows for the evaluation of degrees of relationship which are not perfect, and it is the statistical correlation coefficient which is at the heart of factor-analytic procedures. However, factor analysis deals not with one or two correlations, but with the entire *array of intercorrelations* among many variables. Although factor analysis was first developed in 1904 by Charles Spearman, a British psychologist and statistician, its recent popularity is a result of the availability of high-speed computers, without which much of the current work using the technique would be virtually impossible.

Consider the hypothetical *correlation matrix* which appears in Table 7–9. It contains the correlations of each of seven measures with every other measure. What this matrix tells us is that there is a high positive relationship between a and b (+.70), a and c (+.80), a and d (+.80), b and c (+.90), b and d (+.70), c and d (+.80), e and f (+.80), e and g (+.70), and f and g (+.70), and virtually no systematic relationship (i.e., correlation coefficients in the vicinity of 0) between a and e (−.10), a and f (.00), a and g (.00), b and e (+.10), b and f (+.10), b and g (.00), c and e (−.10), c and f (−.10), c and g (−.10), d and e (.00), d and f (−.10), and d and g (.00).

TABLE 7–9

Hypothetical Correlation Matrix

Measure	a	b	c	d	e	f	g
a	+1.00	+.70	+.80	+.80	−.10	.00	.00
b		+1.00	+.90	+.70	+.10	+.10	.00
c			+1.00	+.80	−.10	−.10	−.10
d				+1.00	.00	−.10	.00
e					+1.00	+.80	+.70
f						+1.00	+.70
g							+1.00

Despite the rather clear-cut nature of the hypothetical correlation matrix and the relatively small number of variables included (it is not uncommon for 100 or more variables to be correlated with one another in factor-analytic studies), the complexities and sheer time needed to summarize and interpret the data contained in the matrix should be apparent from the enumeration of results just presented. One of the major functions of factor analysis is to reduce large sets of data, most often in the form of correlation matrices, to manageable units. By means of complex mathematical formulas, the data are reduced to the smallest number of relatively homogeneous dimensions, called *factors,* which account for the relationships (correlations) among the variables. The following discussion of the hypothetical correlation matrix in Table 7–9 should give the reader a feeling for the basic strategy which underlies factor analysis.

Inspection of the matrix reveals that among the seven measures (*a* through *g*) there is a distinct pattern to be found. Specifically, *a, b, c,* and *d* seem to "go together." They are highly correlated with one another but show little or no relationship (i.e., near 0) to the other three measures. Similarly, *e, f,* and *g* are highly related to one another but not to the other measures. Thus, two units or *factors* emerge from the seven measures. These might be labeled sterilely (e.g., factor *X* and factor *Y*), or we could inspect the several related measures for their common qualities and provide a more meaningful name than *X* or *Y* for the two factors. However, the naming itself would be a *subjective judgment* and not a logical consequence of the statistical procedures involved.

To make our example more concrete, suppose the measures were aptitude tests for academic fields, where *a* = English, *b* = fine arts, *c* = history, *d* = French, *e* = mathematics, *f* = physics, and *g* = engineering. Factor *X* would then consist of English, fine arts, history, and French, and factor *Y* would consist of mathematics, physics, and engineering. In this case, the naming of the factors would be easy, though in practice naming factors is rarely so clear-cut.

A number of personality psychologists have turned to factor analysis as a strategy for directing their research. We shall discuss two of the more prominent of these dispositionalists, Cattell and H. J. Eysenck.

Gattell's Trait Approach

Cattell (1965) proposes that there should be three broad sources of data about personality, which he labels *L*-data, *Q*-data, and *T*-data. *L-data* refer to that information which can be gathered from the life record of the individual and are usually taken from ratings by observers as to the frequency and intensity of occurrence of specific kinds of behavior.

Q-data consist of information gathered from questionnaires and interviews. The common feature of *Q*-data is that the individual answers direct questions about himself, based on his own observations and introspection (e.g., "Do you have trouble making and keeping friends?").

Data gathered from so-called objective tests are referred to as *T-data.* Teachers and educators might well be tempted to call questionnaire and essay data (i.e., *Q*-data) "objective" whenever these are scored in some standardized way so as to lead two or more examiners to exactly the same conclusions. However, Cattell argues that these procedures are often not objective in another sense, since the individual may "give himself airs" or otherwise attempt to fabricate or distort his responses. Cattell (1965) defines an objective test as one in which "the subject is placed in a miniature situation and simply acts . . . [and] *does not know on what aspect of his be-*

havior he is really being evaluated" (p. 104). Cattell and Warburton (1967) have published a compendium of more than 600 tests that meet these criteria of objectivity.

Cattell argues that the three sources of data can and must be integrated to capture the full complexity of human personality. Traditionally, psychologists have looked at only one slice at a time and their experiments, Cattell asserts, have been *univariate*—that is, experiments which vary one (independent) variable and examine its effects on one other (dependent) variable. In contrast, the *multivariate* approach has the advantage that "with sufficient analytical subtlety we can tease out the connexions from the behaviour of the man in his actual life situation—without the false situation of controlling and manipulating" (1965, p. 20). (Cattell calls such research "multivariate experiments," but by the more usual definition [see Chapter 2] they are not really *experiments* at all, for the very reason that they eschew manipulation and control. They are correlational studies.)

Cattell asserts that

> . . . the development of beautiful and complex mathematico-statistical methods like factor analysis has enabled us to take natural data, much as the clinician has long done—except that normals are now included—and to find laws and build sound theories about the structure and functioning of personality (1965, p. 23).

What evidence exists for this assertion?

Three Traits of Personality Derived from L- and Q-Data

In one of Cattell's studies, several hundred young men and women were rated by people who knew them well on 50 different *trait elements,* the elements from which the traits are factor-analytically derived. A sample of eight of these trait elements appears in Table 7–10.

When a set of correlations among the ratings on the 50 trait elements is subjected to a factor analysis, Cattell finds that a number of factors, perhaps as many as 20, emerge.[8] Although 20 factors summarize the personality ratings better than 50 trait elements, 20 bits of information are still not exactly an easily comprehensible summary. Therefore, the next step is to determine the relative importance of each of the 20 factors. For this purpose, they are placed in

---

[8] The number of factors which adequately summarize a given set of data depends upon the nature of the data and the specific mathematical procedures (type of factor analysis) employed. Thus, with a particular set of data, the total number of factors extracted could vary with different factor-analytic procedures.

TABLE 7–10

Eight (of 50) Trait Elements on Which Young Men and Women Were Rated

1. *Adaptable:* flexible; accepts changes of plan easily; satisfied with compromises; is not upset, surprised, baffled, or irritated if things are different from what he expected.

   vs. *Rigid:* insists that things be done the way he has always done them; does not adapt his habits and ways of thinking to those of the group; nonplussed if his routine is upset.

2. *Emotional:* excitable; cries a lot (children), laughs a lot, shows affection, anger, all emotions, to excess.

   vs. *Calm:* stable, shows few signs of emotional excitement of any kind; remains calm, even underreacts, in dispute, danger, social hilarity, etc.

3. *Conscientious:* honest; knows what is right and generally does it, even if no one is watching him; does not tell lies or attempt to deceive others; respects others' property.

   vs. *Unconscientious:* somewhat unscrupulous; not too careful about standards of right and wrong where personal desires are concerned; tells lies and is given to little deceits; does not respect others' property.

4. *Conventional:* conforms to accepted standards, ways of acting, thinking, dressing, etc.; does the "proper" thing; seems distressed if he finds he is being different.

   vs. *Unconventional, eccentric:* acts differently from others: not concerned about wearing the same clothes or doing the same things as others; has somewhat eccentric interests, attitudes, and ways of behaving; goes his own rather peculiar way.

5. *Prone to jealousy:* begrudges the achievement of others; upset when others get attention; and demands more for himself; resentful when attention is given to others.

   vs. *Not jealous:* likes people even if they do better than he does; is not upset when others get attention, but joins in praise.

6. *Considerate, polite:* deferential to needs of others; considers others' feelings; allows them before him in line, gives them the biggest share, etc.

   vs. *Inconsiderate, rude:* insolent, defiant, and "saucy" to elders (in children); ignores feelings of others; gives impression that he goes out of his way to be rude.

7. *Quitting:* gives up before he has thoroughly finished a job; slipshod; works in fits and starts; easily distracted, led away from main purposes by stray impulses or external difficulties.

   vs. *Determined, persevering;* sees a job through in spite of difficulties or temptations; strong-willed; painstaking and thorough; sticks at anything until he achieves his goal.

8. *Tender:* governed by sentiment; intuitive, empathetic, sympathetic; sensitive to the feelings of others; cannot do things if they offend his feelings.

   vs. *Tough, hard:* governed by fact and necessity rather than sentiment; unsympathetic; does not mind upsetting others if that is what has to be done.

Source: Cattell, 1965.

hierarchical order in terms of the degree to which each factor "explains" or "accounts for" all of the trait elements as a group. At the top of the hierarchy would be the factor which represents the greatest single summary of all the data. This factor is assigned the letter *A;* the letter *B* is assigned to the factor which accounts for the next greatest amount of variance of all the trait elements, and so on. Cattell (1965) suggests that this last procedure permits one to look at the obtained patterns of results "without prejudice from earlier clinical notions or traditional popular terms" and notes as an aside that "the investigators of vitamins did just the same, in a parallel situation, where the entities could be identified in terms of their *effects* before truly interpretative chemical labels could be attached to them" (p. 65).

Let us consider the three most important factors (i.e., *A, B,* and *C*) which Cattell has consistently found. As part of the factor analysis, the ratings on each of the 50 trait elements on which the subjects were rated were correlated with each of the factors which had been found. The resulting correlations are technically called *factor loadings.* The elements which *loaded* (correlated) most highly (both in a positive and in a negative direction) with factor *A* are listed in Table 7–11.

TABLE 7–11

Elements (Ratings) Which Load on Source Trait *A:*
Affectothymia vs. Sizothymia

A+ (*Positively Loaded*)		*A—* (*Negatively Loaded*)
Good-natured, easygoing	vs.	Critical, grasping
Cooperative	vs.	Obstructive
Attentive to people	vs.	Cool, aloof
Softhearted	vs.	Hard, precise
Trustful	vs.	Suspicious
Adaptable	vs.	Rigid

Source: Cattell, 1965.

Cattell then inspected information of the type found in Table 7–11 in search of a meaningful name for the factor. He observed that the general characteristics of *A* were similar to the grosser characteristics that Emil Kraepelin[9] had used to distinguish between schizophrenia and the so-called cyclic psychoses. The latter group included manic-depressive psychosis, which we have seen to contrast with schizophrenia in Kretschmer's work. This observation suggested that terms reflecting the parallel might be used—namely, cyclothymia

---

[9] Kraepelin was a German psychiatrist who is largely credited with the traditional (and currently used) scheme of psychiatric classification.

and schizothymia. However, the trait name finally selected was "affectothymia vs. sizothymia." (The more popular label would be "outgoing vs. reserved.")

> . . . since the tests . . . are likely to be recorded for schoolchildren and discussed with parents, it has seemed best to avoid misunderstandings by using finally the new title for it now adopted, namely *sizothymia,* instead of schizothymia, for *sizo,* deriving from the same root as "size" in painting, means "flat" and refers to what psychiatrists call the "flatness of affect," i.e., the absence of lively and vibrant emotion. . . . It is this coldness and aloofness which, more than anything else, characterizes the *normal A* (minus), i.e., the sizothyme. . . . It will also recommend itself to the psychologist to refer to the cyclothyme, when normal, as an affectothyme, because the primary characteristic is affect or emotion, not merely the cyclical ups and down of elation and depression which occur in the abnormal, cyclically insane person (Cattell, 1965, pp. 66–67).

Cattell calls factor *A* (as well as factors *B* and *C*) a *source trait,* indicating that it is an underlying variable which is a source or determinant of overt behavior. He views source traits as the building blocks of personality and maintains that they can be discovered only by factor analysis.

Surface traits are the products of the interaction of source traits. They are clusters of overt behavior which seem to go together, even to the casual observer. However, the behaviors which make up a surface trait do not always vary together and may not have a common cause. For example, success in politics and success in business ventures are sometimes observed to occur in the same people, and their relationship would constitute a surface trait. This surface trait, though, might be caused by a combination of independent source traits, such as affectothymia and shrewdness.

Relative to surface traits, there are only a small number of source traits, and source traits tend to be more stable. Surface traits are primarily descriptive, whereas source traits are explanatory and causal. The distinction between surface and source traits is parallel to Freud's distinction between manifest and latent dream content and Murray's distinction between manifest and latent needs (see Chapter 9).

Let us return to our discussion of factor *A,* affectothymia-sizothymia. If it is a source trait, we would expect that the same pattern of results that emerged from the *L*-data (i.e., the ratings on the 50 trait elements) would appear in *Q*-data. That is, if a trait is really an underlying dimension of personality, it should be reflected in all measures of personality. Sample questionnaire responses which load highly on factor *A* are given in Table 7–12. Considering the *Q*-data, which are summarized in Table 7–12, and referring back to the

TABLE 7–12

Factor *A* in Questionnaire Responses

1.	I would rather work as:		
	(a) An engineer	(b)	*A social science teacher*
2.	I could stand being a hermit		
	(a) True	(b)	*False*
3.	I am careful to turn up when someone expects me		
	(a) *True*	(b)	False
4.	I would prefer to marry someone who is:		
	(a) A thoughtful companion	(b)	*Effective in a social group*
5.	I would prefer to read a book on:		
	(a) *National social service*	(b)	New scientific weapons
6.	I trust strangers:		
	(a) Sometimes	(b)	*Practically always*

Note: A person who selects all the italicized answers has a highly affectothyme temperament, whereas selection of all the nonitalicized responses indicates sizo-thymia. Most people, presumably, would fall between these extremes.
Source: Cattell, 1965.

L-data, Cattell (1965) concludes: "The warm sociability at one pole, and the aloofness and unconcern with people at the other are as evident here as in the observers' ratings" (p. 71).

With respect to the ratings on the 50 trait elements (i.e., *L*-data), Cattell (1965) concludes that the second largest source trait, factor *B*, ". . . looks like nothing less than general intelligence, and correlates well with actual test results" (p. 72).

Concerning the third largest source trait, factor *C*, he notes that

> The essence of *C* factor appears to be an inability to control one's emotions and impulses, especially by finding for them some satisfactory realistic expression. Looked at from the opposite or positive pole, it sharpens and gives scientific substance to the psychoanalytic concept of "ego strength," which it [factor *C*] has come to be called (1965, pp. 73–74).

To illustrate the nature of the source trait "ego-strength" exemplary *L*- and *Q*-data are presented in Table 7–13.

Cattell's dispositional approach to personality is empirical and relatively atheoretical. His contribution has been to "discover," by means of factor analysis, the traits which comprise personality. Cattell's research begins without preconceived theoretical notions as to the nature of the traits which will emerge from the factor-analytic procedures. For example, whereas Cattell's factor *C* turned out to be very similar to the psychoanalytic concept of ego-strength, factor *B*, general intelligence, is clearly not aligned with any particular theo-

TABLE 7–13

L- and *Q*-Data for Source Trait *C*

Behavior Ratings Which Load on C		
C+ (Positively loaded)		C− (Negatively loaded)
Mature	vs.	Unable to tolerate frustration
Steady, persistent	vs.	Changeable
Emotionally calm	vs.	Impulsively emotional
Realistic about problems	vs.	Evasive, avoids necessary decisions
Absence of neurotic fatigue	vs.	Neurotically fatigued (with no real effort)

Factor C Questionnaire Responses

Do you find it difficult to take no for an answer even when what you want to do is obviously impossible?

  (*a*) yes   (*b*) *no*

If you had your life to live over again, would you

  (*a*) *want it to be essentially the same?*   (*b*) plan it very differently?

Do you often have really disturbing dreams?

  (*a*) yes   (*b*) *no*

Do your moods sometimes make you seem unreasonable even to yourself?

  (*a*) yes   (*b*) *no*

Do you feel tired when you've done nothing to justify it?

  (*a*) *rarely*   (*b*) often

Can you change old habits, without relapse, when you decide to?

  (*a*) *yes*   (*b*) no

Note: A person who selects all the italicized answers has high ego-strength, whereas selection of all the nonitalicized responses indicates low ego-strength.
Source: Adapted from Cattell, 1965.

retical position. In the next section, the approach taken by H. J. Eysenck, another prominent dispositional psychologist, will be considered. Like Cattell, Eysenck attempts to discover the basic components of personality in an empirical and atheoretical fashion and relies heavily on factor analysis to accomplish this goal.

Eysenck's Type Approach

Perhaps the most fundamental difference between the dispositional approaches espoused by Cattell and Eysenck lies in the level at which each has chosen to look for the basic dimensions of personality. Cattell's research has revealed a relatively lengthy list of source traits. In contrast, Eysenck's investigations have focused on discovering a small number of basic personality *types*. Types are more global than traits, which Eysenck views as the components that make up types. In turn, traits are based on habitual forms of responding in various situations. And finally, at the most particular level, are a person's specific responses. Eysenck's (1967) overall structure of personality is diagramed in Figure 7–5.

Eysenck's first major search for types was conducted during World

FIGURE 7–5

Eysenck's Hierarchical Model of Personality

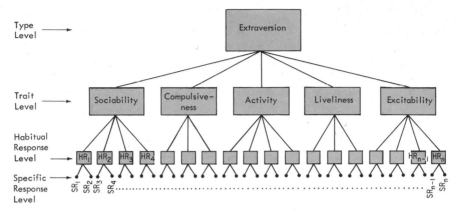

Source: Adapted from Eysenck, 1967.

War II. Applying factor-analytic procedures to a multitude of ratings and classifications of a total of approximately 10,000 subjects, Eysenck identified two major dimensions (factors) of personality: *introversion-extraversion*[10] and *neuroticism*. (Later work suggested the addition of a third dimension, *psychoticism*.)

Factor naming, as we have previously noted, is a subjective procedure divorced from the statistical operations themselves, a point which is well illustrated in the case of Eysenck's introversion-extraversion factor. The major evidence for this dimension came from a study of neurotic soldiers, among whom two groups of symptoms were found which formed the poles of the introversion-extraversion dimension. The "introverts" tended to exhibit anxiety, depression, obsessional tendencies, apathy, irritability, and autonomic dysfunctions, while the "extraverts" were likely to show hypochondriasis (imaginary illnesses), sex anomalies, poor work histories, and low intelligence. The labeling is contrary to many prevalent definitions of introversion and extroversion. For example, Eysenck's label is not intended to connote a dimension of "sociability," though social forwardness is the very dimension which leads the layman to describe someone as an extrovert. In fact, Eysenck suggests that an extravert, according to his system, could be "emotional, shy and reserved."

Neuroticism in Eysenck's system refers to the polar opposite of stability. Eysenck has used numerous sources of data to discriminate neurotics from normals, including psychiatric diagnoses, paper-and-

---

[10] Note that Eysenck's term is *extra*version and not *extro*version.

pencil tests, behavioral tests of such things as suggestibility and manual dexterity, and constitutional differences. Not surprisingly, ratings show neurotics to be distinguishable from normals on such traits as emotional instability, dependence, apprehensiveness, and so on.

The Maudsley Medical Questionnaire[11] is one of the instruments which Eysenck has often used in his personality research. Ten of its 40 items are presented in Table 7–14; neurotics show a higher percentage of endorsement (i.e., responding yes) on these items than normals.

TABLE 7–14

Examples of Items on the Maudsley Medical Questionnaire
(neurotics answer yes to more items than normals)

Do you find it difficult to get into conversation with strangers?	Yes	No
Do you worry too long over humiliating experiences?	Yes	No
Are your feelings easily hurt?	Yes	No
Do ideas run through your head so that you cannot sleep?	Yes	No
Do you sometimes feel happy, sometimes depressed, without any apparent reason?	Yes	No
Do you daydream a lot?	Yes	No
Do you sweat a great deal without exercise?	Yes	No
Do you often feel disgruntled?	Yes	No
Do you often feel self-conscious in the presence of superiors?	Yes	No
Are you troubled with feelings of inferiority?	Yes	No

Source: Eysenck, 1952b.

Self-reported preferences make up a second paper-and-pencil measure used to distinguish between neurotics and normals. It is illustrated by an interesting study which compared the food aversions of the two groups (Gough, 1946). The findings of this study, which appear in Table 7–15 (page 170), clearly reveal that neurotics have considerably more distaste for food than normals, and incidentally provide information about the relative preferences of both groups.

A third measure used by Eysenck, Hull's body sway test of motor suggestibility, also clearly distinguishes between neurotics and normals, not only as dichotomous classes, but also on a continuum from normal to severely neurotic. The subject is merely asked to stand with his eyes closed, his hands at his sides, and his feet together. He listens to the following (recorded) instructions: "You are falling, you are falling forward, you are falling forward all the time. You are falling, you are falling, you are falling now . . ." (Eysenck, 1952b, p. 106). A thread attached to the subject's clothing runs to

[11] Eysenck is director of psychology at the Maudsley Hospital, London, England.

TABLE 7–15

Aversion of Neurotics and Normals for 20 Foods

Food	Percentage of Neurotics Disliking	Percentage of Normals Disliking
Tea	29.1	9.0
Grapefruit juice	38.0	4.3
Bean soup	34.2	5.5
Potato soup	45.6	5.1
Salmon	31.6	8.7
Beefsteak	1.3	0.0
Veal chops	20.3	2.4
Chicken	8.9	1.2
Fried eggs	16.4	1.2
Cottage cheese	51.9	14.6
Swiss cheese	36.7	8.7
Lima beans (broad beans)	24.0	6.7
Cabbage	35.4	12.2
Corn	12.7	1.6
Mushrooms	53.2	25.2
Radishes	26.6	9.8
Tomatoes	11.4	2.4
Cantaloupe	13.9	3.5
Cherries	13.9	0.0
Pears	8.9	0.8

Source: Adapted from Eysenck, 1952b.

a mechanical pointer which indicates on a scale the amount of body sway forward and backward. The data, presented graphically in Figure 7–6 (page 171), clearly indicate that for males and females motor suggestibility increases with increasing neuroticism.

The foregoing investigations of Eysenck and his associates illustrate the strategy he has employed with respect to basic research. Eysenck has argued that his approach may also be fruitfully employed in dealing with practical social problems. We shall take up an example of the application of his type approach to a real-life problem, the employability of "mental defectives."

In considering 104 males who were institutionalized in Britain because they had been "certified" as mental defectives, Eysenck (1952b) observed that

. . . the average level of ability of this group is represented by an I.Q. level of about 75. Thus the average score of this group is well above what one would normally have expected to be the maximum score [for persons called defective]. Indeed, scores as high as I.Q. 120 and above were recorded by isolated individuals . . . (p. 246).

While there are many possible interpretations of these surprising findings, Eysenck (1952b) suggests that they may be explained in terms of his neuroticism dimension.

FIGURE 7–6

Average Suggestibility of Normals and Neurotics Showing Increase in Suggestibility As "Neuroticism" Increases

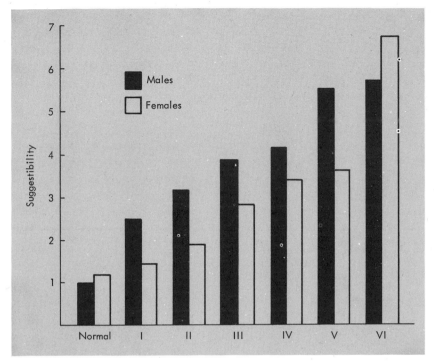

Source: After Eysenck, 1952b.

. . . we must consider the possibility that certification is carried out on the basis, not merely of intellectual defect, but of a combination of mental defect and neuroticism. The child that is merely dull, with an I.Q. of 60 or 65, may easily escape certification; the child that is less dull, but is also suffering from emotional instability, is far more likely to be found an unbearable nuisance by Society, and to be certified a mental defective. . . . High emotional stability could then counterbalance a low I.Q., while low stability would offset even a moderately high I.Q. (p. 247).

On the basis of this reasoning, Eysenck suggested three hypotheses regarding the employability of persons certified as defective: (1) these persons would be variable with respect to neuroticism, (2) neuroticism would be more important than intelligence in successful adjustment to work; and (3) neuroticism can be measured in defectives by the same tests used with normals. These hypotheses were all strongly supported by Eysenck's research. For example, in a study with the sample of 104 men certified as mentally defective, Eysenck

(1952b) employed his usual tests of neuroticism and used a social worker's ratings of work success as the criterion of adjustment to work. The results revealed that "only about one-fourth as much predictive power is given by intelligence tests as by neuroticism tests" (1952b, p. 251). He concludes that "Both society and the defectives themselves would benefit from the introduction of routine tests along the lines suggested . . ." (1952b, p. 251).

8

The
Dispositional
Strategy
SELF-REPORT
PERSONALITY
INVENTORIES

As we saw in the last chapter, many psychologists who study the structure of personality from a trait or type approach have relied heavily on *self-report inventories* for their data. (It should be noted that self-report inventories are also employed in other personality strategies, as will be seen in subsequent chapters.) Self-report inventories are usually composed of a large number of statements or questions which the subject is asked to respond to in terms of a limited number of fixed alternatives, such as "yes-no," "true-false," and "agree-disagree" (occasionally there is a "cannot say" alternative). Typical items are of the following sort:

> I often get mad when things don't turn out as planned.
> I enjoy music and dancing.
> Are you afraid of high places?
> Do you have trouble falling asleep at night?

The items are usually printed in a booklet with separate answer sheets so that the tests can easily be administered to many subjects at once. The use of such procedures is extremely widespread; perhaps as much as two-thirds of the American population will take some sort of self-report personality inventory in their lifetime (cf. Fiske, 1967, 1971).

THE MMPI

The Minnesota Multiphasic Personality Inventory (MMPI), which we have already had occasion to mention, is the most widely used self-report inventory (Edwards & Abbott, 1973), so we shall make it the primary basis for our discussion. The MMPI was developed by S. R. Hathaway, a clinical psychologist, and J. C. McKinley, a neuropsychiatrist, in 1942 in response to a need for a practical and valid test which could classify patients into the existing diagnostic categories of abnormal behavior. Before we examine the manner in which Hathaway and McKinley set about this task, it may be instructive to consider the alternative method of inventory construction which they rejected.

Content Validity and Its Problems

Each psychiatric diagnostic category is defined by its predominating symptoms. Given a list of the symptoms for each classification, the task becomes one of constructing items which will adequately sample the domain of symptoms. For example, an item which reflects the primary symptom of depression would be: "I am often sad." If the domain of symptoms for each category were adequately sampled, the inventory would have *content validity*.

A recent example of a self-report inventory constructed on the basis of content validity is the Wolpe and Lang (1964) Fear Survey Schedule, which was specifically designed for use in assessing objects or situations which cause fear or apprehension in people. The Fear Survey Schedule consists of a list of approximately 75 fears which had been found to be most disturbing to neurotic patients who were treated by Wolpe and his colleagues. Each item is responded to on a five-point scale of fear ranging from "not at all" to "very much." A portion of the Fear Survey Schedule is reproduced in Table 8–1.

The *content validation approach* to inventory construction has a number of difficulties. First, content validity does not speak to the issue of whether a test actually works for the intended purpose. To determine the degree to which the test is successful in classifying patients into diagnostic categories, some means of *external* validation is necessary. For example, the classification obtained by using the test could be compared with that obtained by the independent clinical diagnoses of psychologists. If patients cannot be classified properly by the way they respond to the items, there is little solace in knowing that the test inquired about the full range of symptoms in every diagnostic category. As we shall see shortly, a test with high content validity can fail to work because examinees are not responding to the content of the items but rather to some aspect of the test-taking situation.

Second, an inventory constructed on the basis of content validity may have insufficiently subtle test items. Early test constructors paid little attention to this problem (e.g., the Woodworth Personal Data

TABLE 8–1

Portion of the Fear Survey Schedule

The items in this questionnaire refer to things and experiences that may cause fear or other unpleasant feelings. Write the number of each item in the column that describes how much you are disturbed by it nowadays.

	Not at All	A Little	A Fair Amount	Much	Very Much
1. Noise of vacuum cleaners...........					
2. Open wounds........................					
3. Being alone........................					
4. Being in a strange place............					
5. Loud voices........................					
6. Dead people.......................					
7. Speaking in public.................					
8. Crossing streets....................					
9. People who seem insane...........					
10. Falling.............................					
11. Automobiles.......................					
12. Being teased......................					
13. Dentists...........................					

Source: Wolpe and Lazarus, 1966.

Sheet; Woodworth, 1920), reasoning that a test item which was to measure something ought to "look like" it was doing so. More recently, psychologists have tended to gravitate to the other extreme, maintaining that a test item should be constructed so that the respondent is unaware of what it is purported to measure. One of the principal arguments for the use of subtle test items is that obvious items allow the subject to fake his answers, make a good impression, or otherwise distort his "real" personality. The contemporary use of more subtle items in psychological tests has contributed to the public denunciation in recent years of psychological testing as an invasion of privacy (e.g., investigations by Congress; cf. American Psychological Association, 1965).

Empirical Keying: An Alternative to Content Validation

Sensitive to the limitations of constructing self-report inventories by content validation, Hathaway and McKinley employed a strategy which makes few theoretical assumptions about the items which make up the test. Initially, item selection proceeded along the same lines that are used in the content validation approach. A pool of 1,000 self-descriptive statements was collected from various psychiatric examination forms and procedures, psychiatric textbooks, and previously used inventories. However, rather than stop there.

Hathaway and McKinley administered the 1,000-item inventory to groups of diagnosed psychiatric patients (so classified on the basis of clinical judgments) and groups of normal (nonpatient) subjects. For each of the diagnostic groups and the normal sample, the frequency of endorsement of each item was tabulated. Only those items which clearly differentiated between a diagnostic group and the normal group were retained for the final inventory. For instance, a statement became an item on the Depression scale if, and only if, patients diagnosed as having a depressive disorder endorsed the statement significantly more often than did normal persons. Thus, it was possible for an item which had little content validity to be included on the Depression scale (e.g., "I sometimes tease animals"), or any other scale, of the MMPI. Constructing a test in this manner is referred to as *empirical keying*.

The MMPI consists of 550 statements which deal with such matters as attitudes, educational information, general physical health, sex roles, mood, morale, vocational interests, fears, and preoccupations. There are 4 validity scales and 10 basic clinical scales for which the MMPI is scored. Their characteristics are summarized in Table 8–2. The function of the validity scales is to provide informa-

TABLE 8–2

The Validity and Clinical Scales of the MMPI

Scale Name	Symbol	Sample Item	Interpretation
Cannot say	?	No sample. It is merely the number of items marked in the "cannot say" category or left blank.	This is one of four validity scales, and a high score indicates evasiveness.
Lie	L	I get angry sometimes. (False)*	This is the second validity scale. Persons trying to present themselves in a favorable light (e.g., good, wholesome, honest) obtain high L scale scores.
Frequency	F	Everything tastes the same. (True)	F is the third validity scale. High scores suggest carelessness, confusion, or "fake bad."
Correction	K	I have very few fears compared to my friends. (False)	An elevation on the last validity scale, K, suggests a defensive test-taking attitude. Exceedingly low scores may indicate a lack of ability to deny symptomatology.

TABLE 8–2 (Continued)

Hypochondriasis.......... Hs	I wake up fresh and rested most mornings. (False)	High scorers have been described as cynical and defeatist.
Depression................ D	At times I am full of energy. (False)	High scorers usually are shy, despondent, and distressed.
Hysteria.................. Hy	I have never had a fainting spell. (False)	High scorers tend to complain of multiple symptoms.
Psychopathic deviate..... Pd	I liked school. (False)	Adjectives used to describe some high scorers are adventurous, courageous, and generous.
Masculinity-femininity..... Mf	I like mechanics magazines. (False)	Among males, high scorers have been described as esthetic and sensitive. High-scoring women have been described as rebellious, unrealistic, and indecisive.
Paranoia................. Pa	Someone has it in for me. (True)	High scorers on this scale are characterized as shrewd, guarded, and worrisome.
Psychasthenia........... Pt	I am certainly lacking in self-confidence. (True)	Fearful, rigid, anxious and worrisome are some of the adjectives used to describe high Pt scorers.
Schizophrenia............ Sc	I believe I am a condemned person. (True)	Adjectives such as withdrawn and unusual describe Sc high scorers.
Hypomania.............. Ma	At times my thoughts have raced ahead faster than I could speak them. (True)	High scorers are called sociable, energetic, and impulsive.
Social introversion-extroversion............ Si	I enjoy social gatherings just to be with people. (False)	High scorers: modest, shy, and self-effacing. Low scorers: sociable, colorful, and ambitious.

* The true or false responses within parentheses indicate the scored direction of each of the items.
Source: Adapted from Kleinmuntz, 1967.

tion concerning the validity of the respondent's answers on the clinical scales. For example, an elevated Lie (L) scale indicates that the respondent is attempting to answer the items so as to present himself in a favorable light.

The scoring of the MMPI is straightforward. There are scoring keys which indicate the items which appear on each scale and the scored direction of each item (i.e., true or false). The test can be completely scored by hand in less than 10 minutes and in considerably less time by computer. Interpretation of the scores is not as simple. To arrive at a clinical diagnosis, the *pattern* of scores on the 10 clinical scales is examined. The pattern of scores is often presented graphically, as in Figure 8–1, in what is called a *psychogram,* or *personality profile.* A number of MMPI atlases have been compiled for interpreting profiles (e.g., Marks & Seeman, 1963). These books contain typical profiles and descriptive information about samples of subjects producing each profile. For example, along with

FIGURE 8–1

Sample MMPI Profile (Psychogram)

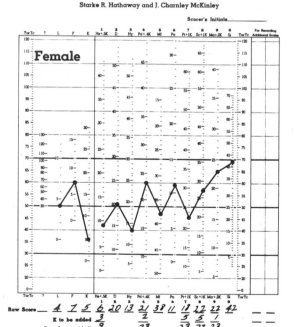

a list of typical and atypical symptoms and behaviors for persons with a given profile, there may be information about the most common diagnostic category of these people, their personal histories, courses of treatment, and so on. While it is rare to find a perfect match of profiles (i.e., identical scores on all the scales), the examiner is helped in finding the "typical" profile in the atlas which will be most like that of his respondent by a series of criteria which must be met for two profiles to be considered similar.

Although the MMPI was originally designed to aid in the diagnosis of psychiatric patients and still serves this function, it has also been used extensively in personality research. For this latter purpose, several hundred additional experimental scales have been developed using the basic 550 items. In many cases, the MMPI items which make up an experimental scale are used alone, as is the case, for example, with the Taylor Manifest Anxiety Scale (Taylor, 1953) which has been used widely in basic research on anxiety.

The CPI

Another example of an empirically keyed self-report personality inventory is the California Psychological Inventory (CPI), which was devised by Harrison Gough (1956) as an MMPI-like scale specifically for use with a normal population. Because of the careful research that went into its construction—including a validation sample of 13,000 normal subjects—the CPI has been hailed as ". . . well on its way to becoming one of the best, if not the best, personality measuring instruments of its kind" (Kleinmuntz, 1967, p. 239).

The CPI contains almost 500 true-false items, about half of which come from the MMPI. Administered, scored, and profiled in much the same way as the MMPI, the CPI contains 3 validity scales and scales for 15 personality traits including dominance, tolerance, self-control, achievement via conformance and achievement via independence, self-acceptance, sense of well-being, responsibility, and flexibility. The scales themselves discriminate well on *non*psychiatric characteristics, such as leadership, and there is much favorable evidence for its validity (Cronbach, 1959; Kleinmuntz, 1967).

FAKING ON PERSONALITY INVENTORIES

People taking tests such as the MMPI have devised various schemes for falsifying their answers (e.g., in order to make a "good impression" when applying for a job or a "bad impression" when being tested for sanity in connection with a murder trial). How successful are these conscious efforts to achieve a desired impression?

Some "fakers," particularly those who overdo it, are likely to be detected by one or more of the validity scales built into most inventories. Still, there appears to be little doubt that, on the average, people can get "better scores" on self-report personality inventories when told to simulate a "nice personality," although there are wide individual differences in the degree to which people succeed in faking good or faking bad (Edwards & Abbott, 1973). There are, moreover, certain other kinds of test-taking attitudes—response sets —which may distort the personality picture presented by self-report inventories such as the MMPI and the CPI.

RESPONSE SETS

Psychologists who use self-report personality inventories often assume that the individual's response to any given item reflects his disposition toward the *content* of the item. For example, it may be important to assume that a person who responds "true" to the statement "I like parties" attends social functions frequently. Are there sources of distortion which can weaken or invalidate this assumption? The answer appears to be yes, since it has been found that respondents with particular test-taking attitudes may not be answering the items in terms of their manifest content. *Response sets,* as these test-taking attitudes are called, are characteristic and consistent ways of responding to items regardless of what the items say. *Response acquiescence* is the tendency to agree with items no matter what their content. *Response deviation* is the tendency to answer items in an uncommon direction. Still another response set which has received much attention in recent years is that of *social desirability,* which is characterized by answering items in the direction which is most socially accepted irrespective of whether that answer is correct for the respondent. For example, an individual who prefers to be alone and dislikes social gatherings might answer "true" to the statement "I like parties" because he feels it is socially desirable to enjoy parties. We shall examine the nature of response sets by looking at social desirability in some detail.

Social Desirability as a Response Set

What evidence is there that social desirability is an important response set? To answer this question, Allen L. Edwards (1953b) performed a straightforward study to assess the relationship between the probability of endorsement of items on a self-report inventory and the social desirability of the items. His hypothesis was: "If the behavior indicated by an inventory item is socially desirable, the subject will tend to attribute it to himself; if it is undesirable, he will not" (1953b, p. 90).

In the first phase of the study, 140 personality trait items, representing 14 of Murray's needs (see Chapter 9), were listed. The list was then given to 152 men and women with instructions to judge the social desirability of each item on a nine-point scale. The instructions presented to subjects are reproduced in Table 8–3. Based on the ratings by the subjects, the position of each personality trait item on a scale of social desirability was calculated.

TABLE 8–3

Instructions Used in Obtaining Judgments of Social Desirability for Personality Statements

---

Below you will find an example of four things that a person says that he likes or would like to do. These likes are called traits. Underneath the list of four traits and opposite the numbers corresponding to each of the traits are nine boxes. These boxes represent different degrees of desirability or undesirability of each trait as it appears in others, as indicated by the adjective at the top. A judge, such as yourself, has made an estimate of the degree of desirability or undesirability of these traits in people by placing an X in the box opposite each trait.

Example 1. To like to punish your enemies.
2. To like to read psychological novels.
3. To like to make excuses for your friends.
4. To like to go out with your friends.

Trait *Undesirable*   *Desirable*

	Extreme	Strong	Moderate	Mild	Neutral	Mild	Moderate	Strong	Extreme
1.		X							
2.					X				
3.							X		
4.									X

The person who judged these traits believes that "to like to punish your enemies" is a definitely undesirable trait in others, "to like to read psychological novels" is neither desirable nor undesirable, "to like to make excuses for your friends" is moderately desirable, and "to like to go out with your friends" is quite a desirable trait in other people.

Indicate your own judgments of the desirability or undesirability of the traits which will be given to you by the examiner in the same manner. *Remember that you are to judge the traits in terms of whether you consider them desirable or undesirable in others.* Be sure to make a judgment about each trait.

Source: Edwards, 1957.

In the second phase of Edwards' study, the same set of personality trait items was presented to a different sample of subjects, 140 premedical and predental students, as part of a battery of tests. This time the items were administered in the form of a personality inventory with instructions to answer "yes" when an item was characteristic of the respondent and "no" when it was not. The proportion of subjects responding "yes" to each item was computed, and these proportions became the probability of endorsement of a given item.

Edwards found that the correlation between the probability of endorsement of each item and the independently determined social desirability scale value of the item was +.87. One statement which had been rated as highly desirable, "I like to be loyal to my friends," was endorsed by 98 percent of the students as an accurate description of themselves. In contrast, the undesirable statement "I like to avoid responsibilities and obligations" was endorsed by only 6 percent of the respondents as describing themselves.

The finding of a strong positive relationship supported Edwards' contention that by knowing where a statement lies on the social desirability-undesirability dimension, ". . . we can then predict, with a high degree of accuracy, the proportion of individuals who will say, in self-description, that the statement does describe them" (1957, p. 3). Using the same basic two-phase design but with different populations of subjects (e.g., Norwegian students; Lovaas, 1956, as cited by Edwards, 1957) and different items (e.g., statements from the MMPI; Hanley, 1956), other investigators have also found a high positive correlation between the proportion of people endorsing a statement and its social desirability. Moreover, these relationships do not appear to be reduced even when the respondents are led to believe that their identities will remain anonymous, thereby supposedly eliminating the subjects' "need" to present themselves in a favorable or socially desirable light. It seems safe to assume that the more socially desirable a statement is, the more likely it is that a respondent will report that it is characteristic of himself.

Given that social desirability is a viable and reliable response set which affects the interpretation of responses on self-report inventories, what is the nature of its influence? At least two possibilities exist. On the one hand, it is possible that subjects taking personality inventories try to make a good impression by describing themselves as possessing more socially desirable traits and fewer socially undesirable traits than they might be found to have if their behavior were evaluated by another method. On the other hand, it may be that behaviors which are judged as desirable in a particular culture are, at the same time, the behaviors which are most common. If this were correct, it would be anticipated that a higher percentage of people would endorse statements which are high on a scale of social desirability than those which are low in social desirability. In this case, subjects would not be misrepresenting themselves. Either of these possibilities or a combination of the two would account for Edwards' findings. Thus, interpreting the responses of subjects to self-report personality inventories may be complicated due to the effects of social desirability (not to mention other response sets).

Controlling for Social Desirability

Several methods have been devised for controlling the influence of social desirability. One approach is to measure the respondent's tendency to answer items on a self-report inventory in the socially desirable direction and to then adjust his score on the inventory to take the degree of this tendency into account.

Another approach involves employing neutral items with respect to social desirability (i.e., statements which are rated in the middle of the social desirability-undesirability scale), as, for example, "I am easily awakened by noise." However, it often proves difficult to find or rewrite items which meet the requirement of neutrality and simultaneously convey the necessary content. It is hard to imagine how one could rewrite the statement "Most of the time I wish I were dead" (an MMPI item which is rated as extremely undesirable; Hanley, 1956) so as to make it more socially desirable without changing the meaning substantially.

A third approach for controlling the effects of social desirability is to use a *forced-choice inventory.* All the statements appearing in the inventory are first scaled for social desirability and then paired according to their scale values. The members of each pair have approximately the same social desirability scale value but different content. Therefore, when the respondent chooses the statement in each pair which is more characteristic of himself, his choice cannot be based on the social desirability of the item. Edwards constructed his Personal Preference Schedule in this way to control for the influence of social desirability. The Personal Preference Schedule is a self-report personality inventory developed for use in counseling and research with nonpsychiatric persons. Examples of items appearing on it are presented in Table 8–4.

TABLE 8–4

Examples of Items from the Edwards Personal Preference Schedule

Alternatives		Items
A	B	A: I like to tell amusing stories and jokes at parties.
		B: I would like to write a great novel or play.
A	B	A: I like to have my work organized and planned before beginning it.
		B: I like to travel and see the country.
A	B	A: I feel like blaming others when things go wrong for me.
		B: I feel that I am inferior to others in most respects.
A	B	A: I like to avoid responsibilities and obligations.
		B: I feel like making fun of people who do things that I regard as stupid.

Source: Edwards, 1953.

RESPONSE STYLES

Fiske and Pearson (1970) note that people can judge the intended domain of a personality test rather accurately and point to the complex implications of this fact. "Like other reactions," they write, "reactions to tests and to test tasks have their personality correlates" (p. 68). In other words, an examinee's response to the fact that he is taking a test may itself be a personality disposition, one which may alter his responses to the particular items on the test. Thus, while some psychologists have endeavored to rid self-report inventories of the distorting influence of response sets, other psychologists have observed that these characteristic modes of responding might not be sources of error at all. This latter group has suggested that it would be more fruitful to look at test-taking attitudes as personality traits. That is, the salient measures of personality in self-report inventories might be *how* an individual responds, rather than *what* he responds to (i.e., the content of the items). Neurotics, for example, are more likely to show extreme response sets than are nonneurotics (Iwawaki & Zax, 1969).

Because an examinee's response tendencies can be viewed either as a source of distortion or error in personality assessment or as an indication of personality dispositions themselves, it is useful to assign different terms to describe each situation. The former are referred to as response *sets,* while the latter are called response *styles* (Jackson & Messick, 1958).[1] We have already examined social desirability as a response set; here we shall consider the evidence for its being a response style.

Social Desirability as a Response Style

Edwards' Approach

In order to measure a person's inclination to respond to self-descriptive statements in the socially desirable direction, Edwards (1953a) developed a Social Desirability (SD) scale. He selected 150 items from the MMPI (from the L, F, and K scales and the Taylor Manifest Anxiety Scale) and asked 10 judges to respond to each of the items in a socially desirable direction. The judges agreed perfectly on 79 of the 150 statements, and these 79 items formed the first SD scale. Later, Edwards reduced the SD scale to 39 items by

---

[1] Some response tendencies probably fall between these categories. Response acquiescence, for example, "may be an internally consistent disposition, [but] it is not a generalized disposition, and occurs more readily when items are weak in content . . . or when subjects are uncertain. . ." (Fiske & Pearson, 1970, pp. 71–72).

selecting those items which showed the greatest differentiation between subjects who had high and low total scores.

Edwards hypothesized: "If the SD scale does provide a measure of the tendency of subjects to give socially desirable responses to statements in self-description, then the correlations of scores on this scale with other personality scales, given under standard instructions, should indicate something of the extent to which the social desirability variable is operating at the time" (1957, pp. 31, 33). A number of studies by Edwards and other investigators (e.g., Edwards, 1953a, 1957; Merrill & Heathers, 1956) have provided evidence supporting this hypothesis. Scales measuring socially desirable traits, such as dominance, responsibility, status, cooperativeness, agreeableness, and objectivity, have been found to be positively correlated with the SD scale. In contrast, scales measuring socially undesirable traits, such as social introversion, neuroticism, hostility, dependency, insecurity, and anxiety, have been found to be negatively correlated with the SD scale (cf. Edwards, 1970).

One possible implication of the correlations found between Edwards' SD scale and other personality scales is that the traits which these scales are measuring are, despite their names (e.g., dominance and social introversion), only different aspects of social desirability. Perhaps it would be more fruitful from the standpoint of predictive and explanatory power and parsimony to view the various traits which have been found to correlate strongly with the SD scale as if they were measures of social desirability. However, several important considerations should be kept in mind. First, correlation does not mean identity. The fact that Drake's Social Introversion Scale (Merrill & Heathers, 1956) and Edwards' SD scale are strongly related (−.90) means only that one can be predicted from the other with a high degree of accuracy. Second, although the relationship *may* occur because both scales measure social desirability, it may also occur because both measure a disposition that is better thought of as social introversion or because of some third variable that is tied to both (see Chapter 2).

Additionally, it appears that the social desirability of an *item* (as averaged across many subjects) does not reflect its social desirability for most people considered as individual examinees. Fiske (1971) observes:

> When correlations are computed for each subject between his own [social desirability] ratings and his endorsements [of personality test items] the values are much lower than the ones for group averages reported by Edwards. Even with these lower but positive relationships for individuals, what is the direction of the influence? Perhaps subjects tend to rate as desirable whatever characteristics

they perceive in themselves, rather than to attribute to themselves those characteristics they deem to be socially desirable (p. 216).

Despite these limitations, proponents of different response styles have endeavored to subsume a variety of traits measured by self-report personality inventories under the rubric of a single response style. Edwards, who has championed the cause of social desirability, is no exception. Consider the persuasive argument he has made for interpreting the trait being measured by the Taylor Manifest Anxiety (MA) Scale as social desirability-undesirability.

The MA scale has been found to be negatively correlated with the SD scale,[2] which means that high anxiety tends to be associated with low social desirability and low anxiety tends to be associated with high social desirability. This finding is not surprising when one examines the items that make up the MA scale. Statements like "I am a very nervous person," "I am certainly lacking in self-confidence," and "I cry easily," which appear on the MA scale, are unquestionably socially undesirable characteristics in our general society. Thus, high scores on the MA scale can be viewed as a function of endorsing these and other socially undesirable statements, whereas low scores on the MA scale would be a function of denying socially undesirable characteristics. (It is interesting to note that for certain subgroups of our culture—such as the residents of mental hospitals or homes for the aged—these socially undesirable characteristics are not as undesirable and may even be construed as socially desirable—for example, because they foster attention and care.)

The MA scale has been used in numerous experimental studies investigating the effect of anxiety on performance to select subjects with high and low anxiety. One finding[3] has been that for certain kinds of verbal learning (such as verbal maze, paired-associate, and serial nonsense-syllable learning) low-anxious subjects make fewer errors and reach a criterion of learning faster (in fewer trials) than high-anxious subjects (e.g., Montague, 1953; Ramond, 1953; Taylor

---

[2] Edwards (1957) reports a correlation of −.84 between the MA scale and the 39-item SD scale and a correlation of −.60 between the MA scale and the 79-item SD scale. The negative relationship between the MA and SD scales, as well as the substantially higher correlation obtained with the shorter SD scale, could be accounted for by the 22 overlapping items on the 39-item SD scale and the MA scale. On the basis of further statistical analyses, Edwards concludes that the negative correlation between the SD scale and the MA scale cannot be accounted for "merely in terms of the item overlap between the two scales" (1957, p. 88 n.).

[3] The relationship between level of anxiety and performance is rather complex, depending, to a large degree, on the nature of the performance task (see Spence & Spence, 1966).

& Spence, 1952). Edwards (1957) attempts to explain these results in terms of social desirability in the following way.

> I believe it possible . . . to describe the low group on the Taylor scale as those who desire to make a good impression on others and the high group as those who are less interested in what others may think of them. I would predict that the group desiring to make a good impression on the Taylor scale, that is to say, those with low scores, might also desire to make a good impression in terms of their performance on the learning task. They are, in other words, perhaps more highly motivated by the desire to "look good," not only in their responses to the Taylor scale, but also in their performance in the learning situation itself. Surely, to be able to learn fast is, in our society, a socially desirable characteristic. If a subject has a strong tendency to give socially desirable responses in self-description, is it unreasonable to believe that he may also reveal this tendency in his behavior in a learning situation where he is aware of what would be considered socially desirable, namely to learn fast, to do his best? The high group, on the other hand, being less interested in making a good impression, showing less of a tendency to give socially desirable responses in self-description, caring less about how others may value them, does not have equal motivation with the low group in the learning situation (p. 89).

Crowne and Marlowe's Approach

One of the major problems with Edwards' SD scale is that social desirability is *confounded* with the content of those items having distinct psychopathological implications. Recall that the items comprising the Edwards SD scale are all drawn from the MMPI, which deals specifically with symptoms of psychiatric disorders. When a subject denies that he is very nervous, has little self-confidence, and cries easily, it is not possible to differentiate whether he is merely responding in the socially acceptable direction or is actually free of these symptoms. In short, there is no way to separate the effects of the content of the items and a respondent's tendency to present himself in a favorable (or unfavorable) light. Thus, when Edwards' SD scale is employed with normal subjects, interpretation of scores is ambiguous.

The Marlowe-Crowne Social Desirability scale was designed specifically to avoid the confounding effects of item content (Crowne & Marlowe, 1960). The criteria for item selection were that *the behaviors in question be sanctioned and approved by our culture but have a low frequency of occurrence.* Additionally, items chosen had to have minimal psychopathological implications. Several examples of items from the final scale (Crowne & Marlowe, 1960) which meet these requirements follow, with the socially desirable response indicated in parentheses.

> On a few occasions, I have given up doing something because I thought too little of my ability. (False)
> No matter who I am talking to, I'm always a good listener. (True)
> There have been occasions when I took advantage of someone. (False) (p. 351)

While never doubting one's own ability, always being a good listener, and never taking advantage of someone else are socially desirable, they are descriptions which do not fit very many of us. Thus, an individual who responds to items on the Marlowe-Crowne SD scale in the socially desirable direction can be said to be presenting himself in a favorable light (i.e., "faking good"), since it is highly improbable that his behavior actually corresponds to his self-report of it. At the same time, when an individual responds in the socially desirable direction, he is not forced to deny pathological symptoms or culturally unsanctioned behavior (as he is on Edwards' SD scale). In our culture there is nothing "wrong" or "sick" with sometimes having little self-confidence, occasionally being a poor listener, and once in a while taking advantage of another person. There is no stigma attached to responding to items on the Marlowe-Crowne scale in the socially undesirable direction. In short, the content of the Marlowe-Crowne SD scale represents ideal behavior—that is, behavior whose presence is praised but whose absence is not punished.

The Marlowe-Crowne and Edwards SD scales are only moderately correlated (+.35) and have no items in common. As would be predicted from the fact that the items on the Marlowe-Crowne scale have substantially less content dealing with psychiatric symptoms than does the Edwards scale, the correlations between the Marlowe-Crowne scale and various MMPI scales are generally lower than the parallel correlations for Edwards' SD scale. It has been suggested that high scores on the Marlowe-Crowne scale reflect the examinee's tendency to adjust his social responses to the unique demands of new situations and not simply a general tendency to give a favorable self-description (Miller, Doob, Butler, & Marlowe, 1965). As we shall see in Chapter 9, Crowne and Marlowe view high scores on their social desirability scale as indicative of a more pervasive personality disposition which they call the *need for social approval*.

EVALUATION OF RESPONSE SETS
AND RESPONSE STYLES

Our discussion of response sets and styles has focused on social desirability and has presented the evidence *for* their existence and validity. While the arguments favoring a response-style interpretation of self-report personality inventories are impressive, they have certainly not gone unchallenged. Indeed, the controversy between a response-style and a content interpretation of self-report inventories has been one of the most pronounced in the recent history of psychology and is still quite alive. Formally, the controversy has taken the form of the presentation of an argument for one position, followed by a rebuttal from the opposition, in turn followed by a defense and counterargument, and so on. The "battle" is reflected in the titles of important works which have addressed the issue, such as *The Challenge of Response Sets* (Block, 1965) and "The Great Response-Style Myth" (Rorer, 1965).

Most probably, people respond to self-report personality inventories *both* in terms of the content of the items and their characteristic styles of responding. Thus, it may prove more fruitful in the long run to examine the *interaction* of these two different sources of variance in self-report inventories.

The polarization which has tended to characterize the debate between a content and response-style interpretation of self-report personality inventories is typical of many controversies in psychology. Psychologists often take extreme stands on issues rather than look for the middle ground between them. (One consequence of this fact is that it becomes possible to classify approaches to personality into opposing strategies, as has been done in this book for heuristic purposes.) Yet, all personality psychologists would no doubt agree that behavior is multiply determined. Therefore, on purely commonsense grounds it would seem more enlightening to search for the interactions among the multiple sources of personality (e.g., traits *and* situational influences rather than traits *versus* situational influences). The approach taken by Henry A. Murray, which is described in the next chapter, is a partial attempt to view personality as an interaction of enduring dispositions within the person and situational forces external to him.

9

The Dispositional Strategy
NEED APPROACHES

Some dispositional views of personality emphasize individual differences in the way people are motivated and the kinds of goals which they seek. From such a vantage point it is argued that differences in the *needs* which people have—both in kind and in amount—propel them to different courses of action and thus give rise to different personalities. In the present chapter we shall consider several dispositional approaches to personality which are distinguished by the fact that they have focused primarily on the identification and measurement of needs as a means to understanding, predicting, and controlling human behavior. The first such approach was formulated by Henry A. Murray.

MURRAY'S PERSONOLOGY[1]

The approach constructed by Murray and his associates[2] beginning in the 1930s deals with "directional forces within the subject, forces which seek out or respond to various objects or total situations in the environment" (1962, p. 24). Positing such forces was not a unique venture. Impelling passions and drives had been suggested

---

[1] Murray and his co-workers defined their area of interest as *personology,* arguing that the phrase " 'the psychology of personality' [is] a clumsy and tautological expression" (1962, p. 4).

[2] Murray's original formulation of his approach was published in 1938 in a volume of more than 700 pages entitled *Explorations in Personality.* Its 1962 reprint is the primary source of information for this section.

by many earlier writers, and the dynamics of Freud's theory were already well known. But Murray sought to do more than acknowledge these forces. He wished to identify and catalog them, to assess them in persons, to determine their relationship to one another, and to take the bold step of writing a comprehensive theory. Recognizing that they did not have "sufficient" data to justify their stand, Murray and his colleagues noted:

> . . . for the present the destiny of personology is best served by giving scope to speculation, perhaps not so much as psycho-analysts allow themselves, but plenty. Hence, in the present volume we have checked self-criticism, ignored various details, winked a little at statistics, and from first to last have never hesitated to offer interpretative hypotheses. Had we made a ritual of rigorous analysis nothing would have filtered through to write about. Speech is healthier than silence, even though one knows that what one says is vague and inconclusive (1962, p. 22).

Primary Constructs

Murray believes that the individual and his environment must be considered together as a person-environment interaction. However, to begin an analysis of this interaction, forces within the individual and forces from the environment are temporarily separated. The former are referred to as *needs* and the latter as *press*.[3]

Needs

A need (*n*) is a theoretical construct, a convenient fiction which is useful only insofar as it helps the psychologist to deal with facts. It is "an organic potentiality or readiness to respond in a certain way under given conditions . . . it is a noun which stands for the fact that a certain trend is apt to recur" (1962, p. 61). So defined, needs are identified with particular effects or temporary end-states (e.g., the need for sex is identified with orgasm). A need must be distinguished from an *actone,* which is a pattern of action (a behavior) which may serve to satisfy a need. An actone may become associated with a need if it is regularly associated with its end-state. For example, verbal "threats" are actones which may function well in the service of a need for power. A given actone can often be used to satisfy a number of different needs (getting married, for example, may directly or indirectly satisfy a person's need for security, sex, and food). Therefore, it is not always possible to identify someone's active needs by observing his behavior. We shall return to the problem of assessing needs in a later section.

---

[3] The plural of "press" is press.

Since need is a theoretical construct rather than something observable, it is incumbent upon the theorist to suggest evidence for its utility, or heuristic value. Murray (1962) cites 23 points of evidence to support the value of the concept of need and to substantiate the claim that needs, rather than observable behaviors (actones), should be the units for the study of personality. Fifteen of the points, which are based on objective data, are included in the following list.

1. Organisms require certain conditions in order to survive. It is apparent, for example, that we all have a "need" for oxygen.
2. For those effects which are universally required by living creatures, a variety of actones may be used. Food may be acquired by growing it, trapping it, stalking it live, or stealing it from a fellow being.
3. In the life of a single individual, we can observe that certain outcomes are regularly attained, but the instrumental actones change markedly with development. "The embryo assimilates food through the umbilical vessels, the infant sucks it from the tendered breast of the mother, the child eats with a spoon what is put before him, and the adult has . . . to get money to buy food" (1962, p. 57).
4. Actones have no intrinsic value. Only those which reliably produce "satisfying" end-states become established.
5. Novel situations often engender a succession of actones, until one is found which produces a desired effect.
6. Some responses can be produced only by novelty (which, of course, is not directly observable). For example, one rarely laughs heartily at a familiar joke.
7. Necessary end-states may be produced by the actones of another person, as in the case of the sick child whose biological requirements are provided by its mother's actions.
8. Persistence would be hard to interpret without positing needs. Humans, for example, often *increase* the intensity of their efforts in the face of opposition.
9. "Complex action is characterized by the occurrence of muscular contractions in widely separated parts of the organism—contractions which manifest synchronous and consecutive coordination. Such organizations of movement must be partially determined by a directional process—which is just what a need, by definition, is" (1962, pp. 61–62).
10. The concept of need is necessary to understand differences in the intensity or duration of goal-directed behavior. Intensity of the actones themselves varies from moment to moment.
11. Actones may be swiftly interrupted by the gratuitous presenta-

tion of end-states, as when the attention of a guest stops a child's crying. If the actone itself were critical, it would presumably have persisted.

12. "That a need is an important determinant of certain kinds of behavior is shown by the fact that when it is neither active nor in a state of readiness, responses to specific stimuli do not occur" (1962, p. 62). For example, directly after a large and filling meal one is not likely to accept an invitation to go out to a local restaurant.

13. If a need is active, then objects or events may be used in novel ways in the service of the need. By way of example, Murray notes that when a boy is quarreling with a playmate and sees an apple, he may well throw it at his antagonist rather than eat it.

14. Organisms sometimes become active *in search of,* as well as *in the presence of,* need-related stimuli. Thus, "an animal will *explore* for food, and a man will *search* for a sex object" (1962, p. 63).

15. Biological causes of activation may be discovered, suggesting a palpable source for need-related behavior.[4]

The remaining eight points which Murray makes in favor of the concept of need are avowedly subjective and emphasize the importance of motivational interpretations in the practical commerce of our daily lives. They can be summarized by the following comment: ". . . no therapist or, indeed, anyone who has to deal in a practical way with human beings, can get along without some notion of motivational force (instinct, purpose, aim, intention, need, drive, impulse, urge, attitude, inclination, wish, desire, or what not) . . ." (Murray, 1962, p. 66).

Having considered Murray's arguments for the value of the concept of need, let us turn to the breakdown of "kinds of needs" that was suggested and to an inspection of the specific needs that were finally posited. The first major division is between the *primary,* or *viscerogenic,* needs and the *secondary,* or *psychogenic,* needs. The viscerogenic needs are best thought of as representing the physical requirements of the organism. There are said to be 12 of them: *n* Air, *n* Water, *n* Food, *n* Sex, *n* Heatavoidance, *n* Lactation, *n* Urination, *n* Defecation, *n* Harmavoidance, *n* Noxavoidance (avoidance of noxious stimuli), *n* Sentience (consciousness), and *n* Coldavoidance. While Murray uses an occasional novel term, there is general

---

[4] At the time Murray was writing, it had only recently been shown that hormonal injections could produce various maternal and sexual behaviors in laboratory animals. Today the argument can also be bolstered by the further discovery of hypothalamic centers of the brain which appear to control thirst, hunger, and perhaps "pleasure."

agreement that this list represents universal, biological requirements of the organism. Further, agreement is relatively easy to obtain on the conditions which will engender one of these needs, both external (e.g., a seductive mate for *n* Sex) or internal (e.g., increased carbon dioxide for *n* Air).

Murray (1962) enumerates 27 psychogenic needs, although they are not entirely independent of one another. The actual list appears in Table 9–1.

Press

Murray and his associates reasoned that needs were but one half of the interactional process that determines behavior and selected the term *press* to represent the complementary, and equally impor-

TABLE 9–1

Murray's List of Psychogenic Needs

Major Category	Need	Behavioral Example
Ambition...................	*n* Achievement	Overcoming obstacles
	n Recognition	Boasting
	n Exhibition	Making efforts to shock or thrill others
	n Acquisition	Acquiring things, by work or stealing
	n Conservance	Repairing possessions
	n Order	Tidying up
	n Retention	Hoarding
	n Construction	Organizing or building something
Defense of status...........	*n* Inviolacy	Maintaining psychological "distance"
	n Infavoidance	Concealing a disfigurement
	n Defendance	Offering explanations or excuses
	n Counteraction	Engaging in acts of retaliation
Response to human power..	*n* Dominance	Dictating to or directing others
	n Deference	Cooperating with others
	n Similance	Imitating others
	n Autonomy	Manifesting defiance of authority
	n Contrariance	Taking unconventional or oppositional views
	n Aggression	Assaulting or belittling others
	n Abasement	Apologizing, confessing, or surrendering
	n Blamavoidance	Inhibiting unconventional impulses
Affection between people...	*n* Affiliation	Joining groups
	n Rejection	Discriminating against or snubbing others
	n Nurturance	"Mothering" a child
	n Succorance	Crying for help
	n Play	Seeking diversion by "having fun"
Exchange of information....	*n* Cognizance	Asking questions
	n Exposition	Lecturing to, or interpreting for, others

Source: Adapted from Murray, 1962.

tant, directional forces provided by objects, situations, or events in the environment. Some common examples of press appear in Table 9–2. Murray distinguished two types of press: *alpha press* and *beta press*. The former represents an objective description of environmental situations (e.g., a certain grade-point average is required for admission to medical school), while the latter represents significant environmental influences as they are perceived by the individual (e.g., "If I don't make the required grade-point average for medical school, I have been a total failure"). For a person to function adequately in an interaction with his environment, there must be reasonable correspondence between his alpha press (objective experience) and his beta press (subjective experience) of the same situation. The case in which alpha press and beta press sharply diverge would be called delusion.

We shall next turn our attention to the two constructs which serve to integrate needs and press.

TABLE 9–2

Common Examples of Press

Press	Example
p Achievement	Others getting good grades
p Order	A messy desk
p Counteraction	Being attacked (verbally or physically)
p Autonomy	Overprotective parents
p Abasement	Doing something wrong
p Affiliation	Friendly companions
p Play	Saturday night
p Cognizance	Not understanding a lecture

Proceedings

Murray suggests that a person's history might well be considered his personality. In order to study a person's history, a continuous process, Murray divides his past into discrete temporal units, called *proceedings,* which serve to integrate the person's needs and press in terms of convenient periods of time. Proceedings may be *external,* involving a stretch of time in which a person is engaged in some sort of overt behavior (e.g., fixing one's car or going on a date), or *internal,* involving a period of time in which there is no overt action (e.g., thinking about how to repair one's car or daydreaming about last weekend's date). While both internal and external proceedings are important for understanding personality, psychologists can only study overt behavior. The external proceeding is "the psychologist's simplest *real entity,* the thing he should observe, analyze, try to reconstruct and represent, if possible, with a model, and thus explain;

it is the thing he attempts to predict, and against which he tests the adequacy of his formulations and hypotheses" (Murray & Kluckhohn, 1953, p. 9).

Although internal and external proceedings are usually closely integrated, at times they may be separate or even disparate. Clearly, if the important proceedings of an individual's life are solely *internal,* his overt behavior may appear quite unsatisfactory from society's point of view. In fact, Murray and Kluckhohn note that it is perhaps completely inaccurate to say that a person exhibiting psychotic behavior has "gone out of his mind." Instead we might well say that he is wholly "in his mind" and "out of the external, objective world."

Proceedings usually occupy relatively short periods of time. Murray and Kluckhohn (1953) suggest that it is also desirable to construe an individual's life according to relatively long periods of time, each of which might be considered a sequence of proceedings. Thus infancy, childhood, adolescence, and so on, constitute convenient and important ways of dividing up an individual's past history.

Unity-Themas

Murray has argued that the period of early childhood may be singularly important in determining an individual's later reactions to needs and press. He found, as a consequence of the efforts to draw personality portraits of his subjects,[5] that often a particular pattern of related needs and press originating in early childhood comes to be a dominant force in the individual's personality. This "key to his unique nature" is called a *unity-thema.* In Murray's (1962) words:

> Experience was to teach us that, though the reasons for many of the subject's responses were mysterious and much of his past entirely out of reach, it was possible to find in most individuals an underlying reaction system, termed by us *unity-thema,* which was the key to his unique nature. I say "key" because if one assumed the activity of this unity-thema many superficially unintelligible actions and expressions became, as it were, psychologically inevitable. A *unity-thema* is a compound of interrelated—collaborating or conflicting—dominant needs that are linked to press to which the individual was exposed on one or more particular occasions, gratifying or trau-

---

[5] The assessments were carried out by a Diagnostic Council of five judges. The council interviewed, tested (with a variety of tests and questionnaires), and independently rated each subject over a period of two years. Finally, "At the end of all the examinations a five-hour meeting was held on each S [subject] at which all the reports and marks were read and discussed and a final mark for each variable was decided upon by majority vote" (Murray, 1962, p. 265).

matic, in early childhood. The thema may stand for a primary infantile experience or a subsequent reaction formation to that experience. But, whatever its nature and genesis, it repeats itself in many forms during later life (pp. 604–5).

Murray's Approach to Personality Assessment

Murray and his colleagues assumed that needs are sometimes *manifest* (observed in overt behavior), sometimes *latent* (inhibited, covert, or imaginal), and that the strength of a need must be measured in both of its forms.

The Assessment of Manifest Needs

The four major criteria for estimating the strength of manifest needs from overt action are: (1) frequency of action, (2) duration of action, (3) intensity of action, and (4) readiness to act. Frequency and duration are simple to measure, since they require only a calendar and a watch. When we say that a friend "needs a lot of sleep," our inference is usually based on these measures and instruments. The third criterion, intensity, may be measured by a graded scaling of responses to a given situation. For example, Murray (1962) suggests the following gradation for *n* Aggression: "criticism given with a smile, a laugh at the O's [other's] expense, a mild insult, a severe accusation, a violent push, a blow in the face, murder" (p. 254). Finally, readiness to act may be measured by the latency of a response (e.g., "I was asleep as soon as my head touched the pillow") or the appropriateness of the object to which it is directed (e.g., it takes a rather hungry man to eat shoe leather).

The Assessment of Latent Needs

Dealing with needs which are not objectified in action is more complicated. Consider the theoretical nature of latent needs.

> The chief differences between an imaginal need and an overt need is that the former enjoys in reading, or represents in fantasy, in speech or in play what the latter objectifies in serious action. Thus, instead of pushing through a difficult enterprise, an S [subject] will have visions of doing it or read books about others doing it; or instead of injuring an enemy, he will express his dislike of him to others or enjoy playing an aggressive role in a play. . . . The term "imaginal need" is convenient for the expression "the amount of need tension that exhibits itself in thought and make-believe action" (Murray, 1962, p. 257).[6]

---

[6] Apart from interest in imaginal or latent needs as phenomena in their own right, Murray (1962) notes: "Also, what is imaginal to-day may be objectified tomorrow" (p. 257).

The logic of assessment of latent needs follows from this description. A strong latent need "is apt to perceive and apperceive what it 'wants' . . . an S [subject] under the influence of a drive has a tendency to 'project' into surrounding objects some of the imagery associated with the drive that is operating" (Murray, 1962, p. 260). This reasoning gave rise to the development of a now widely used projective technique, the Thematic Apperception Test (TAT).

The TAT materials consist of a set of 20 pictures, with separate sets for males and females and for children. Most of the pictures show at least one person, thus providing someone with whom the respondent can presumably empathize. The subject is given the following instructions:

> This is a test of your creative imagination. I shall show you a picture and I want you to make up a plot or story for which it might be used as an illustration. What is the relation of the individuals in the picture? What has happened to them? What are their present thoughts and feelings? What will be the outcome? Do your very best. Since I am asking you to indulge your literary imagination you may make your story as long and detailed as you wish (Murray, 1962, p. 532).

One of the TAT pictures appears in Figure 9–1. (To better understand the discussion which follows, it may be helpful for the reader to respond to the picture, according to the preceding instructions.) Subjects' responses to the TAT cards, which the examiner usually records verbatim, can be scored for the presence of needs as well as press and unity-themes. Both the use of the test and an example of how other data are used to assess personality in terms of Murray's personology can be seen through a brief examination of a case study (Murray, 1962).

The Case of Virt

Virt was a Russian immigrant who came to the United States when he was 11 years old. As a Russian Jew living near the German border during World War I, he had suffered religious persecutions in childhood. Virt's autobiographical account of his childhood experiences is scored (in parentheses) for various press and needs.

> Recollections of those persecutions . . . still prey on my mind: dead bodies with torn limbs dragged in heaps to the cemetery; my uncle forced to dig his own grave before my eyes; my aunt shot in cold blood at my hand; bombs thrown a few feet before me (p Aggression). . . . Suddenly the door [to a cellar in which he and his mother had been trapped without water (p Lack: Water, Food)] was blown open . . . my mother and I stood quite near. I at once ran out to the next building, intent on procuring food and drink . . . I

FIGURE 9–1

Example of a TAT Picture

darted across through the bullets and shrapnel and forced open the door of the next building. Imagine the fright of the inmates. They refused to let me go back (p Dominance: Restraint: Enforced Separation from Mother) (Murray, 1962, p. 535).

Another persistent recollection which Virt reported concerned the time, when he was eight, that his mother left him alone (p Insupport: Separation from Mother) in a Warsaw hotel while she went to get their passports.

"Tired of staying at home, I ventured out," he writes. "I determined in some way or other to go to her" (n Succorance for Mother). He happened to pick up a transfer, took the first car and eventually found his mother. "Lucky for me it was the right car. Otherwise I would have been lost in a strange large city. The surprise of my mother was great when she saw me" (Murray, 1962, p. 535).

Virt was given part of the TAT, and his response to Picture Number 11 (Figure 9–1) follows.

> Mother and boy were living happily. She had no husband (Oedipus complex). Her son was her only support (n Nurturance for Mother). Then the boy got into bad company and participated in a gang robbery, playing a minor part. He was found out and sentenced to five years in prison. Picture represents him parting with his mother. Mother is sad, feeling ashamed of him. Boy is very much ashamed. He cares more about the harm he did his mother than about going to prison. He gets out for good behaviour but the mother dies. He repents for what he has done but he finds that his reputation is lost in the city. No one will employ him. He again meets bad companions and in despair he joins them in crime. However, he meets a girl with whom he falls in love. She suggests that he quit the gang. He decides to quit after one more hold-up. He is caught and sent to prison. In the meantime, the girl has met someone else. When he comes out he is quite old and spends the rest of his life repenting in misery (Murray, 1962, pp. 537–39).

The story is scored for p Dominance ("bad influences" and the externalization of blame), n Acquisition (robbery), p Aggression (the punishment of prison), p Loss (mother's death), n Abasement (the remorse which the boy feels), p Rejection (the girl friend's preference for a rival). The complex theme regarding the boy's mother is repeated with his girl friend (i.e., p Rejection is substituted for p Loss). Murray (1962) argues that the fantasy meaningfully reflects Virt's personality; that is, the boy in the story *is* Virt.

> The subject presents the Son-Lover thema followed by the death of the mother, and later the Love thema followed by desertion. In neither case is union between the lovers achieved. We also find a conflict between mother and son over the question of crime and gang robberies. Since the subject's desire for achievement and marriage are much restricted by poverty, and since his much-respected mother was a smuggler in Russia, we may suppose that temptations to rob and cheat have at times occurred to him.
>
> The conflict of the hero with the mother brings to mind some incidents mentioned by the subject when giving his childhood memories. He said that he had occasionally quarrelled with his mother because she nagged him. Once when he was thirteen he ran away and got a job in Pittsburgh. Another time he ran away to Newport News on account of a romantic longing he had for adventure. In regard to the repentance theme in the . . . story the subject said in his introspections: "That's the way I would feel. If I took my car and stayed out all night I would be ashamed for having hurt my mother (n Nurturance for Mother), not for anything

I might have done. We are really close to each other. She confides everything to me (p Succorance). She doesn't get on well with my father." The subject's conscience is a personal one. It prohibits him from hurting the woman he loves. He is not guided by an impersonal ethical standard (p. 539).

On the basis of Virt's response to TAT Picture Number 11, his responses to four other TAT pictures, and the autobiographical material, Murray (1962) finds "a reverberation of actual experiences and fantasies which occurred in childhood" (p. 544) and suggests that they reflect an underlying unity-theme of "Tragic Love." In this brief example, we have seen the identification of needs, press, proceedings (in the autobiographical passages), and the inference of a fundamental unity-thema.

Major Functions of Personality

What is the role of personality? Most personality psychologists have been content with implicitly assuming that personality serves to guide and determine human behavior. Murray and Kluckhohn (1953) have gone farther and specified six major functions of personality.

Reduction of Need Tension

Among the six major functions of personality, according to Murray and Kluckhohn, the reduction of need tension is the nearest thing to an "all-embracing principle." Needs lead to tension and tension, in turn, leads to tension reduction. What must be attended to and investigated is the initiating state of tension rather than the end-state in which the person finds himself as a result of the increased tension. This orientation, Murray and Kluckhohn (1953) note, can explain some otherwise peculiar events: ". . . we are provided with an explanation of suicide and of certain other apparently anti-biological effects as so many forms of riddance of intolerable suffering. Suicide does not have *adaptive* (survival) value but it does have *adjustive* value for the organism. Suicide is *functional* because it abolishes painful tension" (p. 36).

Generation of Tension

Whereas Murray's personology and Freud's psychoanalysis agree that the reduction of tension is a major function of personality, an important difference between the two theoretical camps becomes evident with a statement of Murray and Kluckhohn's analysis of the second major function of personality, the generation of tension.

Murray and Kluckhohn argue that it is not a tensionless state which is satisfying, as psychoanalysis assumes, but rather it is the *process* of reducing tension which creates satisfaction. We are satisfied to the degree that we are able to reduce the tensions which we experience. The thirstier a man is, the more likely he will be to enjoy a cold beer; the more homesick a person is, the more pleasure he will gain from a letter or telephone call from home; and the lower a student's grade-point average, the more an *A* will be appreciated. "A tensionless state is sometimes the ideal of those who suffer from chronic anxiety or resentment or a frustrated sex drive; but, as a rule, the absence of positive need-tensions—no appetite, no curiosity, no desire for fellowship, no zest—is very distressing" (Murray & Kluckhohn, 1953, p. 36).

Self-Expression

The third major function of personality involves the brief, spontaneous, and free expression of one's most basic nature which all persons experience from time to time. Such self-expression, which may run the gamut from daydreaming to quite intense emotional excitement, is engaged in for no end other than the intrinsic pleasure which it creates.

Scheduling

A fourth major personality function concerns decision-making. Often our decisions involve choices between conflicting goals or aims (e.g., "Should I study on this beautiful spring afternoon, or should I spend the time outside? If I study, should I read my psychology assignment or write my English theme? If I go outside, should I play tennis or go fishing?"). To reduce or resolve such conflicts, we typically schedule our time so that we can satisfy as many of our major needs as possible.

Adjusting of Aspiration Levels

Very few persons are capable of fully satisfying all of their needs. The frustration which accompanies unsatisfied needs often leads persons to adopt a strategy of lowering their levels of aspiration ("Since my high school grades are poor, I'll be content to go to a less prestigious college") or accepting alternative goals ("Since my high school grades are poor, I'll go into my father's business rather than go to college") in an effort to maximize the satisfaction of needs and the attainment of end-states. Murray and Kluckholm (1953) point to the practice of Yoga, in which all external and social needs are rejected, as an example of the extreme use of this strategy. In contrast, they note that democratic ideologies

> . . . have encouraged a high level of extrovert aspiration for every individual (e.g., in the United States: a large fortune, leading to privilege and prestige) and, thus, have opposed the natural tendency to reduce the level after repeated failures. The over-all result, in the United States, has been an extraordinary degree of material progress with a high standard of living, on the one hand, and an equally extraordinary degree of discontent (griping about the lack of material "necessities") on the other. The ideology, in other words, prevents many individuals from achieving happiness (p. 40).

Conforming to Social Expectations

Murray and Kluckhohn believe that the accommodation of the unique individual and his personality to the conventions of society is the "most difficult and painful" of the six major personality functions. Clearly, for society to function smoothly, each individual member must learn to conform to social expectations to some degree. A person who refuses to conform to society's rules, standards, or ideals is likely to be ineffective and unhappy. Nevertheless, there are also undesirable consequences if excessive conformity occurs either in a single individual or in a whole culture. Sometimes, for example, so-called unacceptable behavior is necessary to uphold one's ideals and principles. In fact, many important and ultimately functional social changes required daring nonconformity from members of society. The American Revolution, the Protestant Revolution, and the Industrial Revolution all began because individuals or groups of individuals acted in opposition to usual cultural and social expectations. It is because conformity is both necessary in some realms of behavior and undesirable in others that the regulation of conformity to social expectations is a critical function of personality.

THE NEED TO ACHIEVE

Prominent among the lasting accomplishments of Murray's dispositional approach to personality is the large amount of research which it has stimulated. A prime example is the work of David C. McClelland and his colleagues on the achievement motive. For more than 25 years, McClelland has investigated the need to achieve (i.e., Murray's *n* Achievement) both theoretically and, more recently, from an extremely practical vantage point. While Murray and McClelland share a common bias concerning the nature of human personality, their basic strategies of attacking similar problems differ. Murray chose to catalog and study a large number of needs, whereas McClelland has chosen to focus his attention on a single need. McClelland justifies his approach in the following way:

> . . . concentration on a limited research problem is not necessarily narrowing; it may lead ultimately into the whole of psychology. In personality theory there is inevitably a certain impatience—a desire to solve every problem at once so as to get the "whole" personality in focus. We have proceeded the other way. By concentrating on one problem, on *one motive,* we have found in the course of our study that we have learned not only a lot about the achievement motive but other areas of personality as well (McClelland, Atkinson, Clark, & Lowell, 1953, p. vi) .

Measuring Achievement Motivation

The first step in studying the achievement motive, or any motive or personality variable for that matter, is to develop a way of measuring it. Initial experimentation in measuring the strength of a primary need, *n* Food, showed that sailors who had been deprived of food for varying lengths of time could be reliably differentiated on the basis of their fantasy responses to Murray's TAT (Atkinson & McClelland, 1948) . Following this success, it was decided to try measuring a psychogenic need, *n* Achievement, by the same technique.

Male students[7] who were exposed to various experimental conditions were asked to write stories about four TAT-type pictures. The instructions were very similar to those which Murray used with the TAT, and thus the test was presented to the students as one of creative imagination. The experimental conditions consisted of various achievement-arousing situations (subjects were given success or failure experiences) and nonachievement-arousing situations (the experimental tasks were presented in a casual, relaxed atmosphere) . The stories were scored for a number of different categories related to achievement motivation, and those scoring categories which successfully differentiated subjects who had been exposed to varying degrees of achievement arousal were defined as measures of *n* Achievement.

Research on Achievement Motivation

The basic technique of measuring achievement motivation by fantasy was used subsequently by McClelland and others in a wide

---

[7] Most of the research on the achievement motive has been done with male subjects. The small number of studies which have investigated *n* Achievement in females points, not surprisingly, to sex differences in the mode of expression of the motive.

variety of investigations. The antecedents and development of achievement motivation has been studied, and it appears that the origins of *n* Achievement (abbreviated *n* Ach) are

. . . rooted in early training for independence, subsequent harness-ing of the dispositions so acquired for socially defined achievement situations, support of the n Ach by warm but demanding parental models, and considerable experience with emotional satisfaction in achievement situations. Certainly such a pattern does suggest that the n Achiever should be experienced in maximizing payoffs, relatively free from anxiety about failure, and therefore, efficient at those tasks he chooses to attempt (Birney, 1968, p. 878).

The modified TAT fantasy measure of the achievement motive has made possible a unique type of psychological investigation. Since the scoring system for TAT stories is applicable to any prose ma-terial, McClelland has been able to study *n* Achievement in indi-viduals and groups of individuals who lived in the past but left written accounts of their lives. For example, McClelland and his associates (McClelland et al., 1953) have studied the relationship between independence training and achievement motivation in a number of North American Indian tribes by scoring their folktales for *n* Achievement.

An even more ambitious task in the same vein has involved Mc-Clelland's attempt to explain the economic growth and decline of cultures in terms of the achievement motive. In one aspect of this work, a nation's mean achievement motivation is determined by examining the children's readers of each country for *n* Achievement. By scoring children's stories which were read during the period from 1920 to 1929 in 23 different countries, McClelland (1961) at-tempted to "predict" the economic growth of the countries between 1929 and 1950. The achievement motive found in the children's stories was correlated +.53 with McClelland's index of economic growth, a measure based on changes in the consumption of elec-tricity as related to the deviation from expected growth. McClelland (1961) concludes from this and similar studies that the children's stories reflect ". . . the motivational level of the adults at the time they are published, perhaps particularly of the adults responsible for the education of children . . ." (p. 102).

A Program for Developing Achievement Motivation

More recently, McClelland (1965; McClelland & Winter, 1969) has sought to develop a theory of motive acquisition and a program for increasing human motivation in terms of some very practical problems. Specifically, McClelland has designed a formal course to increase the achievement motivation of individuals (particularly businessmen). Realizing that most psychologists have considered the acquisition of motives in adulthood to be difficult or impossible, McClelland (1965) says:

> . . . we were encouraged by the successful efforts of two quite different groups of "change agents"—operant conditioners [see Chapter 15] and missionaries. . . . The operant conditioners have not been encumbered by any elaborate theoretical apparatus; they do not believe motives exist anyway, and continue demonstrating vigorously that if you want a person to make a response, all you have to do is elicit it and reward it. . . . Like operant conditioners, the missionaries have gone ahead changing people because they have believed it possible . . . common-sense observation yields dozens of cases of adults whose motivational structure has seemed to be quite radically and permanently altered by the educational efforts of the Communist party, Mormon, or other devout missionaries (p. 322).

The supposition that an individual's motivational structure can change in adulthood has several implications for revising traditional theories of motivation. Perhaps the most important of these revisions, according to McClelland, is the proposition that *all human motives are learned;* even motives of biological origin (e.g., hunger or sex) cannot be observed until some learning has occurred so that they are associated with cues which can indicate their presence or absence.

McClelland (1965) formally defines motives as " 'affectively toned associative networks' arranged in a hierarchy of strength or importance within a given individual" (p. 322). Presumably these hierarchies are themselves learned, and defining motives in this way immediately suggests how motives might be changed. Specifically, if motives are viewed as associative networks arranged in a hierarchical order, then the problem of changing motives in adulthood becomes one of introducing new motives or moving up old ones in an individual's existing hierarchy. In short, the problem has now been defined as a problem in learning.

The next step is to determine what kind of learning experiences will increase a particular motive's presence or position in an individual's hierarchy. McClelland's initial efforts drew upon four types of available information. First, experimental work with animals suggested that the appropriate timing of learning sequences and reward for desired responses would both be essential ingredients of any educational program in motivation change. Second, from experiments in human learning, McClelland borrowed such principles as the careful distribution of practice and the recitation, repetition, and attribution of meaning to what is being learned. Third, Mc-

Clelland felt that his courses should have those characteristics which were often said to be effective in psychotherapy. Accordingly, the "teachers" were instructed to be warm, honest, and not overly directive with their "students" (cf. Rogers' client-centered therapy, Chapter 11). Finally, McClelland drew from attitude-change research an emphasis on the importance of such factors as prestige suggestion and affiliation with new reference groups.

The Research Strategy

In borrowing from a wide range of psychological knowledge to find principles for his motive acquisition program, McClelland's initial research strategy can be described as "subtractive" rather than "additive." That is, all possible potent variables are first tried, and later each individual variable is deleted, one at a time, to assess its part in the overall outcome. McClelland (1965) explains the scientific and practical advantages of this "shotgun" strategy.

Despite the fact that many of these variables seem limited in application to the learning situation in which they were studied, we have tried to make use of information from all these sources in designing our "motive acquisition" program and in finding support for the general propositions that have emerged from our studies so far. For our purpose has been above all to produce an effect large enough to be measured. Thus, we have tried to profit by all that is known about how to facilitate learning or produce personality or attitude change. For, if we could not obtain a substantial effect with all factors working to produce it, there would be no point to studying the effects of each factor taken one at a time. Such a strategy also has the practical advantage that we are in the position of doing our best to "deliver the goods" to our course participants since they were giving us their time and attention to take part in a largely untried educational experience (p. 323).

The Program

McClelland's (1965) courses for developing *n* Achievement are typically taught to groups of from 9 to 25 businessmen and over a short but highly concentrated period (the optimal period has been found to be somewhere between 6 and 14 days, 12 to 18 hours per day). Most of the courses have been taught in India, but courses have also been held in the United States, Japan, Mexico, and Spain. As a result of the experience gained from these initial courses, McClelland (1965) has abstracted 12 theoretical propositions or guidelines for motive change. Although these principles have evolved from a program designed to increase a particular motive, McClelland believes that they should be applicable to the development of motivational dispositions in general.

The first thing one must do in any motivational development program is create confidence that the program will work. Proposition 1 states: *"The more reasons an individual has in advance to believe that he can, will, or should develop a motive, the more educational attempts designed to develop that motive are likely to succeed."* McClelland has invoked the scientific authority of research, the prestige of Harvard University (where he was chairman of the Department of Social Relations), and all of the suggestive power which experimenter enthusiasm can produce in "selling" the program and setting high expectations for the participants before the actual training begins.[8]

In Proposition 2, the importance of rational arguments in introducing the purpose of the course is stressed: *"The more an individual perceives that developing a motive is consistent with the demands of reality (and reason), the more educational attempts designed to develop that motive are likely to succeed."*

Proposition 3 provides the first hint of what the training program itself entails. *"The more thoroughly an individual develops and clearly conceptualizes the associative network defining the motive, the more likely he is to develop the motive."* With this principle in mind, it is easy to understand why McClelland chooses an explanation of the meaning of achievement motivation as one of the first steps in training. All participants are asked to take the fantasy test of *n* Achievement at the outset and are taught to score it for themselves. McClelland (1965) says: ". . . we point out that if they think their score is too low, that can be easily remedied, since we teach them how to code and how to write stories saturated with n Achievement; in fact, that is one of the basic purposes of the course: to teach them to think constantly in n Achievement terms" (p. 325). This aspect of the training involves more than merely teaching a label or the rote use of certain expressions. It is an effort to change personal constructs (cf. Kelly, Chapter 12) by substituting "new constructs ('You should become an achiever') for old neurotic or ineffective ones ('rather than being such a slob') . . ." (McClelland, 1965, p. 326).

The next step is to tie changes in thought to changes in action, as seen in Proposition 4: *"The more an individual can link the newly developed network to related actions, the more the change in both thought and action is likely to occur and endure."* Earlier work by McClelland had shown that persons high in achievement motiva-

---

[8] It is interesting to note that what many experimenters consider "error" and try to exclude, McClelland has purposely built into his program.

tion (1) like challenges in their work and prefer moderate risk situations, (2) seek concrete feedback as to how well they are doing, and (3) like to take personal responsibility for achieving work goals. In order to develop these characteristics in the course participants, McClelland makes use of a specially designed business game which allows the participants to learn achievement-oriented actions by both playing the game and observing others play.

> The game is designed to mimic real life: they must order parts to make certain objects (e.g., a Tinker Toy model bridge) after having estimated how many they think they can construct in the time alloted. They have a real chance to take over, plan the whole game, learn from how well they are doing (use of feedback), and show a paper profit or loss at the end. While they are surprised often that they should have to display their real action characteristics this way in public, they usually get emotionally involved in observing how they behave under pressure of a more or less "real" work situation (McClelland, 1965, p. 326).

Behavior developed in the game situation must then be generalized to actual business situations. Accordingly, Proposition 5 states: *"The more an individual can link the newly conceptualized association-action complex (or motive) to events in his everyday life, the more likely the motive complex is to influence his thoughts and actions outside the training experience."* In this regard, examples of career development are explored by means of actual case studies which the group discusses.

However clear it may become to a participant that an achievement orientation is applicable to actual business experience, each participant must be convinced that he, as an individual, is suited to such a way of life. This point is made in Proposition 6: *"The more an individual can perceive and experience the newly conceptualized motive as an improvement in the self-image, the more the motive is likely to influence his future thoughts and actions."* The importance of candid self-appraisal is emphasized to the participants by telling them of an incident which occurred in one of the courses. A participant decided that he did not wish to become an achievement-oriented person. This honest self-evaluation led the man to leave the course, quit his managerial position, and subsequently retire and become a chicken farmer. (This case is the exception rather than the rule, however, since most participants come to view achievement motivation as desirable.) Participants are aided in their evaluation of the influence of increased achievement motivation on their self-images through such techniques as individual counseling, group dynamics sessions, and silent group meditation.

Just as participants must reconcile increased achievement motivation with their self-concepts, so too must they come to feel that their increased *n* Achievement is in line with, or an improvement on, the existing popular or traditional cultural values of their own country. Proposition 7 states: *"The more an individual can perceive and experience the newly conceptualized motive as an improvement on prevailing cultural values, the more the motive is likely to influence his future thoughts and actions."* After having examined their own personal values about achievement motivation, the course participants engage in an analysis of the values of their culture with regard to achievement by analyzing children's stories, myths, popular religion, customs, and so on. For example, in the United States, participants discuss the way in which high achievement motivation can interfere with a person's popularity. Besides rational discussions of such problems, role playing is employed to help the participants understand and accept their new motivational sets in relation to their cultural values.

At the end of the course, each participant writes an essay outlining his aspirations and plans for the next two years. Emphasis is placed on describing one's future realistically and on setting moderate (rather than inordinately high) goals. The essay not only serves to assist participants in making use of the practical implications of the course but also provides a basis for further evaluation of the candidates and the program. During the two-year follow-up period, questionnaires are sent to the course participants every six months, both to remind them of the goals they have set for themselves and to assess their progress. These procedures have led to the formulation of Propositions 8 and 9: *"The more an individual commits himself to achieving concrete goals in life related to the newly formed motives, the more the motive is likely to influence his future thoughts and actions,"* and *"The more an individual keeps a record of his progress toward achieving goals to which he is committed, the more the newly formed motive is likely to influence his future thoughts and actions."*

As mentioned previously, McClelland and his associates have found it helpful for the course instructors (consulting psychologists) to be warm, rewarding, and somewhat nondirective in their dealings with the participants, a result consistent with an earlier study which showed that fathers of high *n* Achievement boys were warmer, more encouraging, and less directive than fathers of boys low on this measure (Rosen & D'Andrade, 1959). Proposition 10 states: *"Changes in motives are more likely to occur in an interpersonal atmosphere in which the individual feels warmly but honestly supported and respected by others as a person capable of guiding and directing his own future behavior."*

The course is structured as a retreat for self-study. Whenever possible, the sessions are conducted in an isolated resort hotel to enhance concentration and exclude outside interference. Furthermore, there is considerable evidence to show that changes in a person's opinions, attitudes, or beliefs are greatly facilitated if he joins a new reference group. In addition to fostering the emergence of a new reference group by having participants study and live together for the duration of the course, McClelland provides signs of identification with the group (e.g., knowledge of the n Achievement coding system and membership certificates). Moreover, he tries to arrange to have all participants in a group come from the same community so that, after leaving the course, the new reference group will remain physically intact and will help maintain the newly acquired motivation. These procedures are reflected in Propositions 11 and 12: *"Changes in motives are more likely to occur the more the setting dramatizes the importance of self-study and lifts it out of the routine of everyday life,"* and *"Changes in motives are more likely to occur and persist if the new motive is a sign of membership in a new reference group."*

Table 9–3 summarizes McClelland's program for motive development in terms of the procedures used (independent variables), the

TABLE 9–3

Variables Hypothesized by McClelland to Affect Motive Change

A Input or Independent Variables	*B* Intervening Variables	*C* Output or Dependent Variables
1. Goal setting for the person (P1, P11)*	Arousal of associative network (salience)	Duration and/or extensiveness of changes in:
2. Acquisition of n Achievement associative network (P2, P3, P4, P5)	Experiencing and labeling the associative network	1. n Achievement associative network
3. Relating new network to superordinate networks	Variety of cues to which network is linked	2. Related actions: use of feedback, moderate risk taking, etc.
Reality (P2)	Interfering associations assimilated or bypassed	3. Innovations (job improvements)
The self (P6)	by reproductive inter-	4. Use of time and money
Cultural values (P7)	ference	5. Entrepreneurial success as defined by
4. Personal goal setting (P8)		nature of job held and
5. Knowlege of progress (P3, P4, P9)		its rewards
6. Personal warmth and support (P10)	Positive affect associated with network	
7. Support of reference group (P11, P12)		

* P1, P11, etc., refer to the numbered propositions in the text.
Source: From McClelland, 1965.

outcomes (dependent variables), and the theoretical processes that are hypothesized to mediate between treatment and results (intervening variables).

Results of the Program

How successful have McClelland's achievement motivation courses been? On a number of concrete, economic measures, it appears that businessmen who participated in the courses increased their achievement motivation substantially more than businessmen who applied for admission but were not accepted (i.e., control subjects). As can be seen in Table 9–4, course participants and controls were similar in the two-year period before the course. However, following the course, significantly more participants than controls were rated as engaging in a high level of business activity (i.e., actions which directly improve business), working longer hours, starting new businesses, and employing more workers in their businesses (McClelland & Winter, 1969).

TABLE 9–4

Examples of the Economic Effects of McClelland's Achievement Motivation Courses

		Before Course 1962–64	After Course 1964–66
1. Rated at highest business activity level*	Participants	18%	51%
	Controls	22%	25%
2. Working longer hours	Participants	7%	20%
	Controls	11%	7%
3. Starting new business	Participants	4%	22%
	Controls	7%	8%
4. Employing more people at end of 2-year period	Participants	35%	59%
	Controls	31%	33%

* Subjects' business activity was rated on a four-point scale, with the highest level being exemplified by an action which directly resulted in an improvement in a business venture (e.g., increased profit).
Source: Data from McClelland and Winter, 1969.

Additionally, it is interesting to examine a case study which illustrates the potential impact of the course.

A short time after participating in one of our courses in India, a 47-year-old businessman rather suddenly and dramatically decided to quit his excellent job and go into the construction business on his own in a big way. A man with some means of his own, he had had a very successful career as employee-relations manager for a large oil firm. His job involved adjusting management-employee difficulties, negotiating union contracts, etc. He was well-to-do, well thought of in his company, and admired in the community, but he was restless because he found his job increasingly boring. At the time of the course his original n Achievement score was not very high and he was thinking of retiring and living in England where his son was studying. In an interview, 8 months later, he said the course had served not so much to "motivate" him but to "crystallize" a lot of ideas he had vaguely or half consciously picked up about work and achievement all through his life. It provided him with a new language (he still talked in terms of standards of excellence, blocks, moderate risk, goal anticipation, etc.), a new construct which served to organize those ideas and explain to him why he was bored with his job, despite his obvious success. He decided he wanted to be an n-Achievement-oriented person, that he would be unhappy in retirement, and that he should take a risk, quit his job, and start in business on his own. He acted on his decision and in 6 months had drawn plans and raised over $1,000,-000 to build the tallest building in his large city to be called the "Everest Apartments." He is extremely happy in his new activity because it means selling, promoting, trying to wangle scarce materials, etc. His first building is partway up and he is planning two more (McClelland, 1965, p. 332).

Alternative Measures of the Need to Achieve

In our discussion of both Murray and McClelland, we have made frequent mention of the TAT. For Murray, the value of this instrument is "its capacity to reveal things that the patient is unwilling to tell or unable to tell because he is unconscious of them" (1951, p. 577). In contrast, McClelland used the TAT to consciously teach people to think and be achievement oriented. A correlational study by Holmes and Tyler (1968) has compared the value of the TAT as an assessment tool with more direct procedures for measuring *n* Achievement, and the results of their study have implications for both the nature of the instrument and the theoretical issue of whether needs are conscious or unconscious.

Using undergraduate males as subjects, Holmes and Tyler selected two types of criterion measures of *n* Achievement: (1) course grades and (2) performance on laboratory tasks (computational and digit symbol[9] tests). Four TAT cards were shown to each subject, and his responses were scored for *n* Achievement both according to a standard system devised by Atkinson (1958) and by having two judges give their *global* impressions of the subjects' responses on a four-point scale. Additionally, two types of self-report measures

---

[9] In the digit symbol test, which is used in some intelligence tests, the subject is presented with a key containing a symbol for each of nine numbers. His task is to substitute the symbols for as many numbers as he can in a fixed time period.

were used. For one, the *self-peer ranking* measure, each subject was asked to list the names of 10 male fellow students whom he knew well. He was then given a description of what is meant by *n* Achievement and asked to rate each of the 10 friends as being higher or lower on *n* Achievement than he felt himself to be. Finally, each subject was asked to state whether he would be likely to work harder or less hard than each friend on an academic task. The second self-report was a *self-rating* measure in which subjects were simply asked to compare their own *n* Achievement with that of "students in general" on a 16-point scale. The correlations between the four assessment measures and the three criteria are presented in Table 9–5. The only correlation that was significantly different from zero was that between self-peer ranking and grades.

TABLE 9–5

Correlations between TAT Scores or Self-Ratings and Criterion Measures of *n* Achievement

	Assessment Method			
	TAT_1 (Atkinson Scoring)	TAT_2 (Global Scoring)	Self-Peer Ranking	Self-Rating
Criterion				
Grades	−.01	−.10	+.33*	+.17
Computational test	−.08	−.05	†	−.14
Digit symbol test	−.01	−.01	†	+.05

* Statistically significant, $p < .005$.
† According to Holmes and Tyler these correlations are not significantly different from zero, but the actual values are not reported.
Source: Prepared from Holmes and Tyler, 1968.

In discussing these results, the investigators make two observations that are particularly relevant to the issues we have been considering. First, they note that the evidence clearly suggests than *n* Achievement is a conscious motive: ". . . when asked properly, Ss [subjects] are able to provide self-assessments which are related to long-term achievement . . . such accurate self-assessments would be impossible in the absence of knowledge about one's achievement motivation, hence it seems clear that Ss are aware of this characteristic" (1968, p. 716).

Second, Holmes and Tyler observe that their findings have substantial implications for more general issues in personality assessment. Their conclusions are consistent with others' arguments for greater reliance on direct assessment (e.g., Mischel, 1968).

> . . . the fact that the ranking measure was more accurate than the projective measure suggests that the ranking measure deserves more

use. Even if the ranking measure were only equally as accurate as the projective measure it would seem preferable to use the ranking measure since it can be administered and scored in only a few minutes by an examiner without any skill or training. This may prove to be a valuable approach for having Ss [subjects] make otherwise difficult abstract self-reports (Holmes & Tyler, 1968, p. 716).

More recently, Holmes (1971) has refined this technique further. Specifically, he noted that one weakness in the self-peer rank method, as he and Tyler originally conceived of it, was that groups of friends tend to be similar on many dimensions (cf. Newcomb, 1961), probably including their level of achievement striving.

> This [similarity] would reduce the accuracy of the measure: The degree to which the scores of two Ss will accurately reflect the difference in their levels of n Ach would be related to the degree to which the Ss used comparable reference points (peers) for reporting . . . if one used a high standard (high n Ach friends) and the other used a low standard (low n Ach friends), the rank scores of the two Ss would not be comparable and therefore of little value in predicting . . . future performance (Holmes, 1971, p. 24).

To test this reasoning, Holmes (1971) replicated the earlier Holmes and Tyler study but with the addition of a new group who rated themselves against the same—"constant"—group of peers (other students from different fraternities and sororities on campus). Relative to subjects in the original—"variable"—peer group, in which each participant compared himself with his own friends, subjects in the constant peer group showed substantial increments in predicting their actual college grades.

In a second study, Holmes (1971) was able to show that the self-peer rankings of sorority pledges during their first three weeks of college predicted their first semester grades as well as standard Scholastic Aptitude Test (SAT) scores (correlations of .54 and .59, respectively). Holmes (1971) concludes that:

> . . . [students] can make judgments about their levels of n Ach which will be predictive of grades even when no grade-relevant information is available to influence their judgments. Further, it is important to note the considerable magnitude of the correlation. This value, based on a simple straightforward measure requiring less than 15 minutes to complete, is higher than most [others] . . . which were arrived at through the more complex and allegedly more sensitive projective techniques (p. 26).

THE NEED FOR SOCIAL APPROVAL

The need for achievement is not the only need which has been the focus of extensive investigations. Similar attention has been given to the need for approval. From their work on social desirability (described in Chapter 8), Crowne and Marlowe (1964) concluded that social desirability is not only a characteristic way of responding on self-report personality inventories (i.e., a response style), but is also one manifestation of a more general personality disposition which they have called the *approval motive*. They reasoned that the tendency of persons to portray themselves in a favorable light reflects a *need for social approval*. To test the utility of this notion in predicting behavior in a variety of situations, Crowne and Marlowe performed a series of experiments in which individuals who were high and low in their need for social approval, as measured by the Marlowe-Crowne SD scale, were compared.

One study (Marlowe & Crowne, 1961) investigated reactions to a long and extremely boring experimental task. The subjects, male undergraduate students, were seen individually by the experimenter, who introduced himself as a psychologist and acted in an aloof manner to accentuate his importance and authority. After a subject completed several questionnaires (the Marlowe-Crowne and Edwards SD scales and the Barron Independence of Judgment scale), the experimenter, in a very businesslike manner, gave him the following instructions:

> Now for the experiment itself. The materials are this box and the twelve spools. I want you to take these spools, one at a time, and place them in the box. When you are finished, empty the box and refill it, one spool at a time. Continue to fill and empty the box until I tell you to stop. Use one hand and work at your own preferred speed.

While the experimenter pretended to record and time the subject's performance, the subject packed and repacked the spools for 25 minutes, at the end of which time he was asked to answer four questions about his personal reaction to the task.

It was predicted that subjects with a high need for social approval would tend to rate the boring task more favorably than would subjects with a low need for social approval. As can be seen in Table 9–6, this is exactly what happened. For each of the questions concerning their reaction to the spool-packing task, the high-need-for-approval group showed a significantly higher (i.e., more favorable) rating than the low-need-for-approval group. Crowne and Marlowe (1964) account for the findings in the following way:

> The experimenters, as a result of their prestige and authoritative manner, reflected in their title, occupation, and behavioral aloofness, were perceived by high-need-for-approval subjects as persons whose favor was worth courting. It seems not unlikely that to many

TABLE 9–6

Differences between High- and Low-*Need-for-Approval* Groups as Expressed in Attitudes toward Spool-Packing

Question	High (N = 30)* Mean	Low (N = 27) Mean	Differ-ence	Statistical Significance
How enjoyable was the task..........	2.17	−0.70	2.87	$p < .01$
How much was learned from the task..............................	5.37	3.22	2.15	$p < .02$
How important was the experiment scientifically.......................	7.37	5.67	1.70	$p < .02$
Desire to participate in a similar experiment........................	3.63	1.67	1.96	$p < .02$

* N = number of subjects.
Source: Adapted from Crowne and Marlowe, 1964.

college students professors are viewed as sources of approval gratification as well as dispensers of academic rewards and punishments. In consequence, our high-need-for-approval subjects were strongly motivated to yield to the demands of the situation and to tell the experimenter that his experiment was interesting, important, personally informative, and worth returning to. In contrast subjects less approval dependent were better able to resist stating what seemed socially appropriate and offered, instead, more realistic appraisals of the experiment. Presumably, the less favorable opinions of low-need-for-approval subjects reflect, in part, the greater freedom of this group from social pressures in the formation and expression of their beliefs (p. 46).

Crowne and Marlowe's explanation in terms of the approval motive certainly accounts for the findings of their experiment in a reasonable and straightforward manner. However, it is legitimate to ask whether there might not be alternative ways of explaining the data. One such alternative construct is *social conformity*. It would be predicted that individuals who tend to yield to social pressure (e.g., by going along with the majority despite feeling that the minority is correct) would evaluate the spool-packing task more favorably than would individuals who tend to resist social pressure. The prestigious experimenter in Marlowe and Crowne's (1961) experiment represented at least an implicit form of social pressure, in that it is not generally considered socially acceptable to tell a college professor that his "ingenious" experiment is uninteresting, unimportant, and not worth an undergraduate's time and effort.

While social conformity and the need for social approval are undoubtedly related concepts, the question arises as to whether they are identical concepts. To answer this question in the experiment

TABLE 9–7

Differences between High- and Low-*Conformity* Groups as Expressed in Attitudes toward Spool-Packing

Question	High (N = 31)* Mean	Low (N = 26) Mean	Differ- ence	Statistical Significance
How enjoyable was the task............	1.31	0.39	0.92	NS†
How much was learned from the task................................	5.27	3.58	1.69	$p < .05$
How important was the experiment scientifically.........................	6.58	6.55	0.03	NS
Desire to participate in a similar experiment.........................	3.19	2.29	0.90	NS

* N = number of subjects.
† NS = not significant.
Source: Adapted from Crowne and Marlowe, 1964.

under discussion, Marlowe and Crowne classified their subjects as high or low in social conformity on the basis of their performance on the Barron Independence of Judgment scale, a paper-and-pencil measure which has been shown to discriminate between conformers and nonconformers. (A typical item on the Barron scale is: "It is easy for me to take orders and do what I am told.") When high and low conformers were compared on their ratings of the spool-packing task, only the question dealing with how much a subject had learned significantly differentiated between the two groups of subjects (see Table 9–7). Recall that the task was rated as more favorable by the high-need-for-approval subjects than by the low-need-for-approval subjects on *all four* of the questions (see Table 9–6). Thus, the concept of approval motive is better at predicting the results of the spool-packing experiment than the concept of conformity. Although there is a moderately high correlation between the Independence of Judgment scale and the Marlowe-Crowne SD scale ($-.54$), the two theoretical concepts are not identical.

If need for approval is related to a paper-and-pencil measure of social conformity, it is even more likely to be related to a situation involving genuine social pressure and actual consequences for conforming. In one experiment reported by Crowne and Marlowe (1964), co-eds were told that they were going to participate in a study of perceptual discrimination. After completing the Marlowe-Crowne SD scale, the subject and four students (two males and two females), who posed as subjects but were actually confederates of the experimenter, were shown a series of 20 slides, each containing two clusters of dots. Each slide was presented for one second, and the subject's task was to tell which of the two clusters of dots was larger. In fact, the discrimination of the larger cluster was virtually unambiguous and required no special ability. Of the 20 trials, 16 were conformity trials" in which the four confederates each gave the *incorrect* answer (i.e., chose the smaller cluster).

The results were clear-cut. As predicted, high-need-for-approval subjects yielded to the majority's incorrect judgments on 59 percent of the critical trials, whereas low-need-for-approval subjects yielded to the majority on 34 percent of the critical trials (a statistically significant difference, $p < .02$). The finding supports Crowne and Marlowe's (1964) contention that social conformity constitutes "a means of satisfying a need for approval from others" (p. 73).

Crowne and Marlowe's efforts to understand the influence of social desirability on self-report inventories began by postulating a propulsive disposition—the approval motive—which would account for the tendency of some people to present themselves in a favorable light. Their basic strategy has been to find the behavioral correlates of the need for social approval outside the sphere of test-taking behavior. Although the study of the need for social approval is by no means finished, Crowne and Marlowe have made it clear that the construct is useful for predicting a variety of behaviors. In addition to having a greater tendency to evaluate a very dull and boring task favorably and to being more conforming—the behavioral correlates which have been discussed—persons with a high need for social approval (as compared to persons with low approval motivation) are more likely to give popular word associations, to set conservative goals in risk-taking situations, to be responsive to social reward in verbal conditioning, and to be susceptible to persuasion.

LIABILITIES OF THE DISPOSITIONAL STRATEGY

Four of the more cogent limitations of the dispositional strategy will be discussed in this section. The dispositional strategy (1) "borrows" its theory from other views, (2) deals only with static man and ignores the significant processes of personality development and change, (3) fails to provide sound criteria regarding when dispositions will and will not be manifest in behavior, and (4) places excessive reliance on the self-report inventory, an assessment tool which has serious limitations for measuring some aspects of personality.

The Dispositional Strategy Lacks Its Own Theoretical Structure

Rather than beginning the quest for critical dimensions of personality from a theoretical base, dispositional psychologists typically search for traits, types, or needs in a "shotgun," empirical fashion. The dispositional strategy has, in fact, given rise to very few theoretical constructs of its own. Instead, dispositional psychologists have had to borrow theoretical ideas from other strategies in order to explain and make sense of orderly patterns uncovered in their research. We saw, for instance, that Cattell used the term "ego strength," borrowed from psychoanalytic theory, to both label and help us understand what he had found in "source trait C."

Even the term "trait" itself was borrowed (from genetics), and it still remains unclear in most discussions how much similarity is intended between the biological and the psychological concept. Both

Allport and Williams, for example, borrow the facts as well as the concepts of biology to argue for a dispositional approach to personality.

When terms such as "ego strength" and "introversion" are employed, empirical findings do in fact find a "theoretical home" and can more easily be associated with other personality variables. The theory employed, however, is not itself a dispositional one; rather, the data have been placed in a foster home. Although dispositional psychologists employ theoretical notions in their work, for the most part they have not developed their own theories of personality and are therefore dependent on other strategies for theoretical progress.

The Dispositional Strategy Deals Only with Static Man

As much as any other strategy, the dispositional view has given rise to longitudinal data—that is, the characteristics of people have been measured at various points in time (e.g., in childhood and again in adulthood), and similarities and differences have been noted. While these data certainly indicate some of the consistency in behavior predicted by the dispositionalist, changes over time are also apparent for most individuals. The dispositional strategy has paid little attention to these changes and has hardly concerned itself with the *processes* that might underlie the initial development or the changing complexion over time of a person's traits, types, or needs. The strategy has generally restricted itself to a *description* of personality, rather than offering an explanation of its dynamic aspects. When and how do source traits develop? Why does one behavior pattern become functionally autonomous and another not? Such questions are not simply unanswered from the dispositional perspective: the strategy does not even call upon the investigator to ask them.

A closely related point is that the dispositional strategy has contributed almost nothing to the important question of how to devise intervention procedures so that undesirable aspects of personality can be changed. Some individuals whose names are associated with the dispositional strategy (e.g., Murray, Eysenck, and McClelland) have been involved in personality change work, but their personality change approaches, like many of their basic theoretical concepts, have been borrowed from other views. Murray, whose approach to personality is based on needs, practiced as a therapist in the Harvard Psychological Clinic using procedures influenced primarily by psychoanalysis; Eysenck, a major advocate of the type approach based on factor analysis, is also one of the most ardent proponents of personality change procedures associated with the behavioral strategy (see Section V); and McClelland's program to foster and increase people's need to achieve is based on principles derived from psychoanalytic, phenomenological, and behavioral personality change principles.

In sum, the dispositional strategy tries to capture and describe *static* man, but ignores the dynamics of development, growth, and change which are also important aspects of personality.

The Dispositional Strategy Fails to Specify When Dispositions Will Be Manifest in Behavior

Recall the last of Allport's eight assumptions of a dispositional approach: "Acts, and even habits, that are inconsistent with a trait are not proof of the nonexistence of the trait." The intent of this assumption is clear: people do not always act consistently, but Allport does not want that fact to vitiate a trait approach. At some point, though, the argument is stretched to absurdity. If *all* of a person's acts are inconsistent with a trait, surely *that* is proof that he does not possess the disposition in question. Otherwise we can describe him in any dispositional way we like, without regard to his behavior. An example would be to say that a minority group has the trait of dishonesty despite the fact that you have always known its members to behave honestly, which is insidious thinking that can become dangerous. How much inconsistency can a dispositional approach endure?

Critics (e.g., Bandura & Walters, 1963; Mischel, 1968; Rotter, 1954) have repeatedly challenged the assumption that human behavior is consistent enough across situations to justify a dispositional view of man, and they have been able to muster both empirical evidence from psychological investigations and compelling everyday examples to support their argument. It is clear, for instance, that the aggressive and forward man at the office may be a milquetoast at home, completely dominated by his wife and children. Overstated, the criticism becomes unfair. Allport's point was that dispositional psychologists do not necessarily claim, for example, that a person with the trait of hostility will be hostile in every situation. But if a hostile person is not hostile in every situation, it is essential to know *when* the characteristic is likely to be operative. A fundamental deficiency of the dispositional strategy is its failure to provide a useful way of describing or predicting in which situations a disposition will and will not be manifest.

The Dispositional Strategy Places Excessive Reliance on Self-Report Inventories

With the possible exception of the psychoanalytic strategy, each of the strategies uses self-report inventories in some form or other. However, these are relied on most heavily in dispositional research, and there is evidence that the reliance may not be justified. Self-reports, while clearly useful to some extent, are more limited than dispositional psychologists recognize.

Faking

In any personality assessment procedure, the assessee can probably succeed to some extent in faking—that is, presenting himself in a different (and usually, but not always, more favorable) light than "the truth" would justify. Self-report inventories, however, are particularly susceptible to dissimulation inasmuch as the absence of an examiner lends a somewhat more impersonal and distant character to the evaluation. The assessee need not fear, for example, that facial expressions or other signs of "nervousness" will give him away when he is making an inaccurate or misleading response by simply checking a category or circling a number.

There have been numerous demonstrations that such faking can be quite successful (e.g., Anastasi, 1968; Noll, 1951; Wesman, 1952). Further, as Anastasi (1968) points out, the problem is compounded because persons of lower educational or intellectual level may be less able to fake. Various corrections, such as the Lie scale on the MMPI, may fail to detect faking by brighter or more insightful assessees while still generally, but unevenly, improving an instrument's validity.

Situational and Set Variables

Test scores of the sort obtained on self-report inventories have been shown repeatedly to be influenced by a wide variety of situational variables, including characteristics of the examiner (e.g., race, age, and sex), the testing conditions, and the stated or presumed purpose of the test.

Closely related to situational influences on self-report assessment are the response sets and styles which were discussed in Chapter 8. While it can be argued that a tendency to give the socially desirable response may itself be a personality disposition, a test that correlates highly with a social desirability scale is not measuring the theoretical construct it was originally designed to measure. Nor is it the case that these aspects of personality are the only viable personality dispositions. Rather, they may simply be the only ones that can be measured by self-report inventories.

Group Validity Data May Not Be Applicable to Individuals

As noted in Chapter 8, many self-report inventories are empirically keyed—the wording or apparent meaning of an item is considered much less important than is the type of criterion (e.g., success in business, good grades in school) with which it correlates. This approach is designed to assure the validity of the test, but because it is based on the *average performance* of many persons it may not result in valid predictions or assessment for *individuals.* Such tests, it may be argued, are *too* nomothetic. Allport (1937), who was one of the few dispositional psychologists to persistently remind his colleagues of the importance of the idiographic perspective, put it this way:

> The stimulus-situation is assumed to be identical for each subject, and his response is assumed to have constant significance. A test will assume, for example—and with some justification in terms of statistical probability—that a person . . . who confesses to keeping a diary is introverted; yet upon closer inspection (which no test can give) it may turn out that the diary is almost wholly an expense account, kept not because of introversion but because of money-mindedness. It is a fallacy to assume that all people have the same psychological reasons for their similar responses (p. 449).

section **IV**

The Phenomenological Strategy

10

The Phenomenological Strategy
INTRODUCTION

If a tree falls in a forest, but no one is there to hear it fall, does it make any sound as it falls? This philosophical and epistemological question addresses the fundamental issue as to whether physical phenomena have reality of their own or whether they must be perceived in order to be real or exist. Psychology is interested in the reality of physical events from the point of view of the perceiver. If a man hears a sound, whether or not that sound has an existence of its own (i.e., independent of the perceiver), then the man's perception and the actions which follow from it lie within the realm of psychology.

How a person reacts to an event in his physical or interpersonal world depends to some degree on the *meaning* that the event has for him. Suppose a man were standing close to the proverbial tree as it fell and heard the sound of the falling tree. If he were a lumberjack, the sound would undoubtedly be familiar to him, and he would hastily retreat to a safe distance. However, to someone who had never before heard the sound of a tree as it begins to fall, the sound might have no special meaning. The sound of the falling tree represents potential danger, yet harm can be avoided only if the person perceives that the danger exists. In most instances people tend to avoid situations which they perceive as potentially harmful. Why, then, do people engage in activities which involve possible danger, such as skiing, sky diving, and driving on freeways? Certainly in these instances the odds of harmful consequences are less than they would be if one stood under a falling tree. But more than that, most people who ski, sky-dive, and drive on freeways do not think about the potential dangers. In effect, they view the activities as safer (or at least as more enjoyable or more necessary) than do those who do not engage in these behaviors. Therefore they too act in accordance with their perceptions.

What has been described in the preceding examples is a *phenomenological* view of man which, in brief, holds that the reality of phenomena is solely a function of the way in which they are observed. What is real to an individual is that which is in his *internal frame of reference,* his subjective world, which includes everything that he is aware of at a particular point in time. There is nothing intrinsically brown, round, or large about a basketball; one must look to the reacting organism to find out the color, shape, and relative size of the object.

From the standpoint of predicting behavior, phenomenological psychology says that effective reality is *reality as it is perceived.* Two people observing the "same" set of circumstances may perceive two very different occurrences, as is so often the case with "eyewitnesses" in traffic accidents.

The implication of a phenomenological orientation for a strategy of personality is that a person's behavior can only be understood from his own point of view. The important object of study then becomes a person's subjective experiences, for it is these experiences that direct his behavior. Subjective experience may or may not coincide with "objective reality," a point which is well illustrated by the case of a young man who had been dreaming about his girl friend. When he was abruptly awakened he found himself embracing, rather passionately, not his girl friend but his mother, who had come into his room to wake him. This embarrassing scene was the result of the boy's subjective experience rather than the objective situation. Clearly, the boy's mother was not his girl friend and was unaccustomed to such amorous attention from her son.

However, there are instances in which what is objectively real is much less clear and, for all practical purposes, what a person perceives, his subjective experience, determines the ultimate reality of the situation for him. Consider the example of Beth, an eight-year-old girl whose family has just moved to a new city. After her first day at the new school, her parents inquire, "How was school today?" "I hated it," says Beth. "The kids are really unfriendly. When I came into the class, all the kids stared at me. They were grinning and thought I was funny looking. Only two kids in the whole class even talked to me at lunch." Now consider how Beth might have *perceived* the same objective situation differently and reported, "I liked it. The kids are really friendly. When I came into the class, they were all interested in me. The kids were looking at me and smiling. And two kids, who I didn't even know, came over to talk to me at lunch!" It is possible that the same objective situation could have led Beth to have had either of these two very different subjective experiences.[1]

From a philosophical standpoint, no practical problems are presented by phenomenology's exclusive concern with subjective knowledge—those things which each individual person knows. But when phenomenology is brought into the realm of psychology, a scientific endeavor which purports to deal with objective knowledge, a dilemma arises. Objective knowledge comes from observations upon which others can agree, whereas subjective knowledge involves only a single person's experiences, of which he alone has direct knowledge. The solution to this predicament which has been adopted by phenomenological psychologists has been to seek what Carl Rogers (1964) has called *phenomenological knowledge*—that is, an understanding of a person as viewed from his own internal frame of reference.

The phenomenological position is often implicit in "everyday psychology." Such common expressions as "Beauty is in the eye of the beholder," "One man's meat is another man's poison," and "Try stepping into the other man's shoes" emphasize the salience of subjective knowledge in determining one's actions and the importance of gaining phenomenological knowledge when trying to understand and predict someone else's behavior. The failure to see things as other people see them gets us into interpersonal difficulties, as when someone makes a joke about an incident which another person takes seriously.

The phenomenological strategy for the study of personality will be illustrated by discussing two basic approaches, the self-actualization approach of Carl Rogers and Abraham Maslow (see Chapter 11) and the Psychology of Personal Constructs, formulated by George Kelly (see Chapter 12). These two positions differ somewhat in their theoretical assumptions about the nature of human personality, the concepts they employ, and the techniques for changing personality which they advocate. Nevertheless, both approaches share some basic suppositions about personality theory, assessment, research, and change, which serve as guides for the scientific and practical endeavors which are derived from them.

---

[1] Another important point which could be gleaned from this example is that Beth's perception of her new classmates affected her behavior which, in turn, influenced how they reacted to her, thereby changing the nature of the objective situation in subsequent interactions.

PHENOMENOLOGICAL PERSONALITY THEORY

Both Rogers and Kelly have proposed broad theories of personality which, at least hypothetically, can account for all of man's diverse behavior. Each of these theories grew, in part, out of the clinical experiences Rogers and Kelly had in dealing with abnormal behavior, and it is therefore no wonder that the theories include both the "healthy" and "sick" side of personality.

In contrast, Maslow's theorizing has been much more delimited. Rather than formulate a comprehensive theory of personality, he focused on theoretical explanations of a few different aspects of human behavior. As a personality theorist, Maslow stands virtually alone in having attended almost exclusively to the positive, or healthy, side of personality. For example, believing that man has a vast potential for growth, Maslow explored the personality of optimal man, man who is close to all he is capable of being. This work on the fully functioning person will be discussed in Chapter 11.

The theories of Rogers, Maslow, and Kelly all focus on "higher" functions of man. Rogers and Maslow's work deals with self-actualization, and Kelly's theory concerns the cognitive templates (constructs) through which people view their experiences. These emphases should be contrasted with the "lower" functions of man, such as drives, needs, and reflexes, which are the focus of other approaches to personality. Each of the phenomenological positions to be discussed takes into account the fact that essential biological needs have to be met before man can concern himself with higher functions, but its theorizing about human personality commences at the point where these have been satisfied.

A common theme running through the theories of Rogers, Maslow, and Kelly is that man is an active, reacting being. In making this assumption, they partially circumvent the basic issue of what motivates man to behave. If man is conceived of as an inert object which must be compelled to action, then it becomes necessary to posit some special force, such as a drive, a trait, or a need, to account for behavior. Each of the phenomenological positions to be discussed begins with the assumption that man is alive and therefore behaves. Each position views man's behavior as active rather than passive—each sees man as reacting to and with his biological makeup and his immediate environment rather than being compelled to action by them.

What Rogers, Maslow, and Kelly do theorize about are the determinants of the directionality of behavior. On a broad scale, why does one man spend much of his life accumulating money while another seeks prestige and fame? In the more narrow sphere of day-to-day endeavors, what factors determine Janet's spending an evening listening to music while her roommate Janyce cleans their apartment? To explain the direction which behavior takes, a general principle is advanced. Rogers and Maslow posit that each person has a tendency to actualize himself in a way that approaches his unique potential. Kelly theorizes that people act in those ways which lead to their being able to predict the events in their lives most accurately. The specifics of how either of these broad principles operates to direct a person's behavior vary with each individual.

The phenomenological approaches to personality not only view man as active but also see him as changing constantly. As Rogers (1961) put it: "Life, at its best, is a flowing, changing process in which nothing is fixed" (p. 27). This dynamic conception of man is wholly consistent with the phenomenological emphasis on the "here and now." In other words, behavior is determined by the individual's phenomenal field at any given point in time. While the phenomenologists certainly acknowledge that past experiences play an important role in shaping present behavior, they view the past only in terms of how it affects present perceptions. Phenomenological theories pay little attention to stable, enduring characteristics of the individual, which are the focus of the dispositional strategy, and to lifelong patterns of action which have originated in early childhood, which are the core of the psychoanalytic strategy.

Does this mean that man's behavior is totally inconsistent and unpredictable? Certainly not. In fact, consistency is an important theme running through the theories of Rogers, Maslow, and Kelly. The theories can be called *holistic,* in that they view and understand each of a person's specific acts in terms of his entire personality. For example, Rogers stresses the importance of consistency between how a person views himself and how he would like to be.

PHENOMENOLOGICAL PERSONALITY ASSESSMENT

The phenomenological strategy is concerned with a person's subjective experiences, with his view of the happenings in his life space. Consequently phenomenological personality assessment necessitates gaining knowledge of private events. Recall that this is also the essential task of psychoanalytic personality assessment.

In both the phenomenological and psychoanalytic strategies, behavior is neither the basic unit of personality nor the exclusive means used to get at personality. Consider the student who does not speak up in a class discussion. What can we infer from this behavior? Would it be a good hunch that he has not read the assignment for the day and therefore is not prepared to participate in the discussion? Or is the student thoroughly familiar with the background reading but reluctant to venture forth in the discussion because he is afraid he will be considered a show-off? Clearly, his behavior on any given day will not answer these questions. The same behavior can have vastly different *meanings* for the same person on different occasions or for two different individuals under the same circumstances. Within broad limits, behavior can yield information about an individual's personality; but for more specific information, the meaning of the behavior for the person must be assessed. In fact, all of phenomenological personality assessment could be said to be aimed at the assessment of *meaning*, for it is the meaning of experiences for people which makes up their personalities and determines their actions.

Seeing the world as another man does is different from making inferences about his behavior which are projections, in the psychoanalytic sense, of the assessor's own view of things rather than an accurate picture of the other person's perspective. This is illustrated by the case of a college student who tells his college-educated parents that he wants to drop out of school because he does not believe he is learning anything worthwhile. His parents reply that they "understand" exactly how he feels. When they were in college, his parents recall, there were times when they were tired and wanted to quit; so why doesn't he take a few days off at the lake and relax, and then he will be ready to complete the semester. Obviously, what the parents "understand" is how *they* felt and not how their son feels. Phenomenological knowledge is a matter of *what the experience means for the person himself* and not what it means for the assessor or for people in general.

The salience of "here and now" experiences in the phenomenological strategy contrasts sharply with psychoanalytic personality assessment. Phenomenological assessment techniques focus on the present. An individual's subjective experiences of the past are important only insofar as they clarify present perceptions. In practice, Rogerian personality assessment almost completely eschews the past and Kellian assessment techniques use the past sparingly.

Phenomenological personality assessment is relatively straightforward, again in contrast to the largely inferential tack employed in the psychoanalytic strategy. The subjective experience itself is taken as the basic datum from which a picture of the individual's total personality is compiled. Of course, subjective experience can never be known fully by anyone but the person having the experience. The basic strategy, then, is to gain phenomenological knowledge—that is, to try to understand another person's subjective experience from his perspective.

Most techniques of personality assessment used within the phenomenological strategy involve self-report measures, especially verbal self-report. These reports of subjective experience are accepted more or less at face value. They are not considered signs or indications of some inferred psychological state (e.g., an intrapsychic conflict) or some underlying disposition (e.g., a trait). The assessment remains on the level of phenomenological knowledge. For example, conscious experiences are taken as direct evidence of important personality functions and are not necessarily viewed as indicators of underlying unconscious processes.

A basic assumption of the phenomenological strategy is that people are generally aware of their subjective experiences. In fact, it is the awareness of these events which is presumed to direct their behavior and is the subject matter of phenomenology. The position of the phenomenological strategy with regard to experiences outside one's awareness (i.e., unconscious) is not that they do not exist but that they do not constitute the major determinants of normal behavior. It should be noted, however, that within both Rogers' and Kelly's approaches, unconscious processes begin to play a greater role as a person's behavior becomes more abnormal or psychologically deviant.

Phenomenological assessment may set up conditions in which the person will be most likely to be open about his experiences. One example of this approach is Rogers' client-centered therapy, in which the therapist attempts to establish an accepting, warm, threat-free atmosphere for the client.

The essence of phenomenological personality assessment involves the assessor's attempt to understand the communication of subjective experiences from the internal frame of reference of the person relating such experiences. This primarily involves what is called empathy, understanding the person's experiences in terms of what they mean for him. It necessitates, among other things, abandoning one's own connotations for the words and phrases the other person uses and one's own interpretation of the experiences related.

Demonstration 10–1

PERCEIVING FROM ANOTHER'S INTERNAL FRAME OF REFERENCE

The reader is invited to try to understand another person's subjective experiences from his internal frame of reference. Below are a series of statements made by a 30-year-old man at the beginning of a therapy session.[2] Assume that you were counseling this man and wanted to let him know by your comments that you were understanding what he was telling you *from his perspective.* Read each statement made by the client and then write down in a sentence or two what response you would make to each of the client's statements. In other words, write the attitudes

---

[2] Statements quoted from Rogers, 1965, pp. 32–33.

or thoughts you have concerning the statement as *you assume the internal frame of reference* of this client.

1. "I thought I'd have something to talk about—then it all goes around in circles. I was trying to think what I was going to say. Then coming here it doesn't work out. . . . I tell you, it seemed that it would be much easier before I came."

2. "I tell you, I just can't make a decision; I don't know what I want. I've tried to reason this thing out logically—tried to figure out which things are important to me."

3. "I thought that there are maybe two things a man might do; he might get married and raise a family. But if he was just a bachelor, just making a living—that isn't very good."

4. "I find myself and my thoughts getting back to the days when I was a kid and I cry very easily. The dam would break through."

5. "I've been in the Army four and a half years. I had no problems then, no hopes, no wishes. My only thought was to get out when peace would come."

TABLE 10–1

Attitudes and Thoughts Representing Internal and External Frames of Reference*

Internal Frame of Reference	*External Frame of Reference*
1. It's really hard for you to get started.	1. Should I help you get started talking? Is your inability to get under way a type of dependence?
2. Decision-making just seems impossible to you.	2. What is the cause of your indecisiveness?
3. You want marriage, but it doesn't seem to you to be much of a possibility.	3. Why are you focusing on marriage and family? You appear to be a bachelor. I didn't know that.
4. You feel yourself brimming over with childish feelings.	4. The crying, the "dam," sound as though you are repressing a great deal.
5. To you the Army represented stagnation.	5. You're a veteran. Were you a psychiatric patient? I feel sorry for anybody who spent four and one-half years in the service.

* Statements quoted or paraphrased from Rogers, 1965, pp. 33–34.

Now compare your attitudes and thoughts with those in Table 10–1 to see what success you had at adopting the client's internal frame of reference. While your thoughts do not have to be identical with those given in the table, they should be of the same general flavor as those in the left-hand column. Rogers (1965) explains why the attitudes in the right-hand column are representative of an external frame of reference by noting that ". . . these are all attitudes which are basically sympathetic. There is nothing 'wrong' with them. They are even attempts to 'understand,' in the sense of 'understanding about,' rather than 'understanding with.' The locus of perceiving is, however, outside of the client" (p. 33).

PHENOMENOLOGICAL RESEARCH

All three of the basic methods of personality research—experimental, correlational, and case study—have been used within the phenomenological strategy, and examples of each will be given in the next two chapters. What characterizes the various types of research endeavors is the focus on subjective experiences and the way people perceive events.

There is a heavy emphasis on idiographic research in the phenomenological strategy. This is in keeping with the idea of conceiving of an individual's personality processes in terms of his subjective phenomenal world, of that which is real to him and him alone. Such idiographic research, of which Maslow's investigations of the self-actualizing man are a good example, most frequently utilizes the case study method. The data from these studies are detailed qualitative descriptions of subjective, intensely personal experiences, and they yield rich, in-depth portraits of single personalities. By selecting for study subjects with particular characteristics (e.g., being highly self-actualized), the data can be combined to produce a composite picture of the nature of that personality characteristic. Thus, what begins as an idiographic investigation, a detailed study of a single individual, can also be used to supply nomothetic information which will be applicable to a great many people.

As is the case in the psychoanalytic strategy, phenomenological research is often related to and done in conjunction with psychotherapy. Historically this is probably due to the fact that theorists such as Rogers, Maslow, and Kelly were clinical psychologists who were actively engaged in psychotherapeutic endeavors as they began to develop their approaches. Additionally, phenomenological approaches to personality have tended to emphasize the application of their theoretical principles to practical human problems.

PHENOMENOLOGICAL PERSONALITY CHANGE

If personality is a function of one's perceptions and one's subjective evaluations of the events in his life, then it follows that in order to modify personality, it is these private experiences which must be altered. In general, this entails a process whereby the person becomes more aware of his subjective experiences and their influence on his behavior. The basic assumption is that when an individual's perception of his life experiences is altered, his behavior will change.

The client[3] takes the major responsibility for changing his per-

---

[3] Phenomenological psychologists use the term *client* more frequently than the term *patient*.

sonality, a fact which evolves directly from phenomenological personality theory. Since man is seen as an active organism, it follows that the client himself will play a major role in altering his personality. Implicit or explicit in phenomenological theories is the assumption that man has the capacity to change his own personality and behavior. Although the specific procedures employed in psychotherapy to encourage self-modification vary with the particular approach, the basic theme of self-determination runs through all phenomenological personality change procedures. Furthermore, the client knows himself and his subjective experiences far better than anyone else could. Therefore, the client, rather than the therapist, should direct the change process.

As would be expected from phenomenological personality theory, the emphasis in therapy is on the present. Usually, the "present" includes the immediate past (e.g., the past few weeks or days), but sometimes the locus of time is the therapy session itself and all that is taking place in it, including the interaction of the client with the therapist and the interaction among clients in group forms of therapy. When that is the case, the expression the "here and now" may be a more accurate description of the locus of time.

The Encounter Group Movement

In recent years there has been a proliferation of techniques aimed at changing personality within groups. Some of the better-known techniques have been called "T-groups," "encounter groups," and "sensitivity training." The formal origin of these groups dates back more than 25 years. In the late 1940s, Kurt Lewin, a noted social psychologist at MIT, and his associates were experimenting with training (the meaning of *T*) groups aimed at developing the interpersonal interaction skills of industrial managers and executives.

> The T group started informally, almost accidently. Lewin originally scheduled it as a casual discussion by group leaders of events occurring in the afternoon workshop. Some group members also attended. This led to direct confrontations, as leaders and participants disagreed in their perceptions of what had occurred in the workshop sessions. The argument moved on to more personal and immediate ground, to what was happening in the "here and now." The group attempted to develop new structures for handling problems as they arose. Out of this developed a new approach to training, an unstructured group centered on the study of its own dynamics. The focus of the group was on the way members interacted in the process of organizing themselves into a group (Schloss, Siroka, & Siroka, 1971, p. 4).

The initial T-groups focused on organizational and human relations skills. In the late 1950s, a second type of group emerged, which shifted the emphasis to the personal growth of the group members. These groups are more likely to be called encounter groups or sensitivity training. They are closer to being a type of psychotherapy than the earlier T-groups, though many of them purport to be designed for "normal" people who are interested in growth experiences, in becoming more aware of themselves and others, and in developing their full potential as human beings.

This group encounter movement, which is part of a larger movement referred to as "humanistic psychology,"[4] has a number of ties with the phenomenological strategy, particularly in its aims. For example, in encounter groups or sensitivity training emphasis is placed on subjective experiences and feelings, understanding others from their perspective, increasing self-awareness and self-acceptance, developing wholeness and consistency within one's personality, and being in the "here and now." The techniques used to bring about such personality changes include not only verbal exchanges among group members but a host of "action" techniques, such as body contact to heighten one's awareness of bodily sensations and physical games to develop trust (e.g., leaning backward until you lose your balance and are caught by another group member).

Because of the recent popularity of encounter-type experiences, people frequently ask what goes on in them. While a description of the general aims and some of the techniques may help to explain what happens (see, for example, Rogers, 1970; Schutz, 1967), the actual experiences of group members are believed to depend upon how the situation is perceived by each individual, which is the essence of the phenomenological position.

Despite the close connection between many of the aims and some of the techniques of sensitivity training and the phenomenological strategy, the theoretical underpinnings of encounter groups are diverse. They include Gestalt therapy (e.g., Perls, 1969) and variations on psychoanalysis (e.g., Berne's [1961, 1964] transactional analysis), as well as the self-actualization approach to personality discussed in the next chapter.

---

[4] Maslow (1962) speaks of humanistic psychology as the "third force" in psychology—a reaction and alternative to psychoanalysis on the one hand and behavioral approaches on the other.

11

The Phenomenological Strategy
SELF-ACTUALIZATION APPROACHES

This chapter will explore the approaches to personality taken by Carl Rogers and Abraham H. Maslow. Rogers has developed a complete strategy for studying personality, including a theory of personality development and functioning, a rationale and specific techniques for assessing personality, an impressive body of research to substantiate the basic propositions and implications of his theory, and a well-known approach to changing personality called client-centered therapy. After discussing Rogers' approach, we shall take a brief look at Maslow's work on fully functioning people. Although Maslow's approach to personality is very similar to that of Rogers, unlike Rogers he did not develop a formal and complete strategy. Instead, Maslow devoted his career to exploring a variety of specific topics of personality, many of which had not been studied previously. His research on fully functioning individuals is among his most notable contributions.

THE BASIC UNDERPINNINGS OF ROGERS' APPROACH

Personality Development

The Actualizing Tendency

Rogers (1959) postulates that all behavior is governed by the *actualizing tendency*, "the inherent tendency of the organism to develop all its capacities in ways which serve to maintain or enhance the organism" (p. 196). At a very basic, organic level this inborn tendency involves the maintenance of the organism by meeting fundamental needs, such as the need for oxygen, water, and food, and the enhancement of the organism by providing for the development and differentiation of the body's organs and functions and its continual growth and regeneration. But of more importance to human personality is the motivation which the actualizing tendency provides for increased autonomy and self-sufficiency, for expanding one's repertoire of experiences, and for creativity.

The actualizing tendency serves as the criterion by which all experiences[1] are evaluated. Through this *organismic valuing process* those experiences which are perceived as maintaining or enhancing the person are evaluated positively and are sought after. Such positive experiences give the person a feeling of satisfaction. In contrast, experiences which are perceived to be in opposition to the maintenance or enhancement of the person are evaluated negatively and are avoided. (It is interesting to note that although Rogers claims to have no theory of learning, his concept of the organismic valuing process seems very much like the reinforcement-based theories of learning and personality discussed in Chapter 15.)

The most important aspect of the actualizing tendency from the standpoint of personality is the tendency toward *self-actualization*. Self-actualization involves all movement of a person in the direction of maintenance and enhancement of the *self*.

The Development of the Self

In early infancy the child perceives all experience, whether it is produced by sensations in his body or by external agents, such as the behavior of his parents, as unitary. The infant makes no distinction between what is "me" and what is "not me." However, as part of the actualizing tendency's process of differentiation, the child soon begins to distinguish between that which is directly part of him and that which is external to him. It is this differentiation which leads to the development of the self. The *self*, or *self-concept* (Rogers uses the terms synonymously), refers to "the organized, consistent conceptual gestalt [whole] composed of perceptions of the characteristics of the 'I' or 'me' and the perceptions of the relationships of the 'I' or 'me' to others and to various aspects of life, together with the values attached to these perceptions" (Rogers, 1959, p. 200). In line with

---

[1] "This term is used to include all that is going on within the envelope of the organism at any given moment which is potentially available to awareness. It includes events of which the individual is unaware, as well as all the phenomena which are in consciousness. . . . It is to be noted that experience refers to the given moment, not to some accumulation of past experience" (Rogers, 1959, p. 197).

Rogers' holistic approach, the self is viewed as a consistent organized whole, which implies that all aspects of the self must be in agreement with one another. For example, a person could think of himself as being both dominant and submissive if, and only if, these two contrasting characteristics could be reconciled. One way to do this would be for the person to perceive some situations (e.g., at home) as being appropriate for domineering behavior and other situations (e.g., at work) as being appropriate for submissiveness. If a reconciliation were not possible, as would be the case if the person felt that one or the other type of behavior was always proper, then the wholeness and consistency of his self would be threatened. The meaning of threat to the self-structure and the defense response which naturally follows will be discussed later.

A person's self-concept includes not only his perception of what he is actually like but also what he thinks he ought to be and would like to be. This latter aspect of the self is called the *ideal self*.

MEASURING THE SELF-CONCEPT VIA THE Q-SORT.   While it is true that a person's self-concept can only be fully known by the person himself, it is possible to gain some understanding of the way an individual views himself. Around 1950, William Stephenson (1953) developed the Q-technique, a method for making comparative judgments which was particularly suitable for the study of an individual's self-concept, especially as it changed (e.g., during the course of psychotherapy). Rogers and his associates were quick to adopt the *Q-sort,* a specific procedure based on Stephenson's general methodology, as one of their basic assessment procedures.

Rogers observed that during the course of psychotherapy a client's[2] self-concept generally underwent change. Usually, at the beginning of therapy there was much divergence between the way in which the client actually viewed himself and the way he would have liked to be (i.e., his ideal self). During psychotherapy these two aspects of the self came closer together. This observation has been amply documented by studies employing the Q-sort.

In a typical study, before entering counseling,[3] clients are given the task of sorting a large number of self-referent statements (e.g., "I am lazy"; "I don't like to be with other people"; "I am generally happy"; "I am a domineering person"). These statements are printed on cards and are placed in a series of piles, each corresponding to a point on a continuum ranging from "very characteristic of me" to "not at all characteristic of me." Usually, the client must sort

---

[2] Rogers has come to use the term *client* to refer to the person with whom the therapist is dealing. See the section on client-centered therapy in this chapter for a discussion of the choice of the term.

[3] Rogers uses the words *counseling* and *psychotherapy* synonymously.

FIGURE 11–1

Example of a Forced Q-Sort Distribution of Self-Referent Statements

	Very characteristic					Neutral					Not characteristic
Pile no.	0	1	2	3	4	5	6	7	8	9	10
No. of statements	2	4	6	12	14	20	14	12	6	4	2

the statements according to some fixed distribution (i.e., a specific number of statements in each pile), as illustrated in Figure 11–1.

The client first sorts the statements under directions to describe himself as he sees himself at the present moment. After this *self-sort* is completed, the client is asked to sort the same statements again. This time, however, he aims to describe his ideal self, the kind of person he would most like to be. This second sort is called the *ideal sort*. The two Q-sorts are then compared by correlating the ratings. Each statement is assigned two numbers, one representing the pile number for the self-sort and the other the pile number for the ideal sort, and it is these numbers that are correlated. The closer each pair of numbers, the more congruent are the perceived self and the ideal self. A positive correlation is indicative of congruence of, a negative correlation of divergence between, the perceived self and the ideal self; in each case the size of the correlation coefficient is an index of the degree of congruence or divergence. Correlation coefficients not significantly different from zero indicate that there is no systematic relationship between the perceived self and the ideal self.

The clients are asked to perform self- and ideal sorts again at several intervals during counseling and at the completion of counseling, and each time the correlation between the two sorts is calculated. It thus becomes possible to determine whether there is a change in the relationship between a client's perceived self and his ideal self over the course of counseling by comparing the correlations between the two sorts.

Demonstration 11–1

THE Q-SORT

To get a better understanding of the Q-sort, the reader is invited to perform two Q-sorts of his interests.

Preparation

1. First, write the name of each of the interests or activities listed in Table 11–1 along with its number on a separate 3 × 5 index card (or any small piece of paper).

TABLE 11–1

List of Activities for Q-Sort Demonstration 11–1

1. Basketball	14. Sewing or knitting
2. Camping or hiking	15. Shopping
3. Card games	16. Singing
4. Dancing	17. Social drinking
5. Dining out	18. Swimming
6. Drawing or painting	19. Talking with friends
7. Going to movies	20. Tennis
8. Going to parties	21. Travel
9. Hunting or fishing	22. Visiting museums or art galleries
10. Listening to music	23. Walking
11. Playing a musical instrument	24. Watching television
12. Politics	25. Writing letters
13. Reading for pleasure	

2. Next, referring to Table 11–2, number nine cards (1–9). On each card write the description of the corresponding degree of interest and the required number of activities which must be sorted into the pile. The first three columns of Table 11–2 provide the descriptions for the nine cards. On a desk or other flat surface, place these cards in numerical order (from left to right), thereby forming a nine-point scale. You are now ready to perform the first Q-sort.

TABLE 11–2

Outline for Q-Sort Demonstration 11–1

Pile No.	Degree of Interest	Required No. in Each Pile	Rank
1	Very strong interest	1	1.0
2	Stong interest	2	2.5
3	Moderate interest	3	5.0
4	Slight interest	4	8.5
5	Ambivalent (neutral)	5	13.0
6	Slight disinterest	4	17.5
7	Moderate disinterest	3	21.0
8	Strong disinterest	2	23.5
9	Very strong disinterest	1	25.0

First Q-Sort

3. To help you sort the activities into nine piles, first divide the 25 activity cards into three broad categories: those activities which you are *definitely interested* in at the present time, those activities which you are

definitely not interested in at present, and those activities which you are *ambivalent* about now.

4. You have just sorted the activities into the three gross categories of definitely interested, ambivalent, and definitely not interested. The Q-sort involves sorting the activities on the nine-point scale which you have set up. Start with the "definitely interested" category and distribute these cards where you feel they belong (i.e., according to how interested you are in the activities *at the present time*). Be sure to adhere to the required number of activities for each pile. Next, do the same with the "definitely not interested" category, and finally, sort the "ambivalent" category. (In this way you will be working for the most part from the extremes to the middle of the scale. This is generally the optimal strategy because more extreme preferences are usually easier to classify than less extreme ones.)

5. Check each pile to see that it contains the correct number of cards.

6. Check the Q-sort to be sure that each activity is in the pile you think it ought to be in.

7. It is now possible to rank the activities from the ones you are most interested in to the ones you are least interested in. The ranks for each pile are given in the last column of Table 11–2[4]. Make a copy of the "Recording Sheet" in Table 11–3 on a piece of lined paper and record the rank of each activity in the column designated "First Sort Rank."

By examining the Q-sort of the activities you have just produced, you can get an idea of what your present interests are, just as a therapist can gain some understanding of a client's self-concept by looking at his Q-sort of self-referent statements. However, usually more than one Q-sort is made, and, indeed, one of the most useful features of the Q-sort is that comparisons between sorts are possible.

Second Q-Sort

8. To make such a comparison, repeat steps 2 through 7, but this time sort the activities with respect to your interests some time *in the past,* say, five years ago. (One alternative would be to have a friend perform the Q-sort of his present interests.) Record the rank of each activity in the column designated "Second Sort Rank" on your Recording Sheet.

Comparison of Q-Sorts

9. You are now prepared to compare the two Q-sorts. Although this can be done by visual inspection alone, correlating the rankings of the activities on the two sorts is a more exact and potentially more meaningful method of comparison. This is easily and quickly done by means of

---

[4] The activity in pile number 1 will be assigned the rank of "1." The next most preferred activity would receive the rank of "2," except that there are two activities designated in pile number 2. Unless activities are ranked within each of the nine categories (a tedious and time-consuming task which, because of the fine discriminations required, may be only arbitrary at best), it must be assumed that the activities within categories are equally preferable. The solution is to assign the average (mean) of the tied ranks. In the case of the two activities in pile number 2, the second and third ranks are tied, which means that each of the activities in this pile will receive the rank of "2.5" (as shown in Table 11–2).

TABLE 11–3

Personality: Strategies for the Study of Man

Sample Recording Sheet for Q-Sort Demonstration 11–1

Activity Number	First Sort Rank	Second Sort Rank	Difference	Difference Squared
1				
2				
3				
4				
5				
6				
7				
8				
9				
10				
11				
12				
13				
14				
15				
16				
17				
18				
19				
20				
21				
22				
23				
24				
25				

Sum of difference squared =

the *rank-order correlation* method, which is outlined in simple, step-by-step fashion below.[5]

(a) For each pair of ranks (i.e., for each activity), calculate the difference between the ranks. The smaller value can always be subtracted from the larger, disregarding algebraic signs (since these values will be squared). Record the differences in the "Difference" column on your Recording Sheet.

(b) Now square each difference and record the squared differences in the last column of the Recording Sheet.

(c) Add all the squared differences found in step (b).

(d) Multiply the sum obtained in step (c) by 6.

---

[5] Lest the reader think that the steps in calculating the rank-order correlation coefficient (*rho*) have been magically rather than mathematically determined, the formula is:

$$rho = 1 - \frac{6\Sigma D^2}{N(N^2 - 1)}$$

where D = differences in ranks of each pair and N = number of pairs of ranks (in the present example $N = 25$). *Rho* is approximately equal to the Pearson product-moment correlation coefficient.

(*e*) Divide the product obtained in step (*d*) by 15,600.

(*f*) Subtract the quotient obtained in step (*e*) from *1.00*. This quantity is the rank-order correlation coefficient, which is designated by the Greek letter *rho.*

If *rho* is positive, your interests have tended to remain the same. The closer *rho* is to +1.00, the greater is the similarity between your interests in the two sorts. If *rho* is negative, then your interests now tend to be different from those you had in the past. The closer *rho* is to −1.00, the more dissimilar are your present interests from your past interests.

The Need for Positive Regard

Rogers postulates that a basic need of all persons is to experience attitudes such as acceptance, respect, sympathy, warmth, and love from significant people in their lives. This *need for positive regard* may be either inborn or learned, and although he tends to favor the latter explanation, Rogers states that its origin is irrelevant to his theory. An interesting aspect of positive regard is its reciprocal nature; that is, when a person becomes aware that he is satisfying another's need for positive regard, his own need is also satisfied.

Most often we receive positive regard for specific things we do, and in this sense positive regard is akin to certain types of positive reward, such as praise or attention. It is possible, however, to give or receive positive regard irrespective of the worth placed on specific aspects of a person's behavior. This means that the person, as a whole, is accepted and respected. Such *unconditional positive regard* is frequently seen in a parent's love for a child when, regardless of the child's specific behavior, he is loved and accepted. It is similar to what Erich Fromm (1963) has called "motherly love," which, in contrast to conditional "fatherly love," is given to the child "because it is her child, not because the child has fulfilled any specific condition, or lived up to any specific expectation" (p. 35). Unconditional positive regard may be given even though all of the recipient's specific behaviors are not valued equally.

The concept of unconditional positive regard, like most concepts in Rogers' personality theory, was developed in the context of psychotherapy. Rogers contends that one of the major requisites for successful psychotherapy is that the therapist "prize" the whole person of the client. The therapist must feel and show unconditional positive regard for the client who is frightened or ashamed of his experiences, as well as for the client who is pleased or satisfied with his experiences. Gradually the client can then feel more acceptant of all his experiences. This makes him more of a whole, or congruent, person who consequently is able to function more effectively.

Positive self-regard develops from the positive attitudes shown toward a person by others. However, rather than coming from other people, the positive regard for one's experiences comes directly from the self. It is as if the self had become a significant other. The development of positive self-regard is another step toward becoming an autonomous person, which is part of the tendency toward self-actualization. When a person perceives his whole self as worthy of positive regard, independent of how he evaluates specific aspects of his behavior, he is experiencing *unconditional positive self-regard*.

Conditions of Worth

It is difficult for significant others to regard all of a child's behavior equally. *Conditions of worth* thus develop "when the positive regard of a significant other is conditional, when the individual feels that in some respects he is prized and in others not" (Rogers, 1959, p. 209). Conditions of worth are the equivalent of internalized values which form the basis of the superego in psychoanalytic theory. It is from this differential assignment of positive regard that the child learns to differentially evaluate his own behavior. The need for positive regard, both from significant others and from one's self, is extremely powerful and consequently can come to supersede the organismic valuing process. That is, independent of whether an experience itself is in any way maintaining or enhancing the organism, an experience may be valued as positive or negative and subsequently either approached or avoided.

Rogers (1959) states, rather categorically, that "a condition of worth, because it disturbs the [organismic] valuing process, prevents the individual from functioning freely and with maximum effectiveness" (p. 210), and he considers conditions of worth as detrimental to the fully functioning person. These points emphasize the primacy of the tendency to actualization in the "normal" development of a person; when conditions of worth become more influential in directing the person's behavior than the organismic valuing process, nature is being tampered with, so to speak.

The Experience of Threat and the Process of Defense

When the self is first formed, it is governed by the organismic valuing process alone, which uses as criteria of evaluation the principles of self-actualization. However, as the need for positive regard becomes important to the individual and conditions of worth become part of his self, conflicts arise between the self and experience. Where unconditional positive regard exists, all experiences are admitted to the individual's awareness and symbolized accurately; if no experience is more or less worthy of positive regard than any other, there is no reason to exclude any experience from awareness. However, if conditions of worth are embodied within the self, awareness of experiences will vary to the extent that they are valued (e.g., mother says it is better to eat oatmeal than ice cream and cake for breakfast). Those experiences which are consistent with the self and its conditions of worth, and thus are valued positively, are allowed to enter awareness and are perceived accurately. Experiences which conflict with the self and its conditions of worth, and therefore are valued negatively, represent a danger to the self-concept and are kept from entering awareness and being accurately perceived.

Suppose a young man has been taught by his parents that each individual has an obligation to be loyal to his country and has come to feel that this is how he should behave. While in college he is exposed to points of view which are in opposition to unconditional support of one's country, especially in the case where the individual citizen feels his country's policies are wrong. The young man is about to be drafted into the army to fight in a war which he feels his country is engaged in unjustly, and he decides to leave his country rather than be drafted. This experience is in direct opposition to his self-concept, which places a high degree of positive self-regard on patriotism, and is therefore threatening to him.

For Rogers, *threat* exists when a person perceives that there is an incongruity between some experience and his self-concept.[6] The person experiences threat as vague uneasiness and tension, which is commonly labeled anxiety. Incongruence between one's self-concept and experience is threatening because the individual's personality is no longer a consistent whole. The young man's behavior is no longer regulated by a unitary force, the actualizing tendency, but is instead governed by several different standards. Rogers (1959) speaks of this division in the following way:

> This, as we see it, is the basic estrangement in man. He has not been true to himself, to his own natural organismic valuing of experience, but for the sake of preserving the positive regard of others has now come to falsify some of the values he experiences and to perceive them only in terms based upon their value to others. Yet this has not been a conscious choice, but a natural—and tragic—development in infancy. The path of development toward psychological maturity, the path of therapy, is the undoing of this estrangement in man's functioning, the dissolving of conditions of worth, the achievement of a self which is congruent with experience, and the restoration of a unified organismic valuing process as the regulator of behavior (pp. 226–7).

---

[6] Incongruity between experience and self-concept need not be perceived at a conscious level. Indeed, Rogers postulates that most frequently the individual is able to discriminate an experience as threatening without the threat's being symbolized in awareness.

It is impossible to conceive of an individual completely devoid of conditions of worth actually existing in the world as we know it. The absence of conditions of worth and the presence of a unified organismic valuing process as the sole regulator of behavior are only goals toward which a person can strive in order to achieve better psychological adjustment. However, to understand how the young man in our example is threatened as a result of the presence of conditions of worth, it would be constructive to consider, hypothetically, how things would have been different had his conditions of worth been absent.

If the young man had been reared in an atmosphere in which all his feelings were accepted and prized, he would have come to value all of his experiences equally, and his behavior would be guided by his organismic valuing process. Under these circumstances, his parents' attitude, and subsequently his own, about patriotism might have been of the following sort: "We all have an obligation to be loyal to our country, but we also have an obligation to follow our consciences in matters of right and wrong. Sometimes these two obligations are in conflict, and we must make a choice between the two. But choosing one does not permanently exclude the other as a course of action at a different time and under other circumstances. Nor does such a decision make one mode of behavior any more worthy than the other. Sometimes it is possible to satisfy one urge and sometimes the other." By retaining his own organismic valuing process of experiences, he could achieve a balance between the two modes of behavior, and his whole, consistent self would remain intact.

Our young man was not fortunate enough to grow up in such utopian circumstances (nor is any person), and so we must turn from the completely theoretical situation to the more practical one which confronts him. Having made the choice to leave his country rather than serve in the army, he is potentially vulnerable to the disorganization of his personality as a result of the existing state of incongruity between his self-concept and his experience. *Anxiety,* the emotional response to threat, serves as a signal that the unified self-concept is in danger of being disorganized if the discrepancy between it and the threatening experience is symbolized accurately (i.e., if the person becomes aware of it).

The person defends himself from this impending danger by a process of defense which attempts to maintain the self as it exists at that time. "This goal is achieved by the perceptual distortion of the experience in awareness, in such a way as to reduce the incongruity between the experience and the structure of the self, or by the denial to awareness of an experience, thus denying any threat to the self" (Rogers, 1959, pp. 204–5).

Rogers' two basic defensive behaviors, *perceptual distortion* and *denial,* can be illustrated in the various alternatives the young man could use to defend himself against his threatening experience, namely, leaving the country to avoid serving in the army. "Rationalization" is a good example of perceptual distortion: "I didn't really leave my country to avoid being drafted. Actually there are many good opportunities for getting ahead in this new country." "Fantasy" is also a mechanism of defense primarily involving distortion: "I am serving my country by looking after its interests in another country." "Reaction formation" involves both distortion and denial: "I didn't want to serve my country in the first place. I've always felt that a man owes nothing to his country." "Projection" also is a composite of the two basic defensive responses to threat: "Look at all those men who have left their country to avoid serving in the army! I'm glad I'm not like them." The ultimate defense would be pure "denial" that the experience ever occurred: "I've never been called to serve in my country's army." In each case, the defensive behavior serves to keep the young man from becoming fully aware of the actual threatening experience, either by distorting the experience so that it is no longer incongruent with his self-concept or by not allowing any aspect of the experience to enter consciousness.

Rogers views psychological adjustment in terms of the degree of congruence between the self and experience. A person who is psychologically well-adjusted is one who perceives himself and his relation to people and objects in his environment as they "really" are (i.e., as an objective observer would see them). At first glance, the preceding statement may appear inconsistent with the salience of subjective experience in the phenomenological strategy. In Rogers' approach it is still subjective experience which is of interest, but psychological adjustment requires a close correspondence between subjective experience and external reality. When this is the case, an individual is *open to experience* rather than threatened by it because experience is in agreement with the perception he has of it. When an experience is in conflict with the perceptions of the self, the threatening experience is prevented from being accurately symbolized by perceptual distortion or denial.

On the basis of these theoretical notions, Chodorkoff (1954, p. 508) derived the following hypotheses about the relationships among self-perception, perceptual defense, and personal adjustment:

1. The greater the agreement between the individual's self-description and an objective description of him, the less perceptual defense he will show.
2. The greater the agreement between the individual's self-description and an objective description of him, the more adequate will be his personal adjustment.

3. The more adequate the personal adjustment of the individual, the less perceptual defense he will show.

To test these hypotheses, Chodorkoff had male undergraduate students serve as subjects. Each student performed a Q-sort of 125 self-descriptive statements under instructions to describe himself. This self-description was compared with another Q-sort of the same statements, made for each subject by two clinically experienced judges. The judges' Q-sort description, which served as the objective description of each individual, was based on information about the subject gleaned from projective techniques administered to each subject, consisting of the Rorschach, the TAT, and a word association test, as well as a biographical inventory.

In the word association test, each subject was presented with 50 emotional words (e.g., whore, bitch, penis) and 50 neutral words (e.g., house, book, tree), and his reaction time to each word was recorded. For each subject, the 10 emotional words having the longest reaction time and the 10 neutral words having the shortest reaction time were used in the perceptual defense test. These 20 words were flashed on a screen in random order by means of a tachistoscope, a device for visually presenting material for brief, controlled durations (e.g., 1/100 second). The exposure time for each word was increased until the word was accurately reported, and this reaction time became the recognition score for each word.

Perceptual defense is a theoretical construct which has been used to denote an unconscious mechanism which resists allowing threatening material to enter consciousness. It was experimentally defined in Chodorkoff's study as the difference between the recognition thresholds for emotional and neutral stimuli. The higher this difference is, the greater is the degree of perceptual defense.

The third variable of interest in Chodorkoff's study, personal adjustment, was rated, from the projective techniques, by the clinically experienced judges.

The hypotheses were evaluated by performing the appropriate correlations. The first hypothesis compared the accuracy of self-description with recognition thresholds, and it was found that the two variables were negatively correlated—high accuracy of self-description tended to be associated with low recognition thresholds for threatening words. The second hypothesis compared accuracy of self-description and personal adjustment ratings and found them to be positively correlated—high accuracy in self-description was associated with good psychological adjustment. To test the third hypothesis, personal adjustment ratings were compared with recognition thresholds; these variables were negatively correlated—greater psychological adjustment was associated with lower thresholds of recognition. Thus, all three hypotheses received support, and Chodorkoff (1954) concluded:

> In a group of Ss [subjects] who show varying degrees of adjustment and defensiveness, one finds that the more inaccurate and faulty the individual's perception of his environment, the more inaccurate and faulty is his perception of himself; and the more inaccurate and faulty the individual's perceptions of himself and his environment, the more inadequate is his personal adjustment (p. 511).

The Process of Breakdown and Disorganization

The discussion of Rogers' theory of personality has focused thus far on "normal" personality development. Even the most psychologically well-adjusted individual is occasionally threatened by an experience which is inconsistent with his self-concept and which forces him to distort or deny the experience. Doubtless most people experience anxiety as part of their daily living. But their anxiety is at a moderate, and therefore tolerable, level due to the fact that the inconsistency between self-concept and experience is correspondingly moderate and their defenses are adequate. When experiences become more than moderately incongruent with the self, or when the incongruent experiences occur frequently, the person feels a level of anxiety that is distinctly unpleasant and may actually interfere with his daily activities. Such individuals are typically labeled "neurotic" and may seek assistance in reducing their anxiety via psychotherapy. However, the neurotic's defenses are still capable of keeping incongruent experiences out of conscious awareness, thereby allowing the self to remain in a whole, if somewhat tenuous, state.

If the inconsistency between self-concept and experience becomes very great, the individual's defenses may be incapable of distorting or denying the experience. The result is that in his defenseless state, the incongruent experience is accurately symbolized in awareness and the consistent, whole self is shattered. A person in such a disorganized state is typically labeled "psychotic" and may exhibit behaviors which, to an observer, seem odd, irrational, or even bizarre. On closer inspection the behaviors may prove to be congruent with the previously denied experiences. The behaviors are odd only insofar as they are incongruent with the way in which the person is seen by others. For example, someone who has rigidly controlled his aggressive tendencies, denying that they were part of his self-concept, may openly display hostility toward people. The person's friends may view the hostility as alien to his personality, whereas, in fact, it was very much a part of his personality, albeit an aspect of which he was unaware.

The Process of Reintegration

While successfully operating defenses are certainly preferable to a disorganized personality, one always pays a price for keeping incongruent experiences from accurate symbolization in awareness (cf. the psychoanalytic concept that libido used for defense mechanisms is not available for other ego functions; Chapter 4). An individual who distorts or denies certain experiences must constantly defend himself against having these experiences come accurately into consciousness. People who are colloquially described as "always on the defensive" illustrate the detrimental consequences of the defensive process. Such people question the meaning and sincerity of even the most innocuous comments made by other people and are quick to respond as if the comments were derogatory toward them. But from their internal frame of reference, the innocent remark of another person *is* derogatory, since it has been perceived in a distorted form.

A person who inaccurately perceives his experiences is not able to function fully. He is not completely open to experience, and thus he misses or must avoid those aspects of life which are potentially threatening to him. Consider the college student who, due to a self-concept which condones only success, is threatened by any situation in which he could potentially fail. By distorting his view of such an event from one which *could* lead to failure to one which is undesirable, he successfully avoids it. Rather than apply to graduate school, he "decides" that he can do just as well with a bachelor's degree; and, anyhow, he might as well be making money while his friends in graduate school must take out loans. Or he may explain that he didn't try out for the football team because being on the team takes too much time.

When there is incongruity between an individual's self and his experience and his defenses are active, it is possible to decrease the self-experience discrepancy by a process of reintegration within the personality. This is achieved by reversing the process of defense; that is, the individual becomes clearly aware of hitherto distorted or denied experiences and, *under certain specific conditions,* he is able to make these experiences part of his self-concept. The student who was threatened by situations in which he might possibly fail could, in the course of reintegration, come to realize that he might not be admitted to graduate school or that he might be cut from the football team, but these possibilities could become acceptable by integrating them into his self-concept. His self-concept would now include a notion such as: "It is not necessary for me to succeed at everything I try," thereby making him less likely to find such situations threatening.

Rogers maintains that this reintegrative process is possible only when there is *a reduction in the person's conditions of worth and an increase in his unconditional positive self-regard.* These essential conditions can occur if the individual is exposed to and perceives the unconditional positive regard of another person. However, unconditional positive regard can only be communicated if a state of *empathy* exists—the other person must accurately perceive the internal frame of reference of the individual. To be empathic, one must feel *as if* he were the other person, but without losing the "as if" quality. Rogers (1959) explains why empathy is necessary for unconditional positive regard:

> If I know little or nothing of you, and experience an unconditional positive regard for you, this means little because further knowledge of you may reveal aspects which I cannot so regard. But if I know you thoroughly, knowing and empathically understanding a wide variety of your feelings and behaviors, and still experience an unconditional positive regard, this is very meaningful. It comes close to being fully known and fully accepted (p. 231).

When a person acquires conditions of worth, he begins to value one experience more than another, and his self-concept comes to include experiences which he values positively and to exclude experiences which he values negatively. Those experiences which have been excluded from the self must be kept from awareness in order to maintain the self as a consistent whole. Thus, the person becomes aware only of the experiences which he regards positively. If, however, all experiences were regarded equally, there would be no conditions of worth. In a state of unconditional positive regard the existing conditions of worth lose their significance and power in directing the person's behavior. The individual becomes open to more experiences, since without conditions of worth all experiences are consistent with the self. For example, a man who values restraint positively and aggression negatively is unable to accurately perceive his need to be aggressive on some occasions. Aggressive behavior is inconsistent with his self-concept "I am a restrained person," which *ipso facto* makes restraint good. If this condition of worth were dissolved, restraint and aggression would have the same unconditional positive value, and they could exist harmoniously within a unified self. Sometimes the man would behave with restraint and at other times aggressively. There is, in effect, no value placed on either mode of behavior, since neither is valued more or less than the other.

As a consequence of the unconditional positive regard shown by another individual, one experiences an increase in his own unconditional positive self-regard which enables him to maintain an openness to experience and a lack of defensiveness when the other person is no longer present. Increased unconditional positive self-regard and the concomitant decrease in conditions of worth are the prerequisites for the reintegration of one's personality. Receiving unconditional positive regard from someone else is not the only way to achieve this, although it is the process by which client-centered therapy is postulated to work.

Before we turn to a discussion of client-centered therapy, a word or two should be said about the many minor personality reintegrations which occur in our daily lives. Such reintegrations are possible without the unconditional positive regard of a significant other *if there is an absence of threat to the self*. Typically, when we are left alone we are able to face minor, inconsistent experiences and to restructure our self-concept to assimilate these experiences. Rogers (1965) gives the following example:

> . . . the child who feels that he is weak and powerless to do a certain task, to build a tower or repair a bicycle, may find, as he works rather hopelessly at the task, that he is successful. This experience is inconsistent with the concept he holds of himself, and may not be integrated at once; but if the child is left to himself he gradually assimilates, upon his own initiative, a revision of his concept of self, that while he is generally weak and powerless, in this respect he has ability. This is the normal way in which, free from threat, new perceptions are assimilated. But if this same child is repeatedly told by his parents that he is competent to do the task, he is likely to deny it, and to prove by his behavior that he is unable to do it. The more forceful intrusion of the notion of his competence constitutes more of a threat to self and is more forcefully resisted (p. 519).

Rogers (1965) maintains that reintegration which occurs without the help of another person is not effective when the inconsistency between the self and experience is large: "It appears possible for the person to face such [large] inconsistency only while in a relationship with another in which he is sure that he will be accepted" (p. 519). The relationship to which Rogers alludes is that found in client-centered therapy.

CLIENT-CENTERED THERAPY

The Meaning of "Client-Centered"

The essence of client-centered therapy[7] is contained in the meaning of its name. Rogers (1965) explains the use of the term *client* in the following way:

---

[7] Client-centered therapy has alternatively been called *nondirective therapy,* since it is the client, not the therapist, who directs the course of treatment.

What term shall be used to indicate the person with whom the therapist is dealing? "Patient," "subject," "counselee," "analysand," are terms which have been used. We have increasingly used the term client, to the point where we have absorbed it into the label of "client-centered therapy." It has been chosen because, in spite of its imperfections of dictionary meaning and derivation, it seems to come closest to conveying the picture of this person as we see it. The client, as the term has acquired its meaning, is one who comes actively and voluntarily to gain help on a problem, but without any notion of surrendering his own responsibility for the situation. It is because the term has these connotations that we have chosen it, since it avoids the connotation that he is sick, or the object of an experiment, and so on (p. 7).

In keeping with Rogers' phenomenological position, psychotherapy is *centered* on the client. It is the client's unique problems, feelings, perceptions, attitudes, and goals which are dealt with in therapy. Therapy can only proceed from the vantage point of the client's internal frame of reference. While the therapist can only hope to gain an incomplete knowledge of his client's subjective experiences, he must through empathic understanding try to learn as much as possible about the way his client views his experiences and the world in general.

Minimal Conditions for the Therapeutic Process

Rogers hypothesizes that there are certain necessary, but not always sufficient, conditions which must be met before the therapeutic process can begin. First, the client must be experiencing some inconsistency between his self-concept and his experiences. Second, the therapist's self-concept and his experiences *in relation to the client* must be congruent. The therapist need not be open to all experiences in his life, but while taking part in the therapeutic relationship he should be relatively free of threatening experiences. Rogers (1959) thinks that the therapist can be most effective when he is "completely and fully himself, with his experience of the moment being accurately symbolized and integrated into the picture he holds of himself" (p. 215). Such a fully functioning therapist is capable of experiencing unconditional positive regard for the client as well as empathic understanding of the client's internal frame of reference. These two essential conditions serve to foster a situation which is free of threat and therefore is maximally conducive to reintegration of the client's personality.

A third prerequisite for the therapeutic process is that the client perceive, at least to some degree, the therapist's unconditional positive regard for him and the therapist's empathic understanding of his outlook. This last condition reemphasizes the importance of viewing the client through his internal frame of reference, since it would not matter how much unconditional positive regard or empathic understanding the therapist experienced for the client if the client did not perceive it.

What is the nature of the evidence to support these hypothesized basic conditions for the therapeutic process? One investigation revealed that less anxious clients have difficulty getting involved in therapy and consequently tend to drop out (Gallagher, 1953), a finding relevant to Rogers' contention that the client should be experiencing some inconsistency between his self and his experience. Seeman's (1954) study of the process and outcome of client-centered therapy showed that both the therapist's liking his client and the client's feeling liked tend to be associated with successful therapy, which indirectly supports Rogers' third hypothesized condition.

Fiedler (1950) compared the relationship established between expert and novice therapists and their clients in three different types of psychotherapy: client-centered, traditional psychoanalytic, and neoanalytic. Four judges listened to recordings of the therapy sessions, and for each session they sorted 75 statements descriptive of the therapeutic relationship (e.g., "Therapist treats patient with much deference"; "Therapist is sympathetic with patient") on a seven-category Q-sort ranging from most characteristic to least characteristic of the session. The results showed that experienced therapists of all three orientations tended to create a relationship in which they demonstrated an understanding of the client's communications from the client's point of view, thereby lending support to the importance of empathic understanding.

The Process of Client-Centered Therapy

In client-centered therapy, the major responsibility for the therapeutic process falls to the client. Rogers' basic philosophy in this regard is that given the proper circumstances, the client will have the capacity to begin to resolve his problems. This is a position which is directly in keeping with Rogers' view of the development of behavioral disorders. Behavioral disorders are a consequence of conflict between a person's two fundamental evaluative processes, one based on the self-actualization tendency—the organismic valuing process—and the other based on the values of other people—conditions of worth. Rogers firmly believes that no behavior disorders would develop if the person were guided solely by the organismic valuing process. It is necessary in client-centered therapy to create a situation in which the client feels free from his conditions of worth, thereby allowing his behavior to be guided by his organismic valuing process. This goal can be achieved in a nonthreatening situation in which the client feels understood (empathic understanding) and accepted as a whole person (unconditional positive regard). Under these conditions the client will be able to accurately examine those experiences which have been inconsistent with his self-concept and of which he was previously unaware because they were either perceived only in a distorted fashion or not at all. How, then, does the therapist create these ideal conditions?

Client-centered therapy proceeds by means of a verbal interchange between the client and the therapist. The therapist shows unconditional positive regard for the client by accepting what the client says without either approval or disapproval. He accepts equally and without evaluation all of the client's feelings and behavior. Typically, this is done by responding to the client's statements with such phrases as "Yes," "I see," and "Mm-hmm."

The therapist communicates his empathic understanding of the client's internal frame of reference primarily on an emotional level and attempts to clarify the client's feelings by synthesizing or reorganizing the feelings which the client has expressed directly or indirectly. Secondarily, the therapist restates on a cognitive or intellectual level the ideas expressed by the client, without any attempt to reorganize the client's statements, so that the feelings involved are clarified. Both types of responses are illustrated in the following excerpt from an actual record of a client-centered therapy session (Snyder, 1947, p. 278). The client is a 20-year-old college girl whose right hand is malformed. See if you can tell which of the therapist's comments involve *clarification of feeling* and which involve *restatement of content.*

> Client (C): After I left here last time—that night during dinner the student dean in our house asked to speak to my roommate. My roommate told me about it afterwards—Miss Hansen asked if I would be embarrassed as hostess at the table. She said she didn't want to hurt me! These darn student deans who think that they must guard us! The other student dean I had before never raised the issue. It makes me so mad!
>
> Therapist (T): You feel that this incident helped to accentuate the difficulty.
>
> C: That was the first time with a student dean. Really though, it struck me very funny. She watches us like a hawk. We can't make a move but she knows it.
>
> T: You resent her activity.
>
> C: I just don't like it on general principles. Oh, I suppose that she was trying to save me embarrassment.
>
> T: You can see why she did that.

C: I think that she is really afraid of us—she's queer. I don't know, but so far as I am concerned, I'm pretty indifferent to her.
    T: You feel that she doesn't affect you one way or the other.[8]

For either type of response to be considered *empathic* understanding, the therapist must experience the cognition or affect from the client's internal frame of reference. This is not easy to do because we are accustomed to viewing others from an *external* frame of reference, as objective, outside observers. It is necessary for the therapist to actively try to stay within his client's subjective world.

The Efficacy of Client-Centered Therapy

Is client-centered therapy effective in producing personality changes? The answer to this question must be sought in empirical studies, and it is very much to Rogers' credit that his approach to personality change has stimulated considerable research. Overall, the existing data indicate that client-centered therapy can produce positive personality changes, usually measured by changes in self-concept, as for example, increased congruity between a client's self and ideal self (e.g., Rogers & Dymond, 1954; Shlien, Mosak, & Dreikurs, 1962). In fact, one reviewer (Bergin, 1966) has concluded that client-centered therapy is, "to date [i.e., 1966], the only school of interview-oriented psychotherapy which has consistently yielded positive outcomes in research studies . . ." (p. 241).

However, a sobering note of caution must be interjected. Whereas there is evidence that client-centered therapy can lead to significant personality changes in a positive direction (when compared with suitable controls), there is also evidence that some of the clients who have undergone client-centered therapy experience negative personality changes. Bergen (1966) notes that in one study (Rogers & Dymond, 1954) almost one-quarter of the client subjects showed a decline in the congruence between their self and ideal self after client-centered therapy. Similar results in the same study have been found in an analysis of changes in maturity, from pretherapy through follow-up, which were assessed independently of the therapists' evaluations of the success of the therapy. Clients whose therapy was judged to have been "unsuccessful" showed a sharp decrease in the level of maturity of their behavior, whereas clients whose therapy had been "successful" showed a definite increase in mature behavior.

It should be noted that client-centered therapy is certainly not the only form of psychotherapy for which a "deterioration effect" has

----

[8] The therapist's first two comments are clarification of feeling, while his last two are restatement of content.

been found (Bergin, 1966). The data are more a warning against the myth that any form of psychotherapy is better than no therapy at all than a condemnation of client-centered therapy in particular. The general findings of psychotherapy research on the effects of client-centered therapy can be summarized as follows. Control subjects who do not receive treatment tend to improve slightly, on the average, and vary little from their group mean. In contrast, there tends to be much more variability among subjects treated by psychotherapy—some clients improve markedly, some remain unchanged, and some get worse. One solution to this perplexing phenomenon is to investigate which clients are most likely to benefit from a given therapeutic orientation, and this is one line of research which is currently under way.

THE FULLY FUNCTIONING PERSON: MASLOW'S RESEARCH

In the preceding discussion of Rogers' approach to personality, the *fully functioning person* has been alluded to a number of times. Such a person is fully self-actualizing: his behavior is regulated by his organismic valuing process, he is open to all experiences, his self-concept is whole and consistent with his experiences, and he is free of threat and anxiety, and hence has no defenses. In short, he epitomizes psychological health or adjustment. Actually, what has just been described is an ideal man, and such a (living) specimen has yet to be found. However, there are some individuals who come close to the goal of complete self-actualization. What would such people be like?

Abraham Maslow, whose approach to personality is very similar to that of Rogers, has tried to answer this intriguing question. Maslow (1972) describes the origin of his studies of the self-actualizing person in the following words:

My investigations on self-actualization were not planned to be research and did not start out as research. They started out as the effort of a young intellectual to try to understand two of his teachers whom he loved, adored, and admired and who were very, very wonderful people. It was a kind of high-IQ devotion. I could not be content simply to adore, but sought to understand why these two people were so different from the run-of-the-mill people in the world. These two people were Ruth Benedict and Max Wertheimer.[9] They were my teachers . . . and they were most remarkable human beings. My training in psychology equipped me not at

---

[9] Ruth Benedict was an anthropologist at Columbia University whose main field of interest was the American Indian. Max Wertheimer was a psychologist who taught at the New School for Social Research and was one of the founders of Gestalt psychology.

all for understanding them. It was as if they were not quite people but something more than people. My own investigation began as a prescientific or nonscientific activity. . . . When I tried to understand them, think about them, and write about them . . . I realized in one wonderful moment that their two patterns could be generalized. I was talking about a kind of person, not about two noncomparable individuals. There was wonderful excitement in that. I tried to see whether this pattern could be found elsewhere, and I did find it elsewhere, in one person after another (pp. 41–42).

Maslow's investigation of self-actualizing persons relies heavily on the case study method and is based on data from a relatively small and select group of subjects, including both living persons and such historical figures as Thomas Jefferson (cf. McClelland's study of achievement motivation in past societies; Chapter 9). In his report of the research, which was first published in 1950, Maslow justified this approach in the following way:

. . . I consider the problem of psychological health to be so pressing, that *any* suggestions, *any* bits of data, however moot, are endowed with great heuristic value. This kind of research is in principle so difficult—involving as it does a kind of lifting oneself by one's axiological bootstraps—that if we were to wait for conventionally reliable data, we should have to wait forever. It seems that the only manly thing to do is not to fear mistakes, to plunge in, to do the best that one can, hoping to learn enough from blunders to correct them eventually. At present the only alternative is simply to refuse to work with the problem. Accordingly, for whatever use can be made of it, the following report is presented with due apologies to those who insist on conventional reliability, validity, sampling, etc. (Maslow, 1963, p. 527).

In keeping with this philosophy, Maslow's research focuses primarily on making observations rather than testing hypotheses, and the resulting observations are admittedly subjective in nature. With this type of qualitative data the ability of the investigator to accurately and graphically summarize his impressions (the basic units of the data) greatly enhances the usefulness of the report. Maslow has a distinct talent in this regard. Accordingly, the present explication of Maslow's 15 most salient characteristics of self-actualizing men relies heavily on direct quotations from Maslow's (1963) highly expressive and communicative language.

To begin with, self-actualizing people can be characterized by their *efficient perception of reality.*

The first form in which this capacity was noticed was an unusual ability to detect the spurious, the fake, and the dishonest in personality, and in general to judge people correctly and efficiently.

. . . As the study progressed, it slowly became apparent that this efficiency extended to many other areas of life—indeed *all* areas that were tested. In art and music, in things of the intellect, in scientific matters, in politics and public affairs, they seemed as a group to be able to see concealed or confused realities more swiftly and more correctly than others. Thus an informal experiment indicated that their predictions of the future from whatever facts were in hand at the time seemed to be more often correct, because less based upon wish, desire, anxiety, fear, or upon generalized, character-determined optimism or pessimism (p. 531).

Maslow observes that fully functioning individuals are characterized by *acceptance* of themselves, of others, and of nature.

They can accept their own human nature in stoic style, with all its shortcomings, with all its discrepancies from the ideal image without feeling real concern. It would convey the wrong impression to say that they are self-satisfied. What we must say rather is that they can take the frailties and sins, weaknesses, and evils of human nature in the same unquestioning spirit with which one accepts the characteristics of nature. One does not complain about water because it is wet, or about rocks because they are hard, or about trees because they are green. As the child looks out upon the world with wide, uncritical innocent eyes, simply noting and observing what is the case, without either arguing the matter or demanding that it be otherwise, so does the self-actualizing person look upon human nature in himself and in others . . . (p. 533).

Although self-actualizing people are *spontaneous,* they are not necessarily the most unconventional people in society.

Their behavior is marked by simplicity and naturalness, and by lack or artificiality or straining for effect. This does not necessarily mean consistently unconventional behavior. . . . It is his impulses, thought, consciousness that are so unusually unconventional, spontaneous, and natural. Apparently recognizing that the world of people in which he lives could not understand or accept this, and since he has no wish to hurt them or fight with them over every triviality, he will go through the ceremonies and rituals of convention with a good-humored shrug and with the best possible grace. Thus I have seen a man accept an honor he laughed at and even despised in private, rather than make an issue of it and hurt the people who thought they were pleasing him (p. 535).

Maslow's subjects are *problem-centered* in the sense that they are

. . . ordinarily concerned with basic issues and eternal questions of the type that we have learned to call philosophical or ethical. Such people live customarily in the widest possible frame of reference. They seem never to get so close to the trees that they fail to see the forest. They work within a framework of values that is broad and not petty, universal and not local, and in terms of a century rather than the moment. In a word, these people are all in one sense or another philosophers, however homely (p. 537).

Self-actualizers appear to have a greater *affinity for solitude and privacy* than the average person and also show a tendency to be *independent from their culture and environment.*

> . . . self-actualizing people are not dependent for their main satisfactions on the real world, or other people or culture or means to ends or, in general, on extrinsic satisfactions. Rather they are dependent for their own development and continued growth on their own potentialities and latent resources. Just as the tree needs sunshine and water and food, so do most people need love, safety, and other basic need gratifications that can come only from without. But once these external satisfiers are obtained, once these inner deficiencies are satiated by outside satisfiers, the true problem of individual development begins . . . self-actualization (p. 539).

Fully functioning persons exhibit a *continued freshness of appreciation* for even the most ordinary events in their lives. They have

> . . . the wonderful capacity to appreciate again and again, freshly and naïvely, the basic goods of life, with awe, pleasure, wonder, and even ecstasy, however stale these experiences may have become to others . . . any sunset may be as beautiful as the first one. . . . For such people, even the casual workaday, moment-to-moment business of living can be thrilling, exciting and ecstatic. These intense feeings do not come all the time; they come occasionally rather than usually, but at the most unexpected moments (pp. 539–40).

They are also likely to experience what Maslow calls *"the oceanic feeling."* This phrase refers to feelings of

> . . . limitless horizons opening up to the vision, the feeling of being simultaneously more powerful and also more helpless than one ever was before, the feeling of great ecstasy and wonder and awe, the loss of placing in time and space with, finally, the conviction that something extremely important and valuable had happened, so that the subject is to some extent transformed and strengthened even in his daily life by such experiences (p. 541).

Self-actualizing people usually have a *genuine desire to help the human race,* although they tend to have *deep ties with relatively few individuals.* As one of Maslow's subjects noted: "I haven't got time for many friends. Nobody has, that is, if they are to be *real* friends" (p. 542).

Maslow describes self-actualizers as being *democratic* in the deepest sense. Besides being free of prejudice with regard to superficial characteristics of people, such as race or political beliefs, they tend to respect all persons. For example, they are willing to learn from anyone who is able to teach them something. At the same time, Maslow says that his subjects do not indiscriminately equalize all human beings. Rather, self-actualizing people, "themselves elite, select for their friends elite, but this is an elite of character, capacity, and talent, rather than of birth, race, blood, name, family, age, youth, fame, or power" (p. 544).

Fully functioning individuals show a keen *ability to discriminate between means and ends.* While they usually focus on ends rather than means, their ends are frequently what most people consider means. That is, they are "somewhat more likely to appreciate for its own sake, and in an absolute way, the doing itself; they can often enjoy for its own sake the getting to some place as well as the arriving. It is occasionally possible for them to make out of the most trivial and routine activity an intrinsically enjoyable game or dance or play" (p. 545).

Maslow's subjects tend to have a *philosophical sense of humor.* Whereas the average man often enjoys humor that pokes fun at some individual's inferiority, that hurts someone, or that is "off-color," the self-actualizing man finds humor dealing with the foolishness of man-in-general appealing. Such thoughtful, philosophical humor typically elicits a smile rather than a laugh.

Not surprisingly, Maslow finds that, without exception, his subjects are characterized by *creativeness.* However, the creativeness manifested by self-actualizing persons is different from unusual talent or genius. Rather, Maslow likens it to the

> . . . naïve and universal creativeness of unspoiled children. It seems to be more a fundamental characteristic of common human nature—a potentiality given to all human beings at birth. Most human beings lose this as they become enculturated, but some few individuals seem either to retain this fresh and naïve, direct way of looking at life, or if they have lost it, as most people do, they later in life recover it (p. 546).

Self-actualizing persons tend to *resist enculturation.* Outwardly, in their dress, speech, and manner of behaving, they remain within the limits of convention. At the same time, they "maintain a certain inner detachment from the culture in which they are immersed" (p. 547). Furthermore, although they are not among those in the forefront of social action, they may be committed to social change, as Maslow points out in the following example.

> One of these subjects, who was a hot rebel in his younger days, a union organizer in the days when this was a highly dangerous occupation, has given up in disgust and hopelessness. As he became resigned to the slowness of social change (in this culture and in this era) he turned finally to education of the young. All the others

show what might be called a calm, long-time concern with culture improvement that seems to me to imply an acceptance of slowness of change along with the unquestioned desirability and necessity of such change (p. 548).

Finally, Maslow makes it clear that self-actualizing persons are indeed "fully functioning" in the sense that, like all of us, they are not perfect.

They too are equipped with silly, wasteful, or thoughtless habits. They can be boring, stubborn, irritating. They are by no means free from a rather superficial vanity, pride, partiality to their own productions, family, friends, and children. Temper outbursts are not rare. Our subjects are occasionally capable of an extraordinary and unexpected ruthlessness. It must be remembered that they are very strong people. This makes it possible for them to display a surgical coldness when this is called for, beyond the power of the average man. The man who found that a long-trusted acquaintance was dishonest cut himself off from this friendship sharply and abruptly and without any pangs whatsoever. Another woman who was married to someone she did not love, when she decided on divorce, did it with a decisiveness that looked almost like ruthlessness. Some of them recover so quickly from the death of people close to them as to seem heartless (pp. 550–51).

12

The Phenomenological Strategy
THE PSYCHOLOGY OF PERSONAL CONSTRUCTS

The Psychology of Personal Constructs differs in a number of respects from the self-actualization approaches described in the previous chapter. Nevertheless, they share many of the same "philosophical" roots of the phenomenological strategy.

In Chapter 1 it was suggested that a theory of personality is very much dependent upon a model of man. That is, the way a theorist views the subject of his study, the human being, will, in large part, determine his theory of personality. But how does one develop a conception of the nature of man? Although we are not generally aware of the ongoing process, all of us develop such conceptions as we view others in our environment and observe our own behavior. For example, both a man who takes advantage of people and a man who has been swindled will probably feel that most persons are opportunists and that such behavior is the norm. George A. Kelly has argued that the personality theorist should view *man in general* in terms of the way *man individually* views, or *construes,* his own behavior.

As a psychologist Kelly was in the business of attempting to predict and control human behavior. In the midst of this endeavor, he found something paradoxical about the way personality psychologists studied man. It was as if the psychologist stood in another world looking down on alien beings who were the subject of his investigations. He would examine these foreign specimens systematically, generate hypotheses about their behavior, and then test these hypotheses in experiments. If the hypotheses were confirmed, the theoretical notions which led to the predictions gained some support.

265

The psychologist went about this business in an intellectual, rational fashion. The beings he was studying, however, were supposed to be neither rational nor intellectual; rather, they seemed to be impelled by dark, mysterious forces which were entirely irrational.

With a little detached thought it became obvious that the psychologist is no different from the people he studies and certainly has no more claim to intellectual and rational powers than any other person. Since the psychologist as a scientist, goes about his daily work theorizing and testing hypotheses in an effort to gain some power of prediction and control over other human beings, one might hypothesize that all men, in their daily interactions with people and things in their environment, behave in a similar way. The young child who has not received the second helping of ice cream he wants and, in an effort to secure it, cuddles up with tearful eyes to a visiting grandparent can be viewed as a scientist at work. The child is acting on the theory, however implicit it may be, that grandparents are likely to be beguiled by affection and also that they tend to be more lenient with second portions of dessert than parents. His hypothesis might be: "I have a better chance of getting that ice cream if I play on grandpa's sympathy." He could then proceed to test this hypothesis, or prediction, by tearfully snuggling up to his grandfather. If it turns out that grandpa somehow succeeds in securing the ice cream for him, then the hypothesis is confirmed and the theory receives some support. In the future he will be more confident in using this theory. If, however, grandpa is not as soft as his grandson thought him to be or is not capable of convincing the parents that a second helping would do no harm, then the hypothesis is not supported. In this case, the child may very well try a new strategy the next time ice cream is served for dessert.

MAN-THE-SCIENTIST

The observation that humans are constantly involved in the prediction and control of events in their environment led Kelly to view man *as if he were a scientist*. Man-the-scientist has many theories about the nature of events in the real world, and it is through these theories that he deals with his environment. Kelly has assumed, it should be noted, that events in the real world actually have existence. That is, they do not just exist in the minds of men. At the same time, man's theories, or conceptions, of these real events also have existence, and they can be the subject of scientific investigation.

Kelly (1955)[1] suggested that "man looks at his world through

---

[1] Kelly's basic statement of his approach to personality is contained in a two-volume work entitled *The Psychology of Personal Constructs* (1955). Its

transparent patterns or templets which he creates and then attempts to fit over the realities of which the world is composed" (pp. 8–9). He called these templets *constructs*. A construct is a representation of some event in the person's environment, a way of looking at something which is then tested against the reality of the environment. Constructs are not abstracted from existing realities; rather, they are imposed *upon* real events: a construct comes from the person who uses it, not from the event it is being used to construe.

Examples of constructs include "just vs. unjust," "stable vs. changing," "liberal vs. conservative," "healthy vs. sick," "flexible vs. dogmatic," "warm vs. aloof," and "heavy vs. light."[2] Such constructs are used by many people to construe events in their lives. However, each construct has a slightly different meaning for each person, and it is only because of the limitations of our language that constructs appear to be common to all people. Every man has his own set of unique *personal constructs*.

A person hypothesizes that a particular construct will adequately fit some event in his environment. He then puts this hypothesis to the test by interacting with the event, be it interpersonal or material in nature, in the manner dictated by the construct. The little boy in the previous example acted in accordance with his construct "Grandparents are benevolent" by first making a specific prediction from this construct (i.e., that he would get a second helping of ice cream by cajoling grandpa) and then acting upon the prediction to test its validity. If a prediction is confirmed, the construct from which it was derived receives support and is therefore maintained as useful. If the construct leads to incorrect predictions, then it is likely to undergo some revision or it may even be discarded altogether. The measure which is used to assess the validity of a construct is its *predictive efficiency*. The more successful a construct is in anticipating events, the greater is its predictive efficiency.

CONSTRUCTIVE ALTERNATIVISM

The Psychology of Personal Constructs is based on the philosophical position of *constructive alternativism,* which Kelly (1955) explains this way:

> . . . there are always some alternative constructions available to choose among in dealing with the world. No one needs to paint

---

first three chapters, which present Kelly's basic theoretical propositions, were reissued as the paperback *A Theory of Personality* (New York: Norton, 1963).

[2] According to Kelly, all constructs are bipolar and dichotomous, and when a construct is used to construe an event, only one pole is being used. This point is discussed fully later in the chapter.

himself into a corner; no one needs to be completely hemmed in by circumstances; no one needs to be the victim of his biography (p. 15).

This position, which imparts free will to man, can be seen as being in striking contrast to the deterministic views of Freud, who saw man as having an unchangeable, partially universal "construct system." Freudian man is very much the victim of his biological endowment (i.e., the drives he is born with are universal) and his experiences in the first few years of life. Kellian man, on the other hand, has his own unique system of constructs and always has the option of changing these ways of construing the world. In fact, according to Kelly, our outlooks (constructs) rarely are the same today as they were yesterday. They are constantly being tested in attempts to anticipate future events. The inevitable failure of our constructs from time to time makes their revision a necessity if we are to construe the world in the most predictively efficient manner. The constructs that undergo the most frequent modification are those that make predictions concerning immediate events and therefore lead to very quick feedback concerning their ability to anticipate the future.

Although events have reality in and of themselves, they do not belong to any construct in particular. In line with constructive alternativism, the same event can be viewed from a variety of different perspectives. One interesting example of how different a situation becomes when it is construed from a different construct involved a patient in a psychiatric hospital (Neale, 1968). The patient's behavior was among the most deviant on the ward, as evidenced by her unintelligible speech, extremely poor personal habits, ludicrous behavior in the presence of other patients and visitors, and occasional violent outbursts. One day the aides dressed the patient in an attractive outfit, including nylon stockings, high heels, lipstick, and makeup, and took her to the beauty parlor to have her hair styled and set. When she returned to the ward several hours later, the patient no longer showed any of the blatantly "abnormal" symptoms which had become her trademark. Whereas she was still a patient in a psychiatric hospital, and in every other respect her circumstances remained unchanged, it was obvious from her behavior that the way she construed herself had definitely changed, if only temporarily.

Properties of Constructs

Each of our constructs has a particular domain of events which may be encompassed by it. This *range of convenience* puts a limit on the usefulness of the construct. The construct "religious vs. not religious" can be used to construe a variety of human behaviors, but it is hardly applicable for talking about the relative merits of American and European sports cars. It is often tempting to generalize beyond the range of convenience of a construct, but a high price of lowered predictive efficiency is usually paid for such generalization.

Although all constructs have a limited range of convenience, the breadth of the range may vary substantially from construct to construct. The construct "good vs. bad" can be used to construe most events in which evaluation is possible and thus has a wide range of convenience. Contrast this with the construct "brave vs. cowardly," which is considerably narrower in its scope of application.

Each construct also has a *focus of convenience* which is the point in the construct's range of convenience at which it is maximally predictive. For example, the focus of convenience of the construct "religious vs. not religious" might be the customs and ceremonies of the church. Although cheating on an examination could be construed as "not religious," it would be more efficiently construed under the construct "honest vs. dishonest." Whereas cheating is an event that is within the *range* of convenience of both constructs, it is the *focus* of convenience only of the latter construct. If our aim is to anticipate Fred's future behavior in a variety of situations, it would be more useful to construe his using concealed class notes during a final examination via the construct "honest vs. dishonest" than by the construct "religious vs. not religious." Using the construct "religious vs. not religious," it would be difficult to predict the frequency of Fred's church attendance from his behavior during the final examination. Presumably, however, using the construct "honest vs. dishonest" would make it easier to anticipate whether Fred would use a fraternity brother's old term paper if he needed an "A" in a course.

Constructs also vary on a dimension of *permeability*. A permeable construct is one that is able to admit new elements to its range of convenience. An impermeable construct is one that has already been used to construe all the elements in its range of convenience and therefore is closed to the construction of new experiences. One person's construct of "good vs. bad symphonic music" might be sufficiently permeable to account for any new piece of music he hears. For example, on hearing "electronic music" for the first time, the person could construe it as either "good" or "bad." Another person's construct of "good vs. bad symphonic music" might be impermeable to any sounds other than those made by traditional orchestral instruments and therefore could not be used to construe electronic music.

There are relative degrees of permeability; constructs range from those which are completely open to new events to those which will admit no new events to their domains.[3] It should be emphasized that the notion of permeability is relevant only to the range of convenience of a given construct. By definition, a construct is impermeable to anything outside its range of convenience.

Motivation: A Rejected Construct

Earliest man construed the physical world in which he lived as one of static objects. Matter was an inert substance which was measured along spatial dimensions (length, width, and depth) and not in terms of temporal dimensions. Later, man became increasingly aware of movement in the universe, but the movement was viewed as being applied to or superimposed upon the inert objects. In an effort to account for motion (something which early man did not need to do since his world was construed as static), physicists came to employ the notion of energy.

Modern psychology, which is barely a century old, has borrowed much from the physical sciences (particularly from physics) with regard to both its view of the world and its methodology. If the physical world was naturally inert and had to be set into motion by some form of energy, it seemed reasonable to psychologists to construe man in the same way. If man is by nature a static being, yet is rarely inactive, what causes or motivates human behavior? To answer this question psychologists have postulated "special enlivening forces," such as motives, drives, needs, instincts, and incentives. Kelly (1960) summarizes the general state of most motivational theories in the following way:

> Motivational theories can be divided into two types, push theories and pull theories. Under push theories we find such terms as drive, motive, or even stimulus. Pull theories use such constructs as purpose, value, or need. In terms of a well-known metaphor, there are the pitchfork theories on the one hand and the carrot theories on the other (p. 50).

The earliest motivational theories were push theories, since they posited forces within the individual that impel him to action. Freud's personality theory, in which man is energized by biological drives, is clearly of this type. Murray has incorporated both push and pull forces within his personality theory in the form of needs (internal motives) and press (external motives). Behavioral approaches

---

[3] Kelly implies that, in practice, few constructs are likely to be completely impermeable. Thus, he noted: "An utterly concrete construct, if there were such a thing, would not be permeable at all, for it would be made up of certain specified events—those and no others" (1955, p. 79).

(see Section V) attribute man's behavior to external, social cues and therefore would be classified as pull theories.

But whether we view man as being pushed by forces within him or pulled by forces in the external world, or as actuated by a combination of pushes and pulls, to construe man in these ways is to relegate him to the realm of purely *reactive* organisms. Indeed, as Kelly and others have found, most people view their fellow human beings (whose behavior they are attempting to predict or control) in just this way, though they probably would be extremely reticent to construe themselves similarly. When a mother wants her child to pick up his toys and wash for dinner, she "knows" that she must somehow *motivate* him. She may do this by means of positive incentives (as, "We're having chocolate ice cream for dessert") or negative incentives (as, "Do what I asked you this minute or your father will spank you"). However, mother does not believe that *she* needs to be motivated to prepare dinner; she just does it!

Early in Kelly's career he traveled through Kansas to provide psychological services to public schools. A frequent complaint of teachers was that particular students were lazy. Laziness, as we commonly use the word, means a lack or minimal amount of action. If a lazy child is viewed in traditional motivational terms, the problem the teacher faces is one of finding suitable incentives—external forms of motivation which can be applied (to a naturally inactive being). What would happen if the teacher simply did not attempt to motivate the student? When Kelly and his associates proposed such a course of action to teachers, they frequently replied that the child would do absolutely nothing—he would just sit. However, when the teachers tried this, more often than not they were surprised to find that their "laziest pupils were those who could produce the most novel ideas . . . that the term 'laziness' had been applied to activities they had simply been unable to understand or appreciate" (Kelly, 1960, pp. 46–47).

It was experiences such as helping teachers *reconstrue* their pupils' behavior which led Kelly to the conclusion that the concept of motivation is redundant. Man is neither inactive nor reactive by nature. The child who was suddenly not being motivated by his teacher did not turn into an inert substance. It appeared, then, that the basic assumption concerning man's essential inertness and the inevitable corollary that the study of the causes of human behavior is synonymous with a search for the energetic forces which motivate man must be called into question. The logical alternative is that man is

. . . motivated for no other reason than that he is alive. . . . Life itself could be defined as a form of process or movement. Thus, in designating man as our object of psychological inquiry, we should be taking it for granted that movement is an essential property of his being, not something that has to be accounted for separately. We should be talking about a form of movement—man—not something that has to be motivated (Kelly, 1960, pp. 49–50).

. . . . Thus, the whole controversy as to what prods an inert organism into action becomes a dead issue. Instead, the organism is delivered fresh into the psychological world alive and struggling (Kelly, 1955, p. 37).

The concept of motivation has been used in psychology to explain two aspects of behavior: why man behaves (is active) at all and, when man is active, why he chooses to move in one direction rather than another. If we accept Kelly's basic notion that man is "already in motion simply by virtue of . . . being alive," it is still necessary to account for the second aspect of behavior—its directionality.

Kelly (1960) envisions man as existing primarily in the dimensions of time and only secondarily in the dimensions of space.

If we want to know why man does what he does, then the terms of our whys should extend themselves in time rather than in space; they should be events rather than things; they should be mileposts rather than destinations. Clearly, man lives in the present. He stands firmly astride the chasm that separates the past from the future. He is the only connecting link between these two universes. . . . To be sure, there are other forms of existence that have belonged to the past and, presumably, will also belong to the future. A rock that has rested firmly for ages may well exist in the future also, but it does not link the past with the future. . . . It does not anticipate; it does not reach out both ways to snatch handfuls from each of the two worlds in order to bring them together and subject them to the same stern laws. Only man does that (p. 56).

Any principle of the directionality of behavior must take into account this "conjunctive vision of man"—man who lives partly in the past, wholly in the present, and partly in the future.

THE FUNDAMENTAL POSTULATE AND ITS COROLLARIES

Kelly's theory is presented in the form of a basic postulate and a series of corollaries which follow from it.

Fundamental Postulate

Kelly's (1955) *Fundamental Postulate* states that: *"A person's processes are psychologically channelized by the ways in which he anticipates events"* (p. 46). Notice at the outset that Kelly focuses on *processes* rather than inert substances. His system is *psychological* and therefore limits its range of convenience to the investigation of human behavior. The word *channelized* denotes the stability of behavior; behavior remains relatively stable across time and situations because it is directed by means of the constructs *(ways)* a person uses to predict *(anticipate)* actual happenings *(events)* in the future. Although Kelly has rejected the traditional psychological view of motivation, it appears that his Fundamental Postulate is actually a motivation-like statement. As Kelly construes man's behavior, the "motive" to predict future events is what directs his activities.

The Construction Corollary

The *Construction Corollary* says: "A person anticipates events by construing their replications" (Kelly, 1955, p. 50). To construe an event means to place an interpretation on it, and it is through such interpretations that man is able to predict events that have not yet occurred. The process of construing involves perceiving not only the similar features which an event has over time but also those features which are *not* characteristic of it. That is, a construct must specify both similarities and contrasts. If the reader will think of some of his own personal constructs, he may not immediately see that differences are implied along with similarities. Constructs such as "good people," "pretty girl," "happy occasion," and "funny movie" appear at the outset to be referring only to similarities among events. However, the contrasts (i.e., "bad people," "homely girl," "sad occasion," and "serious movie") are implicitly there, and must be there, for the construct to be at all useful in anticipating events. In the example of the little boy who wanted more ice cream, the construct was actually "grandpa is benevolent vs. grandpa is not benevolent," although the opposite pole ("grandpa is not benevolent") remained implicit.

Although the *contrast* is often implicitly present when we employ a construct, it is a *sine qua non* and therefore must be capable of being made explicit. Consider the constructs "happy vs. sad" and "good vs. bad" in contrast to "happy vs. euphoric" and "good vs. non-Christian." To state only one of the construct's poles is insufficient; in the present examples, the second set of constructs is as legitimate as the first. The opposite of a concept often differs with the way a person construes things.

The verbal label one puts on a construct should not be confused with the construct itself. The former is generally necessary when a person needs to communicate his construct to others. But all of us have many constructs to which labels in the form of communicable language cannot be applied. Although this may be because the constructs are not well specified, more often than not it is due to the limitations of our language. Children's constructs are frequently at a preverbal level, though they may be no less predictively efficient than those of adults. The old "commonsense" maxim which says that if a person cannot express a thought he really does not have the thought, needs to be called into question. Furthermore, the fact that two constructs have the same label does not necessarily mean that they are equivalent, just as the fact that two constructs are given different labels does not necessarily mean that the constructs are different.

Finally, to fully convey the meaning of the Construction Corollary a word must be said about *replications*.

> Only when man attunes his ear to recurrent themes . . . does his universe begin to make sense to him. Like a musician, he must phrase his experience in order to make sense out of it. The phrases are distinguished events. The separation of events is what man produces for himself when he decides to chop up time into manageable lengths. Within these limited segments, which are based on recurrent themes, man begins to discover the bases for likenesses and differences (Kelly, 1955, p. 52).

No two events are ever identical. In fact, "the appearance of replication is a reflection of . . . [a person's] own fallible construction of what is going on" (Kelly, 1970, p. 11). The packaged peanut butter cookie Judy ate a moment ago is different from the second one she eats and, in general, our taste for and enjoyment of most of the things we like will be slightly different each time we experience them.

But people are much more apt to view two admittedly similar events as the same rather than as different; to do otherwise would make life terribly inconsistent and, more importantly, unpredictable. Thus, although events never exactly duplicate themselves, future events can be predicted if they are construable by the same constructs as their predecessors. Man's task is to search for those themes or characteristics which remain relatively stable over time. He anticipates events by construing those aspects of events which do recur consistently.

The Individuality Corollary

In the *Individuality Corollary,* which states that "persons differ from each other in their construction of events" (1955, p. 55), Kelly emphasizes that each person has a set of unique personal constructs. No two people observing the same event will have exactly the same interpretation of it. The difference between people, therefore, lies in their construing events from different vantage points. Kelly is keenly aware of the uniqueness of each individual but believes that it is possible to ferret out nomothetic laws about human behavior. Just as there are recurrent themes among events which are never exact duplicates of each other, there are characteristics of personal construct systems that repeat themselves across individuals; it is the psychologist's task to search for these.

The Dichotomy Corollary

The *Dichotomy Corollary,* which says, "A person's construct system is composed of a finite number of dichotomous constructs" (p. 59), emphasizes the *bipolar* and *dichotomous* nature of personal constructs. A construct must specify both similarity and difference in order to be able to construe the replication of events.

> Having chosen an aspect with respect to which two events are replications of each other, we find that, by the same token, another event is definitely not a replication of the first two. The person's choice of an aspect determines both what shall be considered similar and what shall be considered contrasting. . . . If we choose an aspect in which A and B are similar, but in contrast to C, it is important to note that it is the same aspect of all three, A, B, *and* C, that forms the basis of the construct (p. 59).

If A and B are men and C is a woman and the aspect which we abstract is sex, we can classify all three in terms of the same aspect. With respect to sex, A and B are alike and C is different. If we introduce still a fourth element, D, a lamp for example, it is apparent that the aspect *sex* is not applicable to construing D. That is, D is outside the range of convenience of the construct "male vs. female."

The idea of dichotomous constructs is perhaps one of the most controversial issues in the Psychology of Personal Constructs. Kelly contends that all human thinking is essentially dichotomous, and this conception is at variance with most contemporary theories of the nature of human thought. If a construct is relevant to a particular event, the event must be placed at *either* one pole of the construct *or* the other. The pole of a construct that is being used at any given moment to construe an event is called the *emergent pole,* while the contrasting pole is called the *implicit pole.*

No problem arises with employing a dichotomy in the case of a construct in which the difference between the poles is unequivocal, as is usually the case with "male vs. female." But although things may be either black or white, they are most often a shade of gray (i.e., neither black nor white). Kelly (1955) was aware of this problem and explained how constructs, which are composed of mutually exclusive alternatives, can be used relativistically: ". . . dichotomous constructs can be built into scales, the scales representing superordinate constructs [see discussion of the Organization Corollary below] which are further abstractions of the separate scalar values. Thus, *more grayness vs. less grayness* is a further abstraction of the construct *black vs. white*" (p. 66).

Kelly's dichotomous constructs do not include both contrasting and irrelevant events. In classical logic, everything that is either the opposite of a concept or simply unrelated to it is lumped together. In that sense, with reference to the concept "automobile," motorcycles, ships, and airplanes *as well as* pickles, pianos, and porcupines are treated as equivalent. In Kelly's system, however, the former objects would be construed at the implicit pole of the construct (i.e., "nonautomobiles"), but the latter objects simply could not be construed by the construct "automobiles vs. nonautomobiles" because they are out of its range of convenience, namely, modes of transportation.

It should be noted that the implicit pole—"nonautomobiles"—is merely a shorthand designation for the opposite of "automobiles." Whereas concepts such as "male," "good," and "living" have contrasts with specific referents in our language, many concepts do not. Therefore, it is often necessary to specify merely the negation of the emergent pole, realizing that it does not include irrelevant elements. Once again, the limitations of language impose artificial restrictions when one attempts to convey the meaning of a personal construct system.

The Range Corollary

Not only do people have a *finite* number of constructs, but, according to the *Range Corollary*, "a construct is convenient for the anticipation of a finite range of events only" (Kelly, 1955, p. 68). This implies that all people encounter events which they are not able to construe. Inevitably there are happenings in one's life which are beyond the range of convenience of all of one's constructs. The effect of being unable to construe an event and, consequently, of being incapable of anticipating it is, in the Psychology of Personal Constructs, what we call *anxiety*.

ANXIETY.   The vague feeling of helplessness which we commonly denote as anxiety is viewed as a result of being unable to anticipate an event because one's available constructs do not apply. When a person has no constructs to interpret an event, he cannot fully comprehend what is happening because it exists without a reference point or meaning for him. Hence, although an anxious individual feels apprehensive or afraid, he is unable to "put his finger" on why he feels that way.

One very prevalent view of mental illness, and most particularly of the so-called neuroses, holds that anxiety is a major causative factor (cf. Freud's position, Chapters 4 and 5). If we accept this view as valid, it is interesting to see how the notion is translated into the concepts of the Psychology of Personal Constructs. The anxious person, rather than being the victim of inner conflicts and dammed-up energy (the psychoanalytic interpretation of neurosis), is one who is having difficulty in construing aspects of his environment. Instead of being overwhelmed by drives which are seeking expression, he is overwhelmed by happenings in his life which he cannot understand (anticipate). Looked at in this latter manner, psychotherapy then becomes a process in which the patient acquires new constructs which will successfully predict the troublesome events or make already existing constructs more permeable so as to admit the new events to their range of convenience. This process will be discussed more fully in a later section.

The Organization Corollary

For Kelly the units of personality are personal constructs. The structure or organization of the personality is determined by the relationship of the constructs to one another. This point is presented in the *Organization Corollary:* "Each person characteristically evolves, for his convenience in anticipating events, a construct system embracing ordinal relationships between constructs" (1955, p. 56). People not only differ in the constructs they use to understand the world, but, perhaps even more importantly, they differ in the way they organize their constructs. It is therefore possible for two people to have similar personal constructs yet have extremely different personalities because their constructs are ordered differently.

Within a person's construct system, constructs are arranged in a hierarchical structure, with most constructs being both subordinate to some constructs and superordinate to others. This type of organization makes it possible for an individual to move from one construct to another in an orderly fashion and to resolve conflicts and inconsistencies among constructs. Consider the relationships among three of David's constructs which are depicted in Figure 12–1. The construct "loving vs. unloving" is superordinate to the constructs "giving vs. selfish" and "pleasant vs. unpleasant," which, for David, are on the same hierarchical level. David has planned to spend the day at the beach with his girl friend and is faced with the dilemma of deciding whether to take along his younger brother as his mother has requested. If his brother should go with them, David would construe himself as "giving" but the day at the beach as "unpleasant." On the other hand, if he chooses to leave his brother at home,

FIGURE 12–1

Hypothetical Relationships among (David's) Three
Personal Constructs

Superordinate construct	**Loving vs. Unloving**
Subordinate constructs*	Giving vs. Selfish Pleasant vs. Unpleasant

* Note: Both subordinate constructs are assumed to be of
equal hierarchical status in this example.

David would construe himself as "selfish" but the day as "pleasant."
To resolve this conflict between two of his constructs, David uses the
superordinate construct "loving vs. unloving" to construe the situation. Both "giving" and "pleasant" are subsumed under the "loving"
pole of the superordinate construct, which makes it possible for
David to construe the event as both "giving" and "pleasant."

A construct system—the ordinal relationships among constructs—
is somewhat more permanent than individual constructs, but it can
change. Sometimes there is even a reversal of superordinate and
subordinate constructs. In the previous example, "giving vs. selfish"
might become superordinate to "loving vs. unloving." Since a person's construct system develops "for his convenience in anticipating
events," predictive efficiency is the criterion for deciding the relative
merit of one hierarchical order of constructs over another.

The Choice Corollary and Elaboration of a Construct System

To predict a person's behavior, it is necessary to know not only
what construct the person will use to construe the relevant events
but also which of the two poles of the dichotomous construct he will
employ. Kelly (1970) deals with this latter problem in his *Choice
Corollary:* "A person chooses for himself that alternative in a dichot-
omized construct through which he anticipates the greater possibility for the elaboration of his system" (p. 15).

There are two basic ways by which one can elaborate his construct system and thereby enhance its ability to anticipate events—
by defining it more precisely and by extending its range of convenience to new events. The meaning of *definition* and *extension* of
a construct system can be understood in terms of two different kinds
of wagers with respect to the anticipation of events. "Definition" involves a relatively safe wager with a modest payoff, while "extension" involves a riskier bet but with a more substantial payoff.

In the case of definition, the person chooses the pole of the
construct that has in the past led to the more accurate prediction
of events similar to the present one and therefore has the higher

probability of predicting the present event. If the prediction is accurate, the construct becomes more explicit by virtue of its having made an additional successful prediction.

In contrast, extension involves choosing the alternative which has the greater probability of expanding the construct so as to include new events (i.e., increasing its range of convenience). In extension the construct is being used either to anticipate a new event or to anticipate a familiar event in a new way, and therefore the probability of success is less than when definition is the goal. However, if the prediction proves to be correct, then the construct becomes more comprehensive.

Kelly (1955) speaks of the difference between definition and extension as one between security and adventure.

> Internal conflict . . . is often a matter of trying to balance off the secure definiteness of a narrowly encompassed world against the uncertain possibilities of life's adventure. One may anticipate events by trying to become more and more certain about fewer and fewer things or by trying to become vaguely aware of more and more things on the misty horizon (p. 67).

The difference between definition and extension can be illustrated by the example of a student who has gotten an "A" in a course entitled "Introduction to Psychology" and must decide whether to take an advanced psychology course or "Introduction to Sociology" next. Because he is already somewhat familiar with the field of psychology, taking an advanced psychology course is more likely to lead to an increase in his understanding of basic psychological concepts and to a good grade. This represents the more secure route of definition. The less secure alternative, extension, would mean launching into the new area of sociology, which is more likely to broaden the student's outlook and knowledge but may lessen his chances of getting a high grade.

Although there is little empirical evidence concerning how or when the decision to define or to extend one's construct system is made, it is probably the case that a person becomes more likely to choose extension of his constructs as his success in anticipation increases. The poorer his constructs are at predicting future events, the more likely he will be to choose definition. Sechrest (1963) gives an interesting example of this principle.

> A young man is more likely to consider asking the new girl in town for a date when he has been relatively successful in his experiences with the old ones, and he is more likely to ask her when the proposed date is for a relatively familiar function. Thus, he may prefer a girl he knows well if he is about to attend his first formal, country club ball (p. 221).

Both definition and extension serve to elaborate a construct, and neither alternative is *ipso facto* the better choice. Elaboration of one's construct system frequently involves both definition and extension, allowing the individual to experiment (extension) in life and at the same time remain within a safe distance of his proven constructs (definition). This strategy for elaboration protects the person from the threatening experience of having his construct system undergo a major change and is analogous to making a moderately risky wager. Whichever path to elaboration is chosen, a person will use that pole of his personal construct which is more likely to elaborate the construct and enhance its efficiency in predicting future events.

Elaboration of one's construct system may come about when natural choice points or dilemmas present themselves. Or, an individual may actively seek experiences which will elaborate his predictive system. The student who does extra work, takes more or unusual courses, asks questions and expresses opinions in large classes, and spends much time after class discussing material with his teachers would exemplify active elaboration. So too would the woman who goes out of her way to meet men, to engage attractive males in conversation, and to arrange for her own dates rather than wait to be asked. In both cases the behavior is likely to be viewed as *aggressive*.

AGGRESSION.   In Personal Construct Theory, aggression refers to the *active* elaboration of one's construct system. Aggression need not be hostile or antisocial in nature. In fact, aggression commonly has two distinct meanings—one involving hostility and attack and the other concerning assertiveness, boldness, and enterprise. It is in the latter sense that aggression is viewed by the Psychology of Personal Constructs, and seen in this way it can have definite positive and adaptive features. In the world of business, for example, aggressiveness is the mark of a successful man or one who is labeled as a "comer."

In the course of actively pursuing the elaboration of his construct system, a person may not take other people's welfare into account and, if that is the case, aggression may have injurious consequences. For instance, the student who talks to his instructor "endlessly" after class may be infringing on the other students' opportunity to see him.

Active elaboration, or aggression, requires setting up choice points in one's life and involving oneself in making decisions and taking action. Not infrequently, other people with whom the person plays roles become inadvertently swept into this whirlwind of action and uncertainty with the result that they are threatened. Specifically, *threat,* in Kelly's theory, is the awareness that a major change in one's construct system is imminent.

The aggressive person—for example the "social pusher"—keeps plunging himself and his associates into ventures which unduly complicate their well-ordered lives. The very fact that he insists on construing himself as belonging to the social group is threatening to those who are already identified with the group. They see, in their impending reciprocal identification with him, a major shift coming up in their own core structures (Kelly, 1955, pp. 509–10).

The Experience Corollary: How a Construct System Changes

A construct system's *raison d'être* is to anticipate events as well as possible. It follows that there would be no reason for making alterations in one's already existing system of constructs if there were no problems in effective prediction. But problems do arise, particularly when new events must be construed. If the novel events show some similarity to those with which the person has had previous experience, then there should be less difficulty in construing them by means of already existing constructs. The more novel an event, the less likely that it can easily be subsumed into the existing construct system.

Persons who tend to have little variation in their daily lives have relatively stable construct systems. Thus, an elderly woman who lives alone, stays in the house most of the time, and follows the same schedule of limited activities (e.g., rise at 7:00, breakfast at 7:45, noon lunch, knit 'til 2:30, tea at 3:00, dinner at 6:30, read until 9:30, and then retire) day after day would be expected to have an extremely stable construct system. Is it any wonder, then, that such a woman would have difficulty finding appropriate constructs to construe such new events as men making extended voyages in space and human organs being transplanted?

Kelly (1955) deals with the change of a construct system in his *Experience Corollary:* "A person's construct system varies as he successively construes the replications of events" (p. 72). As a succession of new events present themselves to be construed in order to be anticipated, a construct system changes. Tentative hypotheses, derived from the constructs, are tested against reality. The feedback as to how well these working hypotheses have predicted future events leads to an alteration of constructs. The altered constructs now are used to generate new hypotheses and, again on the basis of their adequacy, there is progressive change in the system of constructs.

For Kelly (1955), *experience* involves "successive construing of events. It is not constituted merely by the succession of events themselves" (p. 73). Again pointing to the active nature of man, Kelly contends that a person gains little or no experience as a passive observer of events occurring in his environment. If after having witnessed a succession of events, a person still construes the events in the same way, then he has gained no experience. The professor who delivers the same lectures for eight years cannot, according to Kelly's notion of experience, claim that he has had eight years of teaching experience! However, if he uses feedback from his students to modify his lectures and keeps them contemporary with respect to new information, then he would be gaining teaching experience. That is, the professor would be modifying the constructs which he uses to construe the subject matter of his lectures.

HOSTILITY.   When a prediction proves to be accurate, the construct which led to it will be further defined but will remain relatively unchanged and, at least for the moment, no further experimentation need be carried out. If, however, the prediction turns out to be a rather poor prognosticator, three courses of action are available to the individual. He can resign himself to the fact that his prediction was indeed false and that he is therefore in need of a new or revised construct. Or, he can question the validity of his test or the meaning of the results and repeat the test. Finally, he can attempt to change the *events*, rather than his way of looking at them, so that they will conform to his views of them. Hostility is the use of this third alternative to cope with invalidating evidence for one's constructs.

Specifically, Kelly (1955) defines *hostility* as "the continued effort to extort validational evidence in favor of a type of social prediction which has already proved itself a failure" (p. 510). At the outset, this definition seems far afield from the ordinary conceptualization of hostility, which emphasizes the person's intent to do harm. Kelly (1955) attempts to understand hostility "from the point of view of the person who feels it and what it is that he is actually seeking to accomplish . . . [and to view] the injury he may imagine that he would like to inflict upon another person, not as a primary goal in itself, but as an incidental outcome of something more vital that he is trying to accomplish" (p. 510).

When a person's expectations about the material world prove unrealistic, attempting to alter physical objects to meet his expectations is costly, but only to the object and perhaps the person himself. For example, if a man expects that his key will open a particular door but finds that the key does not work, he can obtain another key, insert the key once more, or engage in a variety of behaviors to "prove" that the key does fit the door. If he chooses the last alternative, the most dire consequences would be that in his attempt to force the key to work it will break off in the lock and that he will suffer a few cuts and bruises in the course of his attack on the door.

When predictions are made of another person's behavior, the consequences of choosing to change the event—the other person—

become considerably more significant. Kelly (1955) explains the situation as follows:

> The individual construes another person; he makes a prediction about him; when he turns up contrary evidence, he senses a twinge of anxiety as it appears that the other person may not fall within the range of convenience of his role constructs (or, perhaps, he is threatened by the major revision of his system which the experience indicates may be necessary); then, in order to protect himself either from the anxiety or the threat, he sets out to make the other person into the kind of creature he predicted he was in the first place. This is hostility. The other person is the victim, not so much of the hostile person's fiendishly destructive impulses, as of his frantic and unrealistic efforts to collect on a wager he has already lost (p. 511).

In our daily experiences, we find that hostility is frequently evoked when a person "does not get his own way." Consider the previous example of the little boy who wanted a second helping of ice cream. If his grandfather did not help him get the extra dessert, the boy might "throw a temper tantrum" and hit his grandfather. One way to construe this situation would be that the boy wanted to "get back" at his grandfather, which would be the most frequently given explanation of the boy's behavior. Since the boy's grandfather, like most grandparents, had rarely denied his grandson anything he wanted, it is somewhat unreasonable to conclude that the boy would want to hurt him after just one nonindulgent act on his part. Another interpretation would be that the boy's behavior was aimed at changing his grandfather's "mind."

In this, and many similar circumstances of behavior which we commonly call "hostile," it is more reasonable, on the basis of the facts at hand, to conclude that the hostility is motivated by a desire to have one's prediction validated than to conclude that the person is merely being vindictive. Often, however, when we ask the person why he acted hostilely toward another individual, he will reply with some statement to the effect that he wanted to "get back" at the person who wronged him. Consider Jimmy's report, "Johnny wouldn't let me play in the sandbox, so I hit him."[4] That such statements, which come from children and adults alike, are often made is undoubtedly true, but we need not assume that they are products of "human nature." An alternative hypothesis is that we are *taught* to think in these terms. When a child acts in a hostile manner toward

---

[4] In terms of Kelly's definition of hostility, it is interesting to note that Jimmy's report contains the implicit assumption that hitting Johnny will increase the likelihood that Johnny will let him play in the sandbox, which is consistent with Jimmy's construct that he should be able to play there.

someone else, he is typically told that it is not right to hurt other people and, of even greater significance, that it is wrong to want to do harm to others. If, on the other hand, he were consistently told in childhood that it is wrong to try to change others to suit his own desires, the commonly held conception of hostility might be closer to Kelly's definition.

It is interesting to speculate about the potential consequences of altering child-rearing practices with regard to dealing with hostility. If from an early age children were taught to deal with invalidated predictions by either abandoning their less efficient constructs or by replicating the tests of the constructs rather than with hostility, then we might see a general reduction in tensions among people in future generations.

Hostile behavior, as Kelly construes it, is not a priori undesirable. There are instances in which the best way to deal with invalidation of constructs is to attempt to change the events to meet our expectations rather than to abandon our views to conform to the events. This is the strategy which has been adopted by advocates of social reform who are successful in bringing about change. Supporters of reduced environmental pollution, for example, will be most likely to succeed in their mission by maintaining their construct of the world as being better if people did not destroy the natural environment, rather than to reconstrue the situation.

The Modulation Corollary: When a Construct System Changes

The Modulation Corollary specifies the conditions under which change in a construct system can take place: "The variation in a person's construction system is limited by the permeability of the constructs within whose range of convenience the variants lie" (Kelly, 1955, p. 77). Permeability, it will be recalled, refers to the degree to which a construct is open to the interpretation of new events. The more permeable a person's constructs are, the greater is the change which can potentially occur within the system. The Modulation Corollary specifically addresses itself to an even more basic idea: not only must the person construe the new event, but he must also be able to construe the change itself. That is, the alteration of a construct or group of constructs is an event, and thus for the change to have any influence on the person's behavior, he must already possess a superordinate construct which is capable of construing the change. Kelly (1955) uses the following illustration:

> Suppose a person starts out with a construct of *fear vs. domination* and shifts to a construct of *respect vs. contempt*. Whereas once he divided his acquaintances between those he was afraid of and those whom he could dominate, he may, as he grows more mature, divide

his acquaintances between those whom he respects and those whom he holds in contempt. But, in order for him to make this shift, he needs another construct, within whose range of convenience the *fear vs. domination* construct lies and which is sufficiently permeable to admit the new idea of *respect vs. contempt.* . . . The permeable construct within whose range of convenience the variants lie may be such a notion as that of *maturity vs. childishness* (pp. 81–82).

The Commonality Corollary

If, as was indicated by the Individuality Corollary, differences among people are due to differences in the way they construe events, it follows that similarity between people is a function of similarity in construing events. The *Commonality Corollary*, the Individuality Corollary's counterpart, states: "To the extent that one person employs a construction of experience which is similar to that employed by another, his processes are psychologically similar to those of the other person" (Kelly, 1970, p. 20). This corollary asserts that a person's behavior is governed by his constructs and that two people are likely to behave in similar ways to the extent that they construe events in similar ways.

An interesting implication of the Commonality Corollary concerns the nature of a culture. As the term is generally used, it refers to a group of people who exhibit similar behavior. Typically the common behavior is thought to be the result of similarities in their upbringing and their environment. Kelly (1955) goes several steps further: "People belong to the same cultural group, not merely because they behave alike, nor because they expect the same things of others, but especially because they construe their experience in the same way" (p. 94).

The Sociality Corollary

The *Sociality Corollary* sets forth the basic requirement for an interpersonal relationship: "To the extent that one person construes the construction processes of another, he may play a role in a social process involving the other person" (1955, p. 95). In other words, in order for a person to have a social relationship with another, he must have some understanding of how the other person thinks—he must be able to construe the construct system of the other person. This means that he must be able to predict the ways the other person will anticipate events. Thus, the expression "getting into the other fellow's shoes" could be translated as "getting into the other fellow's constructs."

A *role*, for Kelly (1955), is a "pattern of behavior that follows from a person's understanding of how the others who are associated with him in his task think" (pp. 97–98). According to this definition, the mere fact that two or more people are together, are conversing with one another, or are working on a common task does not mean that an interpersonal relationship exists (i.e., that one or more persons are playing a role in relation to another person in the situation). The basic requirement for playing a role in social situations is that at least one of the individuals present have some understanding of another person's ways of seeing things. Note that there need not be mutual understanding. Indeed, many of our role relationships are one-sided. An optimal relationship, of course, usually involves understanding of one another's views of the world. This understanding may be limited in scope, as in the case of a student-professor relationship which is confined primarily to academic matters; or it may be extremely broad, covering most of each person's construct system, as in a good marital relationship.

People need not have the same constructs in order to be able to subsume the other's constructs within their own systems. As the Commonality Corollary suggests, it is no doubt easier to understand the way another person thinks if one shares similar outlooks with him, but this is certainly not a requirement for effective role playing.

> Consider the differences in the characteristic approaches to life of men and women. None of us would claim, we believe, that men and women construe all aspects of life in the same way. And yet nature has provided us with no finer example of role relationships and constructive social interaction than in the sexes. If we look at the testimony of nature, we shall have to admit that it often takes a man to understand a woman and a woman to understand a man and there is no greater tragedy than the failure to arrive at those understandings which permit this kind of role interrelationship (Kelly, 1955, p. 100).[5]

We play many different roles in our lives—friend, adversary, customer, colleague, student, teacher, lover, playmate. Each of these roles is defined by the person or persons in conjunction with whom it is being played and the particular situation (we often play a variety of roles with the same individual). According to the Psychology of Personal Constructs, there are some roles which a person plays regularly, and these form his *core role*, "that part of a person's role structure by which he maintains himself as an integral being" (Kelly, 1955, p. 503).

---

[5] Has Kelly's example, conceived two decades ago, become antiquated by changing sex roles in our society?

GUILT. When an individual becomes aware that he is deviating from his core role structure, he experiences *guilt*. Defining guilt in this nontraditional manner has the advantage of setting an important human experience apart from conventional notions of evil and punishment which are absolute, value-ladened concepts. In Personal Construct Theory, whether a person feels guilty or not depends upon his core role structure rather than some absolute standard of proper conduct (be it religious or cultural). One man may see as his primary role in life being as good a financial provider for his family as he can. He is likely to experience guilt when he is spending time away from his work, as when he is at home with his family. Another man construes as his core role being an active participant in daily family affairs. When this man is forced to work overtime and be away from his family, he feels guilty.

By now it must be obvious to the reader that Kelly's definitions of such personality concepts as guilt, hostility, aggression, and anxiety are very different from the definitions employed by other personality psychologists as well as from the common dictionary definitions. The uniqueness of his definitions is partially due to their conspicuous independence from value judgments. For example, hostility is neither "good" nor "bad" per se. This absence of evaluation, in combination with Kelly's insistence on understanding another man's personality by construing his constructs, is the essence of the phenomenological strategy. Employing Kelly's definitions would seem to facilitate objectivity in the scientific study of personality and possibly to encourage greater tolerance in everyday interpersonal relations.[6]

THE ASSESSMENT OF PERSONAL CONSTRUCTS—THE ROLE CONSTRUCT REPERTORY TEST

If personality consists of one's personal construct system, then personality assessment must involve a description of personal constructs. Although personal constructs determine behavior, directly observing a person's behavior may not yield valid information about how he is construing the relevant events. People may engage in the same behaviors despite their construing events in very different ways. Take the example of three men who play golf together on Saturday mornings. One of the men views golf as a competitive sport, and each week he looks forward to improving his score and beating his two

---

[6] In our discussion of Kelly's corollaries to his Fundamental Postulate, the *Fragmentation Corollary* has been omitted, and it is given here for the sake of completeness: "A person may successively employ a variety of construction subsystems which are inferentially incompatible with each other" (1955, p. 83).

opponents. For the second man the game of golf is more a means of socializing than an athletic event. The third man construes the Saturday morning golf games as an opportunity to be outdoors and get some exercise. It would be difficult to accurately predict each man's construction of the events taking place from observing his behavior alone.

It is important to digress briefly to stress an issue which is fundamental to the Psychology of Personal Constructs. Of what practical use is knowledge of an individual's personal constructs, over and above knowledge of his behavior? If our interest were only in predicting what each man in the example above would probably be doing the next Saturday morning, the behavioral observation might serve us well. However, knowing the way in which each man construes the Saturday golf game may enable us to predict how he would behave in other situations. For instance, we might predict that the first man would be competitive in his work as well as on the golf course if he uses the same construct to construe both work and golf.

Besides behavioral observation, another way to assess someone's personal constructs would be to ask him directly. But constructs cannot always be communicated in words; when they can be, the meanings of the words are often too broad to give the assessor much specific information about the individual's personal constructs. Furthermore, people are usually not accustomed to construing and communicating their personal constructs.[7]

Kelly has devised a technique for the assessment of personal constructs which surmounts some of the problems associated with behavioral observation and direct inquiry. Called the Role Construct Repertory Test (Rep Test), the technique elicits the constructs which a person uses to construe the important people in his life. A good way to learn about the Rep Test is to actually use the technique, as indicated in Demonstration 12–1, to explore some of your own personal constructs.

Demonstration 12–1

THE ROLE CONSTRUCT REPERTORY TEST

In the Rep Test you will be comparing and contrasting (a process called *sorting*) people (called *figures*) in your life in order to elicit the constructs which you use to construe them.

---

[7] The reader may wish to ascertain the difficulty of this task by attempting to make a list of his personal constructs. It should be noted that the reader is in a substantially better position to do this than most people, since he has already had an introduction to the nature of personal constructs which included numerous examples of such constructs.

Designating Figures

Figure 12–2 is the "grid form" used for the Rep Test. First, draw on a large sheet of paper the grid form exactly as it appears in Figure 12–2. Note that each row of the grid has three circles; double-check to be sure that you have placed the circles for each row in the correct columns.

FIGURE 12–2

Sample Grid Form of the Rep Test for Demonstration 12–1

Column labels: 1 Self, 2 Mother, 3 Father, 4 Brother, 5 Sister, 6 Spouse, 7 Pal, 8 Ex-pal, 9 Rejecting Person, 10 Pitied Person, 11 Threatening Person, 12 Attractive Person, 13 Accepted Teacher, 14 Rejected Teacher, 15 Happy Person

SORT NO.	1	2	3	4	5	6	7	8	9	10	11	12	13	14	15	EMERGENT POLE	IMPLICIT POLE
1									○	○		○					
2		○	○	○													
3				○								○	○				
4		○					○					○					
5	○										○	○					
6					○								○				
7				○				○			○						
8						○				○				○			
9							○	○			○						
10	○			○	○												
11		○	○								○						
12							○			○				○			
13	○						○	○									
14	○	○	○														
15				○					○				○				

Next, turn to Table 12–1 (page 290), which contains 15 role definitions. Read each definition carefully and then write, in the appropriate diagonal space at the top of your grid form, the first name of the person who best fits that role in your life. If you cannot remember the name of the person, put down a word or brief phrase that will bring the person to mind. Do *not* repeat any names; if some person has already been listed, simply make a second choice. Next to the word "Self" write your own name. Then next to the word "Mother" put your mother's name (or the person who has played the part of a mother in your life; see Table 12–1). Continue until all 15 roles have been designated with a specific individual.

Sorting Figures

Now look at the first *row* of the grid form. Note that there are circles in the squares under *columns* 9, 10, and 12. These circles designate the three people whom you are to consider in Sort No. 1 (i.e., Rejecting Person, Pitied Person, and Attractive Person). Think about these three people and decide how *two of them are alike* in some important way that *differentiates them from the third person.* When you have decided the most important way that two of the people are alike but different from the third person,

TABLE 12–1

Definition of Roles for Demonstration 12–1

1. *Self:* Yourself.
2. *Mother:* Your mother or the person who has played the part of a mother in your life.
3. *Father:* Your father or the person who has played the part of a father in your life.
4. *Brother:* Your brother who is nearest your own age, or if you do not have a brother, a boy near your own age who has been most like a brother to you.
5. *Sister:* Your sister who is nearest your own age or, if you do not have a sister, a girl near your own age who has been most like a sister to you.
6. *Spouse:* Your wife (or husband) or, if you are not married, your closest present girl (boy) friend.
7. *Pal:* Your closest present friend of the same sex as yourself.
8. *Ex-Pal:* A person of the same sex as yourself whom you once thought was a close friend but in whom you were badly disappointed later.
9. *Rejecting Person:* A person with whom you have been associated, who, for some unexplained reason, appeared to dislike you.
10. *Pitied Person:* The person whom you would most like to help or for whom you feel most sorry.
11. *Threatening Person:* The person who threatens you the most or the person who makes you feel the most uncomfortable.
12. *Attractive Person:* A person whom you have recently met whom you would like to know better.
13. *Accepted Teacher:* The teacher who influenced you most.
14. *Rejected Teacher:* The teacher whose point of view you have found most objectionable.
15. *Happy Person:* The happiest person whom you know personally.

Source: Kelly, 1955.

put an "X" in each of the two circles which correspond to the two persons who are alike. Do *not* place any mark in the third circle; leave it blank.

Next, in the column marked "Emergent Pole," write the word or short phrase that tells how the two people are alike. Then, in the column marked "Implicit Pole," write a word or short phrase that explains the way the third person is different from the other two.

Finally, consider each of the remaining 12 persons and think about which of them, in addition to the two you have already marked with an "X," also have the characteristic you have designated under the "Emergent Pole." Place an "X" in the square corresponding to the name of each of the other persons who has this characteristic. When you have finished this procedure for the first row (Sort No. 1), go to the second row (Sort No. 2). The process should be repeated until it has been carried out for each of the rows. In summary, the steps to be followed for each of the 15 rows (sorts) are:

1. Consider the three people who are designated by circles under their names. Decide how two of them are alike, in an important way, and different from the third.
2. Put an "X" in the circles corresponding to the two people who are alike and leave the remaining circle blank.
3. In the "Emergent Pole" column, write a brief description of the way the two people are *alike.*
4. In the "Implicit Pole" column, write a brief description of the way the third person is *different* from the two who are alike.
5. Consider the remaining 12 persons and place an "X" in the squares

corresponding to those who can also be characterized by the description in the "Emergent Pole" column.

Discussion

By the time you have completed the Demonstration Rep Test a number of its characteristics should be apparent. Think about how the Rep Test has elicited your constructs. What is the range of convenience of the constructs? Which constructs are relatively permeable, and which relatively impermeable? What relation do these constructs have with one another? Do the sorts compare people randomly, or is there a rationale behind each sort? Finally, you might ask yourself whether the Rep Test has given you any insights into the way you construe your interpersonal world.

The procedure of the Rep Test is similar to a concept formation task. However, instead of sorting objects, the respondent sorts persons (figures) who play important roles in his life. The particular sorts which the examiner asks the subject to make will depend upon the purpose of the assessment procedure. The following are examples of sorts used in Demonstration 12–1 with a brief explanation of each (Kelly, 1955, pp. 275–76).

> *Sort No. 1:* Valency Sort. The client is asked to compare and contrast a person whose rejection of him he cannot quite understand, a person whom he thinks needs him, and a person whom he does not really know well but whom he thinks he would like to know better. All three of these are somewhat phantom figures, and one may expect that in interpreting them the client relies heavily upon projected attitudes.
>
> *Sort No. 3:* Sister Sort. This is an invitation to construe a Sister figure. It provides an opportunity to see the Sister as like the Accepted Teacher and in contrast to the Happy Person, like the Happy Person and in contrast to the Accepted Teacher, or in contrast to both of them.
>
> *Sort No. 5:* Need Sort. The Self is compared and contrasted with the Pitied Person and the Attractive Person. This gives the clinician an opportunity to study the relative subjective and objective reference which the client gives to his personal needs.
>
> *Sort No. 7:* Threat Sort. The client has an opportunity to construe threat in the context of the Brother, Ex-Pal, and Threatening Person.
>
> *Sort No. 11:* Parental Preference Sort. The Mother and Father are placed in context with the Threatening Person.

In the *grid form* of the Rep Test (e.g., Demonstration 12–1), a grid, or matrix, is constructed with significant people in the subject's life on one axis and the constructs he uses to construe them on the other axis. At the intersection of each row and column (of each construct and role title) the subject indicates whether the emergent pole (i.e., that pole which was emergent for the sort) of the construct applies to that person by placing a check mark or "X" there if it does. The absence of a check mark at a particular intersection indicates that the implicit pole is applicable. Each intersect then becomes either an *incident* (i.e., a check mark indicates that the emergent pole applies) or a *void* (i.e., a blank indicates that the implicit pole applies). The requirement that *either* one pole *or* the other applies to a figure is a direct consequence of the dichotomous nature of constructs. Because one of the basic assumptions of the Rep Test is that every construct applies to every figure, the subject examines all the figures and indicates whether the emergent pole can be used to construe each of them.

Capitalizing on the linkage among particular constructs due to their being applied to the same persons, Kelly has devised a "nonparametric factor analysis" to reduce the grid to a few basic dimensions. The basic strategy is similar to factor analysis as it was discussed in Chapter 7. When constructs have approximately the same pattern of incidents and voids, they are said to be *functionally similar* and are represented by a *construct factor*. Whether or not constructs have similar verbal labels applied to them, if they are used to construe most of the same people in the same way, they are equivalent for the function they serve, namely, anticipating future behavior. For constructs to be considered functionally equivalent and represented by a common factor, the check patterns need not be identical, only approximately the same, and Kelly presents a mathematical test for determing this closeness of fit. A similar analysis can be made over the columns of the grid to reduce the information concerning the significant figures in the person's life to more manageable units, with the result being one or more representative *figure factors*.

Several limitations of the Rep Test should be noted. It is true that the Rep Test may often be an effective device for assessing the way a person sees important people in his life. Such information may be extremely helpful in the psychotherapeutic setting, since most human problems concern relationships with other people, particularly those close to us. However, the constructs elicited by the Rep Test are those which the person uses to construe the behavior of others. If the examiner's goal is to predict the behavior of the person himself, then it is necessary to ascertain whether the constructs he applies to others apply to his own behavior as well (Sechrest, 1963).

Though the Rep Test requires that constructs be set down in words, constructs need not be verbalizable. Therefore, it cannot be assumed that the constructs elicited by the test represent all or even the most important of the constructs the person uses to construe the figures in the test.

Finally, even when the person makes his constructs more or less explicitly known by means of verbal labels which appear to have generally accepted meanings, one cannot be sure that the labels do, in fact, have common referents. Constructs such as "successful vs. unsuccessful," "attractive vs. unattractive," and "difficult vs. easy" have highly personalized meanings. Here it is critical to examine how the person uses his constructs, as by looking at the pattern of incidents and voids in the grid form.

EVIDENCE FOR THE PSYCHOLOGY OF PERSONAL CONSTRUCTS

In this section, the nature of the evidence for several of the theoretical propositions of the Psychology of Personal Constructs will be illustrated. We shall examine a few representative studies in order to exemplify the kinds of investigations which have arisen from Kelly's theory.

Individuality Corollary

Kelly asserted in his Individuality Corollary that people differ from one another because, besides having had experience with different events, they construe events differently. Each person, then, has a set of *personal* constructs. It is legitimate to ask how stable or permanent persons' construct systems tend to be. To answer this question, Fjeld and Landfield (1961) asked subjects to take the Rep Test twice. The second time the test was administered, the subjects were instructed not to use the same figures they employed in the first Rep Test, and the trio of role titles which they compared also differed between the two administrations. When the constructs elicited by the two Rep Tests were compared, they were shown to agree substantially, as evidenced by high test-retest reliability (correlation coefficient of +.79). Thus, there is some evidence that the constructs of a given individual are not only stable across time but are also relatively independent of the particular events being construed.

If each person has a unique set of constructs, then it follows that the optimal way to predict his behavior would be to understand his personal constructs as opposed to the constructs which other people use to describe him. To test this hypothesis, Payne (1956) had subjects, in groups of three, predict how the other two people in the triad would complete a questionnaire about social behavior. Each subject was given a list of 15 personal constructs of one of his partners and 15 constructs *about* the other partner which his peers had employed in describing him. Payne found that subjects were significantly more accurate at predicting how another person had responded to the questionnaire when they had access to his own personal constructs.

Experience Corollary

The Experience Corollary says that a person's views of the world change as he reconstrues events over time. The corollary makes sense intuitively, and few psychologists, including those skeptical about Personal Construct Theory, would doubt its validity. (This does not mean, however, that these obvious statements do not need to be tested empirically.) The real value of the Experience Corollary (and of the Individuality Corollary) is that it has stimulated research which has led to findings which are important extensions of the corollary. Three investigations which elucidate some of the conditions for construct change and the nature of that change will be discussed.

In a study of interpersonal perception, Bieri (1953) showed that social interaction between people will produce a change in the way they construe each other. In accordance with the standard design of studies of interpersonal perception, the subjects were first asked to fill out a questionnaire describing an aspect of their behavior. Then they were asked to predict another subject's answers to the questionnaire both before and after a discussion with the other subject. As predicted, subjects came to view the other person as more like themselves after their short social interaction.

Lundy (1952) provided an interesting explanation and extension of Bieri's findings in an investigation of the effect of increased social interaction on the perception of others. The subjects were six patients who were participating in group therapy over a period of four weeks. Each patient predicted the responses of the other five individuals on a questionnaire administered before and after the first session and once a week for the remaining three weeks. Lundy reasoned that before any social interaction, the subjects could only guess how the others would answer the questionnaire. After a minimal amount of interaction, they would assume that the other persons were similar to themselves (Bieri's finding) in an effort to gain some structure. Only after the subjects had gotten to know one another better would they attempt to construe the others differently from themselves. The results supported these hypotheses.

Our final illustration of research related to Kelly's theory is a field study of changes during individual psychotherapy. Tippett (1959) used as subjects patients who had been in therapy at least three months between two administrations of the Rep Test. Her results are particularly enlightening with regard to the predominant topics of discussion during therapy. When the therapist concentrated on the patient's past, the constructs which underwent the most change were those which were predominantly used to construe figures who are generally associated with a person's early life (e.g., parents). When the emphasis was on the present, constructs which were used to construe figures who are usually important to a person later in life (e.g., spouse) tended to be altered. The change in constructs was evidenced both in the verbal labels applied to the constructs and in the pattern of application of the constructs to the figures.

PERSONAL CONSTRUCT PERSONALITY CHANGE

People seek help in making personality changes when they are dissatisfied with the way they are acting or feeling. From the point of view of Personal Construct Theory, a person is likely to become involved in some sort of psychotherapeutic process when he is having difficulty anticipating events in his life.

One possibility is that the person does not have constructs which are useful in viewing some new events in his life. He finds it difficult to deal with these novel events effectively and reports that he feels anxious when confronted with them. This frequently occurs when someone is thrust into a new life situation with little or no knowledge about how to act. Common examples would include going off to college (especially if this is one's first extended period of time away from home), starting on a new job, moving to a new town, getting married or divorced, and having a close relative die. In these cases, the affected individual might have to develop new constructs which are appropriate to and capable of anticipating the new events in his life.

In other instances, it may be sufficient to modify existing personal constructs to make them more predictively efficient. Often a person's views of events are too narrow, which results from using impermeable constructs. The college freshman who earned good grades in high school with only a few hours of studying per week may have construed "good grades with minimal studying" at the "bright" pole of his construct "bright vs. dumb student." When he finds that he is having to spend many more hours studying in college and is still not doing as well as he did in high school, he is confused. The new event, "lower grades and more studying," cannot be subsumed under the "bright" pole of the construct as he has defined it; at the same time, he does not consider himself to be a dumb student. The result is that he feels frustrated, becomes depressed when he thinks that he may not be as bright as he thought he was, and starts avoiding his schoolwork because he becomes anxious when he thinks about it. These "symptoms" are the by-product of an impermeable construct. Using his personal construct "bright vs. dumb student," he is not able to construe the new event in his life, namely, his doing less well academically and studying more hours than previously. However, instead of developing a completely new construct to anticipate his academic behavior, he may find it sufficient to make his existing construct more permeable so that it will be capable of subsuming his present behavior.

Sometimes constructs are inefficient because they are too permeable. This is likely to be the case when a person continues to use an obsolete construct which anticipated events in the past but is no longer appropriate in the present. For instance, construing one's parents as people whose wishes must be acceded to at all times may have been a useful construct when the person was five years old, but at age 25 the construct is likely to interfere with other events in his life (e.g., demands of employer, spouse, friends). One solution to this not uncommon dilemma would be to make a construct like "blind obedience vs. disrespect" less permeable by considering it appropriate for use by only five-year-old children. Since the individual can never be five years old again, this has the effect of "embalming a construct in literalistic impermeability" (Kelly, 1955, p. 592).

In keeping with the basic philosophical position of constructive alternativism, Kelly views psychotherapy as a future-oriented process. In general terms, the aim of psychotherapy is to help the client develop a personal construct system which will enable him to follow his own natural developmental process, much as Rogers advocates. Personality change is conceived as a continuing process of modification as opposed to a process whose goal is a terminal state of well-being or an optimal static construct system. The role of the therapist is to set the stage for such an ongoing program of construct revision by directly and indirectly providing the client with the model of a scientist who formulates hypotheses about future events, tests them, and then revises his theory (construct) in order to increase its predictive efficiency.

The personality change procedures which Kelly advocates do not attempt to change personal constructs directly. Rather, his general approach to modifying constructs involves effecting changes in behavior which, in turn, will lead to a reconstruction of events. According to Kelly, new behaviors which a client performs provide evidence of movement within his construct system; that is, new behaviors indicate that the client is viewing the events in his life somewhat differently. When this occurs, therapeutic progress can be said to have been made. Kelly's assumption that changes in behavior must occur before there can be lasting changes in personality (personal constructs) is very much in keeping with the psychotherapeutic approach of the behavioral strategy (see Section V).

Fixed-Role Therapy

The basic principle of changing behavior in order to modify one's construct system is illustrated in a specific technique developed by Kelly called *fixed-role therapy*. In fixed-role therapy the client is asked to play the role of a fictitious person whose behavior is consistent with a construct system which the therapist hypothesizes it would be beneficial for the client to adopt. The client first writes a self-characterization sketch of himself and completes a number of self-descriptive personality tests, such as incomplete sentences and a Q-sort. On the basis of this information and knowledge of the client's problems, a panel of therapists writes a fixed-role sketch for him. The sketch describes the new role the client is asked to enact. The following is a fixed-role sketch written for a client who characterized himself as passive, self-conscious, shy, and occasionally interpersonally boring and who was having difficulties with his sex-role identity.

Dick Benton[8] is probably the only one of his kind in the world. People are always just a little puzzled as to how to take him. About the time they decide that he is a conventional person with the usual lines of thinking in religion, politics, school, etc., they discover that there is a new side to his personality that they have overlooked. At times, they think that he has a brand-new way of looking at life, a really *fresh* point of view. Some people go through an hour of conversation with him without being particularly impressed; while others find that afterwards they cannot get some of his unusual ideas out of their minds. Every once in a while he throws an idea into a discussion like a bomb with a very slow fuse attached. People don't get it until later.

At times he deliberately makes himself socially inconspicuous. Those are the times when he wishes to listen and learn, rather than to stimulate other people's thinking. He is kindly and gentle with people, even on those occasions when he is challenging their thoughts with utterly new ideas. Because of this, people do not feel hurt by his ideas, even when they seem outrageous.

He is devoted to his wife and she is the only person who always seems to understand what is going on in his mind.

His work in college is somewhat spotted and the courses are interesting to him only to the extent that they give him a new outlook.

All in all, Dick Benton is a combination of gentleness and intellectual unpredictability. He likes to take people as they are but he likes to surprise them with new ideas (Kelly, 1955, p. 421).

---

[8] Each fixed-role sketch is given a name in order to make the character more credible and to facilitate reference to the fixed-role as opposed to the client's customary role.

The fixed-role usually deals with only a few of the client's constructs and thus does not aim at making major personality changes. As a matter of fact, the fixed-role often includes some attributes of the client which are assets to him in order to bolster his efficient constructs and make the role easier and more realistic for him to enact.

The client is not asked to be the person described in the fixed-role sketch, nor is he required to adopt the role as his own. He is merely requested to try acting the role for a period of time. What frequently occurs, though, is that the client ceases to think of his new behavior as a role and begins to consider it as his own, "natural" way of acting. Clients often adapt their fixed-role so that it is more consistent with their other behaviors. The result of fully "getting into" the fixed-role is that the client begins to adopt the constructs which underlie the fixed-role behavior.

LIABILITIES OF THE PHENOMENOLOGICAL STRATEGY

Four liabilities of the phenomenological strategy will now be discussed. Critics have argued that (1) the phenomenological strategy is limited in the scope of the phenomena it studies, (2) phenomenological personality theory does not adequately explain the development of personality, (3) phenomenological personality theory is more descriptive than explanatory, and (4) phenomenological personality assessment places an unjustified credence in self-reports.

The Phenomenological Strategy Is Limited in Scope

The phenomenological strategy focuses on man's conscious experiences of the moment and, in this emphasis, comes close to dealing with those aspects of human behavior which laymen most often think should be the focus of psychological investigations—namely, their subjective experiences. Thus, the phenomenological strategy "makes sense intuitively" and is consistent with commonsense notions of personality.

However, in concentrating on man's conscious, subjective experiences, the phenomenologist has excluded from his study any events of which a person is not immediately aware. Can an individual's behavior be predicted accurately by knowing only what is in his phenomenal field? Can actions be explained without reference to past experiences and influences on which the person is not concentrating at the moment? All the rules which one has learned in the past and which influence his present behavior even though he is not aware of them at the time are common examples of how events outside one's momentary phenomenal field influence behavior. Psychoanalysts would argue even more strongly that events which are out of a person's immediate awareness (i.e., unconscious), perhaps permanently, form the core of personality and play a crucial role in determining behavior.

Besides the limited scope of the phenomenological strategy in general, the two major phenomenological approaches which we considered, those of Rogers and Kelly, have specific limitations which result from their particular emphases. Rogers' phenomenological approach tends to focus on the feeling or emotional aspects of man's behavior while largely ignoring the intellectual, thinking aspects. Interestingly, the bias of Kelly's Psychology of Personal Constructs is exactly opposite; Kelly emphasizes man's cognitive processes and pays little attention to man's emotions.

Phenomenological Theory Does Not Adequately Explain Personality Development

A major weakness of Kelly's Psychology of Personal Constructs is the absence of discussion of how personality develops. Kelly certainly does not believe that man is born with constructs, since constructs develop in order to predict one's experiences, which, it is reasonable to assume, do not begin until birth. But beyond the simple assertion that constructs are learned, there is little in Kelly's theory which speaks to the issue of how they develop. The Psychology of Personal Constructs is applicable only to already-construing-man, man who has developed a set of templates through which to view his experiences. How does a child develop a construct? What factors determine the hierarchical order of his constructs? Are there stages of development in which constructs and the construct system have particular characteristics? Do nonverbal constructs become verbal when the child learns to speak? These and other questions pertinent to personality development are left unanswered by Personal Construct Theory.

In contrast to Kelly's theory, Rogers' theory includes discussion of the development of personality, such as the self-concept and conditions of worth. However, the developmental *process* is not spelled out explicitly. For example, according to Rogers the self-concept develops as part of the actualizing tendency's process of differentiation. But other than specifying that the actualizing tendency is responsible for differentiating psychological functions (presumably, by partialing out "energy" from the actualizing tendency to various functions), Rogers' theory says little about how the process operates.

Another, more serious problem presented by Rogers' theorizing about personality development is that it is no more than theorizing, since there is no empirical evidence to support his notions. Although

Rogers has conducted and inspired a large body of research concerning personality change, there have been no parallel efforts to accumulate evidence regarding the development of the actualizing tendency, the self-concept, conditions of worth, and so on. At the present time, then, it can be said that Rogers' theory of personality development is somewhat vague and unspecified and remains untested.

It is interesting to speculate about the reasons for the relative lack of emphasis given to developmental issues by both Kelly and Rogers. One possibility is that interest in how personality characteristics develop is not in keeping with the phenomenological perspective's emphasis on the individual's present (here-and-now) experiences and his momentary interpretation of them as the primary means of understanding personality.

Phenomenological Personality Theory Is More Descriptive Than Explanatory

A major criticism of phenomenological approaches to personality is that they provide more of a description than an explanation of behavior. Key theoretical concepts such as the self and personal constructs are viewed by some critics (e.g., Skinner, 1964) as only partial explanations. To say that George behaves in a particular manner because of the construct he uses to construe the relevant events or that Carl acts the way he does as a result of his self-actualizing tendency does not explain the person's actions unless the construct or the self-actualizing tendency is, in turn, accounted for. "Personal constructs" and the "self-actualizing tendency" are theoretical constructs which only have the status of what Skinner (1964) has called "mental way stations." They leave unanswered the question of what conditions are responsible for one's personal constructs or one's self-actualizing tendency.

When a theory provides behavioral descriptions without specifying the conditions which determine the behavior described (or without designating the variables which influence the theoretical constructs which are hypothesized to be most directly responsible for the behavior), prediction becomes difficult, if not impossible. The self-actualization approaches of Rogers and Maslow are particularly vulnerable in this regard. Aside from serving to physically sustain life, the nature of the self-actualizing tendency differs from person to person. Each man has a different basic nature, and his behavior is guided by it. Given this strategy, "explanations" of behavior take the form of "Peter is what he is," which of course is merely a tautology ($A = A$) and tells us nothing.

In studying self-actualizing individuals, Maslow ran headlong into this problem. How can self-actualization for a given individual be defined? Is living up to one's potential a sufficient definition (assuming, that is, that one's potential could be measured accurately)? If so, this gives rise to such questions as: Are all people with high IQs who do not attend college non-self-actualizers? Is it possible for a fully actualized person to function at less than his capacity?

Maslow never adequately solved the basic dilemma of definition. He a priori defined certain individuals as self-actualizing, then studied such people, and, from what he learned about them, further described the characteristics of self-actualizers. But this strategy is completely circular and is not different from making such meaningless statements as: "Anxious people are more anxious than nonanxious people." Mere reiteration of one's definition does not elucidate a problem.

To a lesser degree, Kelly's Psychology of Personal Constructs also suffers from the limitation of being more descriptive than explanatory. Kelly's basic statement about the factors which determine behavior is contained in his Fundamental Postulate: "A person's processes are psychologically channelized by the ways in which he anticipates events." Knowing that man constantly strives toward accurate prediction of events gives us little information about the direction of behavior since, as Kelly fully acknowledges in his advocacy of constructive alternativism, a person has open to him a multitude of alternative ways of anticipating events.

Phenomenologists Place an Unjustified Credence in Self-reports

The goal of phenomenological personality assessment is to gain knowledge about a person's subjective experiences, to understand his behavior from his internal frame of reference. Since, by definition, the individual, and he alone, has direct knowledge of these phenomena, phenomenological personality assessment relies on the self-reports of the assessee. The basic assumption of this approach is that people are both willing and able to accurately describe their phenomenological experiences when asked to do so. There are, however, a number of considerations which cast doubt on this assumption and the credence placed in self-reports.

Phenomenological personality assessment is based on the premise that people are aware of ("in touch with") those private experiences which directly influence their behavior. The limitations of this view have already been pointed out above. Also questionable are the person's willingness to reveal his phenomenological experiences to others and his ability to do this accurately.

Abundant evidence exists both from psychological research and everyday observations to suggest that people's self-reports are often distorted in systematic ways. People tend to report those aspects of themselves which they want others to know about, and usually this means that they will distort their personality picture so as to be seen favorably by others. Recall, for example, the influence of response sets, such as social desirability, on self-report inventories (see Chapter 8).

Even if an individual is willing to report his experiences and feelings honestly to someone else, there still remains the problem of his ability to report them accurately, so that the information can be useful to the assessor. We are all aware of the frustrating experience of trying to tell someone else how we are feeling. We struggle ineptly with words such as: "I'm kind of depressed but not really depressed . . . it's more like I'm . . . Oh, I don't know . . . I just can't describe it." A major reason for this failure to communicate resides in the limitations of language.

For language to be useful in allowing an individual to convey information to another person, the words and phrases must have commonly agreed upon and understood referents. However, private experiences frequently do not easily translate themselves into words which fully describe them and, at the same time, communicate that description to another person. What often happens is that the words are understood but the meaning is lost. When language is too imprecise and general, the assessor can base his understanding of words only on his own experiences and perspective, and this does not result in phenomenological knowledge.

section **V**

The
Behavioral
Strategy

13

The
Behavioral
Strategy
INTRODUCTION

All strategies for the study of personality begin with an examination of overt behavior, although in most strategies directly observable behavior is not what is of ultimate interest. A psychoanalytic psychologist collects his subject's dream reports, which can be considered, in and of themselves, as a type of overt, and relatively objective, behavior. If the subject speaks in a clear, audible manner, then any number of observers listening to his report of a dream should be able to record the same dream content. However, the psychoanalyst is not interested in the dream report per se but rather in what the dream content as recalled will reveal about the individual's intrapsychic processes, such as his unconscious wishes and personality conflicts. In much the same way, the dispositional psychologist is ultimately concerned with his subject's need to achieve and will be interested in his performance in a business game as an expression of this need rather than as a sample of how the person will act in similar business situations. And what the phenomenological psychologist is most interested in is the congruence between a subject's self and ideal self rather than the way he sorts self-referent statements into categories.

MAN IS WHAT HE DOES

In contrast to the psychoanalytic, dispositional, and phenomenological strategies, the behavioral strategy for the study of personality is directly and ultimately concerned with overt *behavior* for its own sake. Behavioral personality assessment techniques employ the basic strategy of sampling relevant behavior in an effort to predict similar behavior. A dream report could be used to predict the types of dreams the person is likely to have (or be willing to describe) ; performance in a simulated business task could give the behavioral psychologist information about how the person would probably act in the actual business situation; and the way an individual sorts statements about himself could be used in behavioral personality assessment to predict similar categorizing behavior. In sum, the unit of personality in the behavioral strategy is behavior.

Although behavioral psychologists frequently eschew the term "personality," in fact for them personality is the sum and organization of a person's behavior. "Personality" and "behavior" are closer to being synonymous terms in the behavioral strategy than in any of the other three strategies.

BEHAVIOR IS LEARNED

Besides the focus on behavior, another unifying factor of the behavioral strategy is the emphasis on learning. The basic assumption made by adherents of behavioral approaches to personality is that behavior develops and is modified primarily, though not exclusively, in accordance with principles of learning rather than acquired through heredity and determined biologically. Behavioral approaches differ, however, with respect to the form of learning which is emphasized. The *classical conditioning,* or *respondent,* approach (see Chapter 14) focuses on man's learning new responses by coming to associate a set of circumstances which previously did not elicit a particular reaction with another set of circumstances which had already led to that reaction. For example, a college co-ed who likes to make comments in her classes may have learned that behavior because when she first spoke up in class she was sitting next to a good-looking fellow whose company she enjoyed. In effect, speaking up in class became associated with the handsome fellow and the good feelings which sitting next to him produced in the girl. According to the *operant conditioning,* or *instrumental learning,* approach (see Chapter 15) , behavior is learned as a result of the consequences which the person receives when he performs the behavior. From this perspective, the girl might be said to have developed the habit of making comments in her classes because the first few times she spoke up her handsome friend smiled approvingly at her and remarked that she was smart. The *observational learning,* or *imitation,* approach (see Chapter 16) considers learning to be a function of a person's observations of the behavior of others and its consequences for them. Using this third approach to learning, the girl may have learned to speak up in class because she observed that her good-looking classmate frequently did so and that the teacher appeared pleased when he did.

The three approaches just outlined are paradigms, or theories, of learning. As we have seen, within each paradigm the same behavior can be explained in a somewhat different way, although all the explanations involve learning. The important question is: What are the advantages and disadvantages of construing the development and maintenance of behavior from each perspective? It is important to note, however, that although the distinction among the three paradigms can be useful, especially pedagogically, in real life most behavior is acquired and sustained by a combination of observational, operant, and respondent learning.

BEHAVIORAL THEORY

Parsimony

Behavioral theories of personality usually make relatively few basic assumptions and therefore can be said to be parsimonious. Within a given learning approach, a single set of principles is used to explain a variety of different behaviors. The behavioral explanation of "unexpressed," or "inhibited," behavior is a case in point. "Unexpressed behavior" refers to acts which a person is capable of performing but which he is not performing at present. A simple example of an unexpressed response would be a person's failure to recall a fact which he knows (as evidenced by its being recalled when the appropriate cues are available). In some approaches to personality, particularly the psychoanalytic strategy, unexpressed behavior is explained by assuming first that there are levels of awareness (consciousness) and second that conscious responses are made unconscious by a defensive process, such as repression. Behavioral approaches deal with unexpressed behavior *without recourse to additional assumptions* (i.e., assumptions over and above those invoked to explain expressed behavior). One behavioral explanation holds that an unexpressed response "does not have a qualitatively different nature from any response that has been superseded by an alternative pattern of behavior" (Bandura, 1969, pp. 592–93). On a broader scale, within the behavioral strategy normal and abnormal behavior are postulated to develop, be maintained, and change according to identical principles of learning (e.g., Ullmann & Krasner, 1969). In effect, there is nothing special about abnormal behavior from the standpoint of understanding its basic nature.[1]

---

[1] What is "special" about behavior which is labeled "abnormal" is the consequences which accrue to it (e.g., reactions of other people, the limitations

Emphasis on the External Environment

The behavioral strategy looks to the environment, rather than within the person, for the factors which determine man's behavior. This does not mean that genetic factors, physiology, biological needs, thought processes, and similar intraorganismic variables do not play a role in shaping behavior. It does mean that behavioral approaches hold that personality can be most meaningfully explained (i.e., predicted and controlled) by examining the external influences on man. Specifically, a person's genetic and biological endowment are viewed as primarily setting limits on his abilities and the behaviors he will be able to learn. Within these limits, which are often broad, an individual's personality develops as a result of learning experiences. To borrow Kelly's phrase, the focus of convenience of the behavioral strategy is the external environment, just as the foci of convenience of the psychoanalytic strategy are intrapsychic events, of the dispositional strategy are enduring characteristics, and of the phenomenological strategy are the ways a person perceives his world.

The behavioral strategy is a *deterministic* position, just as the psychoanalytic and dispositional strategies are. However, in contrast to psychoanalytic and dispositional determinism, according to the behavioral strategy the factors which determine behavior lie in the individual's external environment. The nature of behavioral determinism will be illustrated in the discussion of the situational specificity hypothesis which follows.

The Situational Specificity of Behavior

An important corollary of the emphasis placed on environmental factors within the behavioral strategy is an adherence to the *situational specificity* of behavior. All personality theories must account for the relative consistency of people's behavior, and behavioral theories hold that this consistency is a function of environmental cues and consequences. People behave the way they do in response to the demands and characteristics of the particular situation they are in at the moment, including their past experience in similar situations, and therefore their behavior is said to be situation specific. A college student sits quietly at his lectures, engages in casual conversation during his meals at the dorm cafeteria, and loses his voice from yelling at basketball and football games. In each case, the student's verbal behavior is determined by the demands and restric-

the abnormal behavior may place on the person, and the legal ramifications of some abnormal behaviors). For a comprehensive account of the behavioral view of abnormal behavior see Ullmann and Krasner (1969).

tions of the situation. His behavior is *consistent within a given situation,* though not necessarily across situations.

The behavioral psychologist emphasizes how often a person's behavior is *not* consistent across situations. Rather than simply being aggressive or acquiescent, a man may well be aggressive with his subordinates but courteously passive when his own boss comes in to give him orders. Here the situation, and the fact that "one man's boss is another man's employee," clearly controls how the person will act. It is apparent, then, that the situational specificity position contrasts sharply with the generality-consistency assumptions of the dispositional view (see Chapter 6) .

The Nature of Behavioral Concepts

In general, behavioral concepts minimize the use of theoretical constructs and inference.

Minimum of Theoretical Constructs

Compared with the other three personality strategies, relatively few theoretical constructs are employed within the behavioral strategy. For example, behavioral theories do not posit any kind of unifying force or structure for personality. There are no behavioral equivalents of an ego, proprium, or self. Instead, each aspect of personality is viewed semi-independently of all other aspects, which is consistent with the view that behavior is determined by external rather than internal factors.

Consider another more specific illustration of the avoidance of theoretical constructs. "Repression" is a theoretical construct, whereas "not talking about painful past experiences" is not. Behavioral theory is by no means free of theoretical constructs (e.g., reinforcement) , but, as will be apparent in the next three chapters, it avoids explanations via recourse to special entities within the person.

Minimum of Inferences

Since it is behavior per se which is observed and studied in the behavioral strategy, it follows that inferences are minimized. Of course, inference is involved whenever one event is used to yield information about another event. If it is predicted that Mary will arrive at work at 8:00 A.M. on Thursday on the basis of her having arrived at that time on Monday, Tuesday, and Wednesday, Mary's arrival time on Thursday is inferred from her previous behavior in the same situation. What is inferred, however, is on the same level of abstraction as the data from which it is inferred. Future *behavior* is being predicted on the basis of past *behavior*. This one-level inferential process should be contrasted with predicting (inferring) future behavior from a *nonbehavioral* source as would be the case were Mary's punctuality on Thursday to be predicted on the basis of Mary's being a compulsive type of person or on the basis of Mary's superego compelling her to be on time. Behavioral predictions are typically one-level inferences and therefore involve less of an inferential leap than predictions stemming from two-level inferences which are frequently made in the other three strategies.

BEHAVIORAL PERSONALITY ASSESSMENT

Assessment of personality in the behavioral strategy can be characterized as being direct and additive, predominantly ahistorical, and analytic.

Direct and Additive

Since all personality assessment begins with observations of behavior, and since in the behavioral strategy these observations themselves are what is of interest, behavioral personality assessment can be considered *direct*. Unlike indirect approaches to assessment, which *infer* the units of personality (e.g., traits) from observed behavior, the behavioral strategy regards observed behavior itself as the unit of personality. To learn how a person is likely to act when confronted with a stressful situation, the behavioral psychologist observes the person in one or more stressful situations, or, when this is not possible, he inquires how the person has behaved in stress-evoking circumstances in the past.

When self-report measures are used as part of behavioral assessment, the focus is on *direct* assessment of the phenomenon being investigated. The maxim of behavioral self-report measures is: If you want to know something, ask about it directly (cf. phenomenological assessment). For example, the behavioral psychologist studying people's fears might use the Fear Survey Schedule, a self-report inventory (first mentioned in Chapter 8) which asks people to rate the degree of fear they have for a number of different situations and objects. As with all self-report measures, subjects' responses to the Fear Survey Schedule are likely to be influenced by response sets and other extraneous variables and are at best only moderately correlated with actual behavior. Nevertheless, direct self-reports often prove to be a more valid measure of actual behavior than indirect assessment methods, such as projective techniques (e.g., Mischel, 1968).

Behavioral measures are also *additive,* in the following way. If a person reacted to stress by trying to avoid the situation on three separate occasions, this would be a stronger indication that he is likely to react by avoidance in future stressful situations than if he attempted to avoid a stressful event only once.

Ahistorical

In predicting future behavior, the behavioral psychologist relies most heavily on the individual's present and *recent* past behavior as a guide. Consistent with the situational specificity hypothesis, he sees little reason to explore an adult's childhood personality in order to assess his present personality. Events in the remote past, as in childhood for an adult, no doubt have had an influence on his present personality, but this influence is considered minimal in the behavioral strategy for two important reasons. First, the influence is, at the present time, indirect. Although the habit of crying as a reaction to frustrating events in one's life may have been learned by observing one's mother react in this way, that habit will persist in adult life only if it continues to be reinforced (e.g., by a husband's sympathy). (This position is consistent with Allport's notion of functional autonomy, discussed in Chapter 7.) Second, the influence of events in one's remote past has become obscure, and there is no way to reliably assess these events and the nature of their influence. At best, the correlation between past and present personality variables can be obtained, but this relationship is not likely to yield information about causation. Adult obsessive behavior may be correlated with severity of toilet training, but such a relationship does not tell us whether the difficulties a person had with appropriate sphincter control have resulted in his attempts to run his business affairs in a precise and orderly fashion.

Analytic[2]

Behavioral personality assessment proceeds by examining relatively small aspects of a person's total personality. For instance, it would be feasible within the behavioral strategy to study the interpersonal relationships of individuals without delving into their sexual relationships. Sometimes two or more aspects of personality are closely related, and it is therefore necessary to consider them simultaneously in order to fully understand one of them. However, the behavioral approach to personality does not assume a priori that

---

[2] Note that the term *analytic* is used here in the sense of *analysis into component parts* and should not be confused with "psychoanalytic" or "factor analytic."

there is a necessary interdependence among different aspects of personality. This may be contrasted with the holistic approach, espoused by the phenomenological strategy, which maintains that each component of personality must be viewed relative to the entire person. The analytic approach has important implications for both behavioral research and personality change strategies. Specific personality phenomena tend to be studied in greater depth, and efforts are made to change particular behaviors rather than to modify the individual's total personality.

Demonstration 13–1 will give the reader a chance to try out one method of behavioral personality assessment.

Demonstration 13–1

THE OBSERVATION AND RECORDING OF BEHAVIOR

The detailed direct observation and recording of behavior is an essential element of behavioral personality assessment. This Demonstration will give you some practice in observing some of your own behavior, recording it, and then plotting its frequency.

Outline of Procedures

The following steps are involved.

1. *Select a target behavior that you will observe and record.*
2. *Define the unit of behavior* (e.g., number of pages read or cigarettes smoked).
3. *Define the unit of time* (e.g., hours, days).
4. *Make a convenient recording device* (e.g., a 3 × 5 index card marked off in time units). You may also want to keep brief notes of your daily activities.
5. *Observe and record the target behavior.*
6. *Plot the frequency of responses each day.*

Selecting a Target Behavior

The first step is to choose a response. Table 13–1 contains a list of behaviors which are particularly applicable to the purposes of the Demonstration, but you can select another response (perhaps one suggested by the examples in the table) as long as it has several features important for this Demonstration. The response should be relatively easy to observe and record without disrupting the behavior and without taking very much of your time. If the response is emitted at too rapid a rate it may prove difficult to record (e.g., eye blinks). On the other hand, it should occur with reasonable frequency in your life so that it can be observed and recorded. (Buying a new car or getting married would, for most people, not occur often enough to be used in this Demonstration!)

You may find it helpful to select a behavior which you actually wish to increase or decrease, although this is not mandatory. Notice that all the examples in Table 13–1 have this feature. Working with some behavior you want to modify has the advantage that, directly or indirectly, it may help you make the change you desire. The purpose of this Demonstration

TABLE 13–1

Examples of Target Behaviors to Observe and Record for Demonstration 13–1

Behavior	Unit of Behavior	Unit of Time
Reading..............................	Pages	Day or hour
Writing...............................	Lines	Day or hour
Body weight..........................	Pounds (lost or gained)	Week
Jogging..............................	¼ miles	Day
Swimming............................	Laps in a pool	Day
Tardiness............................	Times late for an appointment	Day
Daydreaming.........................	Minutes spent	Day or hour
Talking on the telephone..............	Minutes spent or phone calls	Day or hour
Swearing.............................	Curse words	Day or hour
Foreign language vocabulary..........	Words learned	Day
Studying.............................	Minutes spent	Day
Bull sessions........................	Minutes spent	Day
Drinking		Day or hour
a) Coffee...........................	a) Cups	
b) Beer............................	b) Ounces	
Smoking.............................	Cigarettes	Day or hour

is not to teach you desirable habits or to have you get rid of undesirable ones. Nonetheless, recording of behavior one wishes to modify often changes the rate of emission of the behavior in the desired direction (e.g., Lindsley, 1966). (Although this is not a problem when behavior change is the psychologist's primary goal, it does interfere with obtaining unobtrusive base line measures for research purposes.)

Indirectly, the record you make of your behavior may help you to analyze it, which, in turn, may lead you to think of ways of modifying it. Sup-

FIGURE 13–1

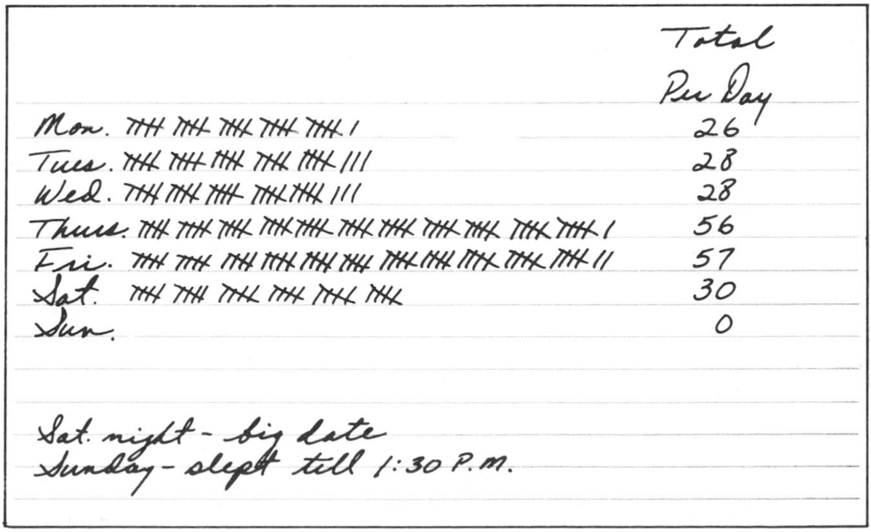

Example of an Index Card Record of Pages Read in a Week for Demonstration 13–1

pose you chose reading as your target behavior because you find that you do not read as much as you need to for your work. You may note that on certain days of the week your reading rate is higher than on other days, and thus you may find it desirable to make a systematic effort to read more on some days. In this regard, it will be helpful to keep a brief diary of the events in your life over the course of your recording in order to help you isolate the events which are associated with a change in response rate.

Observation and Recording

After selecting a target behavior, the next step is to observe it and keep a record of its frequency. This can easily be done by marking off a 3×5 index card in time intervals, and then simply making a tally mark each time you perform the behavior, as is shown in Figure 13–1. At the end of each day (or other unit of time you are using), the total number of tally marks is calculated, and this becomes your rate for the day (e.g., 26 pages read per day).

Graphing the Results of Observation

Each day's rate should then be plotted on a graph to facilitate inspection of the data. As is illustrated in Figure 13–2, the *abscissa,* or horizontal axis, of the graph is marked off in time intervals, such as days or hours. The *ordinate,* or vertical axis, represents the number of responses per unit of time.

As can be seen from the graph, the person read approximately the same number of pages (i.e., between 26 and 28) for the first three days. On Thursday the number of pages nearly doubled, and it remained the same

FIGURE 13–2

Graph of a Week's Reading Behavior (Demonstration 13–1)

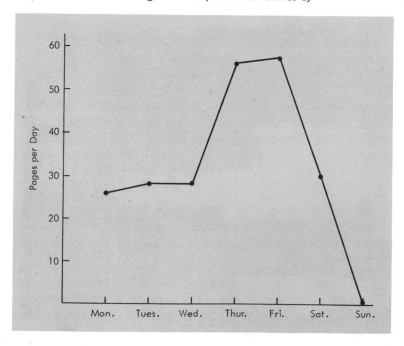

on Friday. On Saturday the number of pages dropped to approximately the Monday-through-Wednesday rate, perhaps because of the interference of the individual's Saturday evening social engagement. And on the seventh day no pages were read (perhaps because the person rested).

BEHAVIORAL RESEARCH

The historical roots of the behavioral strategy are to be found in the laboratories where animal and human learning were being investigated. By way of comparison, recall that the psychoanalytic and phenomenological strategies grew primarily out of observations of human behavior, particularly in a clinical setting, and that the dispositional strategy was an outgrowth of studies of the components of human behavior. The behavioral strategy is a relatively recent descendant of the behavioristic approach to learning; it is partially an attempt to apply principles of learning developed in the laboratory to problems of human personality. Examples include the classical conditioning of attitudes, which is a direct outgrowth of Pavlov's well-known work on the conditioning of salivation in dogs (see Chapter 14) and complex procedures for teaching language to children and adults who do not speak, which were derived from principles developed with pigeons pecking a target in a Skinner box (see Chapter 15).

The experimental method is most frequently used in behavioral personality research because it is particularly suited to the study of specific behaviors under controlled conditions. Rather than examine personality as a single entity, behavioral research investigates small aspects of personality intensively. The research is predominantly nomothetic, although idiographic studies of single subjects are part of behavioral personality change techniques. However, such detailed study of single cases focuses on specific behaviors (e.g., inability to work, difficulties relating to people in authority positions) as opposed to the individual's total personality or global dispositions.

The dependent variables employed in behavioral experimentation tend to be samples of the actual behavior of interest. For example, in behavioral experiments dealing with the factors leading to aggression, the measures of aggression are direct samples of aggressive behavior, such as administering painful electric shock to another person.

BEHAVIORAL PERSONALITY CHANGE

The generic term most frequently used to denote personality change or therapy techniques arising from the behavioral strategy is *behavior modification*. Although most forms of therapy have as their ultimate aim the modification, or change, of behavior, the name "behavior modification" serves to emphasize that in behavioral therapy it is behavior itself which is the primary focus of the change. Another general term used to designate behavioral personality change is *behavior therapy*. There is a third term, "behavior*al* therapy," which we shall use when comparing personality change procedures of the four strategies. All three terms will be employed somewhat interchangeably in subsequent discussion.

Learning and Unlearning

There are many different types of behavior modification techniques, but they all are based on the premise that behavior, be it adaptive or maladaptive in nature, is learned. Problematic or abnormal behavior which necessitates therapeutic intervention is dealt with by having the person either develop new or unpracticed adaptive behaviors or unlearn maladaptive habits.

Target Behaviors

Since personality is viewed in terms of specific behaviors and not in a holistic fashion, it follows that personality change is aimed at modifying specific behaviors rather than the individual's whole personality. Toward this end, behavior modification works on changing selected *target behaviors*. Typically, people come to therapy of any orientation with more than one problem and define their difficulties in vague, general terms. The behavioral therapist first helps the client to specify his problems so that they can be worked with on a behavioral level. For example, clients frequently report feeling "anxious and 'uptight' " much of the time. Through behavioral assessment techniques the therapist will attempt to find the *behavioral referents* of the client's report of anxiety and "uptightness." For one client anxiety may function to keep him away from certain situations (e.g., dates), and for another it may make him perform poorly (e.g., on examinations).

The fact that behavior modification treats specific target behaviors sometimes leads to the *erroneous* conclusion that it cannot deal with multiple problem behaviors and that it changes only simple, relatively straightforward problem behaviors (e.g., snake phobias!). The behavior modification approach works on one or a few target behaviors at a time and, when the required behavior change has taken place, then proceeds to tackle other target behaviors. In practice, behavior modification techniques frequently bring about behavior change in a relatively short period of time—sometimes in one or two sessions and often in as few as a dozen. This makes it possible for multiple target behaviors to be handled sequentially rather than simultaneously. Furthermore, the target behaviors, which are discrete behaviors, form the components of highly complex human behavioral problems. For instance, complicated marital difficulties may necessitate working on such component target behaviors as anxiety about sexual matters, learning interpersonal skills, unlearning dependency behavior, and so on.

Maintaining Conditions

The task of behavioral therapy is to assess those conditions which are currently maintaining the behavior to be changed (the target behavior) and then to modify the maintaining conditions so as to bring about the desired change. Although the target behavior may have originated many years in the past, knowledge about its origin, say in childhood, is not necessary unless the conditions which brought it about initially are the same conditions which account for its present persistence. (Frequently the conditions which first led to the behavior and the factors which are currently maintaining it are different—see above discussion of the ahistorical nature of behavioral assessment.)

The factors which are maintaining a target behavior can often be grouped broadly into two major categories, *antecedent* and *consequent* conditions. Antecedent conditions refer to all the stimuli which are present before the target behavior occurs, including situational cues (e.g., where the target behavior occurs and what is going on at the time), temporal cues (e.g., at what time of day), and interpersonal cues (e.g., who is present and what they are doing). Consequent conditions refer to everything which happens after the target behavior is performed and include both the immediate and the long-range consequences to the individual performing the behavior, as well as to other people and even the physical environment.

To illustrate what is meant by antecedent and consequent conditions, consider the behavior of overeating which Ann would like to change. On the antecedent side of the overeating might be such stimuli as: Ann is at home alone in the evening; she is bored or frustrated; the refrigerator is well stocked with "treats." The consequences of Ann's overeating include: Ann enjoys the treats; she feels guilty; she gains weight; she cannot wear some of her most attractive clothes; her boy friend calls her "chubs." Depending on the specific behavior modification technique employed to deal with Ann's overeating, the emphasis would be on changing the antecedent or the consequent conditions or both.

14

The Behavioral Strategy
THE CLASSICAL CONDITIONING APPROACH

During the early part of the 20th century, the seeds of modern personality psychology were being sown. Freud's position was just gaining prominence, Gestalt psychology (which may be considered a grandfather of the phenomenological approaches) was born, and the behavioristic movement in psychology was announced with enthusiasm and denounced with vigor.

In America, the predominant psychology in the early 1900s was the science of conscious experience. During this period, research with animals was only on the fringes of the prevailing psychology, since it had been generally accepted (from Descartes on) that consciousness in subhuman species could not be logically proved to exist. However, one psychologist, John Broadus Watson, inspired in part by the writings of the Russian physiologist Ivan Pavlov, was conducting experiments with animals and humans which disavowed the importance of consciousness and paved the way for a behavioristic psychology of learning.

HISTORICAL ANTECEDENTS: PAVLOV AND WATSON

Pavlov's Experiments

During the late 19th century Pavlov was investigating the digestive processes of dogs. To his dismay, the results of his studies of the flow of digestive juices were often disrupted by a then unexpected phenomenon which was to become one of the cornerstones of the psychology of learning. Specifically, the dogs often appeared to anticipate the food (meat powder), which Pavlov used to induce salivation, even *before* the salivary flow had been directly stimulated. Initially Pavlov considered these "psychic secretions"[1] a nuisance which should be eliminated.

Upon further consideration, however, Pavlov decided to study the phenomenon on which he had accidentally chanced, rather than simply seek ways to eliminate it. His first approach was introspective, involving an effort to imagine the situation from the dog's point of view. This strategy led up blind alleys (his assistants could not agree on what the dog ought to think or feel) rather than to objective results and was subsequently banned from Pavlov's laboratory (Hyman, 1964). Turning next to a more objective and verifiable approach, Pavlov reasoned that since the salivation occurred with some regularity as he began each experiment, the animal's natural, or reflexive, tendency to respond to the meat powder in its mouth with salivation had somehow also come to be evoked by the mere sight of this food. This latter reaction was not an innate one. It had to be *conditioned,* or acquired, by environmental events which were potentially under experimental control. Following this reasoning, Pavlov began to investigate the manner in which such conditioned responses are formed. He successfully taught dogs to salivate to an impressive variety of signals, including a rotating disk, the sound of a metronome, and the presentation of a light. He also discovered a great deal about how such responses are formed, modified, and extinguished (become less likely to occur).

The experiments conducted by Pavlov followed a paradigm now referred to as *classical conditioning.* The order of events in a typical classical conditioning experiment is as follows.[2] First, a *conditioned stimulus* (CS) is presented, which does not initially produce a reliable response. In many of Pavlov's experiments a light was used for this purpose. Very shortly thereafter (a fraction of a second to no more than a few seconds), a stimulus known to reflexively produce a certain response is introduced. This stimulus is referred to as the *unconditioned stimulus* (UCS), and the response which it produces is the *unconditioned response* (UCR). In many of Pavlov's famous experiments, the meat powder served as the UCS and salivary flow was the UCR. Upon repeated presentations of the CS and UCS (each presentation being referred to as a *trial*), the CS (light) alone began

---

[1] The term is Pavlov's.

[2] While this order is the most effective one for showing a conditioning effect, others have been the subject of experimentation (e.g., trace conditioning involves the termination of the CS before the UCS is presented). Interested readers should consult learning texts such as Kimble's (1961) *Hilgard and Marquis' Conditioning and Learning.*

to produce salivary flow even before the UCS (meat powder) was presented. The salivary flow in this latter condition (which is not necessarily identical to the flow produced by the meat powder) is referred to as the *conditioned response* (CR). The entire process appeared to be an extremely simple and objective way to study the process of learning.

Pavlov's research revealed that a CR is not only developed through the association of the CS and the UCS, but that it must also be maintained by occasional trials in which this association is again presented. When the CS is paired with the UCS on a particular trial, the arrangement is known as *reinforcement*. Although an established CS will continue to produce the CR if the UCS is absent for a number of trials (i.e., is not reinforced), ultimately the CR is likely to weaken or disappear completely. Both the failure to provide reinforcement and the actual diminution of the response have been referred to as *extinction*.

The form of conditioning described above would have limited meaning for our understanding of either human or nonhuman animal behavior if the exact CS used in training were required to produce the CR at a later time. However, both Pavlov's studies and a great deal of subsequent research clearly show that this restriction usually does not hold. Instead, when a CR to one previously neutral stimulus has been developed, stimuli which are similar to (but not identical with) the original CS may also evoke the response; the greater the similarity between the new stimulus and the original stimulus, the greater will be the degree to which the latter can be substituted for the former. This basic phenomenon is known as *generalization,* and the relationship between a new stimulus' similarity to the original CS and its ability to elicit the CR is known as the *generalization gradient*. The concept of generalization has often been invoked in an effort to understand and predict complex human behavior in novel situations, in accordance with the new situations' similarity to familiar ones. For example, people who are afraid of snakes also exhibit emotional reactions to pictures of snakes as measured by their galvanic skin responses (Geer, 1966).

Discrimination may be thought of as the "other side of the coin" to generalization. If the experimental situation is correctly arranged, the subject will learn to respond only to a particular stimulus and not to others that are similar to it. One of Pavlov's most intriguing experiments illustrates how this may occur. The basic procedure was to always reinforce one CS, a luminous circle, but never to reinforce an ellipse with an axes ratio of 2:1. This discrimination was easily formed, so that the dog salivated when the circle was presented but not when the ellipse was presented. Pavlov then proceeded to make the ellipse more and more like a circle (less egg-shaped and more round), and the dog responded remarkably well—up to a point. Finally, however, the two stimuli were so similar (a ratio of 9:8) that the dog could no longer make the discrimination.

> After three weeks of work upon this differentiation not only did the discrimination fail to improve, but it became considerably worse, and finally disappeared altogether. At the same time the whole behaviour of the animal underwent an abrupt change. The hitherto quiet dog began to squeal in its stand, kept wriggling about, tore off with its teeth the apparatus for mechanical stimulation of the skin, and bit through the tubes connecting the animal's room with the observer, a behaviour which never happened before. On being taken to the experimental room the dog now barked violently, which was also contrary to its usual custom; in short it presented all the symptoms of a condition of acute neurosis. On testing the cruder differentiations they were also found to be destroyed . . . (Pavlov, 1927, p. 291).

In addition to demonstrating how discriminations may be developed, the later phases of the above experiment appear to have implications for human behavior. For example, it has been suggested that overaspiring parents, who push their children beyond their capabilities for top grades or other superlative accomplishments, may produce difficulties analogous to the problem encountered by Pavlov's dog.

In the foregoing discussion, we have described the basic principles of classical conditioning and implied that they may be extended to some aspects of human behavior. John Watson was perhaps the first psychologist to take this possibility seriously. An experiment on the classically conditioned emotional reactions of a young child, discussed in the next section, is one of Watson's most widely cited studies.

Watson's Behaviorism

Familiar with Pavlov's work and seeing many of its implications, Watson believed that animal psychologists were not only engaged in scientific research but that they were paving the way for the future of psychology. In contrast to the structuralist school of psychology, so named because it sought to discover the structure of the mind or consciousness, Watson, who founded American *behaviorism,* declared that psychology was the science of behavior. A few excerpts from Watson's first book, *Behavior* (1914), will give the flavor of behaviorism as its founder saw it.

> Psychology as the behaviorist views it is a purely objective experimental branch of natural science. Its theoretical goal is the predic-

tion and control of behavior. . . . The behaviorist attempts to get a unitary scheme of animal response. He recognizes no dividing line between man and brute. The behavior of man, with all of its refinements and complexity, forms only a part of his total field of investigation. . . . It is possible to write a psychology, to define it as . . . the "science of behavior" . . . and never go back upon the definition: never to use the terms consciousness, mental states, mind, content, will, imagery, and the like. . . . Certain stimuli lead . . . organisms to make . . . responses. In a system of psychology completely worked out, given the responses the stimuli can be predicted; given the stimuli the responses can be predicted (pp. 1, 9, 10).

Most of Watson's experimental work focused on simple motor mechanisms, reflexes, and the influence of controlled environmental stimulation upon relatively simple bits of behavior. He did believe, however, that in the long run similar experimental analyses would be possible for the broader study of personality. Watson (1919) rejected "the muddled writings . . . from the hands of many writers upon self, personality and character," referring to those psychologists who found it necessary "to bring into account for self and personality . . . a nucleus, a core, or essence which . . . cannot be expressed in the plain facts of heredity and acquired reactions and their integrations" (p. 396). He eschewed rapid methods of studying personality and stressed the importance of a detailed and thorough analysis of the individual's observable behavior which begins with "discarding of presuppositions." Although he suggested such methods as detailed questioning and systematic naturalistic observation, he favored studying an individual's personality through experimental methods in the laboratory. This last strategy is illustrated by the now famous case of "little Albert," which was published in 1920 by Watson and Rayner.

Albert, an 11-month-old apathetic child, appeared to be afraid of nothing except the loud sound made by striking a steel bar. In order to induce another fear in Albert, Watson and Rayner placed a white rat in front of him and at the same time produced the loud sound he disliked. After a series of seven such presentations, the rat, which had not previously elicited fear in Albert, came to elicit a fear, or avoidance, reaction (e.g., crying, attempts to escape from the situation). Albert also showed fear of other objects that were similar to the rat in various dimensions of appearance, thereby indicating that some stimulus generalization had occurred.[3] Watson and Rayner had in-

---

[3] Most citations of this report consider the experiment a "classic" demonstration of generalization, or spread, of a learned fear of an object to other, similar objects (cf. most introductory psychology textbooks), and Watson and Rayner may have perceived the results that way. Nevertheless, generalization to furry

tended to extinguish the fear which they had produced, but Albert was removed from the laboratory before extinction efforts could be made.

However, there is, in effect, a sequel to the case of little Albert. Three years later Mary Cover Jones (1924b), "with the advice of Dr. John B. Watson," successfully eliminated a child's fear. Jones's subject, Peter, who "seemed almost to be Albert grown a bit older," came to the laboratory already afraid of white rats and other furry objects. When Peter was 2 years and 10 months of age, his fear was quite severe: "Peter was put in a crib in a play room and immediately became absorbed in his toys. A white rat was introduced into the crib from behind. . . . At sight of the rat, Peter screamed and fell flat on his back in a paroxysm of fear . . ." (Jones, 1924b, p. 309).

Peter was even more afraid of a rabbit, and Jones decided to focus on reducing fear of it. Jones's goals for the experiment were first to develop procedures for extinguishing the fear and then to determine whether such procedures applied to one feared object would generalize to other feared objects which had not been directly involved in the treatment. Initially, Peter was exposed to fearless peer models during a daily play period in the laboratory. During these sessions Peter played with three other children, selected because they had a fearless attitude toward furry rodents and appeared in all other respects to show satisfactory adjustment. A rabbit was merely present during a part of each play period. Peter's progress was regularly assessed by exposing him to the rabbit from time to time in the absence of his playmates. Jones (1924b) noted impressive improvement "by more or less regular steps from almost complete terror at sight of the rabbit to a completely positive response with no signs of disturbance" (p. 310). Unfortunately, after seven periods of treatment, and before tests of generalization had begun, Peter contracted scarlet fever and was taken to the hospital for two months.

---

inanimate objects was weak, as the following passage from Watson and Rayner's (1920) report indicates: "When his hand was laid on the wool he immediately withdrew it but did not show the shock that the animals produced. . . . He finally . . . lost some of the negativism to the wool" (p. 7). His newly acquired fear of hair, which has frequently been taken as evidence of generalization, is difficult to interpret. On the one hand, the following incident is reported: "Just in play W. put his head down to see if Albert would play with his hair. Albert was completely negative" (p. 7). On the other hand, ". . . two other observers did the same thing. He began immediately to play with their hair" (p. 7). Finally, to show that the fear had not transferred to completely unratlike objects in the situation, Albert was retested on *his own blocks*. Not surprisingly, he had not come to fear these. A child's own blocks, though admittedly unratlike, may be presumed to have strong positive associations. Thus, Albert's failure to fear his blocks hardly constitutes convincing proof that the acquired fear had not extended to all previously neutral objects in the situation.

When he came back to the laboratory, most of his earlier fear had returned. A nurse reported an incident which may have contributed to the apparent relapse.

> As they were entering a taxi at the door of the hospital, a large dog, running past, jumped at them. Both Peter and the nurse were very much frightened, Peter so much that he lay back in the taxi pale and quiet. . . . This seemed reason enough for his precipitate descent back to the original fear level. Being threatened by a large dog when ill, and in a strange place and being with an adult who also showed fear, was a terrifying situation against which our training could not have fortified him (Jones, 1924b, p. 312).

This setback had one advantage, however. It permitted Jones to examine the efficacy of a more elaborate treatment, which involved both exposure to a fearless peer (which now is called *vicarious extinction* and will be discussed more fully in Chapter 16) and counterconditioning. A session of this procedure began with Peter seated in a high chair eating some food which he liked. The caged rabbit was then brought as close as possible to Peter without interfering with his eating. The procedure was completed with the simultaneous exposure to peer models, as indicated from Jones's (1924b) laboratory notes.

> Lawrence and Peter sitting near together in their high chairs eating candy. Rabbit in cage put down 12 feet away. Peter began to cry. Lawrence said, "Oh, rabbit." Clambered down, ran over and looked in the cage at him. Peter followed close and watched.
> Peter with candy in high chair. Experimenter brought rabbit and sat down in front of the tray with it. Peter cried out, "I don't want him," and withdrew. Rabbit was given to another child sitting near to hold. His holding the rabbit served as a powerful suggestion; Peter wanted the rabbit on his lap, and held it for an instant (p. 313).

Recall that one of Jones's interests was to determine whether the experimental treatments would generalize to other furry objects. Her final description of Peter suggests that this goal was met.

> He showed in the last interview . . . a genuine fondness for the rabbit. What has happened to the fear of the other objects? The fear of the cotton, the fur coat, feathers, was entirely absent at our last interview. He looked at them, handled them, and immediately turned to something which interested him more. The reaction to the rats and the fur rug with the stuffed head was greatly modified and improved. While he did not show the fondness for these that was apparent with the rabbit, he had made a fair adjustment. For example, Peter would pick up the tin box containing the frogs or rats and carry it around the room. When requested, he picked up the fur rug and carried it to the experimenter.

What would Peter do if confronted by a strange animal? At the last interview the experimenter presented a mouse and a tangled mass of angleworms. At first sight, Peter showed slight distress reactions and moved away, but before the period was over he was carrying the worms about and watching the mouse with undisturbed interest. By "unconditioning" Peter to the rabbit, he has apparently been helped to overcome many superfluous fears, some completely, some to a less degree. His tolerance of strange animals and unfamiliar situations has apparently increased (Jones, 1924b, p. 314).

Not until many years later did procedures (and results) similar to those reported by Jones find their way into the mainstream of psychology.

CLASSICAL CONDITIONING AND COMPLEX BEHAVIOR

Since the time of Pavlov's work and Watson's pioneering experiments, the possibility that a process of classical conditioning is responsible for the development of human social behavior has been explored in a variety of settings. The studies have focused on a number of different aspects of personality; in order to illustrate this research, four topics will be presented. The first concerns the classical conditioning of attitudes; the second deals with conditioning techniques for the control of bodily functions; the third involves the possible development of one psychosomatic symptom (asthma attacks) through such conditioning; and the fourth illustrates how derivatives of the classical conditioning paradigm have been employed as therapeutic techniques.

The Classical Conditioning of Attitudes

There are a great variety of social stimuli which elicit evaluative responses from humans. Each of us reacts to the names of certain subgroups, such as cops, jocks, intellectuals, and many others, with an evaluative reaction, or *attitude*. We may also show such reactions to proper names. In extreme cases, attitudes may even develop toward articles of clothing, as illustrated in the following citation from a metropolitan newspaper.

Dear Abby:
My friend fixed me up with a blind date and I should have known the minute he showed up in a bow tie that he couldn't be trusted. I fell for him like a rock. He got me to love him on purpose and then lied to me and cheated on me. Every time I go with a man who wears a bow tie, the same thing happens. I think girls should be warned about men who wear them. (Cited in Bandura, 1968, pp. 306–7.)

In the light of anecdotal examples such as the one above and considering the voluminous amount of research that has shown the power of classical conditioning, it is tempting to hypothesize that many attitudes have been produced by a process of association. In fact, research with humans suggests that this may be the case.

Two relatively early studies by Razran (1938, 1940) were designed to test the hypothesis that responses which are commonly referred to as attitudes could be modified by association with pleasant or unpleasant stimuli. In one of Razran's (1938) studies, 100 judges (whose composition was distributed to correspond to the U.S. adult population in racial and national background, religion, and education) rated photographs of 30 college girls as to their beauty, intelligence, character, entertainingness, ambition, and the degree to which they would be generally liked. Two weeks later the judges were asked to rate the photographs of the girls for a second time but were ostensibly told the names of the girls. Of the surnames chosen, 15 corresponded to ethnic minorities—five Jewish, five Irish, and five Italian—while the remaining 15 were selected from the Social Register and signers of the Declaration of Independence. Liking for the photographs of the girls with minority group names decreased, as did evaluations of their character and beauty. Among other changes observed, assignment of Jewish names produced higher intelligence and ambition ratings, while there were decrements in the intelligence ratings of the Irish- and Italian-named photographs. These biases largely disappeared, however, when the names were presented together with a stimulus which was known to elicit a positive experience. Specifically, Razran employed simple stimulus-pairing, which he referred to as the "luncheon technique." The procedure involved representing the items again while the judges were given a free lunch, thereby presumably conditioning the names to the positive experience of eating.

In another study, Razran (1940) had college students and unemployed workers rate a variety of sociopolitical slogans (such as "Workers of the World, Unite!" and "No Other Ism but Americanism!") on a scale which measured their personal approval of the slogans and the social effectiveness and literary value of each. The slogans were next divided into two sets. Again employing the luncheon technique, one set was repeated for several sessions while the subjects were enjoying a free lunch. The second set, however, was presented as the subjects were required to inhale a number of putrid odors. Nonexperimental slogans were also presented at various times to make conscious recall of the associations more difficult. When Razran readministered the original test of evaluation of the slogans, he found that those associated with the free lunch clearly showed increases in their favorableness, while those associated with the unpleasant odors showed rating decreases. The evidence also suggested that these findings reflected more than mere conscious recall of the positive or negative associations, as disclosed by Razran's (1940) report that ". . . the subjects' knowledge of which slogans were combined with pleasant, and which with unpleasant, stimuli was little above chance" (p. 481). The luncheon technique may be applied in a variety of practical ways. Many businessmen favor the practice of finalizing negotiations over a pleasant meal.

That meanings can be classically conditioned in childhood has been dramatically shown in a series of studies by Nunnally and his associates (Nunnally, Duchnowski, & Parker, 1965; Parker & Nunnally, 1966; Wilson & Nunnally, 1971). In one such study (Nunnally et al., 1965), elementary school children were asked to play a spin-wheel game. Three nonsense syllables appeared randomly on the 18 possible stopping points on the wheel (see Figure 14–1). Each child was asked to spin the wheel 30 times, receiving a different consequence depending on where the wheel stopped: one of the syllable stopping points was associated with a reward (two pennies), another with no consequences, and the third with a negative outcome (the loss of a penny). The question was whether through this

FIGURE 14–1

A Child Playing the Spinning Wheel Game in Nunnally's Classical Conditioning Research

Courtesy Professor Jum C. Nunnally

association the individual nonsense syllables (which were known to be neutral before the game) would take on conditioned meaning or value. The answer was a clear yes.

After playing the game, each participant was shown three stick figures with blank faces; one of the three nonsense syllables—previously associated with a positive, a neutral, or a negative event—appeared below each figure. It was explained to the child that each nonsense syllable was the name of the "boy" above it. The child was read a list of complimentary and derogatory adjectives and asked to attribute each to one of the boys (e.g., "Which is the *friendly* boy?" or "Which is the *mean* boy?"). The results were striking: an average of 4.7 (out of a possible 5) positive evaluations were assigned to the boy whose "name" had been associated with a reward, while *no* positive evaluations were assigned to the boy whose name had been associated with a negative outcome.

Such findings have also been obtained in experimental studies with adults. Consider a pair of investigations by Staats and Staats (1958) which were designed to test the hypothesis that attitudes elicited by socially significant words can be changed through clas-

FIGURE 14–2

A Portion of Staats and Staats's Experimental Results Showing That Attitudes Can Be Classically Conditioned

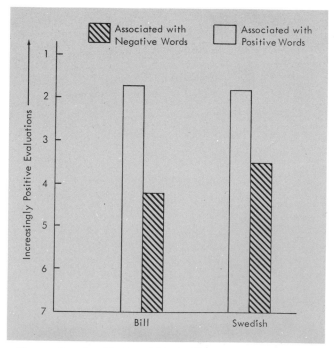

Source: Based on Staats and Staats, 1958.

sical conditioning when other words are used as the unconditioned stimuli. In their first experiment the CS words were national names. Two of these, *Swedish* and *Dutch,* were paired with UCS words already known to elicit either positive (such as *gift, sacred, happy*) or negative (such as *bitter, ugly, failure*) meanings. One group of subjects had *positive* words associated with Dutch and *negative* words with Swedish, whereas for the second group the reverse was true; this *counterbalancing* provided a control for differences in initial attitudes.

In their second experiment, Staats and Staats used proper male names as the CSs, with *Tom* and *Bill* being the names for which evaluative associations were conditioned. The findings of both experiments clearly indicated that the expected conditioning effect occurred since, *within each group,* the negatively conditioned name was rated as the more unpleasant one (see Figure 14–2).

Use of Classical Conditioning Techniques to Control Bodily Functions

Recall that the natural functions of urination and defecation were considered by Freud to have considerable psychological significance. Even if one does not grant that these processes have all the intra-psychic meaning which Freud attributed to them, it is clear that the successful and regular control of the bladder and bowels is necessary for the individual's comfort and health. Moreover, it is sometimes the case that children find it difficult to gain control over both of these functions, and constipation, even in adults, is one of the most widespread functional disorders known to contemporary medicine (Quarti & Renaud, 1964). For these reasons, applied studies of the control of bodily elimination through classical conditioning serve as particularly important examples of the application of the paradigm to human behavior.

Enuresis

An early study (Mowrer & Mowrer, 1938) illustrates the application of classical conditioning to the problem of bed-wetting, tech-nically referred to as *enuresis,* as applied to 30 children between the ages of 3 and 13.[4] The difficulty of the enuretic child, viewed in learning terms, is that the child has not learned to awaken before urination occurs. In other words, for bed-wetting children, the in-ternal stimulation of bladder tension does not produce the necessary response of awakening. The strategy adopted by Mowrer and Mowrer

---

[4] The treatment is specifically *not* recommended for children under three.

to establish the necessary response was to pair the bladder stimulation (CS) with the ringing of a bell (UCS), a stimulus which would inevitably awaken the child (UCR) and permit him to reach the toilet in time.

The subjects slept on a specially prepared pad, consisting of two pieces of bronze screening separated by heavy cotton fabric. When urination occurred, the urine seeped through the fabric and closed an electrical circuit, which, in turn, sounded a bell. Through such repeated pairings, bladder tension alone was able to awaken the child before urination occurred. Bed-wetting was eliminated in all 30 cases, with the maximum period of treatment being two months. Although the Mowrers noted that no severely neurotic or psychotic children were included in the experiment, one of their subjects had an IQ of only 65. He, too, responded satisfactorily. Further, they reported that:

> Personality changes, when they occurred as a result of the application of the present method of treating enuresis, have uniformly been in a favorable direction. In no case has there been any evidence of "symptom substitution." Our results, therefore, do not support the assumption, sometimes made, that any attempt to deal directly with the problem of enuresis will necessarily result in the child's developing "something worse" (1938, p. 451).

Symptom substitution refers to the notion that when a symptom is eliminated without eliminating its cause (e.g., an intrapsychic conflict) another symptom will replace it.

Constipation

Also employing a classical conditioning model, Quarti and Renaud (1964) developed a treatment of constipation. Defecation is stimulated by the massage of a section of the large colon immediately adjacent to the rectal passage. This stimulation constitutes the UCS for defecation, and the treatment depends upon associating it with a convenient CS. For this purpose, Quarti and Renaud devised a special belt, pictured in Figure 14–3, which permits administration of a very mild electric shock to the spinal area. The level of shock used is so mild as to be described by the investigators as "pleasant." The specific treatment, which is self-administered, proceeds as follows:

> The subject to be re-educated continues to take his usual laxatives so as to produce one bowel movement per day. As he goes to the toilet he puts on the apparatus, starts operating it prior to defecation and stops the electric stimulation as soon as evacuation is terminated. . . . Gradually the subject should reduce the quantity of laxatives until he will no longer take any. . . . Once conditioning has been established, which generally happens after 20 to 30

FIGURE 14–3

Apparatus Used for Treatment of Constipation through Classical Conditioning

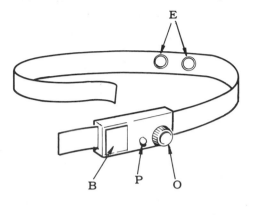

E: Electrodes.
O: On-off switch and intensity control.
P: Pilot.
B: Battery compartment.
Source: Quarti and Renaud, 1964.

applications, the electrical stimulation alone produces defecation according to the individual rhythm of digestion (Quarti & Renaud, 1964, p. 224).

As a final step in Quarti and Renaud's procedure, the subject begins to go to the toilet every day at a given hour, usually immediately after breakfast. Thus, the chosen hour eventually becomes the CS, and the apparatus itself becomes unnecessary. The three cases in which the procedure was reported to have been tried were all successfully treated.

Classical Conditioning and Emotional Reactions

An individual's behavior is often labeled deviant by society when he responds with an intense emotional reaction to stimuli which most people find innocuous. Disorders such as anxiety reactions, insomnia, and a variety of somatic or "nervous" complaints probably fall into this category. Laboratory studies of asthma have suggested, for example, that this disorder may be produced through *aversive classical conditioning* (i.e., the pairing of a neutral stimulus and one that elicits an unpleasant, or aversive, response). Consider a study by Dekker, Pelser, and Groen (1957) which included two subjects who suffered from severe bronchial asthma. The patients repeatedly inhaled an allergen (UCS) to which they were highly sensitive, and which produced an automatic asthmatic attack (UCR). Whereas the neutral solvent (CS) in which these allergens were dissolved did not initially produce any asthmatic symptoms, after repeated trials it came to elicit attacks of asthma (CR) by itself. Moreover, the inhalation of pure oxygen and even the presence of the inhalation mouthpiece (both of which, of course, could not have produced any reaction initially) were now able to provoke severe attacks of asthma that were difficult to distinguish from those which were produced by the allergen itself.

Also consistent with a classical conditioning explanation of asthma is Dekker and Groen's (1956) report that asthma patients, when encouraged to talk freely about the cause of their attacks, list a variety of causative factors, including the sight of dust, watching someone swallow an aspirin, knitting, and sunshine. Such stimuli also elicit asthma attacks in the laboratory from some patients.

> Patient L had told us that she got an asthmatic attack from looking at a goldfish. After a base line had been obtained, a goldfish in a bowl was brought into the room. . . . Under our eyes she developed a severe asthmatic attack with loud wheezing, followed by a gradual remission after the goldfish had been taken from the room. During the next experiment the goldfish was replaced by a plastic toy which was easily recognized as such . . . but a fierce attack resulted. . . . Upon this she told the investigator the following dream, which she had had after the preceding investigation.
> In her home stood a big goldfish bowl. On a shelf high up near the window were her books. In one of them she wanted to read why goldfishes cause asthma. She climbed on a chair and reached for the book, but it was too high. She lost her balance and fell into the goldfish bowl. She gasped for breath behind the glass. The fishes swam around her. Her neck was caught in a streak of water weed. She awoke with an attack of asthma. She also remembered suddenly how when she was a child her mother threw away her bowl of goldfish, which she loved so much. The patient had saved her pocket-money to buy them. Mother threw the fishes into the water closet and flushed them through (Dekker & Groen, 1956, p. 62).

Dekker and his associates were largely unsuccessful in their efforts to treat their asthmatic patients with traditional methods of psychotherapy and called for the development of ". . . a more specific deconditioning therapy that makes the conditioning disappear in the same way in which it came" (Dekker et al., 1957, p. 107). As we shall see shortly, such a therapeutic technique has been developed by Joseph Wolpe.

Wolpe believes that many forms of maladaptive behavior are nothing more than persistent learned habits. For Wolpe, "anxiety" is an inappropriate fear response to situations and events that carry no objective threat to the individual, and it plays a central role in the development and maintenance of neurosis (cf. Freud). Wolpe posits that anxiety is learned by classical conditioning. Specifically, a neutral cue (CS) which is present at the same time that another stimulus (UCS) elicits a fear or anxiety response (UCR), comes to elicit a similar response (CR) on future occasions. This learning paradigm is illustrated in the following prototypal example.

> The child places his hand on the big, black, hot coal stove. He quickly withdraws the painful hand, tearful and fearful. His mother comforts him, but later notes that he keeps away from the stove and seems afraid of it. Clearly, the child has developed a beneficial habit of fearing and avoiding an actually harmful object.
>
> But in some cases the experience also has another and less favorable consequence. Suppose in the mother's bedroom there is a large black chest of drawers. The child may have become afraid of this too—purely on the basis of its *physical resemblance* to the stove— a phenomenon known in psychology as generalization. Fear of the chest of drawers is neurotic because there can be no harm in touching it. It can have several undesirable implications. In the first place, the very presence of an unpleasant emotion like fear is objectionable where it is not appropriate. Secondly, the child is now forced to make a detour if the chest of drawers is in his path; and thirdly, he no longer has easy access to any delectable contents of the drawers, such as candy. In these features of this child's case, we have the model of all neurotic fear reactions (Wolpe & Lazarus, 1966, pp. 17–18).

In this example, an emotional response was conditioned in the child by the association of a painful stimulus with a neutral stimulus. There is evidence that the UCS need not be painful, only unpleasant, for the development of conditioned anxiety.

Geer (1968) used color photographs of victims of violent and sudden death as unconditioned stimuli. The photographs were presented to college students five seconds after the presentation of a tone, an initially neutral stimulus. After 20 such pairings, the previously neutral tone produced galvanic skin responses indicating heightened emotional arousal.

Geer included a "random association" group whose subjects experienced occasional but unpredictable—"random"—pairings (instead of continuous and reliable pairings) of the tone with the photographs of the dead bodies. The random procedure had particularly strong effects in producing emotional arousal in subjects, a finding that may have far-reaching implications.

. . . one could speculate that oppressed groups within a society function in an environment that delivers unpredicted noxious stimuli and that such conditions may result in extensive emotional disturbance. . . . Individuals in long-term stressful conditions characterized by lack of prediction or control may experience considerable disturbance. . . . Certain behavior disorders [may be] states in which the individual is unable to predict the occurrence of noxious stimuli (Geer, 1968, p. 155).

PERSONALITY CHANGE THROUGH COUNTERCONDITIONING

Systematic Desensitization

Wolpe (1958) has developed a technique for alleviating anxiety, called *systematic desensitization,* which is based on the principle of *reciprocal inhibition:* "If a response antagonistic to anxiety can be made to occur in the presence of anxiety-evoking stimuli so that it is accompanied by a complete or partial suppression of the anxiety responses, the bond between these stimuli and the anxiety responses will be weakened" (p. 71). Perhaps the first recorded use of the principle of reciprocal inhibition was Jones's (1924b) attempt to eliminate Peter's fear of rabbits. Recall that one of the techniques Jones employed began with Peter's eating a food which he liked. Then the feared stimulus (a caged rabbit) was gradually brought closer and closer to Peter, without disturbing his eating. In this case, the eating response was antagonistic to the anxiety response.

The technique of systematic desensitization involves three sets of operations. First, the anxious individual must be taught a response which is antagonistic to the response of anxiety. Second, specific details of his anxiety must be assessed and an *anxiety hierarchy* constructed. Once these preliminary procedures have been completed, the actual systematic desensitization can be implemented. This involves the repeated pairing of the response which is antagonistic to anxiety with anxiety-evoking stimuli. Each of these operations will be illustrated in the following sections.

Deep Muscle Relaxation

The response most frequently employed as an antagonist to anxiety is deep muscle relaxation. The physiological concomitants of anxiety (increased heart rate, perspiring, shaking, and so on) are, for the most part, incompatible with a state of deep muscle relaxation. (We never hear someone report that he is both nervous or anxious and relaxed at the same time.)

Relaxation training involves a systematic relaxation of the various skeletal muscle groups (arms, head, neck and shoulders, trunk, hips, and legs). While the specific instructions vary with the particular muscles being relaxed, an excerpt from Wolpe's instructions for relaxation of the arms will serve to illustrate the basic procedure. The subject sits in a comfortable armchair (reclining lounge chairs are often used) with his eyes closed and is given instructions such as the following:

> Settle back as comfortably as you can. Let yourself relax to the best of your ability. . . . Now, as you relax like that, clench your right fist, just clench your fist tighter and tighter, and study the tension as you do so. Keep it clenched and feel the tension in your right fist, hand, forearm . . . and now relax. Let the fingers of your right hand become loose, and observe the contrast in your feelings. . . . Now, let yourself go and try to become more relaxed all over. . . . Once more, clench your right fist really tight . . . hold it, and notice the tension again. . . . Now let go, relax; your fingers straighten out, and you notice the difference once more. . . . Now repeat that with your left fist. Clench your left fist while the rest of your body relaxes; clench that fist tighter and feel the tension . . . and now relax. Again enjoy the contrast. . . . Repeat that once more, clench the left fist, tight and tense. . . . Now do the opposite of tension—relax and feel the difference. Continue relaxing like that for a while. . . . Clench both fists tighter and tighter, both fists tense, forearms tense, study the sensations . . . and relax; straighten out your fingers and feel that relaxation. Continue relaxing your hands and forearms more and more. . . . Now bend your elbows and tense your biceps, tense them harder and study the tension feelings . . . all right, straighten out your arms, let them relax and feel that difference again. Let the relaxation develop. . . . Once more, tense your biceps; hold the tension and observe it carefully. . . . Straighten the arms and relax; relax to the best of your ability. . . . Each time, pay close attention to your feelings when you tense up and when you relax. Now straighten your arms, straighten them so that you feel most tension in the triceps muscles along the back of your arms; stretch your arms and feel that tension. . . . And now relax. Get your arms back into a comfortable position. Let the relaxation proceed on its own. The arms should feel comfortably heavy as you allow them to relax. . . . Straighten the arms once more so that you feel the tension in the triceps muscles; straighten them. Feel that tension . . . and relax. Now let's concentrate on pure relaxation in the arms without any tension. Get your arms comfortable and let them relax further and further. Even when your arms seem fully relaxed, try to go that extra bit further; try to achieve deeper and deeper levels of relaxation (Wolpe & Lazarus, 1966, p. 177).

The number of sessions needed to teach deep muscle relaxation varies from individual to individual, but on the average less than a half-dozen sessions are required if the subject practices the technique for a short time each day at home.

Construction of Anxiety Hierarchies

In order to treat anxiety by systematic desensitization, a detailed and highly specific accounting must be made of those stimuli which elicit anxiety responses. Sometimes a person will come to a therapist with a well-defined fear of a particular class of stimuli or stimulus situations, such as fear of snakes or of going to the dentist. More often, however, people feel anxious at various times but are not aware of the stimulus conditions which precipitate the feeling. In such cases it is the therapist's task to discover, by detailed questioning, the situations which cause anxiety.

When the stimuli which elicit anxiety have been enumerated, they are categorized in terms of common *themes* (e.g., themes relating to fear of being alone or to fear of high places). Within each theme, the stimuli are ordered in terms of the amount of anxiety they evoke in the individual. Examples of such *anxiety hierarchies* are presented in Table 14–1. The ranking of anxiety-evoking situations is a highly individual matter. As is apparent from the "examination" hierarchy in Table 14–1, the same scenes might be ordered dif-

TABLE 14–1

Examples of Anxiety Hierarchies

Examination series
1. On the way to the university on the day of an examination.
2. In the process of answering an examination paper.
3. Before the unopened doors of the examination room.
4. Awaiting the distribution of examination papers.
5. The examination paper lies face down before her.
6. The night before an examination.
7. On the day before an examination.
8. Two days before an examination.
9. Three days before an examination.
10. Four days before an examination.
11. Five days before an examination.
12. A week before an examination.
13. Two weeks before an examination.
14. A month before an examination.

Discord between other people
1. Her mother shouts at a servant.
2. Her young sister whines to her mother.
3. Her sister engages in a dispute with her father.
4. Her mother shouts at her sister.
5. She sees two strangers quarrel.

Source: Wolpe and Lazarus, 1966.

ferently by another person. Exploration of the nature of the person's anxiety and construction of anxiety hierarchies is usually done concurrently with relaxation training.

The Desensitization Process

Relaxation training and construction of appropriate anxiety hierarchies are the prerequisites for the actual procedure of desensitizing the stimuli associated with anxiety. In the desensitization procedure, the subject is instructed to relax his muscles, and he is then asked to visualize or imagine scenes from his anxiety hierarchy, starting with the least anxiety-provoking situation (i.e., the lowest item on each anxiety hierarchy). After each scene has been imagined for a short time, the subject is instructed to "erase" the scene from his mind and continue relaxing. He is asked to signal the therapist if he has felt any anxiety while visualizing the scene. Each scene is repeated, before going on to the next highest scene in the hierarchy, until the subject reports that he experiences no disturbance while visualizing it.

To illustrate the desensitization procedure, a verbatim account of the presentation of scenes during an initial desensitization session is presented below. The subject was a 24-year-old female art student who requested treatment of examination anxiety which had caused her to fail a number of tests. When she discussed her anxiety with the therapist, it was discovered that there were also other stimulus situations which made her anxious. Thus, four different anxiety hierarchies were constructed, two of which appear in Table 14–1. The first scene that she was asked to visualize was a neutral scene (i.e., one that was not expected to elicit anxiety). The next two scenes were the lowest items on their respective anxiety hierarchies (see Table 14–1).[5]

> I am now going to ask you to imagine a number of scenes. You will imagine them clearly and they will generally interfere little, if at all, with your state of relaxation. If, however, at any time you feel disturbed or worried and want to attract my attention, you will be able to do so by raising your left index finger. First I want you to imagine that you are standing at a familiar street corner on a pleasant morning watching the traffic go by. You see cars, motor-

---

[5] The reader may be interested in the outcome of this case. Wolpe and Lazarus (1966) report that a total of 17 desensitization sessions were required for the subject to report no anxiety while visualizing the highest scene on each of her four hierarchies (the two hierarchies presented in Table 14–1 and two additional hierarchies dealing with being scrutinized and devalued by others). The anxiety reduction transferred from the imagined scenes to the actual situations, and she was able to successfully take and pass her examinations.

cycles, trucks, bicycles, people and traffic lights; and you can hear the sounds associated with all these things. (*Pause of about 15 sec.*) Now stop imagining that scene and give all your attention once again to relaxing. If the scene you imagined disturbed you even in the slightest degree I want you to raise your left index finger *now*. (*Patient does not raise finger.*) Now imagine that you are at home studying in the evening. It is the 20th of May, exactly a month before your examination. (*Pause of 5 sec.*) Now stop imagining the scene. Go on relaxing. (*Pause of 10 sec.*) Now imagine the same scene again—a month before your examination. (*Pause of 5 sec.*) Stop imagining the scene and just think of your muscles. Let go, and enjoy your state of calm. (*Pause of 15 sec.*) Now again imagine that you are studying at home a month before your examination. (*Pause of 5 sec.*) Stop the scene, and now think of nothing but your own body. (*Pause of 5 sec.*) If you felt any disturbance whatsoever to the last scene raise your left index finger now. (*Patient raises finger.*) If the amount of disturbance decreased from the first presentation to the third do nothing, otherwise again raise your finger. (*Patient does not raise finger.*) Just keep on relaxing. (*Pause of 15 sec.*) Imagine that you are sitting on a bench at a bus stop and across the road are two strange men whose voices are raised in argument. (*Pause of 10 sec.*) Stop imagining the scene and just relax. (*Pause of 10 sec.*) Now again imagine the scene of these two men arguing across the road. (*Pause of 10 sec.*) Stop the scene and relax. Now I am going to count up to 5 and you will open your eyes, feeling very calm and refreshed (Wolpe & Lazarus, 1966, p. 81) .

Aversive Counterconditioning

We noted earlier that the pairing of a negative experience with a previously neutral or even positive one—aversive classical conditioning—might explain certain behavioral problems, such as asthma, and that even nonpainful but unpleasant stimuli could work in this way. The very same process can be used in reverse; aversive counterconditioning can be employed to eliminate behavior which a person considers undesirable for himself. Lavin, Thorpe, Barker, Blakemore, and Conway (1961) used this strategy to treat a male transvestite, and their case will serve to illustrate the procedure.

The client, a 22-year-old married truck driver, reported that he had experienced the desire to dress as a woman since the age of eight. From the age of 15 and through his military service and marriage, he had derived erotic satisfaction from dressing in female clothes and viewing himself in the mirror. At the same time, he had maintained a good sexual relationship with his wife.

In order to be able to elicit the undesirable behavior systematically (and thus pair it with a negative reaction), Lavin and his associates prepared 35-mm. slides of the client in various stages of female dress and had him make an audio tape recording in which he described these same activities. It was then determined that the presentation of the slides and tape induced sexual excitement.

The treatment involved pairing the transvestic experience with nausea, produced pharmacologically by injection of the drug apomorphine. As soon as the injection began to take effect, the slides and tape were presented, and these stimuli were terminated only after the client began vomiting. This treatment was administered every two hours for six days, a regimen which proved sufficient to completely eliminate the client's desire to don female attire. Systematic follow-up over a six-month period, including interviews with both the client and his wife, suggested that recovery was complete.

The Self-controlled Use of Counterconditioning

A major emphasis of behaviorally oriented therapists has been to teach their clients to administer their own therapy (e.g., Bandura, 1969; Davison, 1968; Davison & Neale, 1974; Goldfried & Merbaum, 1973). One example of this approach, as it applies to the classical conditioning model and its derivatives, is the technique referred to as *orgasmic reorientation*. The basic technique, which is used to treat a variety of sexual problems in males, is the following. First, the client produces an erection, in the privacy of his own home, through any imaginal scene that "works," as by his usual homosexual, sadistic, or masochistic fantasies. The client masturbates and, just before orgasm, he shifts his attention and concentration to a more appropriate sexual stimulus, which initially is an actual picture or photograph (e.g., from *Playboy* magazine). Then, the shift in attention to the appropriate sexual stimulus is introduced earlier and earlier in the masturbational sequence; at the same time, the appropriate stimuli are shifted from pictorial to imaginal ones. Finally, the client is instructed to apply his reoriented sexual interest to his personal sex life.

Orgasmic reorientation was used to treat a young man troubled by sadistic fantasies, who masturbated about five times per week always to the imagined thought of torturing women (Davison, 1968). After a careful clinical interview and an explanation of conditioning procedures, the client was instructed how to proceed on his own.

> When assured of privacy in his dormitory room (primarily on the weekend), he was first to obtain an erection by whatever means possible—undoubtedly with a sadistic fantasy, as he indicated. He was then to begin to masturbate while looking at a picture of a sexy, nude woman (the "target" sexual stimulus); *Playboy* magazine was suggested to him as a good source. If he began losing the

erection, he was to switch back to his sadistic fantasy until he could begin masturbating effectively again. Concentrating again on the *Playboy* picture, he was to continue masturbating, using the fantasy only to regain erection. As orgasm was approaching, he was at all costs to focus on the *Playboy* picture, even if sadistic fantasies began to intrude. It was impressed on him that gains would ensue only when sexual arousal was associated with the picture, and that he need not worry about indulging in sadistic fantasies at this point (Davison, 1968, p. 85).

The first few sessions of therapy went well (e.g., the client was able to masturbate successfully three times over the weekend to a *Playboy* picture without using sadistic fantasies). However, he was still reluctant to ask girls for dates and to give up his sadistic fantasies entirely. A special form of aversive counterconditioning was then instituted in which the client's own imagination (rather than externally administered drugs or electric shock) provided the source of the noxious UCS. Specifically, the client was instructed to close his eyes and

. . . imagine a typical sadistic scene, a pretty girl tied to stakes on the ground and struggling tearfully to extricate herself. While looking at the girl, he was told to imagine someone bringing a branding iron toward his eyes, ultimately searing his eyebrows. A second image was attempted when this proved abortive, namely, being kicked in the groin by a ferocious-looking karate expert. When he reported himself indifferent to this image as well, the therapist depicted to him a large bowl of "soup," composed of steaming urine with reeking fecal boli bobbing around on top. His grimaces, contortions, and groans indicated that an effective image had been found, and the following 5 min. were spent portraying his drinking from the bowl, with accompanying nausea, at all times while peering over the floating debris at the struggling girl. After opening his eyes at the end of the imaginal ordeal, he reported spontaneously that he felt quite nauseated, and some time was spent in casual conversation in order to dispel the mood (Davison, 1968, p. 86).

Within five sessions the client had given up masturbating to sadistic fantasies entirely—he even had difficulty producing such thoughts—and was using thoughts of women and heterosexual scenes to masturbate. Some time after the termination of therapy, he began to date women. Even more impressive, when a relapse occurred, he was able to treat it himself, as may be seen from the following passage from a letter he wrote to the therapist describing the incident and his present state:

". . . I bought an issue of *Playboy* and proceeded to give myself the treatment again. Once again, it worked like a charm. In two weeks, I was back in my reformed state, where I am now. . . . I have no need for sadistic fantasies. . . . I have [also] been pursuing a vigorous (well, vigorous for *me*) program of dating. In this way, I have gotten to know a lot of girls of whose existence I was previously only peripherally aware. As you probably know, I was very shy with girls before; well, now I am not one-fifth as shy as I used to be. In fact, by my old standards, I have become a regular rake!" (Davison, 1968, p. 89).

Effectiveness of Counterconditioning Therapies

Counterconditioning approaches to therapy, and particularly the systematic desensitization technique developed by Wolpe, have been used successfully in treating a variety of disorders, including exhibitionism (e.g., Bond & Hutchison, 1960), chronic frigidity (e.g., Lazarus, 1963), stuttering (e.g., Walton & Mather, 1963), adult phobias (e.g., Rachman, 1959; Ashem, 1963; Clark, 1963), public speaking (e.g., Paul, 1966) and snake (e.g., Davison, 1968) phobias in college students, phobic reactions in schizophrenics (e.g., Cowden & Ford, 1962), and children's phobias (e.g., Lazarus & Abramovitz, 1962). There is little doubt that systematic desensitization has been shown to be a highly efficient and successful treatment method for certain disorders, most particularly phobias, or irrational fears.

There have been a number of direct comparisons of systematic desensitization with traditional insight-oriented psychotherapy (e.g., Lazarus, 1961; Paul, 1966; Paul & Shannon, 1966). In each case, desensitization procedures were found to be more efficacious for the specific problems treated than insight therapy, although these studies have been criticized as being unfair comparisons of the two types of therapy (e.g., Strupp, 1966).

Paul's (1966) study treated college students enrolled in public speaking classes who volunteered to receive help with public speaking anxiety. The five therapists were highly experienced and were predominantly neo-Freudian and Rogerian in therapeutic orientation. Subjects were assigned to one of three treatment groups: (1) modified systematic desensitization; (2) insight-oriented psychotherapy; and (3) attention-placebo treatment, which consisted of providing the subject with the "attention, warmth, and interest of the therapist" along with a "fast-acting tranquilizer" (actually a 2-gram capsule of sodium bicarbonate). Each therapist worked individually with three of the participants in each treatment group for a total of five one-hour sessions ranging over a six-week period. Additionally, two other groups of subjects served as untreated controls.

Paul's dependent variables included a variety of cognitive, physiological, and behavioral measures of anxiety. Systematic desensitization was found to be the most effective treatment (100 percent improvement). The insight-oriented therapy and the attention-placebo treatment did not differ in their effectiveness (47 percent improvement), but they were found to be more effective than no treatment at all (17 percent improvement). Paul reports that the improvement was maintained at a six-week follow-up assessment and that there was no evidence of symptom substitution. A strong replication of Paul's basic finding, controlling for expectancy effects of the subjects, has since appeared (Woy & Efran, 1972), and successful applications of systematic desensitization now number in the hundreds (Davison & Wilson, 1973).

15

The Behavioral Strategy
THE OPERANT CONDITIONING APPROACH

The classical conditioning approach to personality discussed in the last chapter focuses on the conditions which antecede and elicit behavior. The operant conditioning approach deals with the effects of the *consequences* of behavior on its subsequent performance.

Edward L. Thorndike, an American psychologist who is credited with initiating modern laboratory experimentation with animals, was one of the first to call attention to the importance of response consequences for human behavior. At the end of the 19th century, Thorndike was studying what he called *trial-and-error* learning. Hungry kittens were placed in a puzzle box and allowed to escape and secure food when they solved the "combination" which opened the door. The combination involved such behavior as turning buttons, pressing levers, and pulling strings. When an animal was first placed in the puzzle box, it showed much random activity, but in the course of this "aimless" behavior it eventually ("accidentally") performed the response which opened the door. In effect, the animal hit upon the solution to the puzzle box by trial and error. In subsequent trials the animal would perform fewer responses which did not lead to the opening of the door (i.e., make fewer errors) and would reach the solution more quickly. Ultimately, the animal learned to open the door without performing any erroneous responses. Thorndike took this observation as an indication that the correct response had become strongly connected to the problem.

Thorndike assumed that the mechanism which underlay this apparent "stamping in" of the correct response was a function of the consequences which the correct and incorrect responses produced. This idea became formalized in Thorndike's (1898) first formulation of the *law of effect,* which held that the strength of the bond, or connection, between a particular situation and a particular response would be increased if it were followed by a "satisfying state of affairs" (reward) and decreased if it were followed by an "annoying state of affairs" (punishment). In a later formulation of the law of effect, Thorndike expressed the view that rewards were far more powerful than punishments in trial-and-error learning.

SKINNER'S APPROACH

The tradition of behaviorism, which started with the theorizing of Watson and Thorndike, is most often associated today with the name of B. F. Skinner. Although Skinner's research contributions have emphasized the behavior of infrahuman organisms, usually rats or pigeons, he has in his writings (e.g., *Science and Human Behavior* [1953]; *Walden Two* [1948]) made numerous suggestions concerning the application of his findings to human behavior. In *Beyond Freedom and Dignity* (1971), Skinner develops his view of man as an organism whose behavior is primarily determined by *external* environmental influences, particularly the consequences of one's acts, and states the implications of this view for designing a culture which would optimally facilitate human development and growth. In essence, *Beyond Freedom and Dignity* challenges the notion of autonomous man, of man as an organism whose behavior is assumed to be a function of internal influences (e.g., unconscious impulses, traits, self-actualizing tendencies), which is the model of man upon which the psychoanalytic, dispositional, and phenomenological strategies are based.

Psychologists who have followed in the Skinnerian tradition have made remarkable strides in recent years in developing an operant approach to the study of personality which emphasizes: precise, observational personality assessment; applied, yet highly controlled, research; and potent personality change techniques. In the operant approach, there is a close interrelationship among personality assessment, research, and change, while personality theory plays a minor role.

The Atheoretical Nature of the Operant Approach

Skinner has contended throughout his career (his first published book, *The Behavior of Organisms,* appeared in 1938) that psychology in general and the study of learning in particular is not yet at the stage where elaborate, formalized theorizing is justifiable.

Though in principle he is not "antitheory," Skinner thinks that psychology is not ready to establish theories of human personality. Accordingly, Skinner's own research efforts have been directed toward the complete and detailed description of behavior, which he has called the *functional analysis of behavior.* The aim of such functional analyses is to establish empirical relationships among variables. The Skinnerian approach might be summarized by the following maxim, which Skinner (1956) gleaned from Pavlov: "Control your conditions and you will see order."

In keeping with his atheoretical approach, Skinner has eschewed the consideration of all intraorganismic variables. He has rejected the explanation of behavior in terms of theoretical constructs, which he views as convenient but redundant fictions. He has also avoided explanations which are based on the presumed operation of speculative physiological mechanisms. Skinner believes that such "physiologizing" (as in Hebb, 1966) is not only unnecessary and useless, but that it is often only pseudo-theory.

Regarding internal influences on behavior, Skinner (1953) says:

> The practice of looking inside the organism for an explanation of behavior has tended to obscure the variables which are immediately available for a scientific analysis. These variables lie outside the organism, in its immediate environment and in its environmental history. . . . The objection to inner states is not that they do not exist, but that they are not relevant in a functional analysis (pp. 31, 35).

As an alternative, Skinner's approach is concerned with observable phenomena which fall into two main classes—*stimuli,* those observable characteristics of the environment which influence the organism, and *responses,* the overt behavior of the organism. In a sense, Skinnerian psychology deals with an "empty-organism." All variables which come between, or mediate, stimulus and response, and cannot be explained in terms of stimulus or response, are outside the domain of interest of the operant approach. It should be noted, however, that such a position can deal with many of the phenomena which are the basis for positing internal events in other personality approaches. For example, although Skinner would not speak of "hunger" as an explanation for food-seeking, hours of food deprivation may be used to conceptualize the same behavior.

While the operant approach to personality is atheoretical, it is not astrategical. Operant psychologists, including Skinner, do begin with definite assumptions about the nature of behavior which, in effect, constitute a strategy for the study of personality. One such assumption is that the primary determinants of behavior are to be found in one's external environment, particularly in the outcomes of behavior. This assumption gives definite direction to the operant psychologist's investigations. For example, it tells him what types of personality assessment and change techniques are appropriate. Without the plan of attack which a strategy provides, the study of personality would amount to inefficient trial-and-error learning (cf. the role of theory as discussed in Chapter 1).

The Nature of Operant and Respondent Behavior

Skinner (1938) has distinguished between two types of behavior: *operant* and *respondent*.[1] Operant behavior refers to responses which an individual *emits,* and denotes that he is operating on his environment. Such behavior is controlled by the consequences which follow its performance.[2] Operant behavior is also called *instrumental behavior,* a term which draws its meaning from the fact that the performance of the behavior is instrumental in producing some end result. Examples include driving a car, dressing oneself, taking notes in class, and playing tennis. In each case, successful completion of the behavior results in some consequence, and it is to the consequences of an operant that the psychologist directs his attention. His questions are of the form: "What consequences will maintain a given response?" For example, turning the ignition key makes a car start; depressing the accelerator makes the car move; and turning the wheel allows one to avoid the variety of obstacles which appear in the road from time to time. The behavior is under the control of its consequences in the sense that if the consequences are positive, the behavior is more likely to occur again, whereas if they are negative, the behavior is less likely to recur. Much of our behavior has been learned via *operant,* or *instrumental, conditioning.*

Respondent behavior is *elicited* by some identifiable stimulus and thus derives its name from the fact that the subject *responds to* something. The purest examples of respondent behavior are reflexes, such as the pupil of the eye closing down in response to light stimulation, the knee jerk in response to a tap on the patellar tendon, and perspiring in response to heat. Respondents which have been learned, through classical conditioning (see Chapter 14), include blushing when someone tells you that you are attractive and feeling "nervous"

---

[1] The terms *respondent* and *operant* are used both as adjectives, to refer to a type of behavior or procedure ("operant conditioning"), and as nouns, to refer to a specific response which is a member of the class of respondent or operant behavior ("writing one's name is an operant").

[2] Strictly speaking, it is logically impossible for a given response to be controlled by the consequences which accrue to it, since the consequences occur *after* the response is made. It is possible, however, for consequences which accrued to similar responses in the past to affect a given response.

(hands shaking, perspiring, stomach queasy) just before taking an important final examination or giving a speech.

Many behaviors were originally learned as operants but have since come to function as respondents. These behaviors include acts which we colloquially call "reflexes" (since they occur almost automatically), such as stopping when a traffic light turns red and paying close attention to a teacher when he begins to talk about an upcoming examination. In each instance, some stimulus serves as a cue for the response to occur. Such a cue is called a *discriminative stimulus,* and it serves to signal the individual that the particular response is likely to be rewarded, since in the presence of that stimulus it has been rewarded in the past. For example, a sign in a store window saying "Sale" is a discriminative stimulus for walking into the store. (The role played by discriminative stimuli in operant behavior will be discussed more fully in a later section.) While a discriminative stimulus appears to control the response, actually it only sets the occasion for its occurrence. From the operant viewpoint, behavior is controlled by its consequences and not by its antecedents.

The Measurement of Operant Behavior

The most frequently used measure of operant behavior is its *rate of occurrence*. It is an elegantly simple measure because it involves merely counting behavior in specified time intervals; the result is expressed in terms of the number of responses per unit of time (e.g., number of words typed per minute, distractions per hour, kisses per day). Operant data are usually presented graphically in terms of either the number of responses in each time period or the cumulative number of responses in each successive time period. *Cumulative records* are useful in portraying an individual's rate of responding and the change in rate. The steeper the slope (angle) of the cumulative curve, the greater is the rate of responding. Thus, a cumulative curve which comes close to being a vertical line represents a very high rate of responding, while a cumulative curve which approaches a horizontal line represents very little responding. *Acquisition,* or *learning, curves* rise at an angle (the greater the angle, the higher the response rate), whereas *extinction curves* level off. Figure 15–1 (a) (page 350) is a cumulative record of one student's daily studying under three different conditions. Compare it with the conventional record (i.e., noncumulative) in Figure 15–1 (b) (page 351).

The Idiographic Nature of the Operant Approach

Skinner's work has stressed a thorough analysis of an individual subject's behavior. The typical experiment is not concerned with

FIGURE 15–1 (a)

Cumulative Record of Daily Studying

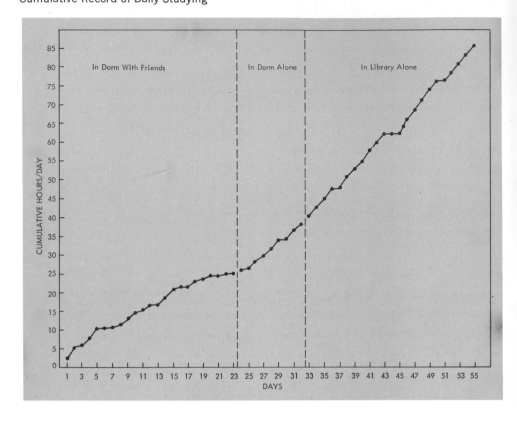

the *average* subject, for the aim of the analysis is to establish experimental control of a particular organism's behavior. Skinner (1956) explains his concentration on the single case as follows:

> In essence, I suddenly found myself face to face with the engineering problem of the animal trainer. When you have the responsibility of making absolutely sure that a given organism will engage in a given sort of behavior at a given time, you quickly grow impatient with theories of learning. Principles, hypotheses, theorems, satisfactory proof at the .05 level of significance . . . nothing could be more irrelevant. No one goes to the circus to see the average dog jump through a hoop significantly oftener than untrained dogs raised under the same circumstances, or to see an elephant demonstrate a principle of behavior (p. 228).

Studying individual subjects within the operant approach is often done by means of a type of single-subject experiment called a *reversal design*. We shall use the example of a subject who wanted to

FIGURE 15–1 (b)

Noncumulative Record of Daily Studying

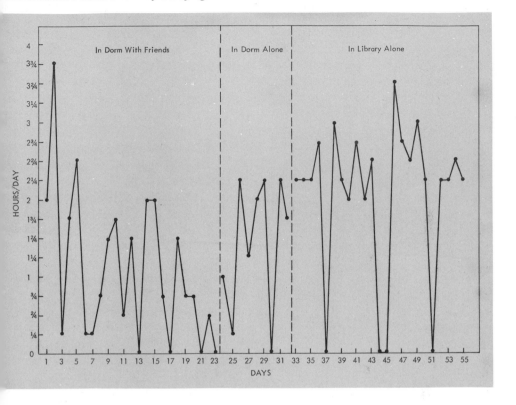

lose weight by exercise to illustrate this type of research. First, a *base line*, or normal, level of the dependent variable (body weight) would be taken for a period of time before the independent variable was introduced. Next, in the *experimental phase* (also called the *conditioning phase*), the independent variable, or experimental manipulation (the exercise program), is instituted. If the independent variable is effective in lowering the subject's weight, the effects will show up as a difference between the subject's weight during the base line and the experimental phase. However, even if the subject's weight does decrease, it is possible that uncontrolled-for changes in the subject's life other than exercise might have caused the observed decrease in weight. For example, the subject may have simply become upset and eaten less during the experimental period because of an up-coming examination.

To check on the likelihood of alternative explanations accounting for the change in the dependent variable, a third part of the exper-

TABLE 15–1

Phases of a Single-Subject Reversal Experiment

	Phase			
	$A_{(1)}$ *Base Line*	$B_{(1)}$ *Conditioning*	$A_{(2)}$ *Reversal*	$B_{(2)}$ *Reconditioning*
Purpose............	Get "normal" comparison	Change behavior	Check whether independent variable caused change	Reinstate change in behavior
Operation...........	(a) Measure behavior	(a) Introduce independent variable (b) Measure behavior	(a) Remove independent variable (b) Measure behavior	(a) Reintroduce independent variable (b) Measure behavior
Expectation*........	—	$B_{(1)} \neq A_{(1)}$†	$A_{(2)} = A_{(1)} \neq B_{(1)}$†	$B_{(2)} = B_{(1)} \neq A_{(1)}$ $\neq A_{(2)}$†

* What will occur if the independent variable is affecting the dependent variable.
† The inequality can be in either direction (i.e., increase or decrease of the dependent variable in the B phases), depending on the nature of the independent and dependent variable.

iment is instituted, the *reversal phase.* During reversal, the experimental manipulation is withdrawn for a time (the exercise program is temporarily suspended) in order to see whether the dependent variable will return to the base line level.

The three phases of the experiment—base line, experimental period, and reversal period—constitute what is called an *ABA* research design. *A* stands for the absence of the independent variable (in the base line and reversal periods), and *B* indicates the presence of the independent variable (in the experimental phase).

Frequently, a fourth phase is added to the ABA design. This is a second experimental period, or *reconditioning phase,* in which the experimental manipulation is reinstated. In the present example this would involve having the subject reinstitute the exercise program. With the addition of the reconditioning phase, the research design can be designated *ABAB.* The reconditioning phase will always be included when the experimental design is being used to assess the effectiveness of a treatment for an actual problem behavior. If an effective treatment has been discovered for a particular problem, it would be unethical, to say the least, to leave the subject in the reversal phase (i.e., at his base line level). Table 15–1 summarizes the four phases of the ABAB design.

THE PRINCIPLE OF REINFORCEMENT

The basic technique of operant conditioning will be described with reference to a single-subject ABAB experiment. Hall, Lund, and Jackson (1968) were interested in increasing the study behavior of elementary school children. One of their subjects, Robbie, disrupted normal class activities and studied very little. In the first phase of the experiment, Robbie was observed unobtrusively during seven 30-minute base line periods in which the pupils were supposed to be working in their seats. Figure 15–2 presents a record of Robbie's study behavior, which was defined as his having his pencil on paper for at least half of a 10-second observation interval. As can be seen in the graph, during the base line observation Robbie engaged in study behavior on the average of 25 percent of the time. The remaining 75 percent of his time was taken up with such behavior as "snapping rubber bands, playing with toys from his pocket, talking and laughing with peers, slowly drinking the half-pint of milk served earlier in the morning, and subsequently playing with the empty carton" (Hall et al., 1968, p. 3). It was also observed during the base line period that for much of his nonstudy behavior Robbie received the attention of his teacher, who urged him to work, put away his playthings, and so on.

Following the base line period, the conditioning phase of the experiment was initiated. Now every time Robbie engaged in one

FIGURE 15–2

A Record of Robbie's Study Behavior

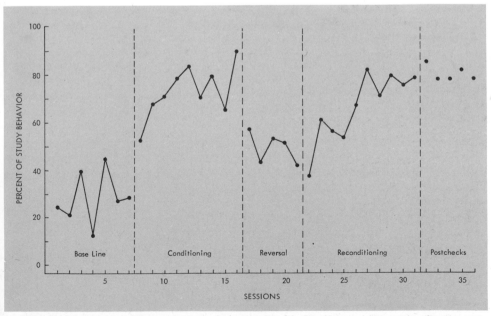

Note: Postcheck observations were made during the 4th, 6th, 7th, 12th, and 14th weeks after the completion of reinforcement conditioning.
Source: Adapted from Hall, Lund, and Jackson, 1968.

minute of continuous study behavior, the observer signaled the teacher, who then promptly rewarded him for the study behavior with her attention. The teacher ignored Robbie at all other times. The results of this procedure were striking, as can be seen in Figure 15–2. When Robbie received attention contingent upon his studying, the amount of studying increased markedly in the first session and continued to rise in subsequent sessions. Robbie spent an average of 71 percent of his time studying during the conditioning phase of the experiment.

The marked change in the amount of Robbie's study behavior can be explained by the *principle of reinforcement:* If the occurrence of an operant is followed by a reinforcing stimulus, the strength of the operant will be increased. A *reinforcer,* or *reinforcing stimulus* (the teacher's attention in the Hall et al. study), is an event which follows a response and increases the probability that the response will occur again.[3]

Some reinforcers require no particular experience to be effective and can thus be referred to as *innate,* or *primary, reinforcers* (e.g., food or sex under appropriate circumstances of deprivation) ; while others have become effective because of experiences in which they were associated with reinforcement. The latter are referred to as *conditioned,* or *secondary, reinforcers,* and they control most of our social behavior. As Reynolds (1968) has noted: "A fraternity pin, meaningless at an earlier age, reinforces the behavior of a teenager. The voice of a dog's master, ineffectual at first, comes to reinforce the dog's behavior. Stock market quotations, at first dull lists of numbers, come to reinforce an investor's behavior" (p. 51).

Two types of reinforcement have been distinguished in the operant paradigm. *Positive reinforcement* refers to the case in which a stimulus is *presented* following an operant (e.g., Robbie's teacher paying attention to Robbie for studying), whereas *negative reinforcement* refers to the case in which a stimulus is *removed* following an operant (e.g., Robbie's teacher ceasing to yell disapprovingly at Robbie when he begins studying). In both cases, if the stimulus event increases the likelihood that the operant will be repeated, reinforcement is said to have occurred.

Returning to Robbie, our now studious subject, it appears that the introduction of reinforcement in the form of the teacher's attention contingent upon study behavior was responsible for the

---

[3] Initial inspection of this definition seems to suggest that it is circular and therefore meaningless. This problem is circumvented, however, when the definition is restricted to *generalized reinforcers,* events which serve to strengthen responses in a variety of situations and with many different people (e.g., social approval or attention).

increased rate of studying. It is important to note that without the base line to which the acquisition rate could be compared, no such statement could be made. However, it is still possible that some other (uncontrolled-for) condition, which occurred during the acquisition phase but not in the base line period, led to Robbie's increased studying (e.g., his parents might have begun to praise him when he reported studying at school). Thus, to increase the probability that Robbie's study behavior was under the control of his teacher's attention, a reversal, or *extinction*,[4] phase was instituted. During this period the teacher refrained from reinforcing Robbie with attention for his study behavior. If study behavior had been under the control of the reinforcement, then when the reinforcement was withdrawn it would be expected that the amount of study behavior would drop off (eventually reaching the base line level). As Figure 15–2 clearly shows, Robbie's study behavior did decline during the reversal period to a mean of 50 percent.

Since the experiment had the practical purpose of increasing Robbie's study behavior, a reconditioning phase was included in which the contingency between study behavior and teacher attention was reintroduced. The result was an increase in Robbie's study rate, which stabilized at a level between 70 and 80 percent (see Figure 15–2). To check on the effectiveness of the operant-conditioning procedures in maintaining Robbie's study behavior, after the last reconditioning session periodic checks were made for the remainder of the school year, the last check being made in the 14th week. These checks indicated that Robbie's studying was being maintained at an average rate of 79 percent (see Figure 15–2). Furthermore, Robbie's teacher reported that the quality of his studying had also improved; he was now completing written assignments and missing fewer words on spelling tests.

Shaping

The general procedures just outlined for the operant conditioning of behavior will work to establish almost any kind of response. Basically, two requirements must be met for operant conditioning to be successful. The reinforcing stimulus used must be a strong incentive for the particular subject being conditioned, and the desired behavior must occur before it can be reinforced. While this latter requirement is certainly an obvious point, it is nevertheless an extremely important one. In the case of behavior which occurs at

---

[4] The term *extinction* has been used to refer to both an *experimental operation* (discontinuation of reinforcement) and a *behavioral outcome* (decreased frequency of responding).

least occasionally, as, for example, Robbie's studying, there is opportunity to reinforce it (although the experimenter may have to wait some time before the behavior is emitted). However, when the base line for a particular behavior which one desires to strengthen is near zero, the standard procedures described above will not work —at least not very efficiently. This is the case with responses which have never been performed before or have not been practiced for a long period of time. It is also frequently true of complex acts; that is, the subject knows how to make each of the simpler component responses but has never put them together to form the complex behavior. For instance, students learning a foreign language frequently know each of the words which make up a sentence but have great difficulty putting them together in a grammatically correct and colloquially acceptable way.

To help circumvent this problem, the experimenter may shape the desired behavior. *Shaping,* which is also called the *method of successive approximation,* involves reinforcing progressively closer and closer approximations of the desired behavior. A common example of shaping is the children's game of "hot and cold," in which one child has to locate a particular object in a room while the other child directs him toward the object by saying "hot" as he gets closer and "cold" when he starts to go farther away. The process of shaping is illustrated schematically in Figure 15–3.

The most complex behaviors can be operantly conditioned by breaking down the behaviors into their component responses and successively reinforcing each of them. Even so-called creative behaviors, which many educators have tended to think of as holistic, unanalyzable, and relatively unteachable (i.e., they are "talents"), can be shaped. Examples of successful shaping include the teaching of such creative behaviors as written composition (Brigham, Graubard, & Stans, 1972) and painting (Turner, 1973).

The procedure of shaping is well illustrated by the following case history of a 40-year-old psychiatric patient who had been completely mute for the 19 years of his hospitalization.

> The S [subject] was brought to a group therapy session with other chronic schizophrenics (who were verbal), but he sat in the position in which he was placed and continued the withdrawal behaviors which characterized him. He remained impassive and stared ahead even when cigarettes, which other members accepted, were offered to him and were waved before his face. At one session, when E [experimenter] removed cigarettes from his pocket, a package of chewing gum accidentally fell out. The S's eyes moved toward the gum and then returned to their usual position. This response was chosen by E as one with which he would start to work, using the method of successive approximation. . . .

FIGURE 15–3

A Diagram Representing the Principle of Shaping

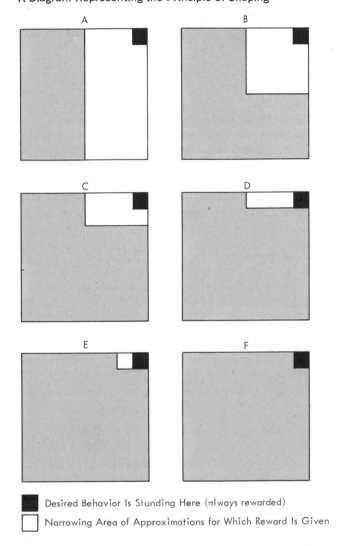

■ Desired Behavior Is Standing Here (always rewarded)

☐ Narrowing Area of Approximations for Which Reward Is Given

The S met individually with E three times a week. Group sessions also continued. The following sequence of procedures was introduced in the private sessions. Although the weeks are numbered consecutively, they did not follow at regular intervals since other duties kept E from seeing S every week.

Weeks 1, 2. A stick of gum was held before S's face, and E waited until S's eyes moved toward it. When this response occurred, E as a consequence gave him the gum. By the end of the second week, response probability in the presence of the gum was increased to such an extent that S's eyes moved toward the gum as soon as it was held up.

Weeks 3, 4. The E now held the gum before S, waiting until he noticed movement in S's lips before giving it to him. Toward the end of the first session of the third week, a lip movement spontaneously occurred, which E promptly reinforced. By the end of this week, both lip movement and eye movement occurred when the gum was held up. The E then withheld giving S the gum until S spontaneously madè a vocalization, at which time E gave S the gum. By the end of this week, holding up the gum readily occasioned eye movement toward it, lip movement, and a vocalization resembling a croak.

Weeks 5, 6. The E held up thè gum, and said, "Say gum, gum," repeating these words each time S vocalized. Giving S the gum was made contingent upon vocalizations increasingly approximating gum. At the sixth session (at the end of Week 6), when E said, "Say gum, gum," S suddenly said, "Gum, please." This response was accompanied by reinstatement of other responses of this class, that is, S answered questions regarding his name and age.

Thereafter, he responded to questions by E both in individual sessions and in group sessions, but answered no one else. Responses to the discriminative stimuli of the room generalized to E on the ward; he greeted E on two occasions in the group room. He read from signs in E's office upon request by E.

Since the response now seemed to be under the strong stimulus control of E, the person, attempt was made to generalize the stimulus to other people. Accordingly, a nurse was brought into the private room; S smiled at her. After a month, he began answering her questions. Later, when he brought his coat to a volunteer worker on the ward, she interpreted the gesture as a desire to go outdoors and conducted him there. Upon informing E of the incident, she was instructed to obey S only as a consequence of explicit verbal requests by him. The S thereafter vocalized requests. These instructions have now been given to other hospital personnel, and S regularly initiates verbal requests when nonverbal requests have no reinforcing consequences. Upon being taken to the commissary, he said, "Ping pong," to the volunteer worker and played a game with her (Isaacs, Thomas, & Goldiamond, 1960, pp. 9–10).

Schedules of Reinforcement

A *schedule of reinforcement* is a statement of the contingency on which reinforcement is received. The most obvious schedule of reinforcement is to provide the subject with reinforcement every time he engages in the behavior which the experimenter desires to increase. This procedure, usually referred to as a *continuous reinforcement* schedule, was used in the examples of Robbie and the mute psychiatric patient. However, continuous reinforcement often does not parallel the sort of experience which is found in actual life situations, and investigators have been especially interested in the effects of reinforcement when it is not available on a continuous basis. Such schedules are referred to as *intermittent,* or *partial,* schedules.

There are four basic schedules of partial reinforcement. Each schedule is characterized by whether the reinforcement is received either after a period of time (*interval* schedule) or after a number of responses (*ratio* schedule) and whether the quantity of time or responses is either a set amount (*fixed* schedule) or a random amount (*variable* schedule). The four schedules of reinforcement which result from the combination of these four possible characteristics are depicted diagrammatically in Figure 15–4.

FIGURE 15–4

The Four Basic Schedules of Partial Reinforcement
(arrows indicate reinforcement)

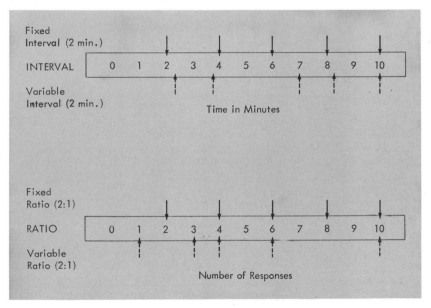

Fixed-Interval Schedules

In a *fixed-interval* schedule, reinforcement is given for the first response made after a prescribed interval of time has elapsed. Numerous life situations appear to operate on fixed-interval schedules, such as college examinations and salary payments. It has sometimes been recommended that infants be fed on a fixed-interval schedule (e.g., every three hours). A fixed-interval schedule produces a reliable pattern of responding that appears "scalloped" when cumulatively graphed (see Figure 15–5). The individual makes few or no responses immediately after a reinforcement but then begins to respond at an accelerated rate until the time for the next reinforcement.

We are more willing to work harder on pay day; absenteeism is less common; the student who has dawdled along all semester suddenly accelerates his study as examination time approaches in order to secure some slight reinforcement at the end of the term; the business man makes a strong effort to "clean up his desk" in time for vacation; most people increase their efforts to make a reinforcing appointment on time (Lundin, 1961, p. 80).

FIGURE 15–5

Stylized Records of Responding under Basic Schedules of Reinforcement

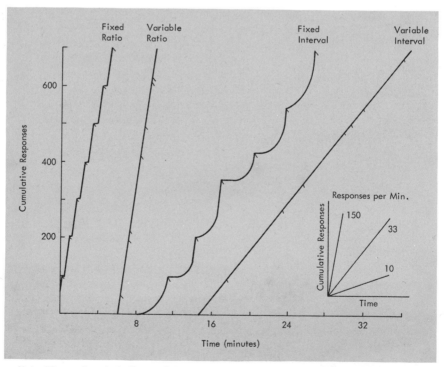

Note: Diagonal marks indicate reinforcement; the slope of various response rates is indicated at lower right. *Fixed Ratio:* high rate, with brief pause following reinforcement and abrupt change to terminal rate. *Variable Ratio:* high sustained rate; no pausing after reinforcement. *Fixed Interval:* low overall response rate due to pause following reinforcement; length of pause increases with length of interval; gradual increase to high terminal rate as interval ends. *Variable Interval:* low sustained rate; no pausing after reinforcement.
    Source: Adapted from Reese, 1966.

Even the United States Congress operates on a fixed-interval schedule (Weisberg & Waldrop, 1972). Bills are passed at a very low rate for the first few months of each session, but as adjournment draws closer the number of bills passed increases sharply, thereby producing the scalloped cumulative record in Figure 15–6.

FIGURE 15–6

Cumulative Number of Bills Passed during the Legislative Sessions of Congress from January 1947 to August 1954

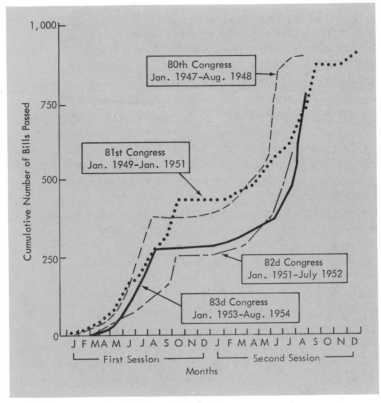

Source: Weisberg and Waldrop, 1972.

Fixed-Ratio Schedules

Fixed-ratio schedules are those in which reinforcement is administered only after a set number of responses have occurred. For example, a fixed ratio of 4:1 refers to a schedule in which after every three unreinforced responses the fourth response is reinforced. Studies with both animals and humans suggest that fixed-ratio schedules can be made to produce considerably higher rates of responding than either continuous reinforcement or fixed-interval schedules (see Figure 15–5; page 360). Moreover, very high ratios can be built up. That is, an experimenter may begin training on a 4:1 schedule and slowly increase the ratio of unreinforced to reinforced responses until the subject is rewarded as infrequently as one response in every thousand (i.e., 1,000:1). Skinner (1953) has noted both the advantages and the dangers of fixed-ratio schedules in maintaining human behavior.

> It is a common schedule in education, where the student is reinforced for completing a project or a paper or some other specific amount of work. It is essentially the basis of professional pay and of selling on commission. In industry it is known as piecework pay. It is a system of reinforcement which naturally recommends itself to employers because the cost of labor required to produce a given result can be calculated in advance. . . . A limiting factor, which makes itself felt in industry, is simple fatigue. The high rate of responding and the long hours of work generated by this schedule can be dangerous to health. This is the main reason why piecework pay is usually strenuously opposed by organized labor.
>
> Another objection to this type of schedule is based upon the possibility that as the rate rises, the reinforcing agency will move to a larger ratio. In the laboratory, after first reinforcing every tenth response and then every fiftieth, we may find it possible to reinforce only every hundredth, although we could not have used this ratio in the beginning. In industry, the employee whose productivity has increased as the result of a piecework schedule may receive so large a weekly wage that the employer feels justified in increasing the number of units of work required for a given unit of pay (pp. 102–3).

Variable-Interval Schedules

In everyday life there is often variability in the schedules on which we are rewarded. A *variable-interval* schedule is one in which the interval between reinforced trials is randomly varied around a specified time value so that *on the average* the individual is rewarded, say, every two minutes. That is, the subject might be reinforced for responses appearing after: 1 minute, $2\frac{1}{4}$ minutes, $1\frac{1}{2}$ minutes, $4\frac{1}{2}$ minutes, $2\frac{1}{2}$ minutes, $\frac{1}{4}$ minute. The average of these six intervals is two minutes. Lundin (1961) gives some interesting examples of commonplace human behavior that is controlled by variable-interval schedules.

> The dating behavior of the college coed often operates on this kind of schedule. Unless she is going steady, when her social engagements are guaranteed (. . . [continuous] reinforcement or fixed

interval), she does not know precisely when the invitations are going to be forthcoming. If she operates as a strong reinforcer for the behavior of the men in her life, the variable interval may be a low one, and she may be called popular. On the other hand if her VI [variable-interval] schedule is a long one (only occasional dates), she waits a long time between invitations, and we may say she is not so popular.

Some kinds of sports activities operate on this schedule, such as hunting and fishing. A fisherman drops in his line, and then he must wait. He does not know precisely when the fish will bite (maybe not at all), nor does he know when the game will fly, even though through past conditioning history he has found certain areas to be situations in which the reinforcements occur. Although these reinforcements of catching the fish or shooting the game are a function of his skill, the aspects of the availability of the reinforcements to him are a function of some undetermined schedule. The enthusiastic sportsman has a regularity of behavior which has had a past history of reinforcement, even though variable (p. 88).

Variable-interval schedules produce steady (but relatively low) response rates, rather than the "scalloped" ones of fixed-interval schedules (see Figure 15–5; page 360) and are highly resistant to extinction.

RESISTANCE TO EXTINCTION. *Resistance to extinction* refers to the persistence of a response after reinforcement for the response has been terminated (i.e., during extinction) and thus serves as a measure of response strength. That is, the stronger a response, the longer it will be emitted without reinforcement. All partial reinforcement schedules tend to lead to greater resistance to extinction than continuous reinforcement, and variable-interval schedules are especially resistant to extinction, as the following case illustrates.

The case involved a 21-month-old child whose bedtime temper tantrums were extinguished by his parents (Williams, 1959). By screaming and crying when they tried to leave, the child had been keeping one of his parents or an aunt, who lived with the family, in his bedroom until he fell asleep. It appeared that the child's behavior was being maintained by the adult's attention (i.e., attention was reinforcing the tantrums). To extinguish this misbehavior, reinforcement was withdrawn. The child was placed in his bed as usual, but now the adult left the room immediately despite the child's crying.

As can be seen in Figure 15–7 (page 364), in the first extinction series (solid line) the child cried for 45 minutes the first time, did not cry at all the second time (it is possible that he was exhausted by the previous crying bout), cried for 10 minutes the third time, and thereafter decreased gradually to no crying. By the 10th trial, the child even smiled when the adult left. However, a week later the child cried when his aunt put him to bed, and she reinforced this be-

FIGURE 15–7

Length of Crying in Two Extinction Series as a Function of Withdrawing Reinforcement

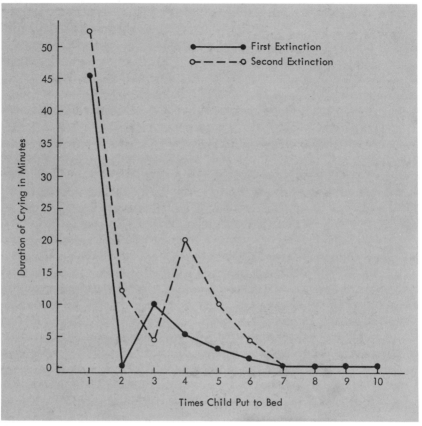

Source: Adapted from Williams, 1959.

havior by remaining in the room until he went to sleep. This *single* reinforcement, which was dispensed on a variable-interval schedule, was sufficient to increase the rate of crying to the preextinction level and to necessitate a second series of extinction trials. As is shown in Figure 15–7 (broken line), the rate of crying reached zero by the seventh trial of the second extinction series, and no additional bedtime tantrums were reported during the following two-year period.

Variable-Ratio Schedules

A *variable-ratio* schedule refers to the situation in which the number of responses required for reinforcement is varied randomly around a particular ratio. For example, a "variable ratio of 20:1" might reinforce a subject after every 19th, 30th, 22d, 14th, 10th, and 25th response (the average being after every 20th response). Variable-ratio schedules are among the most potent for inducing very high, steady rates of responding (see Figure 15–5; page 360) and extreme resistance to extinction.

The extremely high rates that can be generated by these schedules is illustrated in the behavior of the compulsive gambler. Even though the returns are very slim, he never gives up. Families are ruined and fortunes lost; still the high rates of behavior are maintained, often to the exclusion of all alternate forms of activity. Witness the "all night" crap games in which a single person will remain until all his funds and resources are gone. His behavior is terminated only by his inability to perform operations necessary to stay in the game. And even on these occasions, if he can muster more funds by borrowing or stealing, he will return to the game. Although gambling may involve other auxiliary reinforcements, social and personal, the basic rate of behavior is maintained by the schedule itself. The degree of control exercised by such a schedule is tremendous. In these cases almost absolute control has been achieved, so that the behavior becomes as certain as that found in respondent conditioning. The degree of control is often unfortunate and dangerous to the individual and his family, and the paradoxical thing about it is that the controlling agency (unless the gambling devices are "fixed") is the simple factor of chance. For this reason one begins to understand why legalized gambling is prohibited in most states (Lundin, 1961, p. 91).

Schedules of Reinforcement in Daily Activities

Our daily activities are governed by a variety of schedules of reinforcement.

Take, for example, the day-to-day activity of a college student. He eats, sleeps, takes his toilet on a variety of fixed-interval schedules, and does his assignments on ratio schedules. He takes weekly examinations in some courses (fixed interval) and is assigned only term papers in other seminar-type courses (ratio schedule). His social life operates by and large on variable-interval schedules, and much of his verbal behavior is on a . . . [continuous reinforcement] schedule, since people ordinarily speak to him when he addresses them. If he happens to work in his spare time to help pay his way through school, he can earn extra money for typing papers for his fellow students, at so much per page (fixed ratio), or he may prefer to wait on tables in the cafeteria for an hourly wage (fixed interval). He engages in sports and games on some variable-ratio schedules; the more he plays, the more likely he is to win, although the winning is not regular or absolutely predictable (Lundin, 1961, p. 96).

Each of the four basic partial reinforcement schedules and continuous reinforcement can be combined to form multiple schedules (e.g., a fixed-interval followed by a fixed-ratio schedule, as occurs when a salesman begins with a weekly salary and then switches to a commission basis) or concurrent schedules (e.g., a fixed-interval and fixed-ratio schedule both operating at the same time, as is the case when a salesman works for both salary and commission).

The most comprehensive investigation of schedules of reinforcement has been made by Skinner and his associates. The results have been presented in a 739-page book (Ferster & Skinner, 1957) containing 921 cumulative records that illustrate the characteristics of the different schedules. The data consist of a quarter of a billion responses made over the course of 70,000 hours of recording. This monumental work has been criticized on the grounds that the book contains no description or summary of the data (just graphs!) and that the overall research strategy is highly uneconomical. At the same time, proponents of the operant approach have pointed out that "This kind of research is one of the things that reaffirms one's belief in the lawfulness of behavior. There are certain characteristics of responding on each basic schedule, whether the schedule is in effect alone or in combination with others, that have been found for many species of animals, including man" (Reese, 1966, p. 16).

Demonstration 15–1

OPERANT CONDITIONING OF HUMAN BEHAVIOR[5]

The reader may now wish to try his hand at operant conditioning. For this Demonstration you will need to enlist the aid of a friend who is willing to participate. Be sure that the friend has about 45 minutes of free time; otherwise he may remember some pressing engagement at particular phases of the conditioning procedures! You will need a watch or clock with a sweep-second hand, and pencil and paper.

The Response

The first step is to select the response you will teach your subject. Although the procedures to be outlined will work with complex motor or verbal responses as well as simple ones, it may be best to condition a relatively simple response, at least for your first subject. Some suggested responses are listed in Table 15–2. Other than simplicity, the response you choose to condition should meet three additional requirements. First, it should *terminate fairly quickly* so that it can be reinforced. Second, the response should *end where it began*. That is, when the response is completed, the subject should be able to immediately perform the same response again without either your or the subject's having to rearrange the situation. For example, you would not want to condition "opening

[5] The procedures used in Demonstration 15–1 are, in part, adapted from Verplanck, 1956.

TABLE 15–2

Examples of Responses Suitable for Operant Conditioning in
Demonstration 15-1

Motor Responses	Verbal Responses
Opening and closing a book.	Criticizing.
Taking top off a pen and replacing it.	Talking about the future.
Standing up and sitting down.	Talking about schoolwork.
Nodding head.	Using plural nouns.

a book" since it would necessitate closing the book before the subject made the response again. Such rearrangement naturally would be a salient cue for the subject and thus would bias the operant conditioning.[6] Finally, the response should normally *occur at a speed which makes recording feasible.* Finger tapping, for example, would be a poor choice.

Shaping

If the response you select is one your subject makes frequently, then all you have to do is wait until it occurs to reinforce it. If, however, it is an infrequently occurring response, you may have to use shaping procedures. This will necessitate breaking down the total response into logical component-parts. For example, suppose you were going to condition "opening and closing a book." You would first reinforce (reinforcement procedures are discussed later) the first movement your subject makes, since this will start him moving about. *The first movement the subject makes should be the initial component of any motor response.* Next, you might reinforce *movement of either hand, movement of either hand toward the book,* then *touching the book, opening it partway, opening it fully,* and finally, *closing the book.* Similarly, the successive approximations of verbal criticism might be: any verbal utterance, any statement (i.e., as opposed to a question), any negative statement, and finally, any negative statement which is a criticism. Of course, if your subject should combine any of the successive steps, that will make the conditioning of the total response more rapid. Shaping is very much an art, and it is only through practice that you will "get a feel" for the procedure. Figure 15–8 (page 368) illustrates a cumulative record of a response that was initially conditioned by means of shaping.

Reinforcement

Each time the subject makes a correct response (or an approximation of it if shaping procedures are employed), you will say the word "point." A record of the points the subject earns should be clearly visible to him, and this can be conveniently implemented by instructing the subject to make a tally mark on a sheet of paper each time you give him a point. An alternative procedure, which is preferable only if recording points will interrupt the subject's behavior, is for you to record the points on a record sheet which is clearly visible to the subject.

---

[6] If the object were to teach a particular response to someone, rather than to learn about operant conditioning, additional cues which aid the learner would certainly be used (e.g., telling the person what he is to do and modeling the behavior for him).

FIGURE 15–8

Cumulative Record of "Hand Raising" Shaped by Operant Conditioning

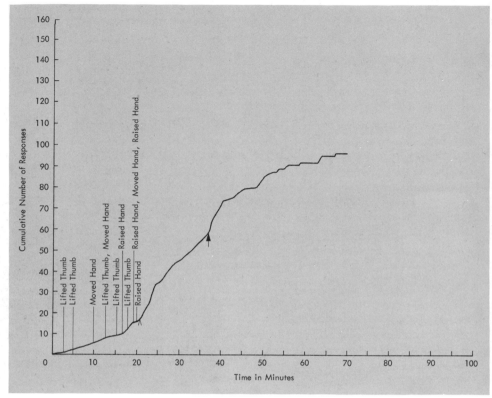

Note: Following the caret (∧) only the complete response was reinforced. Following the arrow (↑) no responses were reinforced (i.e., extinction).
    Source: Verplanck, 1956.

The prompt and accurate administration of reinforcement is the *sine qua non* of operant conditioning. If reinforcement is not administered promptly, then it is likely that one or more other responses will occur between the termination of the target response (i.e., the one which you wish to increase) and the reinforcement. This will make it difficult for the subject to discriminate the response for which reinforcement is contingent. Thus, the reinforcement should be given immediately after the correct response (or an approximation of it) is made. Careful observation of the subject's behavior is necessary to ascertain whether he has made the response as you have defined it.

Procedure

1. *Preparation.* Before your subject arrives for your "experiment," arrange the room so that he will be sitting facing you. Place any equipment needed for the response (e.g., a book for the response illustrated above) in close proximity to the subject. If you are using a room with which the subject is familiar, be sure that the arrangement of the equipment necessary for the response does not look out of the ordinary lest this "give away" the correct response.

2. *Instructions to the Subject.* When your subject arrives, explain to him that you are doing an experiment or project for one of your classes. Then the following instructions should be given: *"Your job is to earn points. I will tell you each time you earn a point and you (I) will record it immediately on this sheet of paper* [hand your subject a pencil and paper] *by making a tally mark for each point you receive. Try to get as many points as you can."* Be sure that you do not give any further instructions to the subject. If he asks you a question, merely tell him: *"I'm sorry, but I'm not permitted to answer any questions. Just work for points and earn as many as you can."*

After the instructions are given to the subject, he may sit motionless and say nothing for several minutes. Sooner or later, however, he will make a response which you will be able to reinforce. Although this initial period of inactivity may be somewhat frustrating for both you and your subject, it should not affect the success of the conditioning. Do *not* try to break the silence or awkward social situation, since this will prejudice the experiment.

Observation and Recording

Once you have given your subject his instructions, your task is simply to observe him very carefully, record the frequency with which he makes the correct response (or an approximation of it), and reinforce his responses. Your record sheet should be modeled after that in Figure 15–9 (page 370). (Do not confuse the subject's record of the points he earns with the record you keep of his behavior and the procedures employed.) Your record sheet should *not* be visible to the subject; using a clipboard will take care of this. When the subject makes a correct response, you must note the 30-second time interval in which it occurred by referring to your watch with a sweep-second hand. The watch should be kept on the clipboard or in such a position that you do not have to move your eyes very far to see the time. You will also indicate on the record sheet whether a reinforcement was given for a response (by circling the check mark—see Figure 15–9), a procedure which is essential when the subject is shifted to a partial reinforcement schedule.

Finally, you must indicate on the record sheet all procedural changes, such as a shift in reinforcement schedule, additional instructions given, and so on. This can easily be done by making a dark, vertical line at the point of change in procedure. As is illustrated in Figure 15–9, a small, lowercase letter is placed adjacent to this line, and it is defined at the bottom of the record sheet in the space provided for comments.

Conditioning

Three phases of conditioning will be used, and the procedures for each are outlined below.

1. *Acquisition: Continuous Reinforcement.* During this phase, each and every correct response (or approximation of it) is given a point. Continuous reinforcement is the most efficient and effective way to establish a response initially. Continuous reinforcement should be given until the *total* response (i.e., not just a component of it) has been reinforced a minimum of 30 times. If, after a number of continuous reinforcements, the subject's rate of responding begins to decrease noticeably, you should simply say: *"Keep earning points."* This statement usually will restore the

FIGURE 15–9

Model Record Sheet for Demonstration 15-1

Response = *looking out the window and then looking back*

✓ = Response   ⊘ = Reinforced Response

30-Second Time Interval	Total For Each Interval	Cumulative	30-Second Time Interval	Total For Each Interval	Cumulative
1.	0	0	25. ✓✓✓	3	66
2.	0	0	26. ✓⊘✓	3	69
3. ⊘ *a*	1	1	27. ✓⊘✓✓	3	72
4.	0	1	28. ⊘✓✓✓	4	76
5. ⊘ ⊘	2	3	29. ✓⊘✓✓	4	80
6.	0	3	30. ✓✓⊘	3	83
7. ⊘⊘	2	5	31. ✓✓✓✓	4	87
8. ⊘⊘	2	7	32. ⊘✓✓	3	90
9. ⊘⊘⊘	3	10	33. ✓✓✓	3	93
10. ⊘⊘⊘⊘	4	14	34. ✓✓✓✓	4	97
11. ⊘⊘⊘	3	17	35. ✓✓✓	3	100
12. ⊘⊘⊘⊘	4	21	36. ✓✓	2	102
13. ⊘⊘⊘⊘	4	25	37. ✓✓	2	104
14. ⊘⊘⊘⊘	4	29	38.	0	104
15. ⊘⊘⊘⊘	4	33	39. ✓✓	2	106
16. ⊘✓✓✓ *c*	3	36	40. ✓✓	2	108
17. ✓⊘	2	38	41. ✓	1	109
18. ✓✓	2	40	42.	0	109
19. ✓✓	2	42	43. ✓	1	110
20. ⊘✓✓✓✓	5	47	44.	0	110
21. ⊘✓✓✓	4	51	45.	0	110
22. ✓⊘✓✓	4	55	46.	0	110
23. ✓✓⊘✓	4	59	47.	0	110
24. ✓✓✓⊘	4	63	48.	0	110

Comments:
a = subject asks what he did to get point
b = start of fixed-ratio 5:1
c = subject asks why I stopped giving points
d = start of extinction

previous response rate. Be sure to indicate on your record sheet the point at which you gave this additional instruction to your subject.

2. Shift to Partial Reinforcement. After the response has been well established (i.e., after a minimum of 30 continuous reinforcements), you will be able to shift your subject to a partial reinforcement schedule with little difficulty. While any of the partial reinforcement schedules discussed earlier in the chapter is applicable, the most convenient for the Demonstration is a *"fixed-ratio 5:1."* That is, reinforce every fifth response. This means that although you will continue *recording* every response the subject makes, only after every five responses will you give him a point. Note also that you will continue to record the responses in the time interval in which they occur, but the five consecutive reponses required for reinforcement to be given need *not* occur in the same time interval. Under this fixed-ratio schedule you should observe that your subject's rate of responding will increase and that there will be a brief pause after each reinforcement (see Figure 15–5 on page 360). Continue on the fixed-ratio 5:1 schedule for a minimum of 10 reinforcements (i.e., 50 responses).

When you shift the subject to a partial reinforcement schedule, you may find that he will begin to emit other responses and make a number of verbal comments (e.g., in the case of a fixed-ratio schedule, counting out loud and statements to the effect that he is receiving points for every five responses). Do not let such behavior changes bother you; just continue with the operant procedures.

3. Extinction. The final phase of the conditioning involves extinction of the response. This is done by completely withdrawing reinforcement for the given response. That is, you will continue to record the number of responses that the subject makes in each 30-second interval, but you will not give him points for any of these responses. Continue the extinction

FIGURE 15–10

Sample Cumulative Record of Data Presented in Figure 15–9

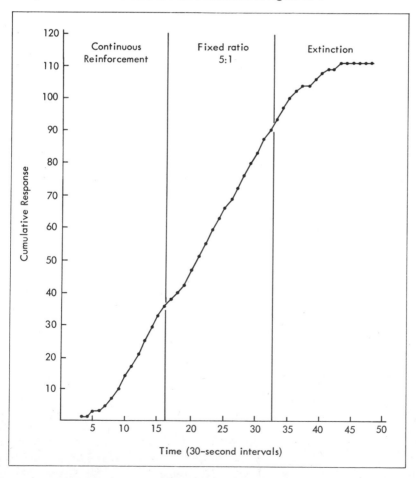

phase until the subject has failed to emit the response during five successive 30-second recording intervals.

Plotting a Cumulative Record

Once the data for the three phases of conditioning have been collected, the frequency of responding can be plotted on a cumulative record similar to that in Figure 15–1 (a) on page 350.

To make a cumulative record, logarithmic paper is best, but any graph paper will do as long as you plan the scale of the ordinate (vertical axis) carefully. That is, it is necessary to make some estimate of the total (cumulative) number of responses for the entire period of recording, so that you can number the ordinate appropriately and not have your cumulative curve run off the top of the paper.

Heavy vertical lines (i.e., parallel to the ordinate) should be drawn on the graph to designate that a new phase of conditioning was instituted. Additionally, you may wish to note with small vertical lines any special changes in procedure and, in the case of shaping, the response component made. You can indicate what occurred at these points either by writing directly on the cumulative record or with a lowercase letter which refers to a statement written at the bottom of the cumulative record. Figure 15–10 is a cumulative record of the data presented in Figure 15–9.

DISCRIMINATION AND STIMULUS CONTROL

The learning of any response involves two aspects. We must not only learn *how* to perform the response but also to discriminate *when* and *where* it is appropriate to emit the response. "Appropriateness" can be defined as those situations which are likely to lead to reinforcement (or, at least, not lead to aversive consequences). *Discriminative stimuli* are those environmental cues which tell us when it is likely that a response will be reinforced. Although operant responses are governed by their consequences, discriminative stimuli serve to set the occasion for their occurrence. Accordingly, behavior which is cued by discriminative stimuli is said to be under *stimulus control.*

Almost all operant behavior is under stimulus control. A professor alluding to an upcoming examination cues students to pay careful attention and take notes; a police car up ahead is often a sufficient discriminative stimulus for decreasing the pressure of one's foot on the accelerator; and the ringing telephone signals us to pick up the receiver and say hello. Other people's behavior often serves as a discriminative stimulus for one's own actions. A girl who sits close to her date while he is driving is usually a discriminative stimulus for the boy to put his arm around her, whereas a girl who sits as close to the door as possible is not.

The same response may be controlled for different people by different discriminative stimuli. In countries where food is scarce, people eat when their stomachs "tell" them that they are hungry, whereas in more affluent societies, such as our own, people tend to eat when the clock "tells" them that it is time to do so.

Problems arise when behavior is under too much stimulus control as well as when it is under too little. In the previous example of shaping the mute psychiatric patient's speech (see page 358), the experimenter became the discriminative stimulus for the patient's talking. In that instance, the patient's behavior was under too much stimulus control, and it was necessary to teach him to *generalize* his speaking in the presence of other discriminative stimuli (e.g., nurses, volunteers).

Fox (1966) has suggested that a good example of behavior which is often under inadequate stimulus control is the study habits of college students.

> The act of studying, regardless of efficiency, is not usually under adequate stimulus control, either by time or by place. The student may study physics at random occasions and at any place he may happen to be on those occasions. Thus, he is subject to all the interfering behaviors conditioned to those occasions. No one occasion becomes uniquely related to study. Even where the student has established regular places and times for study, the immediately preceding occasion is likely to produce behavior competing with that of going to the place of study. He studies physics in the library at ten o'clock if he can resist the reinforcement involved in having coffee with his friends (p. 86).

Fox developed a program to bring the study behavior of students under effective stimulus control, using a variety of operant procedures which have already been discussed. The program will be illustrated by the case of one of the volunteer students with whom he worked.

The student had a 9 o'clock physics class and was then free for an hour at 10 o'clock. He was instructed to go to the library at this time and to begin studying physics. (Students often reported an intention to do just this, but somehow never got around to it.) One of the problems involved in maintaining a schedule, as most readers doubtless know, is that a person is likely to experience some degree of discomfort or perhaps to daydream in such a situation. What does the student do in this instance? The student was instructed to leave his studying and go have coffee with his friends or engage in any other pleasurable activity of his choosing. There was, however, one small restriction—before leaving he was either to read one page of the text carefully or to solve the easiest problem which had been assigned.

On each subsequent day the student was required to read one page more than on the previous day before leaving the study room, and, in this manner he gradually learned to spend the entire hour studying physics. After a week, a second course was similarly scheduled in a different room, and appropriate hours were set. "Eventually, every course was so scheduled, and the student was spending the whole of one hour each day on each course" (Fox, 1966, p. 87).

Each of the steps in this program was dictated by a principle of operant conditioning and therefore serves as a partial review of the preceding sections. First, the counselor assisted the student in making maximal use of available reinforcers. The strategy minimized the aversive situation (a formal option to leave the studying was introduced), and the student did not initially have to entirely forgo the alternative, the positive reward of being with his friends. Second, shaping was used by having the student work up to the full hour of study gradually. Third, a fixed-ratio schedule was employed (so many pages for the reinforcement of leaving the study situation), and the ratio was gradually increased, thereby making studying more resistant to extinction. Finally, the consistent use of a fixed set of stimuli (a particular room and hour of the day) as the occasion for study is in accord with the principles of stimulus control.

THE EFFECTS OF PUNISHMENT

Punishment involves applying aversive consequences to a response in order to reduce (or eliminate) the rate of occurrence of the response. Although in his original formulation of the law of effect Thorndike assumed that reward and punishment worked in "equal and opposite ways," he later concluded that punishment was relatively ineffective. The research which supports this conclusion is almost all based on infrahuman organisms. Simply summarized, a number of experiments have suggested that punishment produces a temporary suppression of operant responding in rats, but that after punishment is terminated punished animals require *more* trials to extinction than those which have not been punished. Overall, the number of trials required for complete extinction (cessation of responding) in punished and nonpunished animals appears to be the same (see Estes, 1944). However, regarding such a generalization, Richard Solomon (1964) has made the following cogent observations: ". . . the attributes of effective punishments vary *across species* and *across stages in maturational development within species*. A toy snake can frighten monkeys. It does not faze a rat. A loud noise terrified Watson's little Albert. To us it is merely a Chinese gong" (p. 241).

Recent human research suggests that punishment can, under some circumstances, be an effective, efficient (Rachman & Teasdale, 1969), and ethically justifiable (Baer, 1970) means of eliminating un-desirable operant behavior. In one such study (Risley, 1968), the subject was a six-year-old girl who was diagnosed as having diffuse brain damage, was hyperactive, and whose only vocalizations were howls, moans, and clicking noises. Her predominant behavior was climbing in high places, although this was interspersed with sitting and rocking. Risley (1968) presents a vivid description of the po-tential hazards of this limited repertoire of behavior.

> Her climbing was a constant source of concern to her parents due to the threat to her life and limb (her body bore multiple scars from past falls; her front teeth were missing, having been left embedded in a two by four inch molding from which she had fallen while climbing outside the second story of her house), and the attendant destruction of furniture in the house. She had attended several schools for special children but had been dropped from each be-cause of these disruptive behaviors and her lack of progress (p. 22).

Initially, Risley attempted a variety of well-established procedures for eliminating the child's potentially harmful climbing behaviors. The first of these was a procedure known as *time-out from positive reinforcement,* or *time-out* for short. Time-out involves the removal of some positive reinforcement, contingent upon the occurrence of the response which is to be eliminated. In this case the subject's physical isolation from social interaction was made a consequence of her climbing behavior. Whenever the little girl climbed, her mother said "No!" sharply, brought her back to the floor, and took her to her bedroom (with no further words and virtually no physi-cal contact) for a 10-minute time-out period. Her mother was also asked to interact with the child as much as possible when she was *not* climbing. After 17 days, no visible diminution of the climbing behavior occurred as a function of the time-out procedure. Simi-larly, it did not appear that the climbing was under the control of any of the reinforcers which were supplied by either the experi-menter or the mother, after an extensive examination of these possi-bilities in the laboratory. Thus, because of the clearly hazardous nature of the behaviors being performed, a form of punishment was applied.

The punishment was administered by a hand-held shock device having an average voltage output of between 300 and 400 volts, and occasionally spikes to more than 1,000 volts. Subjectively, the shock was extremely painful, but using the device produced no negative side effects (e.g., no redness, swelling, or aching). As Risley (1968) noted, "observers of the sessions in which the shocks were applied re-ported that, on the basis of observable autonomic responses . . .

the subject recovered from the shock episodes much faster than the experimenter" (p. 25).

In this study, the contingent application of punishment effectively eliminated the hazardous climbing behavior in a very few sessions. The results are presented as a cumulative record in Figure 15–11. Risley's conclusion appropriately states both the implications and the limitations of the results by noting that his report

> . . . should not be interpreted as a blanket endorsement of punishment with children. In the opinion of the author, the punishment procedures were therapeutically justified for this child. Shock punishment was employed only after other procedures to control disruptive and dangerous behaviors had been extensively but unsuccessfully employed. The possibility of deleterious effects and side effects were thoroughly considered before shock was employed in the home. The benefits to the child, in fact, far exceeded the author's expectations. Of course, no statement about the generality of these findings to other children can yet be made. *However, these findings do serve to limit the generality of extrapolations from past research which contraindicates the use of punishment* (p. 34; italics added).

FIGURE 15–11

Cumulative Record of "Climbing on a Bookcase" Showing the Effects of Punishment

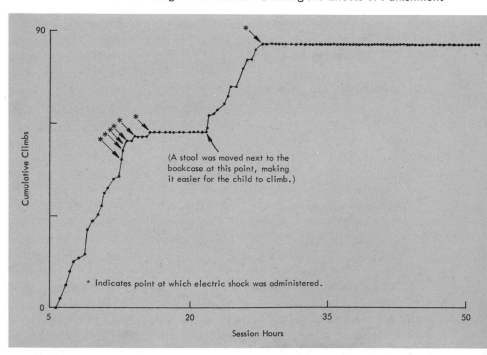

Source: Adapted from Risley, 1968.

THE OPERANT CONDITIONING OF AUTONOMIC RESPONSES

The nervous system (of man and other species) can be divided into a *somatic* and an *autonomic* nervous system. The somatic nervous system is concerned with the sense organs, higher mental processes, and movement of the striated skeletal muscles; the autonomic nervous system controls the smooth muscles of the visceral organs and blood vessels, the heart muscles, and the endocrine glands. Traditionally, the somatic nervous system has been viewed as under voluntary control of the organism and its functions as being modifiable by operant conditioning techniques. In contrast, the autonomic nervous system has been considered involuntary and subject to modification only through classical conditioning techniques. However, evidence accumulated over the past 15 years appears to negate the notion that autonomic functions cannot be instrumentally conditioned. Specifically, a fast-growing body of research has shown that man is capable of learning to control such autonomic responses as salivation, galvanic skin response, heart rate, blood pressure, vasomotor responses (constriction and dilation of blood vessels), penile erection, and brain waves.

Galvanic Skin Response

Kimmel and his associates (Fowler & Kimmel, 1962; Kimmel & Kimmel, 1963) have instrumentally conditioned the galvanic skin response (GSR), the change in the electrical conductivity of the skin, which is a frequently used measure of emotion. In one experimental group, human subjects were seated in a totally dark room and were reinforced for emitting spontaneous GSRs by the brief onset of a light. Each subject in a control group was yoked (matched) with a contingently rewarded subject in terms of the number of reinforcements he received. The only difference between the two groups of subjects was that the yoked controls received the reinforcement at times when they were not emitting spontaneous GSRs (i.e., noncontingently). After an initial period in which both groups of subjects declined in their rate of responding, the experimental group began to increase the frequency of emitted GSRs, while the control group continued to decrease the frequency of GSRs emitted.

Sexual Response

Sexual deviation in men has been diagnosed (e.g., Freund, 1963, 1965, 1967) and treated (e.g., Marks & Gelder, 1967) with the aid of measurements of penile erection, the male's most obvious response to erotic stimulation. In the diagnosis of sexual deviance, a subject may be shown pictures of nude women (normal stimuli) and pictures of nude men and children (deviant stimuli) while the volume of the penis is being monitored by a transducer. Erection to the normal, but not to the deviant, stimuli leads to a diagnosis of normal sexual interests, whereas the reverse leads to a diagnosis of deviant sexual interests. (Interestingly, if the subject responds with an erection to both sets of stimuli, no diagnosis can be made with this technique.) Following diagnosis, treatment may be carried out by punishing subjects with electric shocks for erections they produced while viewing deviant stimuli.

Traditionally, it has been assumed that the suppression of penile erection is not under voluntary control. Accordingly, it was felt that subjects would be unable to avoid producing an erection when shown stimuli which were erotically stimulating to them, and thus they would not be able to fake a normal response to deviant stimuli. However, studies by Rubin and his associates (Henson & Rubin, 1971; Laws & Rubin, 1969) demonstrate that subjects can voluntarily inhibit penile erection, thereby invalidating the diagnosis of sexual deviation in the manner described above.[7]

Laws and Rubin (1969) had normal male subjects watch erotically stimulating movies while the extent of penile erection was being measured. During successive presentations of a film, subjects were either instructed to attempt to inhibit an erection by any means except not watching the film, or instructed to do nothing to avoid getting an erection. To assure that subjects were indeed observing the film, brief light flashes intermittently appeared on the top or bottom of the film on the average of one every 15 seconds, and the subjects were required to push a button located on the arm of the chair in which they were sitting every time they saw a light flash.

Although the ability to inhibit penile erection varied among individuals, all subjects were able to successfully inhibit the response when instructed to do so. The most impressive results are those of two subjects who were shown the same movie nine times in succession, with alternating instructions to either suppress or not suppress penile erection. The data from these two subjects are presented graphically in Figure 15–12.

One possible explanation for these findings is that subjects may not have been attending to the erotic *content* of the films although they attended to the movie screen, as evidenced by their responding

---

[7] This point is not without social implications. In some European countries, the diagnosis of sexual deviance by measuring penile erection in response to various erotic stimuli is accepted as evidence in a court of law for sex crimes and in determining exemption from military duty on grounds of homosexuality.

FIGURE 15–12

Amount of Penile Erection Elicited from Two Subjects by Differential Instructions in Nine Successive Presentations of an Erotic Film

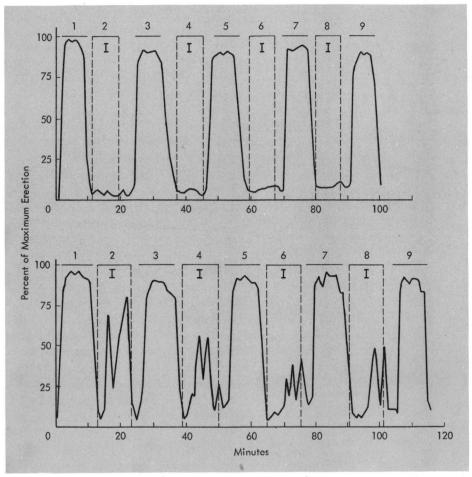

Note: Subjects were instructed to inhibit erection during the presentations enclosed by the dotted lines, and not to inhibit erection during all other presentations.

Source: Laws and Rubin, 1969.

to the intermittent light flashes. Indeed, subjects reported that one way they were able to inhibit penile erection was to think about nonsexual material, such as song lyrics and multiplication tables. Therefore, in a second study (Henson & Rubin, 1971), subjects were asked to verbally describe what was happening in the films and at the same time inhibit penile erection. This procedure not only assured that subjects were attending to the erotic content of the films but also greatly reduced the possibility that subjects were thinking of nonsexual competing material while inhibiting erection.

Despite these stringent controls on the subjects' behavior, all subjects were able to inhibit erection when instructed to do so. Although this study and other investigations have reliably demonstrated that individuals can voluntarily control autonomic functions, how they regulate their autonomic functions remains an open question. So far, most subjects cannot explain the methods by which they achieve control.

What Is Being Conditioned?

Critics (Katkin & Murray, 1968; Kimmel, 1967) of experiments such as those reported above have pointed out that while the responses being conditioned are autonomic, it is possible that the instrumental conditioning of the responses actually involves the conditioning of some somatic response which, in turn, controls the autonomic response (e.g., thinking—a somatic function—about non-sexual things to inhibit penile erection). The only way to categorically refute the somatic mediation hypothesis is to somehow prevent the somatic nervous system from operating. Toward this end, Neal Miller and his colleagues (Miller, 1969) at Rockefeller University have achieved some success in conditioning autonomic responses in subhuman subjects which were injected with curare, a drug which inhibits neural impulses from reaching the skeletal muscles.

Although the issue of somatic mediation in instrumental autonomic conditioning is an important one to the psychologist interested in elucidating the basic learning processes involved, psychologists concerned with the practical implications of *control* of autonomic responses need not be concerned with the underlying mechanism.

Implications for Human Personality

The research on autonomic conditioning, particularly with humans, is still at an early stage, and so few definitive statements can be made regarding it at this time. However, because of the potential importance of the findings thus far for human personality, a brief discussion of some of the possible implications is appropriate.

Psychosomatic Symptoms

A distinction has been made between hysterical symptoms, which primarily involve the somatic nervous system (e.g., paralysis of the legs), and psychosomatic symptoms, which primarily involve the autonomic nervous system (e.g., stomach ulcers). The extant evidence that the functions of the two nervous systems may be modifiable in the same way has led Miller (1969) to speculate about the etiology of psychosomatic symptoms.

> For example, suppose a child is terror-stricken at the thought of going to school in the morning because he is completely unprepared for an important examination. The strong fear elicits a variety of fluctuating autonomic symptoms, such as queasy stomach at one time and pallor and faintness at another; at this point his mother, who is particularly concerned about cardiovascular symptoms, says, "You are sick and must stay home." The child feels a great relief from fear, and this reward should reinforce the cardiovascular responses producing pallor and faintness. If such experiences are repeated frequently enough, the child, theoretically, should learn to respond with that kind of symptom. Similarly, another child whose mother ignored the vasomotor responses but was particularly concerned by signs of gastric distress would learn the latter type of symptom (p. 444).

Individual and Cultural Differences

It is also possible that less extreme emotional reactions than psychosomatic symptoms can be learned in a similar way. Most individuals have characteristic ways of responding to stressful situations. For instance, some people respond to failure with depression and others with anger. It may be that an individual's predominant response to a given situation has been learned because it, rather than some other response, received repeated reinforcement, such as sympathy. Likewise, persons may learn to respond to the same situations in different ways. A young boy who falls while playing with his father may learn to hold back his tears because his father will be disappointed if his son is a "crybaby" but proud if he is a "big boy." The same child may burst out crying when he falls in his mother's presence because he knows that his mother is more concerned about his getting hurt and will reward his tears with sympathy.

The Therapeutic Use of Autonomic Conditioning

Although relatively little therapeutic use of autonomic conditioning has been made so far, its therapeutic potential is impressive. Subjects motivated to eliminate autonomic symptoms (e.g., high blood pressure) may be taught to do so by giving them feedback concerning the changes in their symptom. Success in creating change in the desired direction would serve as a reward, as it did in Rubin's studies cited earlier. Miller (1969) reports that he and his associates have had some success in teaching epileptic patients to inhibit the abnormal brain waves which are thought to cause their seizures. He also suggests the possibility of treating insomnia by reinforcing high-voltage, low-frequency EEGs which characterize sleep. Another potential application of instrumental autonomic conditioning is in the control of the dilation and constriction of cranial blood vessels which accompany migraine headaches.

Although a number of human autonomic functions have repeatedly been operantly conditioned in the laboratory, at the present time the magnitude of the changes produced has often not been sufficient to warrant using the techniques in applied endeavors, such as the therapeutic modification of autonomic functions. (This is an instance of statistical significance but not social significance.) Nevertheless, the area of instrumental autonomic conditioning is one of the latest and most exciting advances in psychology, and the implications and promise it may hold for the understanding and control of human behavior are by no means trivial.

16

The
Behavioral
Strategy
THE
OBSERVATIONAL
LEARNING
APPROACH

In the preceding chapters, we discussed behavioral views of personality which were based on the principles of classical and operant conditioning and which grew more or less directly out of traditional theories of learning and basic experiments in the laboratory (often with infrahuman organisms). The present chapter is concerned with another form of learning, learning by observation, and its unique contributions to human personality and social behavior.

The first treatise on observational learning in this century was Gabriel Tarde's work *The Laws of Imitation,* published in 1903. In this volume, Tarde argued that ". . . the social being, in the degree that he is social, is essentially imitative, and that imitation plays a role in societies analogous to that of heredity in organic life . . ." (p. 11). Tarde was persuaded that everything of social importance is either inventive or imitative and noted that inventions or innovations have no importance whatsoever if they are not emulated by others. It is doubtful, for example, that the *first* voyage from Europe to America was completed by Christopher Columbus. Columbus is nonetheless most often credited with the "discovery" of the American continents because, as a consequence of *his* voyage, subsequent navigators made the trip to them with ever increasing frequency. Had he not been imitated, his voyage would not be socially important. The final thesis of Tarde's argument is nothing less than the statement "society *is* imitation."

Despite Tarde's sweeping generalizations, early psychological analyses of observational learning (e.g., Miller & Dollard, 1941) cast the phenomenon in narrow terms. Imitation was thought to be equated only with simple copying, or matching, of the behavior of others; how people learned a "tendency to imitate" became the major focus of imitation research in the 1940s and 50s.

In recent years, though, there has been a substantial shift away from the mechanistic conceptualization of imitation and toward a broader view of observational learning and imitative behavior. At the same time, both theory and research have burgeoned enormously, so that we can only outline some of the major issues and findings here.

DEFINITIONS AND A THEORETICAL FRAMEWORK

An abundance of terms, with varying meanings, is associated with the word *imitation*. We must, therefore, begin with some definitions.

Overall, our focus of interest is on *observational learning:* the process through which the behavior of one person, an *observer,* changes as a function of merely being exposed to the behavior of another, the *model.* The phenomenon, then, always involves the behavior of at least two participants and therefore embodies the essence of what is "social" about all social learning.

Modeling, as we shall use the term, refers only to the behavior or alleged behavior of the exemplar. (We would *not* say, for example, "The child is modeling [himself after] the adult," but we would say, "The child is imitating the [behavior which the] adult [models].) Specific components of the model's behavior are referred to as *modeling cues.* Such cues are available almost continually in real life. Broadly, they appear in two forms: through the living examples of persons to whom we are exposed directly—instances of *live modeling*—and through examples in such media as movies, television, radio plays, stories, and hearsay descriptions of the behavior of others which we receive secondhand—instances of *symbolic modeling.*

The Acquisition-Performance Distinction

A comprehensive explanation of observational learning must be able to account for the common case in which an individual acquires a response made by a model but does not activate, or perform, the response. A 12-year-old girl, for example, will probably leave the diaper-changing of a "new" brother to her parents and watch the process without participating. Yet on the day when the girl and the infant are left home alone and the need for a change becomes apparent, she will probably perform very well simply because of her repeated observations. With the advent of greater equality of sex roles in the 1970s, many fathers have also begun to use their observationally learned ability (previously latent!) to change diapers. Such instances were first brought to the fore by Albert Bandura and Richard H. Walters, who made the crucial distinction between the "acquisition" and the "performance" of observed responses.

The essential argument is this. People can learn new ways of acting from simply watching others and, for such learning to occur, the observer need only be exposed to the exemplary behavior in such a manner that it can be processed and retained. Still, the availability of observationally learned responses does not necessarily mean that they will be performed at the first opportunity.

To demonstrate the viability of this distinction, Bandura (1965)[1] conducted an experiment now considered a classic. The observers were nursery school boys and girls; modeling cues in the study were provided symbolically by a five-minute film.

> The film began with a scene in which a model walked up to an adult-size plastic Bobo doll and ordered him to clear the way. After glaring for a moment at the noncompliant antagonist the model exhibited four novel aggressive responses each accompanied by a distinctive verbalization.
>
> First, the model laid the Bobo doll on its side, sat on it, and punched it in the nose while remarking, "Pow, right in the nose, boom, boom." The model then raised the doll and pommeled it on the head with a mallet. Each response was accompanied by the verbalization, "Sockeroo . . . stay down." Following the mallet aggression, the model kicked the doll about the room, and these responses were interspersed with the comment, "Fly away." Finally, the model threw rubber balls at the Bobo doll, each strike punctuated with "Bang." This sequence of physically and verbally aggressive behavior was repeated twice (Bandura, 1965, pp. 590–91).

The major independent variable in Bandura's study concerned the consequences which accrued to the model in the film as a result of his aggressive behavior. One group of children simply watched the film, as described above, and thus observed *no consequences* accrue to the model because of his acts. A second group of children saw the same film, but with the addition of a final scene in which the model is rewarded for his aggressive behavior.

> For children in the *model-rewarded* condition, a second adult appeared with an abundant supply of candies and soft drinks. He informed the model that he was a "strong champion" and that his superb aggressive performance clearly deserved a generous treat. He

---

[1] The experiment was first reported in Bandura and Walters' *Social Learning and Personality Development* (1963), where it played a prominent role in their theorizing.

then poured him a large glass of 7-Up, and readily supplied additional energy-building nourishment including chocolate bars, Cracker Jack popcorn, and an assortment of candies. While the model was rapidly consuming the delectable treats, his admirer symbolically reinstated the modeled aggressive responses and engaged in considerable positive social reinforcement (Bandura, 1965, p. 591, italics added).

A third group of children also watched the basic film, but with an added final scene in which the model is punished rather than rewarded for his acts.

> For children in the *model-punished* condition the reinforcing agent appeared on the scene shaking his finger menacingly and commenting reprovingly, "Hey there, you big bully. You quit picking on that clown. I won't tolerate it." As the model drew back he tripped and fell, the other adult sat on the model and spanked him with a rolled-up magazine while reminding him of his aggressive behavior. As the model ran off cowering, the agent forewarned him, "If I catch you doing that again, you big bully, I'll give you a hard spanking. You quit acting that way" (Bandura, 1965, p. 591, italics added).

After exposure to the film, each child was brought into an experimental room which contained a plastic Bobo doll, three balls, a mallet, a pegboard, plastic farm animals, and a dollhouse which was equipped with furniture and a miniature doll family. This wide array of toys permitted the subject to engage either in imitative aggressive responses (i.e., the model's responses) or in alternative nonaggressive and nonimitative forms of behavior. The subject was subsequently left alone with this assortment of equipment for 10 minutes, and his behavior was periodically recorded by judges who observed him from behind a one-way-vision screen. Children's aggressive behaviors in this situation constituted the *performance* measure of the study.

In order to assess the degree to which children could demonstrate or reproduce the modeled behaviors, irrespective of whether they had performed them when alone, the experimenter reentered the room after the performance test, well supplied with sticker pictures and an attractive juice dispenser. He gave the child a small treat of fruit juice and informed him that, for each imitative response he could reproduce, an additional juice treat and sticker would be given. The ability to reproduce the model's behavior in this situation constituted the *acquisition* measure.

The results, shown in Figure 16–1, provide striking support for the view that acquisition and spontaneous performance must be distinguished. In every comparison the children tended to perform

FIGURE 16–1

Results of Bandura's Classic Study on the *Acquisition-Performance* Distinction in Observational Learning

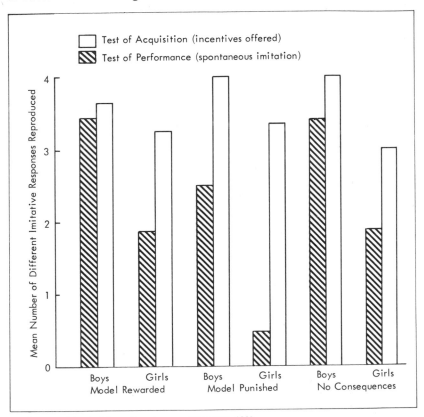

Source: Adapted from Bandura and Walters, 1963.

fewer aggressive behaviors than they had acquired through observation; this was particularly true of children in the *model-punished* condition.

Direct and Indirect Imitative Effects

Just as classical conditioning and instrumental learning show generalization (i.e., extend beyond the situation in which learning occurred originally), observational learning involves more than the recall and exact reproduction of a model's responses. To understand these additional processes, we must distinguish between direct imitative effects and indirect effects which inhibit or disinhibit a large set of responses.

Direct Imitative Effects

We have seen that exposure to a model can lead to relatively exact copying (Bandura, 1965) —that is, to *direct imitation*. It has also been found that observing another's behavior can *reduce* the probability of matching. The child who sees a peer burned by a hot stove will typically become *less* likely to touch the dangerous appliance than previously; he accepts the exemplar's actions and consequences as a guide for what he should not do. Such an outcome may be thought of as *direct counterimitation*.

Indirect Inhibitory and Disinhibitory Imitative Effects

The possible effects of modeling do not end with direct imitation and counterimitation. Modeling cues may also affect observers by suggesting acceptance of a more general class of behaviors, of which the modeling cues are perceived as an example. Consider the child who sees his parents regularly donate money to a variety of charities; subsequently he may become more willing to share his toys with other children or to divide a piece of chocolate cake with his little sister. Similarly, a youngster who observes a variety of models being punished regularly for handing in homework late, talking back to the teacher, and so on, may avoid school "transgressions" which he has never seen modeled (or punished). The former example illustrates *disinhibition* and the latter illustrates *inhibition*.

Observational Learning as a Three-Stage Process

Integrating the various processes which have been described thus far, we can see that Bandura and Walters' original acquisition-performance distinction led to the casting of observational learning as a three-stage process involving *exposure, acquisition,* and subsequent *acceptance* of live- or symbolically modeled responses (Liebert, 1972, 1973). The dynamic, functional manner in which the process works is depicted schematically in Figure 16–2.

Exposure, the first step in the observational learning sequence, is easily arranged in experimental studies; the presentation of precisely controlled modeling cues can be made the independent variable in the laboratory. In correlational field studies, however, determining whether adequate exposure has occurred becomes quite important, as we shall see in a later example dealing with the relationship between TV violence and aggressive behavior.

As implied in Figure 16–2, the possibility exists that a person can be exposed to modeling cues without necessarily acquiring new ways of behaving. People sometimes do not even pay attention to what

FIGURE 16–2

The Three Stages of Observational Learning

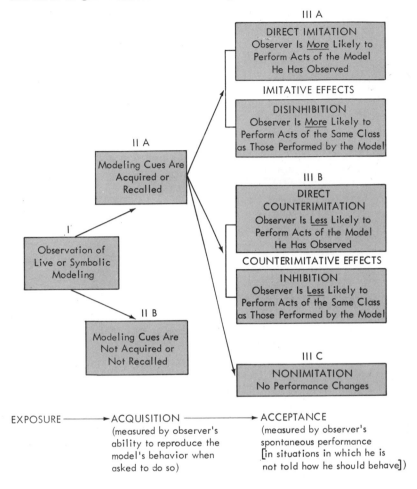

they are shown. In research, *acquisition* has usually been measured as the observer's ability to reproduce or adequately describe the model's behavior when asked to do so; as in Bandura's (1965) study discussed earlier, incentives are often provided to reduce any reluctance to reproduce the model's acts (e.g., because the model had been punished for them).

If both exposure and acquisition have occurred, then our interest turns to the third and final step in the observational learning process: *acceptance*. Acceptance refers to the question of whether or not the observer, having been exposed to and having acquired the modeling cues, now employs or accepts them as a guide for his own actions. As Figure 16–2 shows, there are several ways in which people can accept and use the information obtained by observing others.

When Are Models Attended To and Imitated?

Numerous characteristics of the model, the observer, and the situation will influence the likelihood that a bit of exemplary behavior will be accepted—or even acquired—by the observer. It has been shown, for example, that models who appear to be experienced (e.g., Liebert & Allen, 1969) or competent (e.g., Chalmers, Horne, & Rosenbaum, 1963; Rosenbaum & Tucker, 1962) are more likely to be imitated than those who do not. Conversely, inexperienced observers and observers without a prior commitment to act in certain ways are relatively more likely to imitate models than are observers who are more experienced, committed, or competent (e.g., Davidson & Liebert, 1972; Liebert, Swenson, & Liebert, 1971).

At least in some circumstances, *similarity* between the model and the observer will also foster both learning and acceptance of the model's behavior. Consider, for example, a study conducted by Rosekrans (1967) in which children were exposed to a brief film of a peer model playing a war-strategy game. Subjects in the *high similarity* condition saw a version of the film in which the model was dressed in a Boy Scout uniform, as they were; at the same time, this exemplar was described as being very much like the observers in terms of interests, skills, and place of residence. The film seen by subjects in the *low similarity* condition depicted a peer dressed in street clothes who was described as being quite different from the observers. After exposure to the film, every observer was given an opportunity to play the same game (a test of acceptance) and then asked by the experimenter to demonstrate all of the symbolically modeled behaviors he could remember (a test of acquisition). Rosekrans found that similarity facilitated both acquisition and acceptance of the peer's filmed behavior.

One way of accounting for variations in the degree to which a model's behavior is acquired and accepted by observers is through an informational analysis (Liebert, 1973; Liebert & Allen, 1969; Liebert & Fernandez, 1970a, 1970b). Within this view it is assumed that observers treat modeling cues as information, assessing each bit in terms of its potential value to them. The concept that modeling cues have informational value is viewed as a heuristic one with potentially widespread application. It may be linked with a variety of manipulable variables, and it is closely tied to the three-stage analysis of observational learning. The utility of an informational analysis can be seen in the case of vicarious consequences.

Vicarious Consequences

A central way in which a person's observation of others can furnish information is through the reactions which the modeled behavior is observed to produce in the social environment, as shown, for example, in Bandura's (1965) experiment, described earlier in the chapter. Formally, *vicarious consequences* are said to occur whenever an observer witnesses one or more instrumental acts of a model and subsequently observes the model receiving some external outcome which the observer perceives to be contingent on the model's earlier acts. Two classes of vicarious consequences are: (1) *vicarious reward,* which applies to those outcomes which are presumably perceived by the observer as positive, or desirable, and (2) *vicarious punishment,* which applies to consequences which are likely to be seen by the observer as negative, or undesirable.

An informational analysis of vicarious consequences is based upon the assumption that vicarious consequences, positive or negative, convey two closely related bits of information to observers. Obviously, vicarious consequences provide information as to the kind of effect an action will have—that is, whether the effect will be desirable or undesirable. In this capacity, the information provided by vicarious consequences permits the observer to infer the outcomes which he will receive for similar actions. Many studies have shown that vicarious reward produces direct imitation and disinhibition, while vicarious punishment produces counterimitation and inhibits the performance of responses similar to those of the model (e.g., Bandura, 1969; Liebert & Fernandez, 1970a; Liebert, Sobol, & Copemann, 1972).

In addition to telling the observer the *type* of reaction which some behavior will elicit from others, reward and punishment to a model play an even more fundamental psychological role in learning; they inform the observer that certain actions are particularly likely to get a reaction from others. This information may, in turn, signal the *importance* of what has transpired and thereby increase the likelihood that the observer will attempt to attend to, and try to remember, what he has seen.

In line with the informational analysis of vicarious consequences, several recent experiments have shown that children who see someone else either rewarded or punished for some behavior will show better acquisition of that behavior than children who see the same behavior performed without consequences (e.g., Cheyne, 1971; Liebert & Fernandez, 1969, 1970a; Liebert, Sobol, & Copemann, 1972). We shall describe one of these studies in some detail.

To the extent that seeing someone else rewarded (i.e., vicarious

FIGURE 16–3

Effects of Vicarious Reward on Children's Imitative Learning of a Geography Lesson, as a Function of the Complexity of the Task

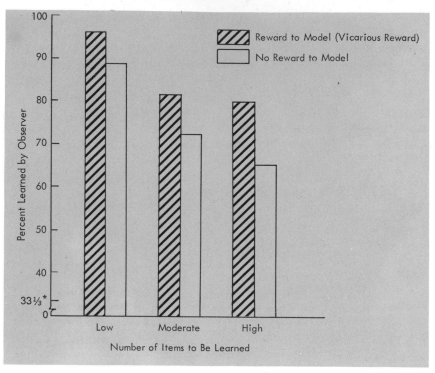

* Chance guessing.
Source: Adapted from Liebert and Fernandez, 1969.

reward) increases the likelihood that a person will pay attention to, and try to remember, what is being done, the question may be asked: "When is capturing the observer's attention likely to be most necessary or important?" Clearly, if what is being demonstrated is intrinsically interesting or fascinating, then no additional features will be necessary in order to assure learning. (This may be the reason that in Bandura's studies of aggression, in which an adult is shown pounding mercilessly on a Bobo doll, learning is equally good with or without vicarious consequences.) Likewise, if the demonstrated behavior is simple, then recall is likely to occur even without any specific effort to capture and hold the observer's attention. On the other hand, when the model's behavior is both relatively uninteresting *and* relatively complex, the effects of vicarious reward should be more important and more critical.

To demonstrate the viability of these suggestions, Liebert and Fernandez (1969) exposed first-grade children to a simulated geography lesson, in which they began by observing an adult model always correctly identify states of the United States from colored slides. Two dimensions of the learning situation were varied in this experiment: the number of items to be learned and whether or not the model was immediately praised by the teacher for correct performance. It was hypothesized that (1) learning by the observer would be better when there were fewer items to be learned and that (2) reward to the model would have its greatest facilitating effect upon the observer's learning when there were more items to be learned. As can be seen from Figure 16–3, both of these hypotheses received clear support.

THE PERVASIVE ROLE OF IMITATION

Most of the research concerned with observational learning has focused either on elucidating the underlying mechanisms of the phenomenon or on exploring the breadth of behaviors in which imitation does, or may, play an important role. Examples of the former type have been discussed thus far. In this section, we turn our attention to the latter focus by indicating some of the areas of personality in which learning by observation has been shown to be potent in the development and modification of behavior.

Imitation and Language

The manner in which children learn to understand and successfully communicate through language is among the most important questions studied by psychologists. The appropriate use of language is central to virtually all aspects of education and social development. Successful and appropriate language communication is also closely linked to the individual's place in society, while the inability to communicate clearly hampers and may virtually eliminate a person's ability to cope with even the simplest educational and social situations.

Traditionally, psychological accounts of language learning have been developed by theorists who have included language learning in their discussions of a general acquisition process (e.g., Miller & Dollard, 1941; Mowrer, 1960; Skinner, 1957). Skinner, for example, believes that language is learned, in large measure, by waiting for children to emit approximations of the forms of speech which are ultimately desired and then by gradual shaping (by parents or other socializing agents) until the correct sounds and sentence forms can be reproduced in appropriate situations with a high degree of fidelity.

In contrast, some psycholinguists (e.g., Chomsky, 1959; Fodor, 1966) have cogently argued that the operant learning theory cannot adequately account for complex verbal behavior. Chomsky (1959) offers the following pregnant critique of a "conditioning" viewpoint:

> . . . it seems quite beyond question that children acquire a good deal of their verbal and nonverbal behavior by casual observation and imitation of adults and other children. It is simply not true that children can learn language only through "meticulous care" on the part of adults who shape their verbal repertoire through careful differential reinforcement, though it may be that such care is often the custom in academic families. It is a common observation that a young child of immigrant parents may learn a second language in the streets, from other children, with amazing rapidity, and that his speech may be completely fluent and correct to the last allophone. . . . A child may pick up a large part of his vocabulary and "feel" for sentence structure from television, from reading, from listening to adults, etc. Even a very young child who has not yet acquired a minimal repertoire from which to form new utterances may imitate a word quite well on an early try, with no attempt on the part of his parents to teach it to him (p. 42) .

Numerous experiments have now disclosed that *principles* for generating novel responses can be acquired through the observation of others (e.g., Bandura & McDonald, 1963; Bandura & Mischel, 1965; Liebert & Ora, 1968; Liebert & Swenson, 1971a, 1971b; Rosenthal & Zimmerman, 1972) . If principles of language usage, rather than mere words, can be shown to be acquired through observational learning, then this would provide at least a partial account of the process of language acquisition.

The classic experiment in this area was conducted by Bandura and Harris (1966) . They were interested in whether second-grade children could make up sentences which included prepositional phrases and the passive voice. The children were tested first during a base rate period and then again after some form of intervening training. The results demonstrated that children showed a greater increment in the production of the relevant construction in their sentences (than did a control group) if they were exposed to a combination of (1) an adult model's production of sentences with and without the relevant construction, (2) reward to both the model and the observer for sentences containing the relevant construction, and (3) attention-focusing instructions.

This study clearly suggests that children's language productions may be modified through modeling in conjunction with other procedures. It is likely, however, that the children in the Bandura and Harris experiment had been exposed to the grammatical constructions many times in their lives prior to entering the experimental situation. Therefore, the question still remained as to whether children could actually acquire new or novel language rules as a function of observation.

Odom, Liebert, and Hill (1968) performed an experiment which was designed to test the possibility that children could abstract and use *new* language rules from the observation of models. Second-grade boys and girls were asked to make up sentences using nouns presented to them on large cards. The subjects were told that any sentence was acceptable, that the sentences did not have to be true, and that they could be either statements or questions. All subjects were given a base rate assessment of their production of prepositional phrases. Children in the two experimental conditions were then exposed to a model who was rewarded for producing particular phrases. In one experimental condition, the children were exposed to modeled prepositional phrases of the usual English form (*preposition-article-noun*, as "The boy went *to the house"*) and were themselves rewarded for using such phrases in the sentences they made up. In the other experimental condition, subjects were exposed to and subsequently rewarded for the production of sentences containing unfamiliar prepositional constructions of the form *article-noun-preposition* (as, "The man was *the door at"*) .

Surprisingly, many children exposed to the *new* rule condition, as well as those exposed to the familiar English rule condition, demonstrated an increase in the frequency with which they used the *familiar* constructions (i.e., preposition-article-noun) relative to children in a control group who saw no model and received no reward. Apparently, instead of abstracting a new rule from the model's productions, the subjects in these conditions in some way "reordered" the unfamiliar language constructions to make them correspond to language rules with which they were already familiar. It is plausible, however, that older children might be able to identify and use the rewarded (unfamiliar) rule.

To test this possibility, Liebert, Odom, Hill, and Huff (1969) employed procedures which were similar to those used by Odom et al., except that children of three age groups participated. These groups consisted of preschool children (mean age = 5.8) , second-grade children (i.e., those of the age previously used; mean age = 8.3) , and young teen-agers (mean age = 14.0). After a base rate period wherein the frequency with which the children produced familiar prepositional constructions was assessed, half of the children in each age group were exposed to a model who produced English rule prepositional phrases and the other half to a model who produced parallel new rule phrases. Following this training, the subjects' production of relevant prepositional phrases was assessed. The most important finding of the study was that the oldest children were able to abstract the new rule through observational learning and were soon using it (see Figure 16–4). A few of the eight-year-olds also occasionally used the new rule, but the youngest children failed to do so.

The studies of imitative language described above all focused on children's acquisition of grammatical rules by observational learning. ing. Investigators have also been interested in whether the *substance* of a child's language can be modified by mere exposure to social models (i.e., without any reinforcement procedures). Rosenthal, Zimmerman, and Durning (1970) studied the kinds of questions preadolescent Mexican-American boys and girls asked about various pictures they were shown. Children in the modeling groups first observed an adult female ask questions about each of the pictures, while children in a control group were simply presented with the pictures and told to ask something about each.

The models were distinguished by the particular *category* of ques-

FIGURE 16–4

Mean Number of New Rule Prepositional Constructions during Base Rate and Training as a Function of Children's Age in Liebert et al.'s Experiment

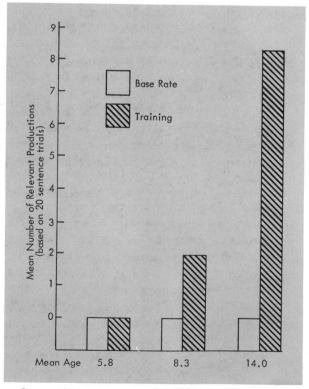

Source: Liebert, Odom, Hill, & Huff, 1969.

tion they asked. The four categories were: physical attributes (e.g., "What shape is that?"), functional characteristics (e.g., "Could you put this in water?"), causal relationships (e.g., "When does the bell on the typewriter ring?"), and judgments involving value or preference (e.g., "Which do you think is the prettiest?"). As predicted, the children in the modeling groups tended to ask questions of the type that had been exemplified by the model. Furthermore, most of these children did not merely copy the model's questions but rather made up questions of their own which were appropriate to the category of questions they had seen modeled.

Self-Control

Theories of personality usually try to account for the fact that most people are able to display a degree of self-control. For example, faced with some sort of immediate incentive to behave in one way, we are able to "control" ourselves and behave in an alternative manner that does not provide as much immediate gratification. There are, in fact, many different types of self-control, but we shall discuss only one: delay of gratification. Like many other forms of behavior, delay of gratification has been shown to be influenced by observational learning.

Delay of Gratification

Delay of gratification refers to the self-imposed postponement of some immediate reward in favor of some potentially more valuable delayed reward. A common example is an individual's decision not to drop out of school for a moderately good job now, but instead to persist in harsh economic circumstances in order to continue his education (which presumably will provide a superior job after training has been completed). A person's ability to delay some small immediate reward for the sake of a larger outcome for which he must wait is a critical prerequisite for the achievement of success in many human endeavors.

That a willingness to delay gratification can be acquired through observational learning has been demonstrated experimentally by Bandura and Mischel (1965). In the first part of their study, fourth- and fifth-grade children were given a delay-of-reward test which involved confronting them with a series of 14 choices between a small immediate reward and a larger postponed reward (e.g., a small candy bar which they could have immediately or a larger one which required a week of waiting). On the basis of this assessment, the children were classified as preferring high-delay of reward or low-delay of reward. The purpose of the study was to demonstrate that these initial preferences could be changed (i.e., from high to low

FIGURE 16–5

Mean Percentage of Immediate-Reward Choices by Children Who Initially Preferred High-Delay and Mean Percentage of Delayed-Reward Choices by Children Who Initially Preferred Low-Delay in Bandura and Mischel's Experiment

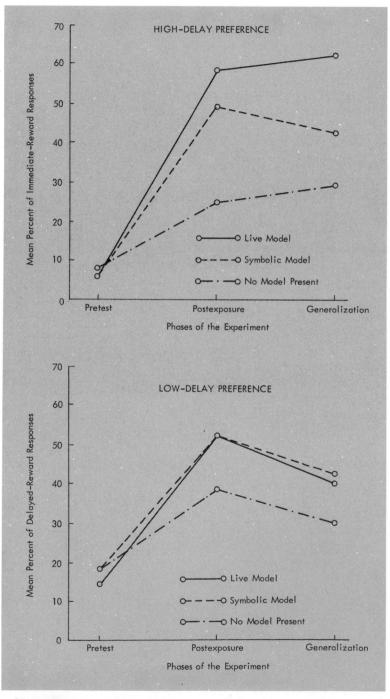

Source: Bandura and Mischel, 1965.

and vice versa) by exposure to an appropriate adult model who made choices between immediate and postponed rewards.[2] Children whose initial preference was for high-delay of reward were exposed to a model who consistently chose the immediate reward item, whereas for those children who preferred low-delay of reward, the model selected the postponed reward item in each case. Additionally, the model briefly summarized his philosophy of life, which embodied the attitude toward delay of reward he was modeling, and occasionally commented on his choice. For instance, when the choice was between a plastic chess set obtainable immediately and a more expensive wooden set which could be obtained in two weeks, the low-delay-of-reward model commented, " 'Chess figures are chess figures. I can get much use out of the plastic ones right away' " (Bandura & Mischel, 1965, p. 701).

Subjects were assigned to one of three conditions. In the *live modeling* condition, the model was actually present. In the *symbolic modeling* condition, the modeling cues were presented in written form. Subjects who were just shown the series of paired objects (*no-model-present* condition) served as controls for the possible effects of mere exposure to rewards on subsequent delay-of-gratification behavior. All the children were then given a delay-of-reward test in the model's absence. To assess the stability of changes in delay-of-reward behavior which occurred as a result of modeling, the subjects were administered a subsequent delay-of-reward measure approximately one month later.

The results of this experiment are presented in Figure 16–5, from which it can be seen that, for both high- and low-delay preference children, modeling produced a marked and moderately stable change in behavior. These data further illustrate the generality of modeling procedures as a potent means of modifying yet another aspect of personality.

Helping Behavior

Helping is one type of social response which has been the focus of many recent studies of observational learning. It has been shown, for example, that children are more likely to contribute some of their earnings (on a bowling game, a perceptual judgment task, or a "job" created for them in the laboratory) if they have seen an adult model do so than if they have not observed the adult (Liebert

---

[2] The items among which the adult model chose were appropriate rewards for adults (chess sets, magazines, and so on) and were different from the items among which the subjects subsequently chose. Thus, the subjects were only able to imitate the *principle* exhibited by the model's behavior and could not merely copy his choices.

& Poulos, 1971; Poulos & Liebert, 1972; Rosenhan & White, 1967) and that the gift-giving of adults is influenced by the size of the contributions made by their co-workers (Blake, Rosenbaum, & Duryea, 1955).

Two reports will serve to illustrate this line of research. Unlike many other studies, the experiments of Bryan and Test (1967) and Hornstein, Fisch, and Holmes (1968) have used "street-corner" rather than laboratory settings to test their hypotheses. Such a strategy places additional demands on the ingenuity of the investigator but significantly broadens the base of evidence for hypotheses which have been supported in the laboratory.

Bryan and Test (1967) conducted a series of naturalistic studies designed to assess the effect of models on helping behavior. In their first experiment, entitled "Lady in Distress: A Flat Tire Study," an undergraduate female was stationed next to a Ford Mustang with a flat tire on the left-rear wheel and an inflated tire leaning beside it. The purpose of the experiment was to determine whether observation of a helping model by passing drivers would increase the likelihood that they would stop and assist the apparently forlorn lady. During the experimental period, an Oldsmobile was located about a quarter of a mile up the road and was clearly visible to motorists driving toward the lady and her disabled Mustang. In this "modeling scene," the Oldsmobile was jacked up, and a young girl was watching while a man changed a flat tire. During the control period, which was held at a comparable time, the modeling scene was absent. The experiment was conducted in a residential area of Los Angeles, and each treatment condition continued for the time required for 1,000 noncommercial vehicles to pass. Although the total number of vehicles which stopped to help was a small percentage of those which passed (fewer than 3 percent), the presence of a model significantly increased the number of drivers who stopped to offer their assistance.

Bryan and Test's second experiment, which they called "Coins in the Kettle," was designed to determine the effects of modeling on donations to a Salvation Army kettle in front of a large department store in Princeton, New Jersey. Once every 60 seconds a man dressed as a white-collar worker (the model) approached the kettle and contributed 5 cents. The first 20 seconds thereafter were considered the modeling period. The third 20-second segment was designated the no-modeling period. It was found that donations occurred significantly more often in the modeling than in the no-modeling periods.

Shoppers who observed the model donate saw, besides the actual donating behavior, the model thanked for his contribution as well as the pleasant interaction which ensued between donator and solicitor (an instance of vicarious reward). Thus, it is possible that observing a charitable model who received *no* social reward for his behavior might not influence the observer. To test this hypothesis, another experiment, "Coins in the Kettle II," was conducted in which the model was not thanked for his contribution. Nonetheless, shoppers donated significantly more often during the modeling periods than during the no-modeling periods.

Overall, Bryan and Test's data clearly demonstrate that modeling can influence helping behavior in naturalistic settings, but they do not elucidate the mechanisms which underlie this process. An experiment by Hornstein et al. (1968) has explored this issue. The study is based on the proposition that "an observer uses the model's experiences as a valid predictor of his own future experiences" (Hornstein et al., 1968, p. 222). This assumption leads to the expectation that when the observer and the model are perceived as *similar,* the observer will see the model's experiences as a valid predictor of what his own experiences would be if he engaged in similar behavior. Thus, in such a case, the observer should be more likely to imitate the model if the model had positive experiences than if he had negative experiences. On the other hand, when the observer and the model are seen as very *dissimilar,* the observer will not consider the model's experiences to be a valid predictor of his own. In this instance, the observer should be no more likely to imitate the model if the model had positive experiences than if he had negative experiences.

To test these hypotheses, Hornstein et al. inconspicuously dropped addressed but unstamped envelopes containing a man's wallet and a letter on the sidewalk in a midtown Manhattan business district. The wallet's contents, for all subjects, were shrewdly designed to create the impression of an "average" owner, Michael Erwin. It contained $2 in cash, an identification card, postage stamps, membership cards for two fictitious organizations, a receipt for a rented tuxedo, the calling cards of a florist and a podiatrist, and other nondescript contents that contributed to its "legitimacy."

A typewritten letter, which provided the modeling cues, gave the impression that the wallet had been lost *twice.* When the wallet was lost initially, its finder (the model) put the wallet in an envelope to be mailed to its owner, enclosing a letter describing his feelings about finding and returning it. However, before he could mail it, the well-intentioned finder lost the wallet himself. The pedestrian who found the letter a "second" time, and who thereby became a subject in the experiment, had to decide between returning the wallet (and imitating his predecessor's prosocial behavior) and keeping the wallet and the money for himself.

To manipulate the similarity of observer and model, the letter was either written in familiar English (*similar model* condition) or

TABLE 16–1

The Letters Used by Hornstein et al. to Manipulate the Feelings of Its Original Finder (Model) and His Similarity to the Second Finder (Subject)

Letter Condition	Model Condition	
	Similar	*Dissimiliar*
*Neutral**	Dear Mr. Erwin: I found your wallet which I am returning. Everything is here just as I found it.	Dear Mr. Erwin: I am visit your country finding your ways not familiar and strange. But I find your wallet which I here return. Everythings is here just as I find it.
Positive†	I must say that it has been a pleasure to be able to help somebody in the small things that make life nicer. It's really been no problem at all and I'm glad to be able to help.	It great pleasure to help somebody with tiny things which make life nicer. It is not problem at all and I glad to be able help.
Negative†	I must say that taking responsibility for the wallet and having to return it has been a great inconvenience. I was quite annoyed at having to bother with the whole problem of returning it. I hope you appreciate the efforts that I have gone through.	To take responsibility for wallet and necessity to return it is great inconvenience. Is annoyance to bother with whole problem of return and hope you appreciate effort I went to.

* The neutral letter said no more than this.
† The positive and negative letters began with the neutral statement.
Source: Hornstein, Fisch, and Holmes, 1968.

in an ungrammatical, broken English which created the impression of a foreign writer (*dissimilar model* condition). In each of these conditions, the letter described the writer's feeling of pleasure at returning the wallet (*positive letter* condition), expressed his annoyance at being bothered (*negative letter* condition), or did not reveal his feelings (*neutral letter* condition). The letters used are presented in Table 16–1.

The percentage of wallets returned in each group is presented in Table 16–2, from which it is clear that the researchers' predictions were supported. When the letter was apparently written by a similar model, positive and neutral experiences produced more returns than

TABLE 16–2

Percentage of Wallets Returned Intact in the Hornstein et al. Experiment as a Function of the Subject's Similarity to and the Feelings of the Model

Letter Condition	Model Condition	
	Similar	*Dissimilar*
Neutral	60.0	26.7
Positive	70.0	33.3
Negative	10.0	40.0

Source: Adapted from Hornstein, Fisch, and Holmes, 1968.

negative experiences, whereas there were no such differences for the dissimilar model condition. The study further demonstrates the role of modeling in naturalistic situations, and illustrates how two characteristics of the model, his similarity to the observer and his feelings, may mediate such an effect.

Observational Learning and TV Violence

Not all observational learning leads to socially positive outcomes. People can learn undesirable and antisocial forms of behavior through the same processes which impart self-control and an increased willingness to share with others. Violence in television entertainment has long been suspected of having such a negative impact. The effects of TV violence, particularly on children, have recently been explored through application of the three-stage observational learning framework discussed earlier.

Exposure to Aggression

Following the scheme shown in Figure 16–2 (page 389), the first question concerns exposure. How much violence is shown on commercial television entertainment? The answer is found in careful and extensive surveys by Gerbner (1972a, 1972b), which indicate that the frequency of overt physical violence during prime time and Saturday morning network programs has been such that, in 1969, eight out of 10 programs contained violence, with the frequency of violence episodes running about eight per program hour. Children's cartoons, which have long been the most violent programs, actually increased their lead in violence portrayals over a three-year period (1967–69). Nor have there been significant changes in the more recent past. Gerbner's (1972a) analysis of the 1970 and 1971 season reveals that ". . . new programs in 1971 spearheaded the trend toward more lethal violence by depicting record high proportions of screen killers" (p. 3). Clearly, the first stage of the observational learning of aggression from television, exposure to TV violence, does occur.

Acquisition of Aggressive Responses

A series of experiments by Bandura and his associates (e.g., Bandura, 1965 [described earlier in the chapter], 1969) has thoroughly documented the enormous power of the television-like format in teaching novel forms of aggressive behavior. Evidence shows, too, that aggressive responses acquired in this way can be recalled for long periods of time. Hicks (1965, 1968), for example, found that young children who viewed a simulated television program of aggressive acts showed substantial acquisition of these behaviors after a single viewing, and retention of the ability to perform them was still in evidence when the children were tested again, without further exposure, six and eight months later. There is no doubt, then, that children can acquire a good deal of the aggressive repertoire they see on television entertainment.

Acceptance of Aggression

Given that the requirements of exposure and acquisition have been met, we turn next to the evidence regarding children's acceptance of aggression observed on television as a guide for their own behavior.

DIRECT IMITATION OF AGGRESSION. For the past two decades American newspapers have reported a succession of documented cases of crime and violence whose perpetrators imitated them directly from TV models. The perpetrators include the successful imitator of the TV version of "The Doomsday Flight," who was paid a $500,000 plane ransom by Qantas Airways, and a youngster who poisoned the family dinner with ground glass after observing the successful use of this tactic on a television crime show (Schramm, Lyle, & Parker, 1961). Laboratory studies have also demonstrated that children will directly imitate aggressive acts which they have seen and that they may choose human as well as inanimate victims (Bandura, Ross, & Ross, 1961, 1963; Hanratty, Liebert, Morris, & Fernandez, 1969; Hanratty, O'Neal, & Sulzer, 1972; Savitsky, Rogers, Izard, & Liebert, 1971).

DISINHIBITION OF AGGRESSION. Direct imitation requires that the situation be virtually identical with the one observed. Since real-life circumstances usually do not mirror those of television (e.g., few children have access to pistols, swords, torture chambers, laser guns, and other TV-aggrandized implements or facilities), the demonstration of disinhibitory effects has been a central research issue. To illustrate the typical finding, we turn to a study by Steuer, Applefield, and Smith (1971).

Designed to show the absolute degree of control which television violence can have on naturally occurring aggressive behavior, this study involved 10 preschool boys and girls who knew each other before the study began. First, the children were matched into pairs on the basis of the amount of time they spent watching television at home. Next, to establish the degree to which aggressive behavior occurred among these youngsters *before* any modification of their television "diets," each child was carefully observed in play with other children, for 10 sessions, and the frequency of his aggressive responses was recorded. Steuer and her associates used a stringent measure of physical interpersonal aggression, including hitting or pushing another child, kicking another child, assaultive contact with another child (e.g., squeezing, choking, or holding down), and throwing an object at another child from a distance of at least one foot.

Next, on 11 different days, one child in each pair observed a single aggressive television program taken directly from Saturday morning program offerings, while the other member of the pair observed a nonaggressive television program. Observations of the children at play during the course of the study provided continuous measures of interpersonal aggression for each group. By the end of 11 sessions—a total of less than two hours of television exposure—the children exposed to TV violence had become more aggressive toward one another than had their control counterparts, who had been exposed to neutral fare.

These results are not unique. More than 50 studies of TV violence, involving more than 10,000 children from every type of social background, have been conducted. Research procedures have covered the full range from partialed correlational studies (e.g., Chaffee & McLeod, 1971) to laboratory studies of disinhibition with actual TV sequences (e.g., Liebert & Baron, 1972) to longer-term field experimental studies (e.g., Stein & Friedrich, 1972). The regular finding is this: viewing TV violence is positively and causally related to children's aggressive behavior.

TV violence presents the ideal circumstance for both the learning of a variety of aggressive behaviors and informing observers that violence "pays." The usual, and most effective, solution to interpersonal conflict on television is through violence (Gerbner, 1972b). Indeed, the medium has provided a superb example of consistent multiple modeling of violence and aggression.

Network officials, however, have sometimes justified television violence because the "bad guy" is punished for his behavior. The argument deserves a closer look. The usual program sequence involves aggression by the villain through which he achieves his immediate objectives, such as securing the plans for the latest nuclear weapon. Then the hero catches up with and punishes the villain, by shooting, beating, or otherwise physically vanquishing him. The hero is not punished for these glamorized acts of brutality. Rather, he is rewarded with a promotion, a blonde, or a bottle of champagne; if he is lucky, he may get all three, plus a vacation in the sun.

THERAPEUTIC USES OF MODELING

As we have seen, there have been a large number of investigations of basic imitative phenomena in recent years. Not surprisingly, a major offshoot of these enterprises has been a parallel effort to apply emerging principles and procedures to personality change.

The Role of Modeling in Counseling

Modeling procedures are being employed increasingly in counseling (e.g., Krumboltz & Thoresen, 1969). For example, a series of well-designed studies by Krumboltz and his associates (Krumboltz & Schroeder, 1965; Krumboltz & Thoresen, 1964; Krumboltz, Varenhorst, & Thoresen, 1967) has shown that through modeling techniques it is possible to increase the degree to which high school students seek appropriate occupational and educational information.

One study (Krumboltz & Thoresen, 1964) compared a combination of modeling and reinforcement with reinforcement alone. Subjects in *model-reinforcement counseling* were initially exposed to a 16-minute tape recording of a counseling interview in which a male student discussed what he planned to do after high school and, in doing so, frequently verbalized information-seeking responses which the model counselor (i.e., in the tape) rewarded. After listening to the tape, subjects discussed their own future plans, and the counselor rewarded information-seeking responses both verbally ("mm-hmm," "excellent ideas," and so on) and nonverbally (smiling, head nodding, and the like). This direct conditioning procedure constituted the treatment for the subjects in the *reinforcement-counseling* condition. Subjects in the *control-film discussion* condition watched a film (unrelated to information-seeking behavior) which they then discussed with the counselor. The dependent measures consisted of the frequency and variety of *actual* information-seeking behavior (e.g., writing for a college catalog) during a three-week period. The results of the experiment revealed that the model-reinforcement condition proved to be most influential, followed by the reinforcement condition.

Modeling Used in Conjunction with Operant Techniques

Modeling procedures have frequently been used in conjunction with operant conditioning techniques (see Chapter 15) in the treatment of various behavioral deficiencies. A major limitation of the operant approach in establishing behavior is that the desired response (or an approximation of it) must occur before it can be rewarded. In the case of such persons as autistic children, mental retardates, and psychotic adults (who often have very limited behavioral repertoires), it is highly uneconomical to wait for responses which have a low probability of occurrence to be emitted (e.g., speech in a mute child). In such instances, modeling has served a crucial role in eliciting the desired response. Ivar Lovaas (1968), a psychologist who pioneered in working with autistic children to teach them speech and social behaviors, has commented: "In retrospect, it seems virtually impossible to have brought about certain behavioral changes . . . without an imitation approach" (p. 118).

The general procedure for eliciting a response through modeling involves an experimenter demonstrating the desired response for the subject (e.g., emitting a word or phrase) and rewarding him (as with food or verbal praise) if the response is imitated within a set time interval. An important consequence of this procedure seems to be that imitation itself becomes conditioned. Thus, one technique employed to teach complex behaviors is to first train subjects to imitate a series of simple responses which may have little or no social usefulness (e.g., touching one's head). Then this *generalized imitation* is used to teach more complex and useful skills, such as speech, brushing one's teeth, and the like (e.g., Lovaas, Freitas, Nelson, & Whalen, 1967). The modeling of a response is usually accompanied by a verbal request or question. The experimenter may say: "What is this? This is a *book.*" It is hoped that eventually the imitative control of the response can be "faded out," so that the response will come under the control of verbal statements alone. Metz (1965) has noted two "side effects" of conditioning generalized imitation in autistic children:

> . . . as appropriate learning occurred, "inappropriate" motor and emotional behavior spontaneously disappeared. Not only did the children learn to do what was required by the task, but appropriate emotional responses also seemed to appear. For example, the children expressed joy or delight upon "solving" a problem, an affect rarely seen in these children in other situations. . . . Temper tantrums and "rituals" disappeared even though food and tokens were sometimes withheld for long periods of time . . . (p. 398).

Metz's observations point to important therapeutic benefits besides the acquisition of new responses. The combination of modeling and of reward contingent upon imitation appears to be an effective means of giving these children success experiences, which, in turn, contribute to heightening their self-esteem.

One team of researchers (Phillips, Liebert, & Poulos, 1973) has recently developed a "language training packet" for children with IQs under 35 which can be administered by teachers with relatively little special training or experience. The program consists of units (e.g., Unit I is "Foods We Eat"; Unit II is "Clothes We Wear"), each containing 24 lessons. The teacher is provided with manuals, written in simple language, which present (1) an introduction to basic reinforcement and modeling techniques, (2) an explanation of specific techniques aimed at teaching language skills and developing appropriate classroom behavior, (3) detailed lesson plans, and (4) testing instructions that provide for the continual evaluation of the students' progress. The program itself can best be seen through part of the investigators' description of one of the units, as employed in a large school for the mentally retarded in Tennessee.

Each class worked through 24 "Clothes We Wear" lessons, where a lesson could be completed in one class period or extended over several days. The first 12 lessons primarily emphasized identification of items. An item to be learned would be displayed, the class told its name, and asked to give the name back. [The teacher] . . . began a lesson or the introduction of a new procedure by asking the most competent children to answer first, in order to promote imitation from the others. If she received no responses, she would give the correct response and reinforce herself, then attempt the question again. Various discriminative attributes of the particular item were pointed out and emphasized (e.g., "a shirt has a collar that goes around your neck and buttons; it is made of light material"). Children were encouraged to try it on and to point to the same item that they were wearing. Then, each child came to the table and was asked to pick out the item from the others; the position of the items was randomly rearranged with each new attempt. The rest of the class was often included and various games were made out of this activity. Other games were also employed, such as a race to find the item named in a grab-box or to pick it out of magazine pictures. All appropriate responses were rewarded with food and enthusiastic praise (Phillips et al., 1973, p. 612).

Intervention of this sort has proved to be highly successful. In the Tennessee study, four different experimental groups were initially matched with controls from the same institution, making direct comparisons possible. Some of the results are presented in Table 16–3, in which the differences between the combined experimental and control groups were statistically significant. Equally important are factors which cannot be reduced to a numerical description.

Most participants had been institutionalized early in life and many were mute or near-mute, making only incomprehensible sounds. Several also suffered from various physical disorders, were not toilet trained, and displayed behavior problems. Nevertheless, there are reports of striking improvements, such as children speaking for the first time during their 2-mo. training experience. It should also be noted that increased identification skills alone are useful in an institution oriented toward promoting self-help. Beyond the increases in language-oriented skills, it is important that children learned to participate in classes, began interacting with each other as well as with staff members (often a novel experience), and seemed to enjoy

TABLE 16–3

Mean Percentage Improvement in Correct
Verbalizations of Real Clothing Items (between
Pre- and Posttest) for Experimental and
Control Groups in Phillips et al.'s Study of
Language Training

Group	Percentage of Improvement
Experimental 1	18.8
Control 1	0.0
Experimental 2	21.7
Control 2	6.7
Experimental 3	8.3
Control 3	6.9
Experimental 4	43.3
Control 4	5.0

Note: Each group included between four and six
children.
Source: Phillips, Liebert, & Poulos, 1973.

their classes. Behavior problems were minimal . . . (Phillips et al.,
1973, pp. 614–15) .

The Application of Modeling to Problems of the Disadvantaged and Handicapped

One important application of modeling techniques has been the
use of appropriate role models to enhance the self-esteem and raise
the level of occupational aspiration of black students (e.g., Henderson, 1967; Smith, 1967) . Smith (1967) describes an informal project
in which successful adult blacks spoke monthly over the course of
the school year about their early life and present work to black freshman high school students. The purpose of the project was both to
model achievement by blacks and to illustrate professions to which
blacks could aspire. Several of the models—a teacher, an engineer,
a lawyer, an anthropologist, and a poetess—were former slum dwell-
ers who had overcome adverse circumstances to reach their present
status. At the same time, they were credible models, since aspiring to
be a teacher is within the realm of possibility for the average student, whereas being as successful as Willie Mays or Martin Luther
King may not be. Smith reports that he observed an increase in
pupils' self-esteem over the course of the project.

Kliebhan (1966, 1967) employed modeling and goal-setting to increase the performance of retarded adolescents in an occupational
workshop. The subjects in the modeling group were exposed to a
nonretarded model (a college student) who performed the work
task, which consisted of attaching samples of tape to pages of a sales-

man's advertising booklet. The subjects were told initially: " 'Terry will show you how to do the task. . . . He's doing a fine job. . . . Watch him . . .' " (Kliebhan, 1967, p. 222). When compared to control subjects who received only verbal instructions regarding the task, subjects who worked in the presence of the model showed an increase in productivity.

Vicarious Extinction of Avoidance Responses

In a growing number of well-controlled studies, behaviorally oriented therapists have confirmed and extended a suggestion that Jones (1924a, 1924b; see Chapter 14) made 50 years ago: avoidance behavior in children (and adults) can be vicariously extinguished by observing appropriate models make approach responses to feared objects or situations without (the models) incurring any adverse consequences.

In an early study involving this problem (Bandura, Grusec, & Menlove, 1967), the strength of nursery school children's fear of dogs was assessed before and immediately after treatment, as well as approximately one month later, by asking the children to perform 14 graded tasks involving progressively more interaction with a dog. One group of children observed a fearless peer make successively more intimate approach responses to a dog in the context of a jovial party (*modeling-positive context*). A second group observed responses by the same model but without the positive party atmosphere (*modeling-neutral context*). To control for the effect of exposure to the dog and the positive atmosphere itself, a third group participated in the parties with the dog, but in the absence of the model (*exposure-positive context*). Finally, to check on the influence of the presence of the dog as well as to control for possible benefits of the positive experiences and interaction with friendly experimenters, a fourth group of children merely participated in the party (*positive context*). All groups met for eight sessions. Both modeling conditions were found to be more effective than either control condition in reducing avoidance behavior, as measured by the number of tasks the four groups of children completed.

Continuing this line of research, Bandura and Menlove (1968) presented the modeling sequences by means of films in order to explore the potential therapeutic use of such symbolic modeling. All subjects were shown a series of eight three-minute movies on four alternate days. Children in the *single-model* condition saw a fearless five-year-old model make successively more intimate contacts with a single dog. The subjects in the *multiple-model* condition saw several models (differing in age and sex) interact with a variety of dogs. The size and fearsomeness of the dogs were gradually increased, as was the boldness of the approach responses made by the models. A third group of children, who saw movies of amusement parks for an equal amount of time, served as *controls*. The results, which are depicted graphically in Figure 16–6, indicated that both the single-model and the multiple-model conditions significantly increased approach responses but that only the latter treatment reduced the children's fears to the extent that they were able to perform the most intimate interaction with the dog. Furthermore, whereas the single-model group merely maintained its level of approach behavior after the treatment, the multiple-model children became even bolder over time.

FIGURE 16–6

Median Approach Scores for Children in Each of the Three Conditions of Bandura and Menlove's Experiment

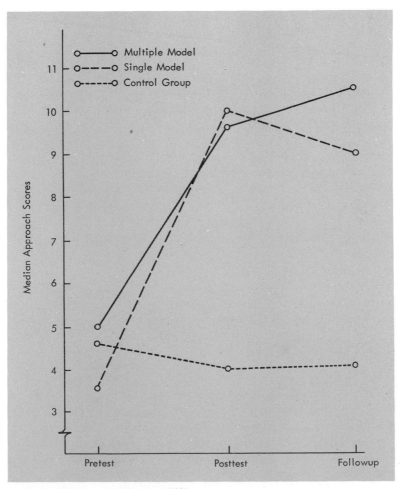

Source: Bandura and Menlove, 1968.

Similar therapeutic modeling effects have also been shown with adults. For example, Spiegler, Liebert, McMains, and Fernandez (1969) produced a 14-minute modeling film to be used in reducing fear of nonpoisonous snakes in adults. The film first presents the meeting of an attractive female undergraduate (Model One) and a female herpetologist (Model Two). In successive scenes of the film, Model One gradually learns to approach and handle several snakes by following Model Two's demonstration of each behavior. As the film progresses, Model One, who was initially fearful, becomes noticeably more confident in handling the snakes and appears to be enjoying the procedure increasingly. While wearing gloves, Model One learns to stroke and pick up a small snake and then repeats this procedure with a larger snake. Next, Model One removes the gloves and repeats these successively more difficult tasks bare-handed. Model One is later shown confidently holding the larger snake. Finally, Model One holds the snake close to her face in an affectionate gesture while it curls itself around her neck, imitating Model Two's example. An accompanying narration verbally describes what the film depicts and also includes information about snakes and their handling. A series of three experiments (Spiegler et al., 1969) has demonstrated the utility of exposure to such a film in reducing persistent avoidance of harmless snakes.

In the third of these experiments, adults from the community-at-large (6 men and 15 women) were recruited by a newspaper advertisement asking for persons who were afraid of snakes and willing to participate in a study of new treatment methods. These subjects were selected by means of a graduated behavioral test. In turn, participants were asked to (1) enter a room containing a caged 2-foot water snake, (2) walk to the cage (a distance of about 15 feet), (3) put on a pair of gloves, (4) remove the lid of the cage and look in, (5) reach into the cage and stroke the snake, (6) pick up the snake, (7) remove the gloves, (8) stroke the snake, and finally (9) hold the snake bare-handed. The subjects were also briefly interviewed and given comparable expectancies about treatment. They were then matched for level of avoidance behavior (as measured by the initial behavioral test) and assigned to one of three treatment groups.

Several subjects in the previous experiments had commented that, although the film seemed to help in overcoming their fear, they became somewhat "anxious" while watching *some* of the scenes. It was reasoned that if the participants were relaxed while viewing the film, its effectiveness would be enhanced. Thus, in the present experiment, subjects in the *film-plus-relaxation* group were taught deep muscle relaxation (similar to that used in systematic desensitization; see Chapter 14) by means of a 50-minute prerecorded tape and then shown the modeling film. A second group was shown the *film* only. A third group was given just the *relaxation* training and, like the film-plus-relaxation group, was instructed to practice relaxation and to use it in future encounters with snakes. All subjects were treated in groups, and the treatments were administered in two sessions, one week apart.

Posttreatment behavioral tests were individually administered after the first treatment session, before and after the second session, and one week after the second session, with a new and substantially larger snake as a test for generalization. The results of these tests are presented in Figure 16–7.

As predicted, the addition of relaxation training to the modeling film substantially enhanced its effectiveness. Subjects in the film-plus-relaxation condition performed significantly better after the first treatment and on all subsequent tests than participants in either

FIGURE 16–7

Mean Number of Behavioral Tests Passed in the Third Experimental Test of Spiegler et al.'s Film as a Function of Treatment Condition

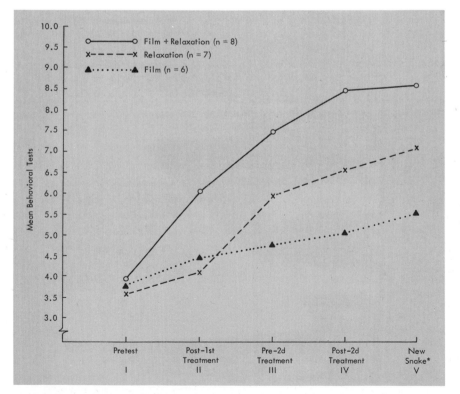

* Two subjects were unable to attend the final assessment (V), thereby reducing the number of subjects in the Film + Relaxation (*n* = 7) and Film (*n* = 5) conditions.
Source: Spiegler, Liebert, McMains, and Fernandez, 1969.

of the other two conditions. As in the first two experiments, there was a significant decrease in avoidance behavior after only a single presentation of the modeling film, and a second exposure to the film served to enhance its effectiveness. Finally, it is important to note that no performance loss resulted from introducing the new and larger snake.

Few demonstrations of the potential therapeutic power of modeling have been more dramatic than an experiment by O'Connor (1969). O'Connor, who was interested in social isolation among preschoolers, identified 13 nursery school children who almost never interacted with their peers. Six of the isolates were arbitrarily chosen for treatment, while the remaining seven served as a control for possible changes over time. The treatment consisted of viewing a brief film (less than 20 minutes in length) on a large TV console.

The film portrayed a sequence of 11 scenes in which children interacted in a nursery school setting. In each of these episodes, a child is shown first observing the interaction of others and then

FIGURE 16–8

Mean Number of Social Interactions Displayed by Children in the Modeling and Control Conditions, before and after the Experimental Sessions

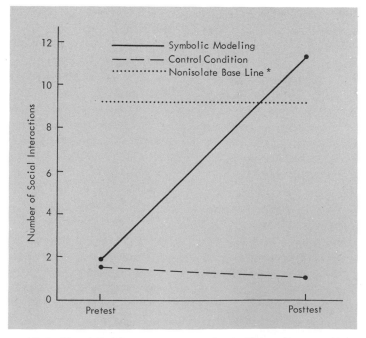

* Note: The dotted line represents the level of interactions manifested by 26 nonisolate children who were observed during the pretest phase of the study.
Source: O'Connor, 1969.

joining in the social activities, with reinforcing consequences ensuing. The other children, for example, offer him play material, talk to him, smile and generally respond in a positive manner to his advances into the activity. The scenes were graduated on a dimension of threat in terms of the vigor of the social activity and the size of the group. The initial scenes involve very calm activities such as sharing a book or toy while two children are seated at a table. In the terminal scenes, as many as six children are shown gleefully tossing play equipment around the room (O'Connor, 1969, p. 18).

Subjects in the control group saw a film of comparable length, but it was about dolphins and thus could not teach any pertinent social lessons.

The effect of this single treatment was such that the previously isolate children were soon engaging in as many or more social interactions as were children who had been nonisolates in the first place (see Figure 16–8). A follow-up at the end of the school year disclosed that five of the six treated children continued to be socially active, while the control children were still rated as extreme isolates by their teachers.

LIABILITIES OF THE BEHAVIORAL STRATEGY

In this section we shall describe four limitations of the behavioral strategy. They are that the behavioral strategy (1) relies too heavily on the concept of learning, to the exclusion of other processes that also have an important influence on personality, (2) extrapolates from laboratory experimentation to complex human behavior without justification, (3) falsely assumes that behavioral personality theory is validated because behavioral personality change techniques work, and (4) places excessive credence in situational tests.

The Behavioral Strategy Relies Too Heavily on the Concept of Learning

The behavioral strategy approaches personality phenomena with the fundamental assumption that *behavior is learned.* While it is certainly useful to think of *some* aspects of personality in terms of learning, it is equally clear that a complete theory of personality will have to explain some of its subject matter in other ways. We have seen, for example, that there is strong evidence for a major hereditary component in certain types of abnormal behavior even when relevant learning opportunities are held constant (see Chapter 7). The behavioral strategy makes little allowance for hereditary influences or for other biologically based individual differences that exist either before or apart from learning processes. It is not merely that a behavioral approach does not use genetic and dispositional notions; the behavioral approach tends to be *anti*dispositional and *anti*genetic and thus may be viewed as narrow and provincial. Levy (1970) has described the liability this way:

> Personality theorists who have adopted a learning approach have defined their domain of interest as "the study of learned behavior." . . . Although this is a perfectly defensible position, it restricts the range of behavioral phenomena that can be studied and the kinds of explanations that can be proposed . . . some possible qualities of behavior commonly associated with personality must be either ignored or inadequately explained as a consequence (p. 433).

The Behavioral Strategy Extrapolates from Laboratory Experimentation without Justification

The behavioral strategy differs markedly from the other three strategies in its research emphasis. Correlational and case studies are rare; the favored method is the controlled laboratory experiment. As was noted in Chapter 2, this research method is most conducive to drawing conclusions regarding cause and effect relationships. Despite the definite assets of the experimental method, critics often point out that the precision and rigor claimed for experimental research which is used to support a behavioral view of personality is more illusory than real. The error in the behaviorist's argument lies not in how well his research is designed but in the way in which he extrapolates or generalizes from its findings.

Consider the example of classical conditioning. There is no doubt that the phenomenon Pavlov originally observed in dogs is real. It can be repeated in almost any laboratory, and, what is more, much is known about the variables that "control" such conditioning. But does this enormous body of research with subhuman animals in specially contrived laboratory arrangements truly parallel issues in personality, such as the "conditioning" of attitudes? In fact, many patterns are not parallel. Timing, for example, which is critical in the pairing of the CS and UCS when conditioning dogs or rats (seconds, and sometimes fractions of seconds, may determine whether conditioning occurs) is less essential in humans, who are capable of symbolically "bridging the gap" between two events which are separated in time. So, too, classical conditioning of laboratory animals almost always displays a gradual acquisition curve. Is this analogous to "conditioned" emotional reactions in humans (e.g., intense fear) which are based on a single exposure to a noxious stimulus? Critics argue that classical conditioning in humans is quite different from that in lower species. There may be a variety of emotional, cognitive, and dispositional components which are simply ignored by referring to highly controlled and often artificial experimental situations which gloss over the complexities of real life.

Even when human subjects are studied, the artificiality of most experiments may artifactually produce simple learning responses. The laboratory situation, in effect, "decorticates" the subject in that it restricts his alternatives so as to make more complex responses impossible. Even if an adult *can* learn prejudicial responses because a name or a word is paired repeatedly in the laboratory with some discrete unpleasant event (e.g., an electric shock or a noxious sound or word), that hardly means that most—or even any—real-life prejudices are learned this way. Demonstrations that any particular set of learning principles accounts for complex human behavior require more than analogies to laboratory findings occurring under highly restricted conditions.

The Behavioral Strategy Falsely Assumes That Its Theory Is Validated Because Behavior Therapy Is Effective

Behaviorally oriented psychologists take great pride in the success of behavior therapy techniques and often claim or imply that these successes demonstrate the validity of behavioral personality theory. The logic of this assumption can be questioned. The situation is similar to that of a person who takes aspirin for a headache; generally, the medicine will relieve the pain and thus "cure" the ailment. Still, the fact that introducing acetylsalicylic acid (aspirin) into the bloodstream eliminated the discomfort hardly means that the pain was caused by a lack of acetylsalicylic acid in the first place. Likewise, the fact that a learning–behaviorally based treatment eliminates a psychological problem does not logically imply that the problem was caused by the reverse learning process. Simply because an unrealistic fear can be eliminated by counterconditioning does not prove that it was *acquired* through conditioning.

Some critics have argued that no theory of learning (and certainly no single theory) underlies behavioral change techniques; rather, behavior therapists can be said to have achieved a "nontheoretical amalgamation of pragmatic principles" (Weitzman, 1967, p. 303) from which their procedures derive strength. Weitzman suggests, for example, that the effectiveness of systematic desensitization can be explained in terms of a variety of nonbehavioral theories, such as psychoanalysis.

This liability takes on even greater force when one observes that behavioral theories of personality are not responsible for behavioral change techniques, inasmuch as the change techniques antedate contemporary behavioral approaches by many years. Breger and McGaugh (1966), two strong critics of the entire behavioral movement, write:

> . . . it is clear that the techniques in question were in existence long before . . . learning theory. Pfaundler described an apparatus for treating enuresis in 1904 that greatly resembled Mowrer's con-

ditioning technique [described on pages 331–32 of this book], and Nye, a pediatrician, outlined a proposed method for treating enuresis in 1830 that included all of the elements of "conditioning" therapy. . . . Circus animal trainers used "operant" and "shaping" techniques for centuries. [Therefore] . . . it is not true that learning theory has been necessary or even very important in *developing* the specific techniques in question (p. 171).

The Behavioral Strategy Places Excessive Credence in Situational Tests

Behavioral psychologists often use situational tests in their assessment of personality. An individual's personality (behavior) is assessed by observing him in situations which are similar to the ones which are of interest. For instance, if we were concerned with learning how a person responds to failure, we might place him in several situations in which he fails at some task and observe and measure his reactions. (This tact should be contrasted with such personality assessment procedures as having the subject respond to written questions about his reactions to failure, measuring his need to achieve and avoid failure by having him write stories in response to TAT cards, and so on.) Situational tests make sense "intuitively," inasmuch as it would seem that measuring what a person actually does is an "obvious" way of determining what he will do. Partially because situational tests often have high face validity (i.e., they look like they measure what is being tested for), there has been little systematic evaluation of such techniques of personality assessment.

Perhaps the most extensive development and use of situational tests occurred during World War II, when the American and British armed forces were faced with the task of selecting suitable officer candidates (Morris, 1949) and men for military intelligence assignments (OSS Assessment Staff, 1948). In general, the reliability of these tests was not very high (e.g., the ratings given men at different "assessment stations" were not consistent). Neither was the predictive validity of the situational tests, their ability to predict those candidates who subsequently performed well on assignments, as high as had been hoped (Anastasi, 1968; Morris, 1949). The disappointing performance of situational tests in selecting personnel in the wartime situation is no doubt partially attributable to factors which were independent of the techniques themselves, such as the less than ideal circumstances of having to develop mass assessment procedures very quickly. On the other hand, some of the failure may be due to the general problems which inhere in situational tests.

One difficulty is that the act of observation by psychologists and the stresses of being "on the spot" to perform in a test situation alter the behavior of the assessee to an unknown degree. Anyone who has "flubbed" a demonstration of something he knows how to do very well just because it *was* a demonstration understands how this can happen. At the other extreme, some people may perform more competently or diligently than they are likely to in the actual situation because they know they are being assessed or merely watched. The teacher who enthusiastically encourages her first-grade students while the school principal is sitting at a desk in the back of her room shows that she *can* put forth an impressive effort under observation; whether she *will* do so as conscientiously when only the children are present cannot be judged on that basis alone.

A related problem that arises with situational tests is that the "role-playing" component which many of them have may involve somewhat different abilities than are called for in the corresponding life situations. For example, the man who is best able to *pretend* that he is a strong leader under test conditions may not prove to be the most effective leader in the field when he is faced with real, rather than fictitious, enemies.

Finally, situational tests may not be "lifelike" enough to have adequate predictive validity. A person who demonstrates that he is able to pick up a harmless snake in the laboratory and reports that he is no longer afraid of snakes may still show considerable fear if he unexpectedly encounters a reptile on a solitary country lane. Indeed, such a possibility should be considered all the more likely by the behavioral strategy because of its emphasis on situation specificity.

References

Allport, G. W. *Personality: A psychological interpretation*. New York: Holt, 1937.

Allport, G. W. *Personality and social encounter: Selected essays*. Boston: Beacon Press, 1960.

Allport, G. W. *Pattern and growth in personality*. New York: Holt, Rinehart & Winston, 1961.

Allport, G. W. *Letters from Jenny*. New York: Harcourt, Brace & World, 1965.

Allport, G. W. Traits revisited. *American Psychologist,* 1966, **21,** 1–10.

Allport, G. W., & Allport, F. H. *The A–S reaction study*. Boston: Houghton Mifflin, 1928.

American Psychological Association. Special issue: Testing and public policy. *American Psychologist,* 1965, **20,** 857–993.

Anastasi, A. *Psychological testing*. (3d ed.) New York: Macmillan, 1968.

Asch, S. E. Studies of independence and conformity: A minority of one against a unanimous majority. *Psychological Monographs,* 1956, **70** (9, Whole No. 416).

Aserinsky, E., & Kleitman, N. Regularly occurring periods of eye motility, and concomitant phenomena, during sleep. *Science,* 1953, **118,** 273–74.

Aserinsky, E., & Kleitman, N. Two types of ocular motility occurring in sleep. *Journal of Applied Physiology,* 1955, **8,** 1–10.

Ashem, B. The treatment of a disaster phobia by systematic desensitization. *Behaviour Research and Therapy,* 1963, **1,** 81–84.

Atkinson, J. W. (Ed.) *Motives in fantasy, action, and society*. Princeton, N.J.: Van Nostrand, 1958.

Atkinson, J. W., & McClelland, D. C.   The projective expression of needs, II. The effect of different intensities of the hunger drive on thematic apperception. *Journal of Experimental Psychology,* 1948, **38,** 643–58.

Ayllon, T.   Some behavioral problems associated with eating in chronic schizophrenic patients. In L. P. Ullmann & L. Krasner (Eds.), *Case studies in behavior modification.* New York: Holt, Rinehart & Winston, 1965. Pp. 73–77.

Baer, D. M.   A case for the selective reinforcement of punishment. In C. Neuringer & J. L. Michael (Eds.), *Behavior modification in clinical psychology.* New York: Appleton-Century-Crofts, 1970. Pp. 243–49.

Bandura, A.   Influence of models' reinforcement contingencies on the acquisition of imitative responses. *Journal of Personality and Social Psychology,* 1965, **1,** 589–95.

Bandura, A.   *Principles of behavior modification.* New York: Holt, Rinehart & Winston, 1969.

Bandura, A., Grusec, J. E., & Menlove, F. L.   Vicarious extinction of avoidance behavior through symbolic modeling. *Journal of Personality and Social Psychology,* 1967, **5,** 16–22.

Bandura, A., & Harris, M. B.   Modification of syntactic style. *Journal of Experimental Child Psychology,* 1966, **4,** 341–52.

Bandura, A., & McDonald, F. J.   The influence of social reinforcement and the behavior of models in shaping children's moral judgments. *Journal of Abnormal and Social Psychology,* 1963, **67,** 274–81.

Bandura, A., & Menlove, F. L.   Factors determining vicarious extinction of avoidance behavior through symbolic modeling. *Journal of Personality and Social Psychology,* 1968, **8,** 99–108.

Bandura, A., & Mischel, W.   Modification of self-imposed delay of reward through exposure to live and symbolic models. *Journal of Personality and Social Psychology,* 1965, **2,** 698–705.

Bandura, A., Ross, D., & Ross, S.   Transmission of aggression through imitation of aggressive models. *Journal of Abnormal and Social Psychology,* 1961, **63,** 575–82.

Bandura, A., Ross, D., & Ross, S.   Imitation of film-mediated aggressive models. *Journal of Abnormal and Social Psychology,* 1963, **66,** 3–11.

Bandura, A., & Walters, R. H.   *Social learning and personality development.* New York: Holt, Rinehart & Winston, 1963.

Bergin, A. E.   Some implications of psychotherapy research for therapeutic practice. *Journal of Abnormal Psychology,* 1966, **71,** 235–46.

Berne, E.   *Transactional analysis in psychotherapy.* New York: Grove Press, 1961.

Berne, E.   *Games people play.* New York: Grove Press, 1964.

Bieri, J.   Changes in interpersonal perceptions following social interaction. *Journal of Abnormal and Social Psychology,* 1953, **48,** 61–66.

Birney, R. C.   Research on the achievement motive. In E. F. Borgatta &

W. W. Lambert (Eds.), *Handbook of personality theory and research.* Chicago: Rand McNally, 1968. Pp. 857–89.

Birns, B.   Individual differences in human neonates' responses to stimulation. *Child Development,* 1965, **36,** 249–56.

Blake, R., Rosenbaum, M., & Duryea, R. A.   Gift-giving as a function of group standards. *Human Relations,* 1955, **8,** 61–73.

Block, J.   *The challenge of response sets.* New York: Appleton-Century-Crofts, 1965.

Blum, G. S.   A study of the psychoanalytic theory of psychosexual development. *Genetic Psychological Monographs,* 1949, **39,** 3–99.

Blum, G. S.   *The Blacky Pictures: A technique for the exploration of personality dynamics.* New York: Psychological Corporation, 1950.

Blum, G. S., & Miller, D. R.   Exploring the psychoanalytic theory of oral character. *Journal of Personality,* 1952, **20,** 287–304.

Bond, I. K., & Hutchison, H. C.   Application of reciprocal inhibition therapy to exhibitionism. *Canadian Medical Association Journal,* 1960, **83,** 23–25.

Breger, L., & McGaugh, J. L.   Learning theory and behavior therapy: A reply to Rachman and Eysenck. *Psychological Bulletin,* 1966, **65,** 170–173.

Brenner, C.   *An elementary textbook of psychoanalysis.* Garden City, N.Y.: Doubleday Anchor Books, 1957.

Brigham, T. A., Graubard, P. S., & Stans, A.   Analysis of the effects of sequential reinforcement contingencies on aspects of composition. *Journal of Applied Behavior Analysis,* 1972, **5,** 421–29.

Brill, A. A.   *Lectures on psychoanalytic psychiatry.* New York: Vintage Books, 1955.

Brown, N. O.   *Life against death.* New York: Random House, 1959.

Brown, R.   *Social psychology.* New York: Free Press, 1965.

Bryan, J. H., & Test, M. A.   Models and helping: Naturalistic studies in aiding behavior. *Journal of Personality and Social Psychology,* 1967, **6,** 400–407.

Burnham, J. C.   Historical background for the study of personality. In E. F. Borgatta & W. W. Lambert (Eds.), *Handbook of personality theory and research.* Chicago: Rand McNally, 1968. Pp. 3–81.

Buros, O. K. (Ed.)   *The sixth mental measurements yearbook.* Highland Park, N.J.: Gryphon Press, 1965.

Campbell, D. T., & Fiske, D. W.   Convergent and discriminant validation by the multitrait-multimethod matrix. *Psychological Bulletin,* 1959, **56,** 81–105.

Cattell, R. B.   *Personality.* New York: McGraw-Hill, 1950.

Cattell, R. B.   *Personality and motivation structure and measurement.* Yonkers, N.Y.: New World Book, 1957.

Cattell, R. B.   *The scientific analysis of personality.* Baltimore: Penguin Books, 1965.

Cattell, R. B., & Warburton, F. W.   *Objective personality and motivation tests: A theoretical introduction and practical compendium.* Urbana: University of Illinois Press, 1967.

Chaffee, S. H., & McLeod, J. M.   Adolescents, parents, and television violence. In G. A. Comstock (Chm.), The early window: The role of television in childhood. Symposium presented at the meeting of the American Psychological Association, Washington, D.C., September 1971.

Chalmers, D. K., Horne, W. C., & Rosenbaum, M. E.   Social agreement and the learning of matching behavior. *Journal of Abnormal and Social Psychology,* 1963, **66,** 556–61.

Cheyne, J. A.   Effects of imitation of different reinforcement combinations to a model. *Journal of Experimental Child Psychology,* 1971, **12,** 258–69.

Chodorkoff, B.   Self-perception, perceptual defense, and adjustment. *Journal of Abnormal and Social Psychology,* 1954, **49,** 508–12.

Chomsky, N.   Review of B. F. Skinner's *Verbal Behavior. Language,* 1959, **35,** 26–58.

Clark, D. F.   The treatment of a monosymptomatic phobia by systematic desensitization. *Behaviour Research and Therapy,* 1963, **1,** 63–68.

Cowden, R. C., & Ford, L. I.   Systematic desensitization with phobic schizophrenics. *American Journal of Psychiatry,* 1962, **119,** 241–45.

Cronbach, L. J.   Statistical methods applied to Rorschach scores: A review. *Psychological Bulletin,* 1949, **46,** 393–429.

Cronbach, L. J.   Review of the California Psychological Inventory. In O. K. Buros (Ed.), *Fifth mental measurements yearbook.* Highland Park, N.J.: Gryphon Press, 1959. Pp. 97–99.

Crowne, D. P., & Marlowe, D.   A new scale of social desirability independent of psychopathology. *Journal of Consulting Psychology,* 1960, **24,** 349–54.

Crowne, D. P., & Marlowe, D.   *The approval motive: Studies in evaluative dependence.* New York: Wiley, 1964.

Darley, J. M., & Latané, B.   Bystander intervention in emergencies: Diffusion of responsibility. *Journal of Personality and Social Psychology,* 1968, **8,** 377–83.

Davidson, E. S., & Liebert, R. M.   Effects of prior commitment on children's evaluation and imitation of a peer model's perceptual judgments. *Perceptual and Motor Skills,* 1972, **35,** 825–26.

Davison, G. C.   Case report: Elimination of a sadistic fantasy by a client-controlled counter-conditioning technique. *Journal of Abnormal Psychology,* 1968, **73,** 84–90.

Davison, G. C., & Neale, J. M.   *Abnormal psychology: An experimental-clinical approach.* New York: Wiley, 1974.

Davison, G. C., & Wilson, G. T.   Processes of fear-reduction in systematic desensitization: Cognitive and social reinforcement factors in humans. *Behavior Therapy,* 1973, **4,** 1–21.

Dekker, E., & Groen, J. Reproducible psychogenic attacks of asthma: A laboratory study. *Journal of Psychosomatic Research,* 1956, **1,** 58–67.

Dekker, E., Pelser, H. E., & Groen, J. Conditioning as a cause of asthmatic attacks. *Journal of Psychosomatic Research,* 1957, **2,** 97–108.

Dement, W. C. An essay on dreams: The role of physiology in understanding their nature. In *New directions in psychology.* Vol. 2. New York: Holt, Rinehart & Winston, 1965. Pp. 135–257.

Dement, W. C., & Kleitman, N. The relation of the eye movements during sleep to dream activity: An objective method for the study of dreaming. *Journal of Experimental Psychology,* 1957, **53,** 339–46.

Dement, W. C., & Wolpert, E. The relation of eye movements, body motility, and external stimuli to dream content. *Journal of Experimental Psychology,* 1958, **55,** 543–53.

D'Zurilla, T. Recall efficiency and mediating cognitive events in "experimental repression." *Journal of Personality and Social Psychology,* 1965, **37,** 253–56.

Edwards, A. L. *Manual for Edwards Personal Preference Schedule.* New York: Psychological Corporation, 1953. (a)

Edwards, A. L. The relationship between the judged desirability of a trait and the probability that the trait will be endorsed. *Journal of Applied Psychology,* 1953, **37,** 90–93. (b)

Edwards, A. L. *The social desirability variable in personality research.* New York: Dryden, 1957.

Edwards, A. L. *The measurement of personality traits by scales and inventories.* New York: Holt, Rinehart & Winston, 1970.

Edwards, A. L., & Abbott, R. D. Measurement of personality traits: theory and technique. In P. H. Mussen & M. R. Rosenzweig (Eds.), *Annual Review of Psychology.* Vol. 24. Palo Alto, Calif.: Annual Reviews, 1973. Pp. 241–78.

Engstrom, W. C., & Power, M. E. A revision of the study of values for use in magazine readership research. *Journal of Applied Psychology,* 1959, **43,** 74–78.

Erikson, E. H. The dream specimen of psychoanalysis. *Journal of the American Psychoanalytic Association,* 1954, **2,** 5–56.

Erikson, E. H. *Childhood and society.* New York: Norton, 1963.

Eron, L. Relationship of TV viewing habits and aggressive behavior in children. *Journal of Abnormal and Social Psychology,* 1963, **67,** 193–96.

Estes, W. K. An experimental study of punishment. *Psychological Monographs,* 1944, **57** (3, Whole No. 263).

Eysenck, H. J. *Dimensions of personality.* London: Routledge & Kegan Paul, 1948.

Eysenck, H. J. The effects of psychotherapy: An evaluation. *Journal of Consulting Psychology,* 1952, **16,** 319–24. (a)

Eysenck, H. J. *The scientific study of personality.* London: Routledge & Kegan Paul, 1952. (b)

Eysenck, H. J.   The effects of psychotherapy. In H. J. Eysenck (Ed.), *Handbook of abnormal psychology.* New York: Basic Books, 1961. Pp. 697–725.

Eysenck, H. J.   *The biological basis of personality.* Springfield, Ill.: Charles C Thomas, 1967.

Feldman, F.   Results of psychoanalysis in clinic case assignments. *Journal of the American Psychoanalytic Association,* 1968, **16,** 274–300.

Ferster, C. B., & Skinner, B. F.   *Schedules of reinforcement.* New York: Appleton-Century-Crofts, 1957.

Fiedler, F. E.   A comparison of therapeutic relationships in psychoanalytic, non-directive, and Adlerian therapy. *Journal of Consulting Psychology,* 1950, **14,** 436–45.

Fisher, C., Gross, J., & Zuch, J.   Cycle of penile erection synchronous with dreaming (REM) sleep. *Archives of General Psychiatry,* 1965, **12,** 29–45.

Fiske, D. W.   The subject reacts to tests. *American Psychologist,* 1967, **22,** 287–96.

Fiske, D. W.   *Measuring the concepts of personality.* Chicago: Aldine, 1971.

Fiske, D. W., & Pearson, P. H.   Theory and techniques of personality measurement. *Annual Review of Psychology,* Vol. 21. Palo Alto, Calif.: Annual Reviews, 1970. Pp. 49–86.

Fjeld, S. P., & Landfield, A. W.   Personal construct consistency. *Psychological Reports,* 1961, **8,** 127–29.

Fodor, J. A.   How to learn to talk: Some simple ways. In F. Smith & G. A. Miller (Eds.), *The genesis of language.* Cambridge: MIT Press, 1966. Pp. 105–28.

Fodor, N.   *The search for the beloved.* New York: Hermitage, 1949.

Foulkes, D.   *The psychology of sleep.* New York: Scribner, 1966.

Fowler, R. L., & Kimmel, H. D.   Operant conditioning of the G. S. R. *Journal of Experimental Psychology,* 1962, **63,** 563–67.

Fox, L.   Effecting the use of efficient study habits. In R. Ulrich, T. Stachnik, & J. Mabry (Eds.), *Control of human behavior.* Glenview, Ill.: Scott Foresman, 1966.

Freedman, D. G., & Keller, B.   Inheritance of behavior in infants. *Science,* 1963, **140,** 196–98.

French, T., & Fromm, Erika.   *Dream interpretation.* New York: Basic Books, 1964.

Freud, S.   *Psychopathology of everyday life.* A. A. Brill (Trans.). New York: New American Library, 1951.

Freud, S.   *The analysis of a phobia in a five-year old boy.* Vol. 10. *The standard edition of the complete psychological works of Sigmund Freud.* J. Strachey (Trans. and Ed.). London: Hogarth Press, 1957.

Freud, S.   *Jokes and their relation to the unconscious.* Vol. 8. *The standard edition of the complete psychological works of Sigmund Freud.* J. Strachey (Trans. and Ed.). New York: Norton, 1960.

Freud, S.   *The interpretation of dreams.* J. Strachey (Trans. and Ed.). New York: Science Editions, 1961.

Freud, S.   *Introductory lectures on psycho-analysis.* Vol. 15. *The standard edition of the complete psychological works of Sigmund Freud.* J. Strachey (Trans. and Ed.). London: Hogarth Press, 1963.

Freud, S.   *New introductory lectures on psychoanalysis.* New York: Norton, 1965.

Freund, K. A.   A laboratory method for diagnosing predominance of homo- or hetero-erotic interest in the male. *Behaviour Research and Therapy,* 1963, **1,** 85–93.

Freund, K. A.   Diagnosing heterosexual pedophilia by means of a test for sexual interest. *Behaviour Research and Therapy,* 1965, **3,** 229–34.

Freund, K. A.   Diagnosing homo- or heterosexuality and erotic age preference by means of a psychophysiological test. *Behaviour Research and Therapy,* 1967, **5,** 209–28.

Fromm, E.   *The art of loving.* New York: Bantam Books, 1963.

Gallagher, J. J.   The problem of escaping clients in non-directive counseling. In W. U. Snyder (Ed.), *Group report of a program of research in psychotherapy.* Psychotherapy Research Group, Pennsylvania State University, 1953. Pp. 21–38.

Geer, J. H.   Fear and autonomic arousal. *Journal of Abnormal Psychology,* 1966, 71, 253–55.

Geer, J. H.   A test of the classical conditioning model of emotion: The use of nonpainful aversive stimuli as unconditioned stimuli in a conditioning procedure. *Journal of Personality and Social Psychology,* 1968, **10,** 148–56.

Gerbner, G.   The violence profile: Some indicators of the trends in and the symbolic structure of network television drama 1967–1971. Unpublished manuscript, The Annenberg School of Communications, University of Pennsylvania, 1972. (a)

Gerbner, G.   Violence in television drama: Trends and symbolic functions. In G. A. Comstock & E. A. Rubinstein (Eds.), *Television and social behavior. Vol. 1. Media content and control.* Washington, D.C.: U.S. Government Printing Office, 1972. Pp. 28–187. (b)

Glover, E.   *On the early development of mind.* New York: Hillary, 1956.

Goldfried, M. R., & Merbaum, M. (Eds.)   *Behavior change through self-control.* New York: Holt, Rinehart & Winston, 1973.

Gollob, H. F., & Levine, J.   Distraction as a factor in the enjoyment of aggressive humor. *Journal of Personality and Social Psychology,* 1967, **5,** 368–72.

Gottesman, I. I.   Heritability of personality. *Psychological Monographs,* 1963, **77,** (9, Whole No. 572).

Gough, H. G.   An additional study of food aversions. *Journal of Abnormal and Social Psychology,* 1946, **41,** 86–88.

Gough, H. G.   *California Psychological Inventory.* Palo Alto: Consulting Psychologists Press, 1956.

Grieser, C., Greenberg, R., & Harrison, R. H.   The adaptive function of sleep: The differential effects of sleep and dreaming on recall. *Journal of Abnormal Psychology,* 1972, **80,** 280–86.

Guilford, J. P.   *Personality.* New York: McGraw-Hill, 1959.

Hall, C. S.   *A primer of Freudian psychology.* New York: New American Library, 1955.

Hall, C. S., & Van de Castle, R. L.   An empirical investigation of the castration complex in dreams. *Journal of Personality,* 1963, **33,** 20–29.

Hall, R. V., Lund, D., & Jackson, D.   Effects of teacher attention on study behavior. *Journal of Applied Behavior Analysis,* 1968, **1,** 1–12.

Hanley, C.   Social desirability and responses to items from three MMPI scales: D, Sc, and K. *Journal of Applied Psychology,* 1956, **40,** 324–28.

Hanratty, M. A., Liebert, R. M., Morris, L. W., & Fernandez, L.E.   Imitation of film-mediated aggression against live and inanimate victims. *Proceedings of the 77th Annual Convention of the American Psychological Association,* 1969, **4,** 457–58.

Hanratty, M. A., O'Neal, E., & Sulzer, J. L.   The effect of frustration upon imitation of aggression. *Journal of Personality and Social Psychology,* 1972, **21,** 30–34.

Hathaway, S. R., & McKinley, J. C.   *Minnesota Multiphasic Personality Inventory.* Minneapolis: University of Minnesota Press, 1942.

Hebb, D. O.   *A textbook of psychology.* (2d ed.) Philadelphia: Saunders, 1966.

Henderson, G.   Role models for lower class Negro boys. *Personnel and Guidance Journal,* 1967, **46,** 6–10.

Henson, D. E., & Rubin, H. B.   Voluntary control of eroticism. *Journal of Applied Behavior Analysis,* 1971, **4,** 37–44.

Heston, L. L.   Psychiatric disorders in foster home reared children of schizophrenic mothers. *British Journal of Psychiatry,* 1966, **112,** 819–25.

Heston, L. L., & Denney, D.   Interactions between early life experience and biological factors in schizophrenia. *Journal of Psychiatric Research,* 1968, **6,** 363–76.

Hicks, D.   Imitation and retention of film-mediated aggressive peer and adult models. *Journal of Personality and Social Psychology,* 1965, **2,** 97–100.

Hicks, D.   Short and long-term retention of affectively varied modeled behavior. *Psychonomic Science,* 1968, **11,** 369–70.

Holmes, D. S.   Conscious self-appraisal of achievement motivation: The self-peer rank method revisited. *Journal of Consulting and Clinical Psychology,* 1971, **36,** 23–26.

Holmes, D. S. Repression or interference? A further investigation. *Journal of Personality and Social Psychology,* 1972, **22,** 163–70.

Holmes, D. S., & Schallow, J. Reduced recall after ego threat: Repression or response competition? *Journal of Personality and Social Psychology,* 1969, **13,** 145–52.

Holmes, D. S., & Tyler, J. D. Direct versus projective measurement of achievement motivation. *Journal of Consulting and Clinical Psychology,* 1968, **32,** 712–17.

Hornstein, H. A., Fisch, E., & Holmes, M. Influence of a model's feeling about his behavior and his relevance as a comparison other on observers' helping behavior. *Journal of Personality and Social Psychology,* 1968, **10,** 222–26.

Hyman, R. *The nature of psychological inquiry.* Englewood Cliffs, N.J.: Prentice-Hall, 1964.

Isaacs, W., Thomas, J., & Goldiamond, I. Application of operant conditioning to reinstate verbal behavior in psychotics. *Journal of Speech and Hearing Disorders,* 1960, **25,** 8–12.

Iwawaki, S., & Zax, M. Personality dimensions and extreme response tendency. *Psychological Reports,* 1969, **27,** 359–63.

Jackson, D. D. (Ed.) *The etiology of schizophrenia.* New York: Basic Books, 1960.

Jackson, D. N., & Messick, S. Content and style in personality assessment. *Psychological Bulletin,* 1958, **55,** 243–52.

Johnson, G. B. Penis envy or pencil needing? *Psychological Reports,* 1966, **19,** 758.

Jones, M. C. The elimination of children's fear. *Journal of Experimental Psychology,* 1924, **7,** 382–90. (a)

Jones, M. C. A laboratory study of fear: The case of Peter. *Pedagogical Seminar,* 1924, **31,** 308–15. (b)

Katkin, E. S., & Murray, E. N. Instrumental conditioning of autonomically mediated behavior: Theoretical and methodological issues. *Psychological Bulletin,* 1968, **70,** 52–68.

Kelly, G. A. *The psychology of personal constructs.* New York: Norton, 1955.

Kelly, G. A. Man's construction of his alternatives. In G. Lindzey (Ed.), *Assessment of human motives.* New York: Grove Press, 1960.

Kelly, G. A. *A theory of personality.* New York: Norton, 1963.

Kelly, G. A. A brief introduction to personal construct theory. In D. Bannister (Ed.), *Perspectives in personal construct theory.* New York: Academic Press, 1970. Pp. 1–29.

Kimble, G. A. *Hilgard and Marquis' conditioning and learning.* (2d ed.) New York: Appleton-Century-Crofts, 1961.

Kimmel, H. D. Instrumental conditioning of autonomically mediated behavior. *Psychological Bulletin,* 1967, **67,** 337–45.

Kimmel, E., & Kimmel, H. D.   Replication of operant conditioning of the G. S. R. *Journal of Experimental Psychology,* 1963, **65,** 212–13.

Kleinmuntz, B.   *Personality measurement: An introduction.* Homewood, Ill.: Dorsey Press, 1967.

Kliebhan, J. M.   *The effects of goal-setting and modeling on the performance of retarded adolescents in an occupational workshop.* (Doctoral dissertation, University of Illinois.) Ann Arbor, Mich.: University Microfilms, 1966, No. 66–12.

Kliebhan, J. M.   Effects of goal-setting and modeling on job performance of retarded adolescents. *American Journal of Mental Deficiency,* 1967, **72,** 220–26.

Kline, P.   *Fact and fantasy in Freudian theory.* London: Methuen, 1972.

Klopfer, B., & Davidson, H. H.   *The Rorschach technique: An introductory manual.* New York: Harcourt, Brace & World, 1962.

Kretschmer, E.   *Physique and character: An investigation of the nature of constitution and of the theory of temperament.* W. J. H. Sprott (Trans.) . New York: Harcourt, 1926.

Krumboltz, J. D., & Schroeder, W. W.   Promoting career planning through reinforcement. *Personnel and Guidance Journal,* 1965, **44,** 19–26.

Krumboltz, J. D., & Thoresen, C. E.   The effect of behavioral counseling in group and individual settings on information seeking behavior. *Journal of Counseling Psychology,* 1964, **11,** 324–33.

Krumboltz, J. D., & Thoresen, C. E. (Eds.)   *Behavioral counseling: Cases and techniques.* New York: Rinehart & Winston, 1969.

Krumboltz, J. D., Varenhorst, B. B., & Thoresen, C. E.   Nonverbal factors in the effectiveness of models in counseling. *Journal of Counseling Psychology,* 1967, **14,** 412–18.

Lavin, N. I., Thorpe, J. G., Barker, J. C., Blakemore, C. B., & Conway, C. G.   Behavior therapy in a case of transvestism. *Journal of Nervous and Mental Disease,* 1961, **133,** 346–53.

Laws, D. R., & Rubin, H. B.   Instructional control of an autonomic sexual response. *Journal of Applied Behavior Analysis,* 1969, **2,** 93–99.

Lazarus, A. A.   Group therapy of phobic disorders by systematic desensitization. *Journal of Abnormal and Social Psychology,* 1961, **63,** 504.

Lazarus, A. A.   The treatment of chronic frigidity by systematic desensitization. *Journal of Nervous and Mental Disease,* 1963, **136,** 272.

Lazarus, A. A., & Abramovitz, A.   The use of "emotive imagery" in the treatment of children's phobias. *Journal of Mental Science,* 1962, **108,** 191.

Lefkowitz, M. M., Eron, L. D., Walder, L. O., & Huesmann, L. R.   Television violence and child aggression: A follow-up study. In G. A. Comstock & E. A. Rubinstein (Eds.) , *Television and social behavior.* Vol. 3. *Television and adolescent aggressiveness.* Washington, D.C.: U.S. Government Printing Office, 1972. Pp. 35–135.

Lessler, K. Cultural and Freudian dimensions of sexual symbols. *Journal of Consulting Psychology,* 1964, **28,** 46–53.

Levy, L. H. *Conceptions of personality: Theories and research.* New York: Random House, 1970.

Liebert, D. E., Swenson, S. A., & Liebert, R. M. Risk taken by the opponent and experience of subject as determinants of imitation in a competitive situation. *Perceptual and Motor Skills,* 1971, **32,** 719–22.

Liebert, R. M. Television and social learning: Some relationships between viewing violence and behaving aggressively. In J. P. Murray, E. A. Rubinstein, & G. A. Comstock (Eds.), *Television and social behavior.* Vol. 2. *Television and social learning.* Washington, D.C.: U.S. Government Printing Office, 1972. Pp. 1–34.

Liebert, R. M. Observational learning: Some social applications. In P. J. Elich (Ed.) *The fourth western symposium on learning.* Bellingham, Washington: Western Washington State College, 1973, 59–73.

Liebert, R. M., & Allen, M. K. Effects of a model's experience on children's imitation. *Psychonomic Science,* 1969, **14,** 198.

Liebert, R. M., & Baron, R. A. Some immediate effects of televised violence on children's behavior. *Developmental Psychology,* 1972, **6,** 469–75.

Liebert, R. M., & Fernandez, L. E. Vicarious reward and task complexity as determinants of imitative learning. *Psychological Reports,* 1969, **25,** 531–34.

Liebert, R. M., & Fernandez, L. E. Effects of vicarious consequences on imitative performance. *Child Development,* 1970, 41, 847–52. (a)

Liebert, R. M., & Fernandez, L. E. Imitation as a function of vicarious and direct reward. *Developmental Psychology,* 1970, **2,** 230–32. (b)

Liebert, R. M., Neale, J. M., & Davidson, E. S. *The early window: Effects of television on children and youth.* New York: Pergamon Press, 1973.

Liebert, R. M., Odom, R. D., Hill, J. H., & Huff, R. L. The effects of age and rule familiarity on the production of modeled language constructions. *Developmental Psychology,* 1969, **1,** 108–12.

Liebert, R. M., & Ora, J. P. Children's adoption of self-reward patterns: Incentive level and method of transmission. *Child Development,* 1968, **39,** 537–44.

Liebert, R. M., & Poulos, R. W. Eliciting the norm of giving: Effects of modeling and the presence of a witness on children's sharing behavior. *Proceedings of the 79th Annual Convention of the American Psychological Association,* 1971, **6,** 345–46.

Liebert, R. M., Sobol, M. P., & Copemann, C. D. Effects of vicarious consequences and race of model upon imitative performance. *Developmental Psychology,* 1972, **6,** 453–56.

Liebert, R. M., & Swenson, S. A. Abstraction, inference, and the process of imitative learning. *Developmental Psychology,* 1971, **5,** 500–504. (a)

Liebert, R. M., & Swenson, S. A.   Association and abstraction as mechanisms of imitative learning. *Developmental Psychology,* 1971, **4**, 289–94. (b)

Lindsley, O. R.   An experiment with parents handling behavior at home. *Johnstone Bulletin* (Johnstone Training Center, Bordentown, N.J.), 1966, **9**, 27–36.

Lindzey, G., & Herman, P. S.   Thematic Apperception Test: A note on reliability and situational validity. *Journal of Projective Techniques,* 1955, **19**, 36–42.

Lorand, S.   *Technique of psychoanalytic therapy.* New York: International Universities Press, 1946.

Lovaas, O. I.   Some studies on the treatment of childhood schizophrenia. In J. Schlein (Ed.), *Research in psychotherapy.* Washington, D.C.: American Psychological Association, 1968. Pp. 103–21.

Lovaas, O. I., Freitas, L., Nelson, K., & Whalen, C.   The establishment of imitation and its use for the development of complex behavior in schizophrenic children. *Behaviour Research and Therapy,* 1967, **5**, 171–81.

Lundin, R. W.   *Personality.* New York: Macmillan, 1961.

Lundy, R. M.   Changes in interpersonal perception associated with group-therapy. Unpublished master's thesis, Ohio State University, 1952.

MacCorquodale, K., & Meehl, P. E.   On a distinction between hypothetical constructs and intervening variables. *Psychological Review,* 1948, **55**, 95–107.

Marks, I. M., & Gelder, M. G.   Transvestism and fetishism: Clinical and psychological changes during faradic aversion. *British Journal of Psychology,* 1967, **113**, 711–29.

Marks, P. A., & Seeman, W.   *An atlas for use with the MMPI: Actuarial description of abnormal personality.* Baltimore: Williams & Wilkins, 1963.

Marlowe, D., & Crowne, D. P.   Social desirability and response to perceived situational demands. *Journal of Consulting Psychology,* 1961, **25**, 109–15.

Masling, J.   The influence of situational and interpersonal variables in projective testing. *Psychological Bulletin,* 1960, **56**, 65–85.

Maslow, A. H.   *Toward a psychology of being.* Princeton, N.J.: Van Nostrand, 1962.

Maslow, A. H.   Self-actualizing people. In G. B. Levitas (Ed.), *The world of psychology.* Vol. 2. New York: Braziller, 1963.

Maslow, A. H.   Self-actualizing and beyond. In A. H. Maslow, *The farther reaches of human nature.* New York: Viking Press, 1972. Pp. 41–53.

McClelland, D. C.   *The achieving society.* Princeton, N.J.: Van Nostrand, 1961.

McClelland, D. C. Toward a theory of motive acquisition. *American Psychologist,* 1965, **20,** 321–33.

McClelland, D. C., Atkinson, J. W., Clark, R. A., & Lowell, E. L. *The achievement motive.* New York: Appleton-Century-Crofts, 1953.

McClelland, D. C., & Winter, D. G. *Motivating economic achievement.* New York: Free Press, 1969.

McKee, J. P., & Sherriffs, A. C. The differential evaluation of males and females. *Journal of Personality,* 1957, **25,** 356–71.

Merrill, R. M., & Heathers, L. B. The relation of the MMPI to the Edwards Personal Preference Schedule on a college counseling center sample. *Journal of Consulting Psychology,* 1956, **20,** 310–14.

Metz, J. R. Conditioning generalized imitation in autistic children. *Journal of Experimental Child Psychology,* 1965. **2,** 389–99.

Miller, N. E. Liberalization of basic S-R concepts: Extensions to conflict behavior, motivation, and social learning. In S. Koch (Ed.), *Psychology: A study of a science.* Vol. 2. New York: McGraw-Hill, 1959. Pp. 196–292.

Miller, N. E. Learning of visceral and glandular responses. *Science,* 1969, **163,** 434–45.

Miller, N. E., & Dollard, J. *Social learning and imitation.* New Haven, Conn.: Yale University Press, 1941.

Miller, N., Doob, A. N., Butler, D. C., & Marlowe, D. The tendency to agree: Situational determinants and social desirability. *Journal of Experimental Research in Personality,* 1965, **1,** 78–83.

Mischel, W. *Personality and assessment.* New York: Wiley, 1968.

Mischel, W. *Introduction to personality.* New York: Holt, Rinehart & Winston, 1971.

Montague, E. K. The role of anxiety in serial rote learning. *Journal of Experimental Psychology,* 1953, **45,** 91–96.

Morris, B. S. Officer selection in the British Army, 1942–1945. *Occupational Psychology,* 1949, **23,** 219–34.

Mowrer, O. H. *Learning theory and the symbolic processes.* New York: Wiley, 1960.

Mowrer, O. H. The behavioral vs. disease model of psychopathology—Do we need new patterns of training and treatment? Paper presented at the meeting of the Association for the Advancement of Behavior Therapy, Washington, D.C., September 1969.

Mowrer, O. H., & Mowrer, W. M. Enuresis—a method for its study and treatment. *American Journal of Orthopsychiatry,* 1938, **8,** 436–59.

Mullahy, P. *Oedipus myth and complex.* New York: Grove Press, 1948.

Murray, H. A. Uses of the Thematic Apperception Test. *American Journal of Psychiatry,* 1951, **107,** 577–81.

Murray, H. A. *Explorations in personality.* New York: Science Editions, 1962.

Murray, H. A., & Kluckhohn, C.   Outline of a conception of personality. In C. Kluckhohn & H. A. Murray with the collaboration of D. M. Schneider (Eds.), *Personality in nature, society, and culture.* New York: Knopf, 1953.

Myerson, A.   The attitude of neurologists, psychiatrists, and psychologists towards psychoanalysis. *American Journal of Psychiatry,* 1939, **96,** 623–41.

Neale, J. M.   Personal communication, 1968.

Neale, J. M., & Liebert, R. M.   *Science and behavior: An introduction to methods of research.* Englewood Cliffs, N.J.: Prentice-Hall, 1973.

Nisenson, S., & DeWitt, W. A.   *Illustrated minute biographies.* New York: Grosset & Dunlap, 1949.

Noll, V. H.   Simulation by college students of a prescribed pattern on a personality scale. *Educational and Psychological Measurement,* 1951, **11,** 478–88.

Nunnally, J. C., Duchnowski, A. J., & Parker, R. K.   Association of neutral objects with rewards: Effect on verbal evaluation, reward expectancy, and selective attention. *Journal of Personality and Social Psychology,* 1965, **1,** 270–74.

O'Connor, R. D.   Modification of social withdrawal through symbolic modeling. *Journal of Applied Behavior Analysis,* 1969, **2,** 15–22.

Odom, R. D., Liebert, R. M., & Hill, J. H.   The effects of modeling cues, reward, and attentional set on the production of grammatical and ungrammatical syntactic constructions. *Journal of Experimental Child Psychology,* 1968, **6,** 131–40.

Offenkrantz, W., & Rechtschaffen, A.   Clinical studies of sequential dreams. *Archives of General Psychiatry,* 1963, **8,** 497–508.

OSS Assessment Staff.   *Assessment of men.* New York: Holt, Rinehart & Winston, 1948.

Parker, R. K., & Nunnally, J. C.   Association of neutral objects with rewards: Effects of reward schedules on reward expectancy, verbal evaluation, and selective attention. *Journal of Experimental Child Psychology,* 1966, **3,** 324–32.

Passini, F. T., & Norman, W. T.   A universal conception of personality structure? *Journal of Personality and Social Psychology,* 1966, **4,** 44–49.

Paul, G. L.   *Insight versus desensitization in psychotherapy.* Stanford, Calif.: Stanford University Press, 1966.

Paul, G. L., & Shannon, D. T.   Treatment of anxiety through systematic desensitization in therapy groups. *Journal of Abnormal Psychology,* 1966, **71,** 124–35.

Pavlov, I. P.   *Conditioned reflexes.* New York: Liveright, 1927.

Pawlik, K., & Cattell, R. B.   Third-order factors in objective personality tests. *British Journal of Psychology,* 1964, **55,** 1–18.

Payne, D. E.   Role constructs versus part constructs and interpersonal understanding. Unpublished doctoral dissertation, Ohio State University, 1956.

Perls, F. S. *Gestalt therapy verbatim.* Lafayette, Calif.: Real People Press, 1969.

Phillips, S., Liebert, R. M., & Poulos, R. W. Employing paraprofessional teachers in a group language training program for severely and profoundly retarded children. *Perceptual and Motor Skills,* 1973, **36,** 607–16.

Poulos, R. W., & Liebert, R. M. Influence of modeling, exhortative verbalization, and surveillance on children's sharing. *Developmental Psychology,* 1972, **6,** 402–408.

Quarti, C., & Renaud, J. A new treatment of constipation by conditioning: A preliminary report. In C. M. Franks (Ed.), *Conditioning techniques in clinical practice and research.* New York: Springer, 1964. Pp. 219–27.

Rachman, S. The treatment of anxiety and phobic reactions by systematic desensitization psychotherapy. *Journal of Abnormal and Social Psychology,* 1959, **58,** 259–63.

Rachman, S., & Teasdale, J. *Aversion therapy and behavior disorders: An analysis.* Coral Gables, Fla.: University of Miami Press, 1969.

Ramond, C. K. Anxiety and task as determiners of verbal performance. *Journal of Experimental Psychology,* 1953, **46,** 120–24.

Rank, O. *The trauma of birth.* New York: Harcourt, Brace, 1929.

Razran, G. S. Conditioning away social bias by the luncheon technique. *Psychological Bulletin,* 1938, **35,** 693.

Razran, G. S. Conditioned response changes in rating and appraising sociopolitical slogans. *Psychological Bulletin,* 1940, **37,** 481.

Reese, E. P. The analysis of human operant behavior. In J. A. Vernon (Ed.), *Introduction to psychology: A self-selection textbook.* Dubuque, Iowa: Brown, 1966.

Reynolds, G. S. *A primer of operant conditioning.* Glenveiw, Ill.: Scott Foresman, 1968.

Risley, T. R. The effects and side effects of punishing the autistic behaviors of a deviant child. *Journal of Applied Behavior Analysis,* 1968, **1,** 21–34.

Rogers, C. R. *Counseling and psychotherapy: Newer concepts in practice.* Boston: Houghton Mifflin, 1942.

Rogers, C. R. A theory of therapy, personality, and interpersonal relationships, as developed in the client-centered framework. In S. Koch (Ed.), *Psychology: A study of a science.* Vol. 3. New York: McGraw-Hill, 1959. Pp. 184–256.

Rogers, C. R. *On becoming a person.* Boston: Houghton Mifflin, 1961.

Rogers, C. R. Toward a science of the person. In T. W. Wann (Ed.), *Behaviorism and phenomenology.* Chicago: University of Chicago Press, 1964. Pp. 109–33.

Rogers, C. R. *Client-centered therapy.* Boston: Houghton Mifflin, 1965.

Rogers, C. R. *Carl Rogers on encounter groups.* New York: Harper & Row, 1970.

Rogers, C. R., & Dymond, R. F. (Eds.) *Psychotherapy and personality change.* Chicago: University of Chicago Press, 1954.

Rorer, L. G. The great response-style myth. *Psychological Bulletin,* 1965, **63**, 129–56.

Rosekrans, M. A. Imitation in children as a function of perceived similarity and vicarious reinforcement. *Journal of Personality and Social Psychology,* 1967, **7**, 307–15.

Rosen, B. C., & D'Andrade, R. G. The psychosocial origins of achievement motivation. *Sociometry,* 1959, **22**, 185–218.

Rosenbaum, M. E., & Tucker, I. F. Competence of the model and the learning of imitation and nonimitation. *Journal of Experimental Psychology,* 1962, **63**, 183–90.

Rosenhan, D., & White, G. M. Observation and rehearsal as determinants of pro-social behavior. *Journal of Personality and Social Psychology,* 1967, **5**, 424–31.

Rosenthal, T. L., & Zimmerman, B. J. Modeling by exemplification and instruction in training conservation. *Developmental Psychology,* 1972, **6**, 392–401.

Rosenthal, T. L., Zimmerman, B. J., & Durning, K. Observationally induced changes in children's interrogative classes. *Journal of Personality and Social Psychology,* 1970, **16**, 681–88.

Ross, A. O. Deviant case analysis: A neglected approach to behavior research. *Perceptual and Motor Skills,* 1963, **16**, 337–40.

Rotter, J. B. *Social learning and clinical psychology.* Englewood Cliffs, N. J.: Prentice-Hall, 1954.

Sanford, N. Personality: Its place in psychology. In S. Koch (Ed.), *Psychology: A study of a science.* Vol. 5. New York: McGraw-Hill, 1963. Pp. 488–592.

Sarnoff, I., & Corwin, S. M. Castration anxiety and the fear of death. *Journal of Personality,* 1959, **27**, 374–85.

Savitsky, J .C., Rogers, R. W., Izard, C. E., & Liebert, R. M. The role of frustration and anger in the imitation of filmed aggression against a human victim. *Psychological Reports,* 1971, **29**, 807–10.

Scarr, S. Social introversion-extroversion as a heritable response. *Child Development,* 1969, **40**, 823–32.

Schaefer, W. S., & Bayley, N. Maternal behavior, child behavior, and their intercorrelations from infancy through adolescence. *Monographs of the Society for Research in Child Development,* 1963, **28**, 1–27.

Schafer, R. Review of S. Deri's *Introduction to the Szondi Test: Theory and Practice. Journal of Abnormal and Social Psychology,* 1950, **45**, 184–88.

Schloss, G. A. Siroka, R. W., & Siroka, E. K. Some contemporary origins of the personal growth group. In R. W. Siroka, E. K. Siroka, & G. A.

Schloss (Eds.), *Sensitivity training and group encounter: An introduction.* New York: Grosset & Dunlap, 1971. Pp. 3–10.

Schramm, W., Lyle, J., & Parker, E.   *Television in the lives of our children.* Stanford, Calif.: Stanford University Press, 1961.

Schutz, W. C.   *Joy: Expanding human awareness.* New York: Grove Press, 1967.

Sears, R. R.   *Survey of objective studies of psychoanalytic concepts.* New York: Social Science Research Council, Bulletin 51, 1943.

Sechrest, L.   The psychology of personal constructs: George Kelly. In J. M. Wepman & R. W. Heine (Eds.), *Concepts of personality.* Chicago: Aldine, 1963. Pp. 206–33.

Seeman, J.   Counselor judgements of therapeutic process and outcome. In C. R. Rogers & R. F. Dymond (Eds.), *Psychotherapy and personality change.* Chicago: University of Chicago Press, 1954. Pp. 99–108.

Sheldon, W. H.   *The varieties of temperament: A psychology of constitutional differences.* New York: Harper, 1942.

Shlien, J. M., Mosak, H. H., & Dreikurs, R.   Effect of time limits: A comparison of two psychotherapies. *Journal of Counseling Psychology,* 1962, **9**, 31–34.

Shurcliff, A.   Judged humor, arousal, and the relief theory. *Journal of Personality and Social Psychology,* 1968, **8**, 360–63.

Singer, D. L., Gollob, H., & Levine, J.   Inhibitions and the enjoyment of aggressive humor: An experimental investigation. Paper presented at the meeting of the Eastern Psychological Association, New York, 1966.

Skinner, B. F.   *The behavior of organisms.* New York: Appleton-Century-Crofts, 1938.

Skinner, B. F.   *Walden two.* New York: Macmillan, 1948.

Skinner, B. F.   *Science and human behavior.* New York: Macmillan, 1953.

Skinner, B. F.   A case history in scientific method. *American Psychologist,* 1956, **11**, 221–33.

Skinner, B. F.   *Verbal behavior.* New York: Appleton-Century-Crofts, 1957.

Skinner, B. F.   Behaviorism at fifty. In T. W. Wann (Ed.), *Behaviorism and phenomenology.* Chicago: University of Chicago Press, 1964. Pp. 79–108.

Skinner, B. F.   *Beyond freedom and dignity.* New York: Knopf, 1971.

Smith, D. H.   A speaker's models project to enhance pupils' self-esteem. *Journal of Negro Education,* 1967, **36**, 177–80.

Smoking and health: Report of the advisory committee to the Surgeon General of the Public Health Service. Washington, D.C.: U.S. Department of Health, Education, and Welfare, Public Health Service, 1964.

Snyder, C. R., & Larson, G. R.   A further look at student acceptance of general personality interpretations. *Journal of Consulting and Clinical Psychology*, 1972, **38**, 384–88.

Snyder, F.   The organismic state associated with dreaming. In N. W. Greenfield (Ed.), *Psychoanalysis and current biological thought.* Madison: University of Wisconsin Press, 1965. Pp. 275–315.

Snyder, W. U. (Ed.)   *Casebook of non-directive counseling.* Boston: Houghton Mifflin, 1947.

Solomon, R. L.   Punishment. *American Psychologist,* 1964, **19**, 239–53.

Spence, J. T., & Spence, K. W.   The motivational components of manifest anxiety: Drive and drive stimuli. In C. D. Spielberger (Ed.), *Anxiety and behavior.* New York: Academic Press, 1966. Pp. 291–326.

Spiegler, M. D.   Classroom approach teaches patients independence skills. *Hospital and Community Psychiatry,* 1973, **24**, 216–21.

Spiegler, M. D., Liebert, R. M., McMains, M. J. & Fernandez, L. E.   Experimental development of a modeling treatment to extinguish persistent avoidance behavior. In R. D. Rubin & C. M. Franks (Eds.), *Advances in behavior therapy, 1968.* New York: Academic Press, 1969. Pp. 45–51.

Staats, A. W., & Staats, C. K.   Attitudes established by classical conditioning. *Journal of Abnormal and Social Psychology,* 1958, **57**, 37–40.

Stein, A. H., & Friedrich, L. K.   Television content and young children's behavior. In J. P. Murray, E. A. Rubinstein, & G. A. Comstock (Eds.), *Television and social behavior.* Vol. 2. *Television and social learning.* Washington D.C.: U.S. Government Printing Office, 1972. Pp. 202–317.

Stephenson, W.   *The study of behavior.* Chicago: University of Chicago Press, 1953.

Steuer, F. B., Applefield, J. M., & Smith, R.   Televised aggression and the interpersonal aggression of preschool children. *Journal of Experimental Child Psychology,* 1971, **11**, 442–47.

Strupp, H. H.   Who needs intrapsychic factors in clinical psychology? Paper presented at the Albert Einstein College of Medicine, New York, 1966.

Strupp, H. H.   *An introduction to Freud and modern psychoanalysis.* Woodbury, N.Y.: Barron's Educational Series, 1967.

Tarde, G.   *The laws of imitation.* New York: Henry Holt, 1903.

Taylor, J. A.   A personality scale of manifest anxiety. *Journal of Abnormal and Social Psychology,* 1953, **48**, 285–90.

Taylor, J. A., & Spence, K. W.   The relationship of anxiety level to performance in serial learning. *Journal of Experimental Psychology,* 1952, **44**, 61–64.

Thigpen, C. H., & Cleckley, H.   A case of multiple personality. *Journal of Abnormal and Social Psychology,* 1954, **49**, 135–51.

Thomas, A., Chess, S., & Birch, H. G.   The origin of personality. *Scientific American,* 1970, **223**, 102–9.

Thorndike, E. L.   Animal intelligence: An experimental study of the associative processes in animals. *Psychological Review,* 1898, **2** (Monogr. Suppl. 8).

Tippett, J. S. A study of change process during psychotherapy. Unpublished doctoral dissertation, Ohio State University, 1959.

Turner, A. J. Personal communication, 1973.

Ullmann, L. P., & Krasner, L. *A psychological approach to abnormal behavior.* Englewood Cliffs, N.J.: Prentice-Hall, 1969.

Ulrich, R. E., Stachnik, T. J., & Stainton, N. R. Student acceptance of generalized personality interpretations. *Psychological Reports,* 1963, **13,** 831–34.

Van de Castle, R. L. *The psychology of dreaming.* New York: General Learning Press, 1971.

Vandenberg, S. G. Contributions to twin research in psychology. *Psychological Bulletin,* 1966, **66,** 327–52.

Verplanck, W. S. The operant conditioning of human motor behavior. *Psychological Bulletin,* 1956, **53,** 70–83.

Walton, D., & Mather, M. D. The relevance of generalized techniques to the treatment of stammering and phobic symptoms. *Behaviour Research and Therapy,* 1963, **1,** 121–25.

Watson, J. B. *Behavior: An introduction to comparative psychology.* New York: Holt, 1914.

Watson, J. B. *Psychology from the standpoint of a behaviorist.* Philadelphia: Lippincott, 1919.

Watson, J. B., & Rayner, R. Conditioned emotional reactions. *Journal of Experimental Psychology,* 1920, **3,** 1–14.

Weisberg, P., & Waldrop, P. B. Fixed-interval work habits of Congress. *Journal of Applied Behavior Analysis,* 1972, **5,** 93–97.

Weitzman, B. Behavior therapy and psychotherapy. *Psychological Review,* 1967, **74,** 300–317.

Weitzmann, E. A note on the EEG and eye movements during behavioral sleep in monkeys. *EEG Clinical Neurophysiology,* 1961, **13,** 790–94.

Wesman, A. G. Faking personality test scores in a simulated employment situation. *Journal of Applied Psychology,* 1952, **36,** 112–13.

Williams, C. D. The elimination of tantrum behavior by extinction procedures: Case report. *Journal of Abnormal and Social Psychology,* 1959, **59,** 269.

Williams, R. J. The biological approach to the study of personality. In T. Millon (Ed.), *Theories of psychopathology.* Philadelphia: Saunders, 1967. Pp. 19–31.

Wilson, W. C. Extrinsic religious values and prejudice. *Journal of Abnormal and Social Psychology,* 1960, **60,** 286–88.

Wilson, W. H., & Nunnally, J. C. A naturalistic investigation of acquired meaning in children. *Psychonomic Science,* 1971, **23,** 149–50.

Wolman, B. B. *The unconscious mind: The meaning of Freudian psychology.* Englewood Cliffs, N.J.: Prentice-Hall, 1968.

Wolpe, J. *Psychotherapy by reciprocal inhibition.* Stanford, Calif.: Stanford University Press, 1958.

Wolpe, J., & Lang, P. J. A fear survey schedule for use in behaviour therapy. *Behaviour Research and Therapy,* 1964, **2,** 27–30.

Wolpe, J., & Lazarus, A. A. *Behavior therapy techniques: A guide to the treatment of neurosis.* New York: Pergamon Press, 1966.

Woodworth, R. S. *Personal data sheet.* Chicago: Stoelting, 1920.

Worchel, P. Anxiety and repression. *Journal of Abnormal and Social Psychology,* 1955, **51,** 201–5.

Woy, J. R., & Efran, J. S. Systematic desensitization and expectancy in the treatment of speaking anxiety. *Behaviour Research and Therapy,* 1972, **10,** 43–49.

Zax, M., & Strickler, G. *Patterns of psychopathology.* New York: Macmillan, 1963.

Zeller, A. An experimental analogue of repression: II. The effect of individual failure and success on memory measured by relearning. *Journal of Experimental Psychology,* 1950, **40,** 411–22.

Zeller, A. An experimental analogue of repression: III. The effect of induced failure and success on memory measured by recall. *Journal of Experimental Psychology,* 1951, **42,** 32–38.

Zucker, R. A., Manosevitz, M., & Lanyon, R. I. Birth order, anxiety, and affiliation during a crisis. *Journal of Personality and Social Psychology,* 1968, **8,** 354–59.

Author Index

Subject Index

Methods of personality research
  case study, 32–37
  correlational, 24–31
  experimental, 19–24
Minnesota Multiphasic Personality
  Inventory (MMPI), 147, 173–79,
  182–84, 187
Modeling, 384
  cues, definition of, 384
  live, 384, 399
  multiple, 410
  symbolic, 384, 399
Models, and imitation, 384
Modulation Corollary, G. A. Kelly's,
  284–85
Monozygotic twins, 142
Moral anxiety, 74
Motives, Kelly's view, 270–72; *see also*
  Achievement motive; Approval
  motive; Functional autonomy;
  Thematic Apperception Test
Multiple determination of behavior,
  28
Multivariate research, 158–72

N

n achievement; *see* Need for achieve-
  ment
n approval; *see* Need for social ap-
  proval
Need for achievement, 203–15
Need for social approval, 188, 215–19
Needs, 181, 191–94, 270
  latent, 197–201
  manifest, 197
  primary (viscerogenic), 193
  secondary (psychogenic), 193–94
Negative correlation, 25
Neoanalysts; *see* Neo-Freudians
Neo-Freudians, 41
Neurosis, 103, 105, 116, 323
Neurotic anxiety, 74
Neuroticism, 168, 171
Nomothetic approach, 8, 152, 224
Nonadditive model, of personality as-
  sessment, 48
Nondirective therapy; *see* Client-cen-
  tered therapy
Nonrapid eye movements (NREM),
  94–97; *see also* Dreams and
  dreaming

O

Objective anxiety, 74
Observational learning, 308, 384
Oedipus complex, 58–61, 70, 106, 112;
  see also Oedipal conflicts
Oedipal conflicts, 88; *see also* Oedipus
  complex
Oedipal intensity, 102
Operant behavior, definition of, 348
Operant conditioning, 308
Opposites (in dream work), 85
Oral eroticism, 56, 102
Oral sadism, 56
Oral stage, 56–57; *see also* Psycho-
  sexual development
Organismic valuing process, 239, 248
Organization Corollary, G. A. Kelly's,
  276–78
Orgasmic reorientation, 341
Overdetermination, 85
Overindulgence, 56

P

Paradoxical sleep, 93
Partial schedule; *see* Intermittent
  schedule of reinforcement
Pavlovian conditioning; *see* Classical
  conditioning
Penile erection, and operant condi-
  tioning, 377–80
Penis envy, 61, 102; *see also* Oedipus
  complex
Perceptual defense, 249
Perceptual distortion, 249
Permeability, of personal constructs,
  269, 284
Persona, 1
Personal constructs, 229; definition of,
  267
Personal dispositions; *see* Individual
  traits, G. W. Allport's view
Personality, definition of, 6–7
  G. W. Allport's, 6
  U. Bronfenbrenner's, 7
  R. B. Cattell's, 7
  H. J. Eysenck's, 6–7
  E. R. Hilgard's, 7
  T. Newcomb's, 6
  H. S. Sullivan's, 7
Personality profile; *see* Psychogram
Personology, H. A. Murray's, 190–203

This book has been set in 11 and 10 point Baskerville, leaded 1 point. Section and chapter numbers are in 16, 42, and 48 point Helvetica; section and chapter titles are in 18 point Helvetica Medium. The size of the type page is 27 x 46½ picas.